D1616220

Kung Fu Elements

Wushu Training and Martial Arts Application Manual

中國武術

功夫及踢打摔拿實用訓練

梁守渝，吳文慶著

By

Shou-Yu Liang

&

Wen-Ching Wu

Edited by

Denise Breiter-Wu

The Way of the Dragon Publishing, Rhode Island, U.S.A.

Published by:

龍 The Way of the Dragon Publishing

P. O. Box 14561

East Providence, RI 02914-0561

United States of America

www.waydragon.com

First Printing 2001

Printed in the United States of America

9 8 7 6 5 4 3 2 1

Publisher's Cataloging-in-Publication Data

Wu, Wen-Ching, 1964-

Kung fu elements: wushu training and martial arts application manual/by Wen-Ching Wu and Shou-Yu Liang

illus. p. cm.

Includes bibliographical references, index, appendixes, and glossary.

ISBN 1-889659-17-7

1. Kung fu. 2. Martial arts. 3. Wrestling--China. 4. Hand-to-hand fighting, Oriental. 5. Exercise. 6. Ch'i kung. I. Title. II. Liang, Shou-Yu.

796.8159 99-76911

Table of Contents

Table of Contents (cont.)

Acknowledgments

There are many friends and students of the authors that have helped in completing this book. The authors would like to acknowledge them and thank them for their help. Thank you to Sarah Alexander for proofreading and preparing the Publisher's Cataloging-in-Publication Data. Thank you to Frank Whitsitt-Lynch, Robert Ross, and Thomas Uva for proofreading. Also, we would like to thank our current students for their continual support and encouragement!

In addition to the authors, there are many friends and students of the authors that have modeled in the main part of this book. The authors would like to acknowledge them and thank them for their assistance. Thank you!

Helen Liang—Model in Chapters 1 and 2, wearing a traditional Wushu outfit.

Maria Liang—Model in Chapters 1 and 2, wearing a traditional Wushu outfit.

Bruce Fontaine—Model in Chapters 1 and 2, wearing a traditional Wushu outfit.

Kelly Maclean—Model in Chapters 1 and 2, wearing a traditional Wushu outfit.

Siu Hung Huen—Model in Chapters 1 and 2, wearing a traditional Wushu outfit.

Irene Chen—Model in Chapter 1, wearing a traditional Wushu outfit.

Katrina Leung—Model in Chapter 1, wearing a traditional Wushu outfit.

Fred Whiting—Model in Chapters 1 and 2, wearing a traditional Wushu outfit.

Howie Leung—Model in Chapters 1, 2, and 3, wearing a traditional Wushu outfit and a Sanshou competition outfit.

Mo Hui—Model in Chapter 2, wearing a traditional Wushu outfit.

Narcyz Latecki—Model in Chapter 2 wearing a traditional Wushu outfit.

Pete Sihan Lin—Model in Chapter 2, wearing a traditional Wushu outfit.

Michael Levenston—Model in Chapter 3, wearing a Wushu Sanshou Dao uniform.

Rudy Ott—Model in Chapter 3, wearing a Sanshou competition outfit.

Barry Farrands—Model in Chapters 4 and 6, wearing a training outfit.

Sanford Lee—Model in Chapters 5 and 6, wearing a training outfit.

Preface by:

Shou-Yu Liang

As Wushu (Chinese martial arts) continues to spread all over the world, it has become increasingly popular. Currently, there are over 100 nations with Wushu participants. Since the International Wushu Invitational held in 1985 in China, more and more International Wushu competitions are being held worldwide.

Our goal in writing this book is to present essential information to our readers and to answer the questions: What is Wushu and what are the contents of Wushu training? It is our attempt to write the best possible training reference that we are able to write at the present time, for anyone interested in learning Wushu. It is our hope that this book will be a stepping stone, assisting you to higher achievements.

Wushu in ancient China was known as Wuyi (martial skill). During the 1920's, it was renamed Guoshu (national art). These are all official terms used to refer to Chinese martial arts. The term Kung Fu (gongfu) was also used in conjunction with the training of Wushu. Kung Fu is a term describing the level of achievement (good or poor) an individual has. It also refers to the time and effort an individual invests in their training. Because of this, the term Kung Fu is often used in combination with Wushu. Historical factors have caused much confusion with the proper use of these terms, so it is understandable why many people may be confused by the proper use of these terms.

Thirty years ago in China, due to political changes and the Cultural Revolution, every corner of the society was adversely affected. The damage done was especially apparent in the traditional cultures. Wushu was not an exception. At the time, Wushu was considered a bad component of Chinese culture, and practitioners were considered enemies of the state. All fighting arts, routine practice, and wrestling were forbidden.

After the Cultural Revolution, selected Wushu training was permitted. However, the fighting component (Sanshou) was still not allowed. Fortunately, Wushu is diverse and has many other components that could be promoted. Wushu routines could be compiled into very graceful, artistic forms. The government, at that time, encouraged and promoted this area of Wushu which resulted in what is known as Modern Wushu or Contemporary Wushu. Every year for more than twenty years, there have been competitions in China in the areas of barehanded and weapon routines. Today, Wushu competition routines have also become a performing art. In the 1970's, the Beijing Wushu Team began to perform Wushu routines in other nations.

Contemporary Wushu performance routines emphasize fundamental training along with increasing the degree of difficulty of the movements. It is especially advantageous to a developing youth's flexibility, speed, jumping ability, and physical strength. The general public has been very receptive to these routines, especially the parents of the developing youth. The training is both beneficial to the youth's mental and physical health.

In the 1960s, traditional Wushu was suppressed, especially in the area of Sanshou (free fighting training). Sanshou training was nowhere to be found in public places. However, China is a vast nation with over a billion people; it was not possible for any one person, or the government to truly prevent people from continuing with their traditional Wushu training.

Throughout Chinese history, many dynasties have tried to prevent civilians from practicing Wushu, and confiscated all metal weapons. But this didn't stop people from continuing their training and passing on the art to future generations. During the Cultural Revolution, my friends and I continued to train traditional Wushu in the remote villages and in hidden corners of the streets. Knowing that traditional Wushu training was a Chinese tradition, witnesses in these areas did not report us. The only problem with the training of traditional Wushu was that it was forbidden to be publicized.

After the Cultural Revolution, the Chinese government appointed me as a professional coach, coaching Contemporary Wushu. Therefore, I also put my effort in training many different types of performance routines. I realized that the emphasis and training of Contemporary Wushu were all very good. In fact, all the training methods were derived from traditional training methods. Using the Contemporary Wushu training methods as a first step to training developing youths, will give them a solid foundation. With a solid foundation, they can learn traditional Wushu components with ease.

While teaching at my appointed posts, I also continued to train with my traditional Wushu friends in Sanshou, shuaijiao (takedown), qinna (grapppling), weapon sparring, and Taiji Push Hands. Drawing from my experiences in both traditional Wushu and Contemporary Wushu training, I began to teach my students a combination of both. All of my students are well-rounded in their ability. They have received awards in Contemporary Wushu performance, and are equally competent in Sanshou and shuaijiao. In 1979, after all the areas of my personal and coaching abilities were considered, I was selected as one of the top Coaches of Excellence in China.

When I first arrived in North America at the beginning of the 1980's, I met numerous Chinese individuals who had practiced Wushu and Taijiquan. Some of them said to me, "It is not possible for one person to learn so much. It must have just been for fun ..." Some of these individuals who have made this type of statement are individuals that have spent their lifetime learning one thing, but are still terrible at it. Even though, some individuals have practiced

Taijiquan for over 20 years, they are still very awkward in their movements, and still have little or no understanding of Push Hands. When they encounter someone with good Push Hands skill, they immediately lose their balance. It is no wonder that such an individual can't conceive of the idea that any one person can learn many Wushu styles and attain many abilities. They didn't understand the complementary concept. One type of martial ability can complement the other type, and vise versa. Individuals with well-rounded ability are numerous in China.

Those who have dedicated their life to Wushu should have a deep understanding of and proficiency in all aspects of Wushu. It is true that one person can't master everything, but one should at least be aware of and understand the concepts. The barehanded applications of traditional Wushu, include ti (kicking), da (use of arm strikes), shuai (takedown), na (grappling), and tuishou (push hands). In addition to the above, there is also the training of Wushu Qigong. The weapon applications, include splitting, chopping, spearing, pointing, sweeping, etc. One must be familiar with all the barehanded applications and the different types of weapon applications. Every style of Wushu has had a glorious past. It does not matter what style you are studying, when you have achieved the highest attainment in that style, it will be the same as with other styles.

In China today, every province has two different Wushu teams. One is the Wushu Performance Team and the other is the Wushu Sanshou Team. The performance team trains different routines for competitions and for performances. The Sanshou team trains for fighting competitions. Both teams have high standards. Together both types of teams have a strong influence to other nation's Wushu development. However, there is a tendency for the performance team members to lack fighting ability, and for the Sanshou team members to lack the ability to do Wushu routines. This problem has resulted in the separation of Wushu into two types of arts. This is causing a misunderstanding of the term Wushu.

Conversely, outside of China, Wushu traditions have been preserved. Many well trained Sanshou fighters are also excellent performers. I am joyful and pleased to be able to witness this development in International and World Wushu Competitions.

I would like to take this opportunity to give thanks to my grandfather, the late Grandmaster Liang, Zhi-Xiang, for initiating my Wushu and qigong training. Thanks to my father, Liang, Zuo-Feng; and my mother Huang, Zhe-Xi for nurturing my growth. Thanks to my uncle, Liang, De-Xin and my aunt, Tang, Ying-Hua for providing me with an opportunity to come and prosper in North America. Thanks to my wife, Xiang-Yong for her years of support and understanding which have helped me with my career and success. Thanks to my lovely daughters, Helen and Maria for their love. Thanks to all my relatives, students, and friends that have helped and supported me, especially to

Wen-Ching for writing another book with me, and to his wife, Denise for her hard work in editing this book.

Shou-Yu Liang

Summer 2001

Preface by:

Wen-Ching Wu

Martial arts has been an integral part of human existence since the dawn of time and contains valuable lessons that can prepare us to deal with challenges in life. It has served us well throughout the millenniums both as a means of self-defense and as a way to discipline our mind, body, and spirit. It is said that the greatest value one can attain in martial arts training is "the will to exert and strive hard without stopping in anything." Through the conditioning of our body, we discipline our mind and gain a greater understanding of ourselves. By understanding ourselves, we learn to live in harmony with our emotions and our environment. This cultivation of the *whole being* gives us the serenity to carry out our life tasks.

One of the most common questions a beginning martial artist has, is "How long will it take me to get a black belt?" This is a question that will depend on the effort the practitioner invests in his or her training. In the past, traditional martial arts systems did not use a belt as a rank. Belts or sashes were used to help hold the clothing together. As a student progressed in their training, their clothing would age, fade, or discolor. If the belt was white, after many years of training, it would become old and no longer as white as when they started. That was an indication of the length of time that had passed—an indication of one's experience, one's true rank.

In traditional Chinese martial arts training, belts or sashes had many uses. Besides using it to hold your outfit together; it was also used as a weapon, used to protect your internal organs when generating power, and to hold herbs. It was not meant to be used as a ranking system. Today, ranking with the different colored belts or sashes has been adopted by most Asian martial arts systems, including the Chinese martial arts. The implication of the belt or sash is a symbol of an *individual's* achievement. This achievement is attained with *time and effort* invested in one's practice. The more time you invest in your training, the higher your rank will be, because you have more *experience* and have higher *attainments* than you had yesterday.

When we look beyond the superficial colors of the belt, we realize that true attainment is internal, not what is visible to others. It is not the color of the belt that makes a martial artist, it is what one has attained since the beginning of one's training that is the true *measure* of one's *rank*. It is how much we have understood and mastered in our own mind and body.

Mr. Wu Yu-Kuang (父親吳餘光先生), &
Ms. Fan Chiu-Mei (母親范秋妹女士)

Practicing martial arts on your own is a very important part of your growth and development, but it can't replace direct instruction from a capable teacher. By practicing, learning, and observing the teacher, you can learn many of the inherent virtues of martial arts, that can't be fully expressed in books. A teacher's example is an expression of their virtues and contains many of their life experiences and spiritual lessons. These martial art virtues are the binding force that integrates the physical with the mental. Reciting or memorizing the virtues alone does not give a person virtue. The virtues only become inherent when one lives them. When a teacher's or a student's actions defy these virtues, it makes these qualities meaningless.

Great teachers are those who express their lives with virtue without pretense. They use a martial arts code of ethics as a guide, not as a method of control over their students. They know that human beings are all equal. No one person is *better* than the next. An individual may be more evolved, more knowledgeable, have a higher IQ, be physically stronger, but it does not make the individual *superior* to others. It is simply the *state* from which we are to learn in this life. In fact, when a teacher takes on a disciple, the teacher addresses the student humbly as *tudi* (徒弟), meaning disciple younger brother. It is like taking on a younger brother! The disciple, however, addresses the teacher respectfully as *shifu* (師父), meaning teacher father.

It is the teacher's responsibility to pass on knowledge. However, the teacher can't make the student learn, nor can the teacher simply give his or her knowledge and ability to the student. The student has the responsibility to train and assimilate the knowledge and ability by himself. As the student continues to improve physically, and manifest proper martial ethics with increasing patience, humility, respectfulness, honesty, a bond of trust will develop between the teacher and the student. This will facilitate an exchange of mutually beneficial energy and bridge the continuous lineage of martial arts.

A teacher has to be willing to teach, and the student has to be willing to learn for the knowledge to flow and interchange freely and effectively. A feeling of trust is the bridge that allows this flow of knowledge and energy be-

Master Liang Shou-Yu (恩師梁守渝大師), &
Ms. Liang Xiang-Yong (師母梁向勇女士)

Dr. Wu Chengde (義父吳誠德教授), &
Professor Wang Jurong (義母王菊蓉教授)

tween a teacher and student. It takes time to build this bond. If the student has broken the bond of trust, it will take a long time to rebuild that connection. If the teacher has broken that trust, it may be time for the student to move on. A teacher's virtuous character is an example and inspiration for a student's continual learning. The student's virtue, dedication, and willingness to train hard, are his or her keys to higher attainments.

I am a fortunate person with a wonderful family, inspirational teachers, and supportive friends and students. Everywhere I go and whatever I do, I have the support that I need to carry out my goals. I would like to take this opportunity to express my sincere appreciation to all the people that have helped me throughout the years. Thank you!

A special thanks goes to my parents, Yu-Kuang and Chiu-Mei Wu; my teacher and mentor, Master Shou-Yu Liang and Mrs. Xiang-Yong Liang; and my adopted parents, Professor Jurong Wang and Dr. Chengde Wu. These three couples have had a tremendous affect on my life. They have been the standards for which I model my life both professionally and personally. They are shining examples of truly achieved individuals, not just in their ability and knowledge, but also in their way of being. They live their lives in harmony with each other and with their surroundings, and manifest a great integrity of virtues in the way they live their lives. I am fortunate and proud to be their son and student.

It is their love, inspiration, and teaching that gives me the greatest aspiration to continue my personal studies and continue with my work. They have provided me with the opportunity to explore the universe and have given me unconditional love and support, which has helped shape my present character and has helped me attain my current achievements.

Thanks to my wonderful wife, whom I love with all my heart. No amount of words can fully express my love and appreciation for her, and for assisting me in my work. It is her countless hours of editing my English that makes this books easier to read and understand. Thanks to my son, Andrew, for being the joy of my life.

Once again, it is with great honor to be able to write another book with Master Liang. It is his vast experience and guidance that has given the depth and insights to this book. Over the years, Master Liang has guided me and provided me with a resource of physical and intellectual lessons which have been invaluable, but it is the spiritual lessons and talks that we have shared which are immeasurable to my growth. Words can't fully express my appreciation and seem to belittle my gratitude. Nevertheless, I would like to take this opportunity to extend my heartfelt thanks to Master Liang. Thank you ... Master Liang.

He is my teacher, but he is also my friend. During our times together, he often uses the expression, "We will cultivate together.", "We will mutually learn from each other.", and "We will mutually help each other." He has so much to offer, yet he is also willing to listen to the little that I may be able to offer back to him.

When a teacher shows mutual respect for a student, it is not an elevation of the student's status. It is a humbling experience for the student. When a teacher with decades of more experience than the student is humble, how can a student with much less experience be arrogant when he/she also has the respect of the teacher.

Today, we are fortunate to have access to the many treasures Wushu has to offer, especially since in the past it was very secretive and available only to a select group of individuals. We may not be able to master the entire spectrum of Chinese martial arts systems, but we can keep on learning and training as much as we can. Just as it is not possible to master it all, it is also not possible to cover it all. In this book, we will present as much relevant information as is needed to give you a clear and concise concept of the training in Chinese martial arts. It is our hope that this book will serve you well in your continual journey of learning and training.

Life is a spiritual experience with many lessons to learn. Kung Fu has been instrumental in my learning and sharing of my experiences with others. It has been a way of life for me. Through Kung Fu, I have become more aware of my being. It has helped me develop my character, my self-reliance, and my confidence to stand up for my beliefs. By not letting my own or other's ignorance or jealousy be an obstacle to my growth, I have opened new doors for my advancement. It is my hope that you will also be able to attain similar or greater benefits than I have, and that this book will assist you in your continual search for self-awareness and the betterment of your being.

Wen-Ching Wu

Summer 2001

武術

Introduction:

Essential Elements

There are many martial arts systems being trained by millions of people all over the world. To master any martial art system requires similar dedication and training. Proficiency does not depend on which system you choose to study, because it is not the system that makes you proficient in martial arts. Your proficiency and attainment will depend on the effort you put into your training. This attainment is the definition of Kung Fu.

Kung Fu (功夫) literally means an attainment of, or the level of one's ability in something. In the Southern Chinese dialect and in the English language, it is often taken to mean Chinese martial arts. In actuality, any accomplishment one has attained is called Kung Fu (gongfu). For example, Van Gogh had good Kung Fu in painting, and Beethoven had good Kung Fu in music.

In order for anyone to attain proficiency in Chinese martial arts, they have to invest time and effort into their training. Because the dedication and discipline in perfecting the mental, physical, and spiritual requirements of being a true martial artist are very demanding, the term Kung Fu has become synonymous for Chinese martial arts.

The proper term for Chinese martial arts is *Wushu* (武術). The Chinese character for *wu* (武) is made up of two parts. The first part means *to stop* (止) and the second part means a *lance* (戈), a spear-like weapon used in war and fighting. *Shu* means *art*. Therefore, a definition of Chinese martial arts is the *art of stopping war and fighting* or *the art of stopping violence*. It is said, combine the character *to stop* with the character *lance* to make the character *martial*. This Chinese martial arts idiom implies that true bravery is the ability to cease fighting before it starts.

Purpose and Philosophy

Chinese civilization and its perspective of life are heavily integrated with nature. Their philosophy stresses the importance and the belief in the "Unification of the heavens and humans (天人合一)", a harmonious relationship between the environment and human existence. Wushu is the essence of Chinese civilization and is a major component of the Chinese social, historical, cultural, scientific, military, medical, psychological, and educational developments. From this perspective of harmonious integration, Wushu is more than just a combat readiness training. It is also a life nourishing, mental, spiritual, and educational training.

Harmonious integration, on an individual level, is about the integration of the whole person. The importance of the physical postures and movements are highly integrated with the vitality of spirit. Wushu emphasizes "training the muscles/tendons, bones, and skin externally; training *qi* internally (外練筋骨皮，內練一口氣)". Qi, in this case, refers to breathing; and the internal energy (內氣) controlled, regulated, and developed by focused intention. With the proper integration of the mental and the physical, the whole body can fully express powerful martial movements. When one aspect reaches the target, all other aspects also reach the target. All styles of Wushu emphasize this harmonious integration. Each style, of course, has their own integrated expression.

In Wushu, we train the physical to aid the shapeless; cultivate the shapeless to care for the physical. The training of Wushu gives one the necessary conditioning to master one's own physical body, and gain a greater understanding of the inner workings of the mind and spirit. Both the health of the mind and the physical body are important aspects in martial arts training. A well trained martial artist, without a calm mind, is like a time bomb ready to explode. Without a good character and physical health, one would not be able to achieve a high level in Chinese martial arts. When one trains martial arts and ends up with ill health; or becomes violent, aggressive, and undisciplined, one has deviated from the traditional training and value of martial arts.

On the interpersonal level, Wushu training is also about working on social harmony. Students respect their teachers and their teachings. The relationship between a student and a teacher is unlike that in other physical pursuits. Their training stresses righteousness, humility, loyalty, honesty, trustworthiness, integrity, modesty, kindness, and courteousness. Students are expected to be ethical before learning the martial components of Wushu. With proper martial ethics and with the spirit of benevolence as a guide, Wushu practitioners are working toward attaining harmonious social relationships.

Not deviating from the philosophy of harmony, martial artists uphold martial ethics (武德), the moral values and stepping stones for high goals in martial attainment. They are a *guide* for martial artists, not *rules* that restrict the development of individuality. With martial ethics, a martial artist has the proper mind set to achieve high standards mentally and physically. Martial ethics are to be followed willingly, not imposed as rules. Today, many of the once understood and followed virtues have been written down, as a wonderful reminder of the practices and virtues of Wushu. The unfortunate part, as Laozi stated in the *Daodejing* (道德經), is that when the rules of conduct have to be written down and imposed, and tagged with punishments for offenders, society has already degenerated.

The training of Wushu combat skills are also based on traditional Chinese philosophy. There is an understanding that in many situations, the seemingly soft and weak are more resilient than the hard and strong. An example of this is a piece of grass which can withstand a powerful wind storm, where as, a tree can be broken by the wind storm. Another example of this is how flowing water can crush and move strong obstacles in its path. In the training of applications, the emphasis is placed on how to utilize a seemingly disadvantageous position against an obviously stronger adversary; how to use the opponent's strength against him, how to redirect his strength against him; and how to minimize force to move a powerful attack. This type of development has given the shorter less muscular men and women the boost they need to continue their training, knowing that they can be victorious over an adversary despite being smaller and physically not as strong. In fact, there have been many female practitioners who have attained greater advancements than many male practitioners.

The study of martial arts prepares a person for war and fighting. However, war and fighting have never permanently solved any conflict. They only temporarily restrain and mask the conflict, and perpetuate future disasters. Our ancestors have learned the value of peace from the cruelty of war. They realized that the best defense was prevention. The truly courageous martial artist is the one who knows how to prevent a fight before it starts. All the training you have done has been to prepare you for possible conflicts, and to develop your confidence and a clear mind to know when to and when not to use your ability. This is the mastery of your *heart* (心) and *intellect* (意), the combination of which is true wisdom.

One of the obvious reasons for martial arts training is for self-defense. However, many people often misunderstand self-defense as kicks or punches. Good self-defense does not necessarily need to use kicks and punches. Avoidance is more effective than frontal confrontation. A smart mind is often better than an invincible technique. It is far better to avoid a confrontation with proper mental and physical training. Martial artists learn to discipline their minds and condition their bodies to prevent and avoid violent situations before they occur. However, if a situation does demand combative measures, they are ready to react properly from their training.

There are many ways to stop violence. Fighting is not a permanent solution for settling a dispute. A martial artist who is comfortable with his or herself, does not have to prove to anyone that they know how to fight. Their fighting ability is their own to keep, not to prove to others. They don't need the praise of others to be comfortable with themselves and their abilities. A true martial artist is the first to walk away from a fight because they do not have to prove to others what they can do. They don't give in to peer pressure because they are the masters of their own mind and emotions, not dependent on what others say about them.

The knowledge and ability to defend oneself from natural and man-made disasters strengthens and develops the will to stand up to the sometimes cruel and devastating environment in which we live; it develops the strength to not be afraid of the wickedness of stronger and evil people; and it develops bravery to continue with one's own conviction to become successful in whatever one puts their mind to. The expression, "the will to exert and strive hard without stopping at any obstacle (自強不息)", is one of the greatest attainments one can achieve in martial arts training.

The many possible and valuable mental, spiritual, and physical advantages of Wushu training have attracted Wushu practitioners from over 100 nations. Among the 100 nations, there are over 70 nations that regularly hold Wushu competitions with their own Wushu teams. Nations around the world are applying Wushu in the pursuit of greater health, for discipline, for self-defense, for training military and police officers, for cultural and holiday demonstrations, and for routine and fighting competitions. The extensiveness of Wushu has attracted practitioners from all walks of life and all age groups of men and women. Once a practitioner is attracted to Wushu, their commitment to Wushu often becomes a lifelong study.

Combat Psychology and Training Emphasis

In Wushu combat, one must have a strong foundation, proficient technical skills, as well as, a set of practical combat strategies. *Sunzi's Art of War* (孫子兵法) is a valuable reference and utilized by many Wushu practitioners. It is a military strategy book written during the Spring-Autumn and the Warring Kingdoms era and is regarded as the "First book of military strategy (世界第一兵書)." This book has been highly regarded by military strategists around the globe for the past two millenniums.

Since the beginning of human civilization, there have been wars and conflicts between people. Wars have been an integral part of human history. Nations and dynasties were founded or ended by war. Because of the cruelty and the threat of war that prevails in our lives, it is no wonder that many books about the strategies of war have been written from many different perspectives.

Sunzi was the most outstanding military strategist in Chinese history. He lived during the most war infested time in Chinese history, the Spring-Autumn era. His thirteen chapters about the strategies of war are the most complete and systematic works about the proper attitude and strategies of war. On a grand scale, *Sunzi's Art of War* is about the strategy of war. On a personal level, it is also about conflict resolution and how to effectively deal with conflicts, if the situation should arise.

There are always some losses when countries engage in war. Therefore, the best strategy is to win, without actually having to engage in war. Sunzi believed that to engage in battles and to win one hundred times is not a good strategy. Having your opponent surrender to you, without having to actually engage in a bloody combat, is the best approach.

Sunzi advocated cautiousness with respect to combat. Being cautious does not mean to be afraid of war, nor does it undermine the outcome of war. Sunzi stated, "Leaders should not go into war when angered; generals should not go to war when irritated; act when there is an advantage, stop when there is a disadvantage. Anger can be restored back to joy, and irritation can be restored back to pleasantry; the death of a nation can't be recovered, and the loss of life can't be revived. Therefore, wise leaders are cautious, and competent generals are careful..." War is like gambling with one's national interest and people's lives. Personal conflict is also a gamble, because there are so many possible reactions and consequences to our actions.

Sunzi also advocated both self-understanding and awareness, as well as, the understanding and awareness of one's opponents. He stated, "When you know your own ability and know your opponent's ability, you can engage in one hundred battles without danger (知己知彼，百戰不殆). When you lack the knowledge of your opponent's ability and only know your own ability, the chance of winning and losing is half and half (不知彼而知己，一勝一負). When you lack the understanding of your own ability and your opponent's ability, it is a losing battle (不知彼，不知己，每戰必敗)."

Knowing yourself is about understanding your martial ability, your power, your endurance, and continuing to improve yourself. Knowing the capabilities of your enemy will allow you to take advantage of your enemy's weaknesses and avoid his strengths. In order to be victorious in combat, one needs be able to utilize one's abilities and continue to eliminate one's weaknesses. If one only knows of the enemy's weaknesses but does not have the ability to take advantage of them, this knowledge is useless. When you are aware of your abilities and your opponent's abilities, you have already won, because you are mentally and physically prepared for the conflict. That is, you have already won before engaging in combat. Never fight a fight that you are not prepared to fight.

Sometimes, it is not possible to know the abilities of your opponent until you are actually engaged in combat. To fully understand what you are able to apply, it is necessary that you also understand what your opponent can do. In this case, you may need to use different methods to figure out his agility, reaction, strengths, and weaknesses. Do not overestimate your ability. That is arrogance; and arrogance is a recipe for loss. Do not underestimate your ability either. Underestimating your ability is a weakness and a sign of fear. When you are afraid during combat, you have already placed yourself at a psychological disadvantage.

Sunzi also advocated controlling the situation, being the active one instead of the reactive one. When you do engage your opponent, the only reason to engage should be to strike back. Being in the passive, reactive position you are likely to be hit eventually. If you control the situation, you will have the upper hand, the winning hand. We will discuss more about combat strategies in Chapter 3.

There are many areas that a practitioner can focus on to become a well-rounded martial artist. The barehanded applications of Wushu generally include four elements. They are: *ti*, the use of the legs for kicking; *da*, the use of the arms for striking; *shuai*, the use of take down techniques; and *na*, the use of controlling techniques to immobilize the opponent. In actual combat, there are both defensive and offensive strategies, which include variations of advancing and retreating, movement and stillness, fast and slow movements, hard and soft movements, and consequential and inconsequential movements. Based on these variations, the practical applications of *ti*, *da*, *shuai*, and *na* were created.

Ti (踢) or kicking is used both as an offensive, as well as, a defensive technique. An offensive kick is any movement of the leg with the intent to distress your opponent. A defensive technique is mostly used for deflecting or blocking the opponent's kicks. Kicks are either accomplished with one leg off the ground or both legs off the ground to kick. This makes the body less stable than when both feet are on the ground. Besides the kicking drills, dynamic balancing and jumping drills are important to accomplish effective kicks.

Da (打) refers to the many shapes of the hand, as well as, the many defensive and offensive maneuvers of the hands and the arms. It also refers to the use of intentional collision techniques to knock down the opponent. Even though, the hands are usually not as powerful as the legs, they are by far much more versatile than the legs. The hands and legs are both an important part of a good application. There is a saying in Chinese martial arts that states, "The hands are like a double swing door that opens up for the legs to kick the opponent". This implies the importance of hand and arm maneuvers to set up strategies to allow the stronger legs to deliver a powerful application.

Shuai (摔) is short for *shuaijiao* (摔跤) or take down. In Wushu fighting applications, a more specific shuaijiao approach is used. It is called *kuaijiao* (快跤), meaning *fast take down*. In actual combat, kicks and punches become less effective at very close range. It is then necessary to use take down techniques to subdue your opponent.

Na (拿) is short for qinna, which literally means to seize and to capture. The objective of qinna is to control one section of the opponent's body to immobilize the opponent's entire body; or to escape and counter control your opponent. The proper application of qinna allows you to subdue your opponent without having to injure your opponent. It also gives you the option to seriously injure your opponent when the situation requires such a measure.

Within the training of ti, da, shuai, and na, are many other components to enhance their effectiveness. Such as, the ability to apply Cavity Press or Dianxue (Dim Mak), the ability to neutralize an opponent's force, and of course, one must have power.

The term used in describing power emission in the practice or application of martial arts is *fajin* (發勁). The character *fa* literally means to emit, and the character *jin* is an expression of power. Fajin is accomplished by consciously focusing the mind along with the proper coordination of breathing, alignment, the relaxing and contracting of muscles, and internal energy.

When speaking of power in Wushu, li (力) and jin (勁) are specific terms used to describe and distinguish differences in power. Li refers to muscular strength. It is like the strength of an oxen pulling a heavy object or the force of a pneumatic car lift in a garage, lifting a car. Jin refers to integrated power that can be focused to a section of the body and released like an explosion. It is like the release of power of a crouching tiger suddenly leaping up to catch its prey or a jack hammer pulverizing concrete. Jin can be expressed in multiple directions, can be flexibly applied, and can vary in the way it is released.

Compressed air is like unrefined li, when released steadily, it can lift or push heavy cars, or crush steel. When compressed air is channeled and released in pulses, it is like jin that has been refined and focused. Li is the foundation of jin. With proper training, an individual with a lot of li has the potential to release a tremendous amount of jin. To convert li into jin, the whole body must be coordinated and move in unison. The different sections of the body must be able to superimpose the power of each section, focus it, and release it like an explosion.

In general, the body movements must be smooth and coordinated to be able to express jin. Additionally, the muscles must be able to contract and release fast with the right timing. Before jin is released, the muscles are relaxed. At the instant of jin release, the muscles suddenly tighten on impact, then relax again. Wushu practitioners are expected to be able to utilize their li and release a focused jin activated from all over the body. We will discuss and introduce the many strength building and power training methods in Chapter 6.

Body Mechanics and Artistic Expressions

The philosophy of harmony incorporates an elegant artistic expression, as well as, proper body mechanics. The rhythm of Wushu movements requires that to extend, one must first condense. To go left, first go right. To open, first close. To rise, first sink. To tighten, first loosen. This method of attaining the objective by first beginning with the opposite can be traced back to the philosophy of Laozi. Wushu movements also require that hard and soft compliment each other; offensive implies defense; and defense implies offense. This understanding of the opposing, yet interdependent, aspects are adapted from the philosophy and harmonious integration of *yin-yang* (陰陽).

Proper body mechanics are necessary to utilize the body's potential. In Wushu, natural scenery and animals are often used to describe movements and proper body mechanics. The *Twelve Models* (十二型) describe the postures and movements as, "*Move like a tidal wave, still as a great mountain, jump like an ape, land like a magpie, balance like a rooster, stand like a pine tree, spin like a wheel, bend like a bow, light as a leaf, heavy as iron, suspend like an eagle, and fast like the wind.*"

"*Move like a tidal wave* (動如濤)" describes the powerful, rhythmic, and controlled force of your movement.

"*Still as a great mountain* (靜如嶽)" describes the strength of a still posture with an immovable foundation like that of a great mountain; and expresses a majestic presence.

"*Jump like an ape* (起如猿)" describes the alertness and agility of your movements, like that of an ape in a movement involving jumping.

"*Land like a magpie* (落如鵲)" describes the lightness and stability of a magpie when landing on a tree branch.

"*Balance like a rooster* (立如雞)" describes a one legged standing posture that moves, then stops; similar to the stillness and alertness of a rooster in motion, then coming to an abrupt stop.

"*Stand like a pine tree* (站如松)" describes a standing posture with both feet on the floor. Even though you are standing still, your posture emanates the strength of a pine tree.

"*Spin like a wheel* (轉如輪)" describes a rotational movement, like that of a spinning car wheel with the rotation axle well defined and controlled.

"*Bend like a bow* (折如弓)" describes the storage of potential power in a bending or twisting posture, resembling a strung bow ready to release an arrow.

"*Light as a leaf* (輕如葉)" describes the lightness of the body gliding effortlessly from one location to the next.

"*Heavy as iron* (重如鐵)" describes an expression of seriousness, but not vicious and out of control.

"*Suspend like an eagle* (緩如鷹)" describes an animated state like that of an eagle flying and searching for food on the ground. It is alert and concentrated, not simply moving aimlessly.

"*Fast like the wind* (快如風)" describes fast, sharp, and swiftly accomplished movements.

Wushu training also includes sets of principles that the martial arts masters of old discovered and have passed on to their students. One such set of principles is the *Eight Principles of Integration* (八法) which refers to the four physical movements of your arms (手), your eyes (眼), your upper body (身法), and your stepping (步); and the four manifestations of your vitality (精神), your breathing & qi (氣), your expression of power (力), and your overall expression (功). The requirements of these eight areas are summarized in the phrase, "*punch like a shooting comet, eyes flash an like electric current, waist turns like a moving snake, steps should be rooted; vitality of spirit should be full and focused, breathing should be sunken, power should be smooth, delivery should be thorough*". This phrase is a principle regarding the integration of the *whole* body.

"*Punch like a shooting comet* (拳如流星)" is a requirement of the upper limbs. It requires that the movements of the arms be as fast as a shooting comet. Every movement, including the subtle and intricate movements of the palms and wrists, no matter how small, must be clearly and swiftly executed.

"*Eyes flash like an electric current* (眼似電)" is a requirement for the head. The movement of your head provides the range of view for your eyes. To be able to react to your opponent's intentions or movements, an alert and swift movement of your head can enhance your reaction speed.

"*Waist turns like a moving snake* (腰如蛇行)" is a requirement for the torso. The upper body movements and the transmission of power from the legs are generally controlled and directed by the waist. The coordination of the vertebrae, and various muscles in the torso play an important role in the many variations of bending, twisting, and jerking movements. The fluid movement of your waist makes it possible to transmit power.

"*Steps should be rooted* (步賽黏)" is a requirement for the stepping movements of the legs. Stepping in martial arts is harder to master than punching. Stepping must not only be fast; it must also provide a firm foundation for the upper body. It is said that, "*If stepping is not stable, then the punch will be scattered; and if the stepping is not fast, then the punch will be slow* (步不穩則拳亂，步不快則拳慢)." Another saying in Wushu states, "*Apply the hands 30% of the time, and apply stepping 70% of the time; to become victorious, one must rely on the unity of the hands and stepping* (手打三分步打七，勝人重在手步齊)." This saying stresses the relative importance of the hands and legs, as well as, the importance of the legs to set up the proper distance for the arms to be effective. It is important that the hands and legs are integrated and coordinated to accomplish proper defensive and offensive techniques.

"*Vitality of spirit should be full and focused* (精要充沛)" is a requirement for mental and spiritual expression. If your mind is not focused and lacks vitality, then your movements will lack energy and appear lifeless.

"*Breathing should be sunken* (氣宜沉)" is a requirement for your breathing pattern. The term sunken implies that breathing should include the abdomen. With abdominal breathing, martial artists tap into the energy (qi) center for stronger power emission. Breathing is also closely related to the endurance of an individual, since our body converts oxygen into energy that is used for metabolic functions. The proper coordination of inhalations and exhalations with each defensive and offensive application, not only provides for higher endurance, but it also makes it possible to deliver applications more effectively and more powerfully.

"*Power should be smooth* (力要順達)" is a requirement for power emission. Martial artists must be able to emit jin. Without jin, the movements are useless in combat. Also, if jin is not executed properly, the movements will be stiff and power will stay within the body. For jin to be expressed properly, each section of the body must react and relate to the other sections.

"*Delivery should be thorough* (功宜純)" refers to the integrated expression of all other parts of the *Eight Principles of Integration*; including power, endurance, speed, agility, and technique. Every move in your training must be delivered with proper focus to reach its maximum potential. Your practice should be purposeful, alert, and filled with vitality.

A Brief History of Wushu

China is located in the southeastern part of the Asian continent, with an area of ten million, four hundred, and sixty thousand square kilometers (10,460,000 KM^2) and a population of 1.2 billion people. This is about 20% of the world's population. It is a diverse nation with over fifty ethnic groups including the Han, Manchu, Mongol, Hui, and Tibetan. The vast land mass and diverse ethnic groups have made it difficult to keep clear records over the thousands of years of Chinese civilization. Chart I-1 lists a brief chronology of Chinese dynasties tracing back about five thousand years.

Due to the uncertain origins and as a tribute to the ancestors of China, many social organizations, including Chinese martial arts systems, credited the founder of their systems to well-known and respected historical figures in Chinese history. Taijiquan is one such example which gives credit to a Daoist priest as the originator. Shaolin Wushu is another example which gives credit to Bodhidharma as the originator. Similarly in Traditional Chinese Medicine, the *Yellow Emperor's Internal Classics* (黄帝内經) is ascribed to the Yellow Emperor.

The lack of written records in the past has created many discrepancies in the history of Wushu. Since many highly accomplished martial artists in ancient China were unable to read or write, the only way they passed down their art was by word of mouth and from teacher to student. In the written records that were found, valuable information was missing, or it contained mistakes, or it was unclear due to the diversity of dialects and customs in China. Also, martial artists of different styles were very conservative and secretive about their system, which created even more mystery in the history of Chinese martial arts. Many martial artists in ancient China were persecuted by the government and sought after by their enemies. To escape government persecution and enemies seeking revenge, many changed their names, or became hermits, creating additional confusion to the history of Wushu. The Chinese government, archeologists, historians, and martial artists have all made attempts to clarify the many discrepancies of Wushu during recent years. From their research and our understanding of the past, the origin of Wushu can be traced back to prehistoric times.

Our ancestors' need to hunt for food, to protect themselves from wild animals, and to guard against tribal attacks gradually developed into combative skills. As time went on, they developed their survival instincts into skilled abilities. This was the beginning of Wushu. Defensive and offensive techniques were constantly being developed through combat, and passed on from one generation to the next. These valuable survival experiences eventually became known as Wushu.

Chinese Chronology

Fuxi 伏羲		2852 B.C.
Shennong 神農		2773 B.C.
Huangdi (Yellow Emperor) 黃帝		2697 B.C.
Shaohao 少昊		2597 B.C.
Zhuanxu 顓頊		2513 B.C.
Yao 堯		2356 B.C.
Shun 舜		2255 B.C.
Xia Dynasty 夏		2205-1766 B.C.
Shang (Yin) Dynasty 商		1766-1123 B.C.
Zhou Dynasty 周		1122-249 B.C.
Spring-Autumn and Warring Kingdoms 春秋戰國		722-221 B.C.
Spring-Autumn 春秋	(722-480 B.C.)	
Warring Kingdoms 戰國	(403-221 B.C.)	
Qin Dynasty 秦		221-207 B.C.
Han Dynasty 漢		206 B.C.-7 A.D.
Eastern Han Dynasty 西漢		25-220 A.D.
Three Kingdoms Period 三國		220-265 A.D.
Shu Dynasty 蜀	(221-264 A.D.)	
Wei Dynasty 魏	(220-265 A.D.)	
Wu Dynasty 吳	(222-280 A.D.)	
J'in Dynasty 晉		265-317 A.D.
Eastern J'in Dynasty 東晉		317-420 A.D.
Southern and Northern Dynasties 南北朝		386-589 A.D.
Southern Dynasties 南朝	(420-589 A.D.)	
Former Song Dynasty 宋（劉）	(420-479 A.D.)	
Southern Qi Dynasty 南齊	(479-502 A.D.)	
Southern Liang Dynasty 南梁	(502-557 A.D.)	
Southern Chen Dynasty 南陳	(557-589 A.D.)	
Northern Dynasties 北朝	(386-581 A.D.)	
Northern Wei Dynasty 北魏	(386-535 A.D.)	
Eastern Wei Dynasty 東魏	(534-550 A.D.)	
Western Wei Dynasty 西魏	(535-556 A.D.)	
Northern Qi Dynasty 北齊	(550-577 A.D.)	
Northern Zhou Dynasty 北周	(557-581 A.D.)	
Sui Dynasty 隨		590-618 A.D.
Tang Dynasty 唐		618-906 A.D.
Five Dynasties 五代		907-960 A.D.
Later Liang Dynasty 後梁	(907-923 A.D.)	
Later Tang Dynasty 後唐	(923-936 A.D.)	
Later J'in Dynasty 後晉	(936-947 A.D.)	
Later Han Dynasty 後漢	(947-950 A.D.)	
Later Zhou Dynasty 後周	(951-960 A.D.)	
Liao Dynasty 遼		907-1125 A.D.
Northern Song Dynasty 宋		960-1126 A.D.
Western Xia Dynasty 西夏		990-1127 A.D.
Southern Song Dynasty 南宋		1127-1279 A.D.
Jin Dynasty 金		1115-1234 A.D.
Yuan Dynasty 元		1260-1368 A.D.
Ming Dynasty 明		1368-1644 A.D.
Qing Dynasty 清		1644-1912 A.D.
China		1912-

Chart I-1: Chinese Chronology

As ancient civilization continued to develop, specialized labor prompted the need for education for doing special tasks. Wushu, as well as other skilled jobs, became a well organized social and military organization for self-defense or for attaining specific objectives.

Besides using Wushu to tame nature (farming, hunting, etc.) and for combat, Wushu was also used to strengthen the physical body, increase endurance, and prevent diseases. Chinese historical records indicate that prehistoric leaders encouraged their troops to engage in fighting drills with imaginary opponents. Gradually, these drills were put together and became what is known today as Wushu routines or sports activities.

When China reached the feudal Spring-Autumn (722-480 B.C.) and Warring Kingdom (403-221 B.C.) period, the entire Chinese civilization encountered many new changes in the political, economical, cultural, and Wushu development. The new changes in that era significantly influenced the development of Chinese civilization. The perpetual struggle for power and wars between the different kingdoms brought out many incredible strategic martial artists that left lasting imprints on the history of Chinese civilization. *Sunzi's Art of War* (孫子兵法) by Sunzi was one book of strategy that created a significant influence on the development of Wushu.

The Chinese empire was unified in 221 B.C. when the First Emperor of the Qin Dynasty (221-207 B.C.) took control of the six surrounding kingdoms and established the first multiethnic central government in the history of China. From the Qin to the Early Han Dynasty (206 B.C.- 7 A.D.), and to the Later Han Dynasty (25-220 A.D.), the development under the unified empires flourished and provided an intermittent, but extended time of peace. This also gave Wushu a chance to develop outside of the military. The developments both in the military and in the civilian population continued to influence and enhance each other throughout history.

The first Shaolin Temple was built after China split into the Northern and Southern Dynasties. In 495 A.D., Emperor Xiaowen of the Northern Wei Dynasty (386-535 A.D.) commissioned the building of the Henan Shaolin Temple for the Indian priest, Batuo, who had come to China to spread the teachings of Buddhism. In 527 A.D., another Buddhist priest, Bodhidharma (470-543 A.D.), came to China and settled in the Shaolin Temple. Historical records indicate that Bodhidharma meditated in the cave next to the temple for nine years and came up with many realizations that he passed on to his followers. From then on, the teachings of the Shaolin Temple flourished and Bodhidharma became known as the first generation of Chinese *Chan* (禪).

It is unknown whether or not Bodhidharma knew any martial arts at all, nor did people know exactly from whom or where the Shaolin martial arts originated. Since Bodhidharma is the father of Chinese Chan Buddhism, to honor him and for a lack of a better choice, later generations credited him as the originator of Shaolin Kung Fu. Today, historians believe that Shaolin martial arts were brought to the Shaolin Temple by the many martial artists that sought spiritual sanctuary there; and in return they taught the monks how to defend themselves and strengthen their bodies through the practice of martial arts.

Shaolin martial arts became well known to Chinese society at the beginning of the Tang Dynasty (618-906 A.D.). At that time, thirteen martial monks from the Shaolin Temple assisted Li Shi-Ming in his struggle to gain control and reestablish order in the empire. Li later succeeded his father and became the emperor of the unified Tang Dynasty. During the Tang Dynasty (618-906 A.D.), specific requirements and testing procedures were established to award government positions and titles to qualified martial artists. This type of testing and selecting process for government positions was a catalyst in Wushu development.

In the Ming Dynasty (1368-1644 A.D.), Wushu reached a peak. Many different systems of marital arts were well developed. Specific training philosophies and theories, along with the requirements for the body, spirit, and power were recorded. This well organized system encouraged even more people to study Wushu. In-depth books about Wushu were being published now more than in any era before. These materials significantly increased the development of the martial techniques and health aspects of Wushu.

In his book, *New Book of Effective Disciplines* (紀效新書), Qi Ji-Guang, a well-known Wushu expert and writer of the time, was the first to distinguish between the Short Range Types and the Long Fist Types of Wushu styles. It was in his book that the Wushu Sanshou elements; *ti*, *da*, *shuai*, *na*, were coined.

Before the Ming Dynasty, Wushu development was done primarily in the military and was designed for large scale military combat. Their main focus at that time was on practical weapon techniques. In the era before guns, Wushu was crucial to the winning or losing of battles. As military Wushu spread to the civilian population and was influenced further by other cultural factors, Wushu development began taking on its modern form during the Ming Dynasty.

When the Qing Dynasty (1644-1912 A.D.) took control of the Chinese empire, many patriots of the defeated Ming Dynasty went into hiding and organized counterrevolutions against the Qing Dynasty. According to legend, some of these Ming Dynasty patriots hid and planned their counterattack in the Shaolin Temple. Fearing that the Ming loyalists would set up a counterrevolution against the new Qing Dynasty, the Qing Emperors forbad civilians from learning Wushu. Accusing the Shaolin Temple of harboring the defeated Ming Dynasty loyalists, the Shaolin Temple was burned down by the Qing army twice. This forced many martial monks out of the Shaolin Temple, initiating the wide spread of Shaolin martial arts all over the empire.

During the later part of the Qing Dynasty, training with guns gradually replaced the training of Wushu in the military. However, Wushu continued to develop with the general public. During that period of time, the late great Wushu fighter, Huo Yuan-Jia (1857-1909), defeated numerous foreign challengers, and became a living legend and a hero to the people of the weakened and downtrodden Qing empire. In 1909, Huo Yuan-Jia founded the Jinwu Physical Education School in Shanghai. Unfortunately, his untimely death in the same year prevented him from personally carrying on his work. In 1910, with the support of the many contemporary masters of the time, the school was renamed the Jinwu Athletic Association. Branches of the Jinwu Athletic Association were formed in many provinces, as well as, in Hong Kong and nations in Southeastern Asia.

In 1912, the Qing Empire was overthrown and replaced by a democratic government named the Republic of China. The restriction on Wushu training for civilians was removed, and the practice of Wushu reached another height. In 1926, the term Wushu was officially changed to *Guoshu* (國術), meaning national martial art. In the following year, the Guoshu Research Group was formed in Nanjing, and in 1928, it was renamed the Central Guoshu Institute. The first group of students were referred to as the "Professor Training Class", with the goal of nurturing martial arts teachers. The institute was also instrumental for creating martial arts magazines and books, for organizing competitions, and for organizing a Wushu team. In 1936, the Wushu team performed in the 11th Olympics held in Germany, where their Wushu performance amazed the world.

Efforts were also made to systematically organize and teach the diverse Wushu styles for younger generations to learn, as well as, and to continue its development. The Central Guoshu Institute included the notable great Wushu teachers, Wang Ziping (1881-1973) and Yang Chengfu (1883-1936). The Central Guoshu Institute was relocated to Chongqing City, Sichuan Province in 1943 during the Chinese civil war, and was finally closed in 1949.

The New China or the People's Republic of China, took control of the government in 1949 and ended the Chinese civil war. The term *Guoshu* was abolished and the term Wushu was brought back. However, outside of mainland China, places like Taiwan and Hong Kong still use the term *Guoshu*.

In the 1950's, the National Athletic Committee of the People's Republic of China developed many new routines which led to the standardization of Wushu. These new routines were used for popularizing Wushu and as a foundation for Wushu training. In 1959, the *Wushu Competition Rules* were formulated and began to divide Wushu into categories. The types of Wushu styles were being distinguished and each type was placed in its own division for competition. This allowed each type to be judged more objectively.

From 1952 to 1956, Wushu was actively publicized. Research and teacher training was being done to promote Wushu. Old masters were officially invited to teach the younger generations. Physical education colleges began to include

Wushu training as part of the curriculum. In 1956, the first official rules for Wushu competition were compiled. Specific requirements on the content, time, space, etc. were written for Nanquan (南拳, Southern Style), Changquan (長拳, Long Fist), and Taijiquan (太極拳).

These new rules encouraged individuals to create their own routines, giving the athletes the liberty to create without hindrance. The degree of difficulty in Wushu increased and gradually developed many new stylistic characteristics that were more suited for young athletes.

The most significant developments in the Wushu divisions were in the Long Fist type and weapon categories. To attain higher scores, many competitors gradually replaced the traditional routines with newly created routines that included many acrobatic maneuvers. These new routines still met the competition requirements while increasing the artistic expression of each movement. The freedom to create also developed an individual's unique physical potential. These routines are now known as *Contemporary Wushu* routines which were distinguished from *Traditional Wushu* or Kung Fu routines.

The newly created Contemporary Wushu routines were more artistically expressive in performance than Traditional Wushu routines. Unfortunately, many of these new routines lacked the offensive and defensive characteristics of Traditional Wushu routines. Therefore, in the years that followed, competition rules were modified to limit movements that did not have martial applications and to limit the frequency of repeated movements.

In 1957, Wushu was officially listed as a competition category in China's national athletic competitions. From this point on, every year there have been national Wushu competitions and performances. Beginning in the 1960's, provinces, counties, and cities all over China began to organize their own Wushu teams. High schools and grade schools began to include Wushu as a part of their physical education programs.

In 1960, the first National Wushu team of the New China performed in Burma. The Head coach was the late great Wushu grandmaster, Wang Ziping (王子平); and the first women Wushu professor and coach ever to lead a Wushu team to perform outside of China, Professor Wang Jurong (王菊蓉). Since then, more and more teams have been sent out to international sports communities all over the world.

Starting in 1966, a set back to Wushu occurred during the 10 years of the Cultural Revolution. Along with many other arts and culture, Wushu received a severe blow and destruction. The older generation masters were persecuted, martial arts books were destroyed, weapons were confiscated, and fighting arts were forbidden to be discussed.

After the Cultural Revolution, in order to recover and restore some of the loss of Wushu styles, the National Athletic Committee began a national research and gathering of Wushu remnants. Teams of Wushu Research groups were formed both in the provinces and in the cities across China. A dedicated team of Wushu Investigators and Researchers was formed to investigate in all of the provinces in China and to organize the scattered and once lost Wushu styles.

Beginning in 1979, besides continuing the annual national competitions, an annual National Wushu Exhibition was organized. Individuals that competed at the national level, had already competed in many local, city, provincial, and regional competitions. During the National Wushu Exhibitions, many of the once believed to be lost styles began to resurface. Since the 1980's, significant efforts were being placed on organizing and finding traditional Wushu. Valuable Wushu information and styles that were on the verge of perishing were finally being preserved.

Today, all provinces in China have their own professional Wushu team. Every city and region have professional coaches. Among the over one thousand cities and counties in China with amateur Physical Education Schools, all of them have Wushu training classes for children and adults, and all of the expenses are paid by the government.

China has been sending Wushu coaches to nations all over the world to teach Wushu. Tens of thousands of people now go to China to further their Wushu studies. Aside from China, Wushu competitions are being organized throughout the world. The standards of the competitors are improving every year. Many countries are now sending teams to compete in China, winning medals, and amazing the Chinese audience with their ability and captivating performances. Nations worldwide are now working on introducing Wushu at the Olympics.

Wushu has become an international sport that all people can learn and use to attain its inherent benefits. Since the development of firearms, the actual use of Wushu for combat has greatly decreased, but the application of Wushu continues. Aside from a means of self-defense, Wushu has also been developed into a sport capable of improving a participant's health and fitness, while improving their reaction time, jumping ability, balance, flexibility, coordination, power, and speed. Even athletes from other sports are taking up Wushu training to complement their physical pursuits and to improve the quality of their performance. Today, Wushu is also a performing art. The performance of a superb Wushu participant can captivate and mesmerize an audience.

Classification of Styles

Throughout history there have been many ways to classify Wushu into different categories. However, it wasn't until the Qing Dynasty that more and more Wushu styles were becoming distinctive and apparent. Some classified Buddhist (Shaolin, 少林) Wushu into Chujia (出家, Ordained monk practicing Wushu) or Zaijia (在家, Buddhist lay person practicing Wushu). Some classified the styles with compact movements from Southern China as Nanquan (南拳, Southern Style), and the styles with extended movements from Northern China as Beipai (北派, Northern Style).

Other terms such as Shaolin (少林), Wudang (武當), or Emei (峨嵋) Styles are commonly used to refer to styles originating from the Shaolin Temple, Wudang Mountain area, and the Emei Mountain area, respectively. In 1928, the Central Guoshu Institute (中央國術館) used Wudang and Shaolin as a way to classify the different styles of Wushu. The Wudang division included: Taijiquan (太極拳), Xingyiquan (形意拳), and Baguazhang (八卦掌). The Shaolin division included: Shaolinquan (少林拳), Chaquan (查拳), Tantui (彈腿), Bajiquan (八極拳), and Piguaquan (劈挂拳).

Today, one of the most common ways to classify Wushu styles, is based on their training approaches, as Internal or External Styles. The terms *Internal Style* (内家拳) or *External Style* (外家拳) are figures of speech in the martial arts community, used to distinguish their stylistic emphasis. As a martial art, the general philosophy and purpose of the Internal and External Styles are the same, with differences only in their stylistic approaches.

The well-known Internal Styles today include: Taijiquan (太極拳), Xingyiquan (形意拳), Baguazhang (八卦掌), Liuhebafa (六合八法), along with many others. Taijiquan is perhaps the most well-known due to it's health and healing benefits. Most people that practice Taijiquan today are not very concerned with the martial aspects of this art, they practice Taijiquan for its healing potential. The well-known External Styles today include: Shaolinquan (少林拳), Chaquan (查拳), Huaquan (華拳), Hongquan (紅拳), Paoquan (炮拳), Chuojiaoquan (戳脚拳), Fanziquan (翻子拳), and many others.

Further classifications can be made under the Internal and External Styles. For example, Taijiquan is classified as an Internal Style, and can be further distinguished into Chen (陳), Yang (楊), Wu (吳), W'u (武), Sun (孫), and other styles. The External Styles can be further distinguished into Northern or Southern Styles. The Northern Styles refer to the External Styles that have their origin above the Yangtze River (長江, Changjiang) in China. The Southern Styles refer to the External Styles that have their origin located south of the Yangtze River. Drawing I-1 shows a map of China with the location of the two largest rivers in China.

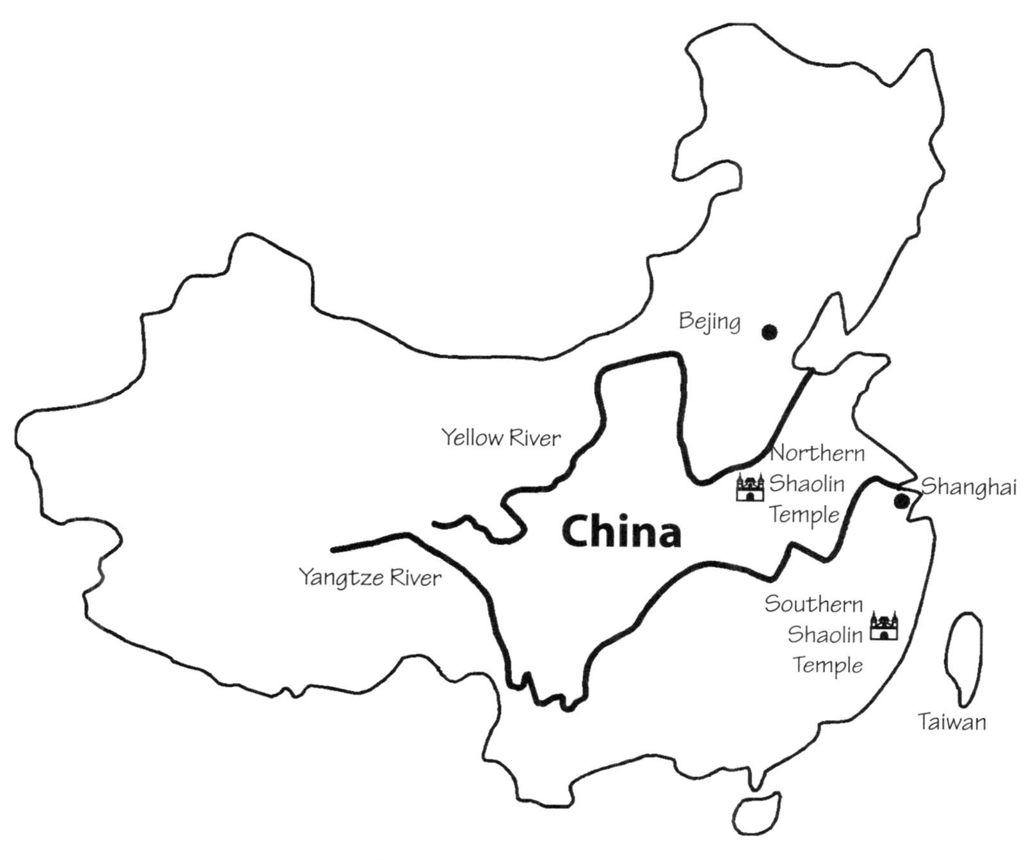

Drawing I-1: Map of China

Wushu styles have been further classified by the characteristics of their movements. They are categorized under one of the five types:

1. Circular Movement and Soft Appearance Type refers to almost all styles classified as an Internal Style. An exception is Xingyiquan which is classified as a Short Range Type. Most of the movements in this type are circular in nature and have a soft, but energetic appearance.
2. Long Fist Type refers to Wushu styles that emphasize their kicking abilities and are capable of striking the opponent from a distance. It is characterized by rapid advancing and retreating movements. One of the common phrases used in Long Fist training states, "*The hands are like double swing doors that open up for the legs to kick the opponent* (手是兩扇門，全憑腿打人)." The term Long Fist is used in contrast to the close range applications used in the Short Range Type.
3. Long Range Type refers to styles that use their long reach to engage their opponent. Tongbeiquan and Piquaquan are typical examples of this type. Even though it's emphasis is on long range

applications similar to Long Fist Type, its movement characteristics differ from the Long Fist Type styles.

4. Short Range Type refers to styles that emphasize close range fighting applications. It is used in contrast to the Long Fist Type which emphasizes striking from a longer distance. Xingyiquan, Bajiquan, and most Southern Styles are of the Short Range Type. This type of Wushu style is characterized by rapid, compact, and closed range strikes.
5. Imitation Type refers to styles that imitate the characteristics of an animal or a person in a specific state. Praying Mantis, Monkey, and Drunken Styles are typical examples of this type.

A more detailed modern classification divides Wushu into different training and competition categories.

1. The Barehanded Routine Component. This component is further categorized into different types of styles:
   a. Changquan (Long Fist) Type includes well-known styles of Northern Chinese origin such as Chaquan, Huaquan, Hongquan, Paoquan, Chuojiaoquan, Fanziquan, Shaolinquan, etc.
   b. Taijiquan Type includes the well-known Chen, Yang, Wu, W'u, and Sun Style Taijiquan; and 24 Posture Taijiquan, 48 Posture Taijiquan, and 88 Posture Taijiquan, etc.
   c. Nanquan (Southern) Type refers to Southern Styles originating in the southern regions of China. It includes countless number of styles. In the Guangzhou (Canton) Province alone, there are over 400 Nanquan Type styles.
   d. Xingyiquan Type refers to the style that uses Santishi (Three Body Posture); Pi, Zuan, Beng, Pao, Heng; and the 12 animal characteristics and intentions in its movements.
   e. Baguazhang Type refers to the style that uses various palm changes; and focuses on circular stepping, continuous movements, and agile stepping and body movements.
   f. Imitation Type refers to the styles that literally imitate the movements of animals or different states of a person, and name the style with the animal name itself. These styles include: Tanglangquan (Preying Mantis Style), Yingzhuaquan (Eagle Claw Style), Huquan (Tiger Style), Zuiquan (Drunken Style), Shequan (Snake Style), and many others.
   g. Other Type includes the styles that do not fit within the other types, and have their own unique characteristics. They include: Liuhebafa, Bajiquan, Gongliquan, Tongbeiquan,

Wujiquan, Liangyiquan, Sixiangquan, and many others.

2. The Weapon Routine Component includes over 400 plus types of weapons. The common weapons used in competition include: saber, sword, spear, staff, long handled saber, double saber, double swords, double hooked swords, double spears, nine sectional chain, rope dart, and many others.

3. Sparring Set Component refers to two or more people following a set routine to train their defensive and offensive skills. These routines include combinations of various barehanded against barehanded or weapon routines.

4. Group Routine Component refers to many people performing the same barehanded or weapon routines with or without music.

5. Application Component is further categorized into different types of applications including:

   a. Sparring with specific guidelines (with or without protective gear)

   b. Taiji Push Hands

   c. Qinna

   d. Shuaijiao

   e. Free sparring (including ti, da, shuai, na, and Push Hands skills)

   f. Short weapon sparring

   g. Long weapon sparring.

6. Wushu Qigong Component. Most styles of Wushu include their own method of Wushu Qigong training to increase their defensive, as well as, their offensive application abilities. Wushu Qigong is excellent for maintaining health; strengthening the internal organs, bones, and tendons; and to lessen training related injuries (for more information about Wushu Qigong, please refer to the book *Qigong Empowerment* by the authors).

The modern classifications placed on the different styles of Chinese martial arts are for the purpose of clarifying Chinese martial arts systems, identifying their unique stylistic emphasis, and for competition categorizing. It is intended to assist in the preservation of these arts, not as a dividing or limiting factor. To become proficient in Wushu, one will have to train hard in his or her chosen style and learn to absorb the essence of the other styles in order to enhance one's main style. The essence of other styles can greatly improve one's learning and training in a particular style, because the root is the same for all Chinese martial arts styles.

A Brief Outline of This Book

This book has been written as a guide for anyone interested in martial arts. It is designed to help build a solid and well-rounded foundation and is intended to be used as a reference for the beginning to advanced martial artist. The information presented is useful for all Chinese martial arts systems. Mastering the training in this book will help build a solid foundation in your martial arts training and facilitate your advancement to higher levels.

Chapter 1 focuses on methods to build a strong foundation. This chapter includes methods to increase your flexibility; develop stable stances, agile steps, and proper arm movements; develop the integration of your body movements; and improve your balance.

Chapter 2 focuses on developing powerful kicks. This chapter includes jumping drills, basic and advance kicks, and other drills to improve your physical ability.

Chapter 3 focuses on free fighting applications, including a discussion on the proper strategies, the many uses of the arms and legs in fighting applications, and many effective fighting combinations.

Chapter 4 focuses on takedown techniques, including a discussion on the use of levers to apply an effective takedown and many techniques that utilize the lever principle.

Chapter 5 focuses on qinna applications. The techniques are explained in detail from neutralizing, controlling, to trouble-shooting for possible problems in applications.

Chapter 6 focuses on training the arms and the legs to be strong like iron for effective applications, including Iron Arm, Iron Sand Palm, Red Sand Palm, and Cavity Press Finger Training. This chapter includes vocal, visual, and auditory training; jin training; and Light Body training.

Chapter 7 focuses on Cavity Press, including a theoretical discussion about Dianxue, numbing points, knockout points, points to deter an opponent used in fighting, and examples of vital points used in different Wushu styles.

We have included two appendixes at the end of the book. Appendix A contains an extensive glossary about many Wushu styles, Wushu practitioners, Wushu weapons, and Wushu terms that practitioners of Chinese martial arts can use as a reference. Next to the description of the styles and weapons we have included many valuable photos we have obtained from practitioners of these styles and weapons. Appendix B contains a list of some traditional herbal formulas used for Wushu training.

基本功

Chapter 1:

Building a Strong Foundation

The foundation drills in Wushu are for overall body conditioning, yet develops power, speed, flexibility, jumping ability, quick reactions, control of one's body, agility, and coordination. The drills generally include the training of the shoulders, arms, waist, legs, hands, stances, stepping, jumping, and balancing. The training can be isolated to one section or part of the body, or can integrate different sections of the body.

The purpose of the fundamental drills are to help the practitioner attain a well rounded and conditioned body for all other aspects of Wushu training, including barehanded routines and weapon routines. It is also an important step in the preparation for self-defense and combat readiness. With a good foundation, all the necessary components required for free fighting, including ti, da, shuai, and na, will be enhanced and improved.

Regular training of the fundamental drills will strengthen the joints, increase flexibility and agility of the ligaments, and heighten the control of the muscles and it's elasticity. A well conditioned body will improve the body's ability to express the Wushu movements more effectively and can reduce the chances of unnecessary injuries that may occur during training.

Many people feel that basic drills are boring, hard, and a waste of time. These people tend to want to start their Wushu training with routines and fighting right away. Unfortunately, many of these people find that they lack the coordination and proper body conditioning to excel to a high level and end up with injuries. Many give up their training due to injuries or due to a lack of advancement after a long period of stagnation. These individuals often have to restart their training with basic drills. All highly accomplished martial artists have strong foundations developed through repetitious foundation drills. There are many foundation drills. It is not easy to master all the drills. Therefore, the approach should be to focus on the drills that are most beneficial for developing the less adequate areas of your body.

We live in a fast paced society that demands quick results. However, not everything can be rushed to reach fruition. Wushu is one thing that can't be rushed. Starting your sparring and routine training without a solid foundation will limit higher accomplishments. Starting your martial arts training with sparring and routine training may provide some visible quick results. Unfortunately, without a strong foundation, the coordination and proper body conditioning required to excel to high levels will be hindered.

This chapter focuses on increasing your flexibility; basic arm, waist, and leg movements; and strength building. Flexibility will increase your mobility and overall range of motion, improve the muscles' ability to contract and relax, and improve the muscles' elasticity. One's flexibility directly affects one's movements. In martial arts, one's flexibility and range of motion can effectively increase one's striking distance, and the ability to neutralize and avoid an opponent's attacks. Flexibility training generally includes the shoulders, back, waist, and legs.

The basic arm, waist, and leg maneuvers include stances, stepping patterns, coordination drills, balance drills, and strength and endurance building drills. These drills will set a good foundation for you, and provide a guarantee for furthering your achievements in Kung Fu. When training these drills, repetition is necessary to improve the fluidity of your movements. Continuous and dedicated training will make these movements become a part of your body's automatic response. Practice 10 to 20 repetitions of each during your training session. Concentrate and be alert, do not simply go over the movements mechanically.

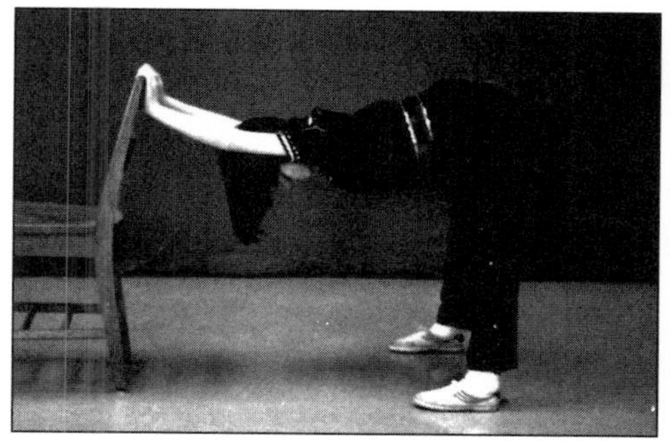

Figure 1-1

Figure 1-2

1.1. Increase Your Flexibility

Preparing Your Upper Body for Action

Shoulder exercises are used for improving the shoulders' flexibility, increasing the range of motion, developing strength; and improving the arms' agility, extension, and rotation ability.

1. Stretch the Shoulders (*yajian* 壓肩):

Drill 1: Grab a hold of something stable that is about your waist height with both hands. Place your feet about shoulder width apart and bend your upper body forward. Keep both of your arms and your legs straight (Figure 1-1).

Drill 2: Two people may also do the stretch by holding onto each other's arms (Figure 1-2).

When stretching the shoulders, rhythmically bounce your shoulders up and down. Focus on the downward movement of the shoulders, and gradually increase the depth of the downward pressure over time.

Figure 1-3

Figure 1-4

Figure 1-5

2. Swing the Arms (*lunbi* 掄臂):

One Arm Backward Swing: Stand in a left Bow Stance and place your left hand on top of your left knee, and extend your right arm over your head (Figure 1-3). Keep your upper body straight while swinging your right arm in a vertical circle (Figures 1-4 and 1-5). After you have done this about 20 times, change sides, and swing the other arm.

One Arm Forward Swing: Same starting posture as in the Backward Swing. Swing your arm in a vertical circle forward. After you have done this about 20 times, change sides, and swing the other arm.

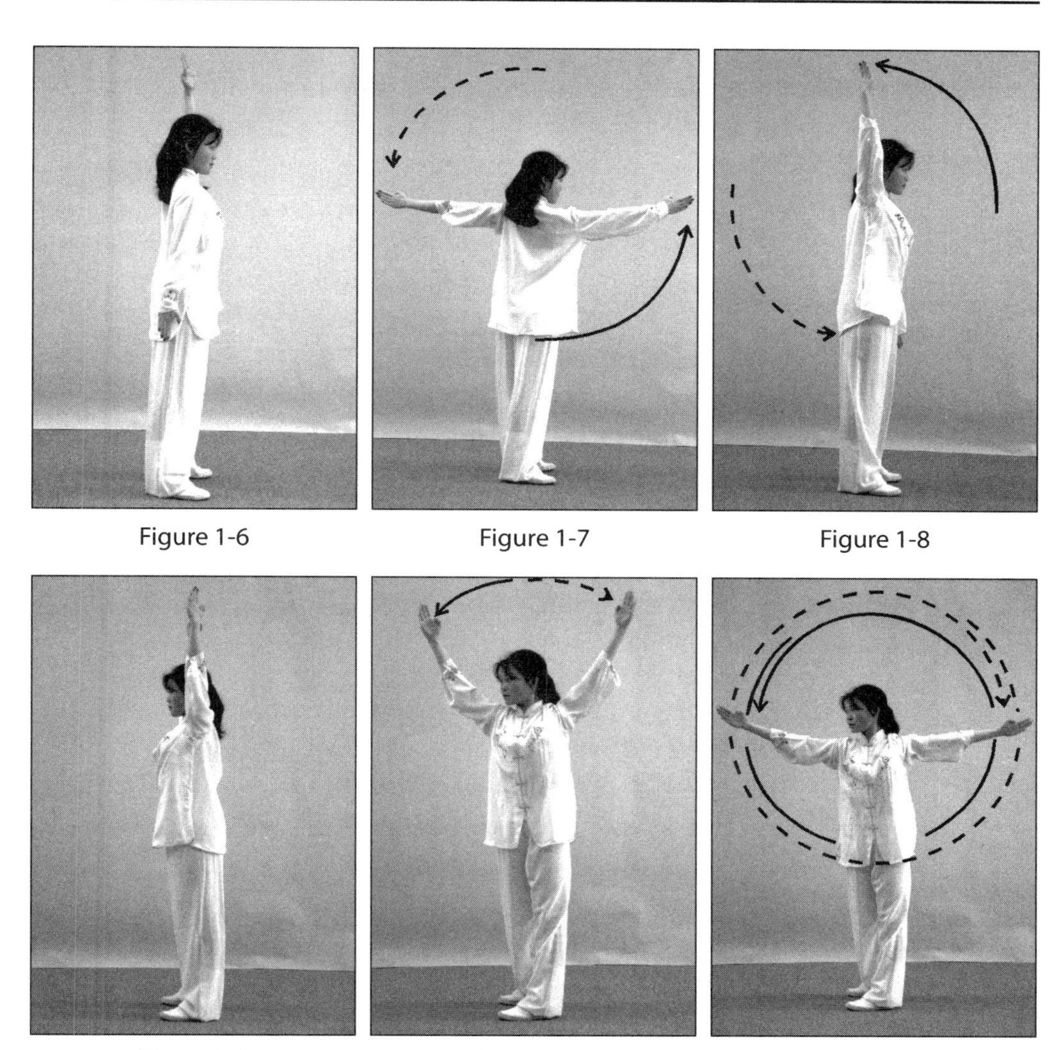

Figure 1-6 Figure 1-7 Figure 1-8

Figure 1-9 Figure 1-10 Figure 1-11

Both Arms Backward Swing: Stand straight with your feet about one shoulder width apart. Raise one arm up over your head and the other next to your side pointing down (Figure 1-6). Keep your arms pointing in the opposite directions and swing the arms in a vertical circle backwards (Figures 1-7 and 1-8).

Both Arms Forward Swing: Same starting posture as in the Backward Swing, except swing your arms in a verticle circle forwards.

Both Arms Forward and Backward Simultaneous Swing: Extend both arms over your head (Figure 1-9). Lower your arms in opposite directions, down then back up, while keeping the arms in a vertical plane (Figures 1-10 and 1-11).

Figure 1-12

Figure 1-13

Both Arms Cross Swing: Stand with your feet about one shoulder width apart. Extend your right arm straight to your right and place your left hand next to your right upper arm (Figure 1-12). Swing your arms up and across your head to the other side by extending your left arm and placing your right hand next to your left upper arm (Figure 1-13). Alternate from side to side.

During the arm swings, relax the shoulders and keep the swinging arm straight. Gradually increase the speed of the swing. Do each swing about 20 times or until your fingers are slightly numb after each exercise.

3. Stretch the Back and Waist:

The waist is the connector of the upper and the lower body. There is a saying in Wushu, *"If one trains the martial arts without training the waist, their accomplishment will never be high* 練拳不練腰，終究藝不高." In the training of Wushu, the waist is the key to the proper expression of the movement.

Forward Back Stretch (*qianfuyao* 前俯腰): Stand with your feet together and interlock your fingers. Stretch your arms up then bend from your waist and push your palms down towards the floor as low as you can (Figure 1-14). Then release the fingers and grab a hold of your heels with your hands, and bring your chest as close to your thighs as you can (Figure 1-15). Hold this position for about 30 seconds before standing up.

Instead of holding your heels, you may also place your palms on either side of your feet for about 30 seconds each side (Figure 1-16).

Figure 1-14

Figure 1-15

Figure 1-16

Figure 1-17

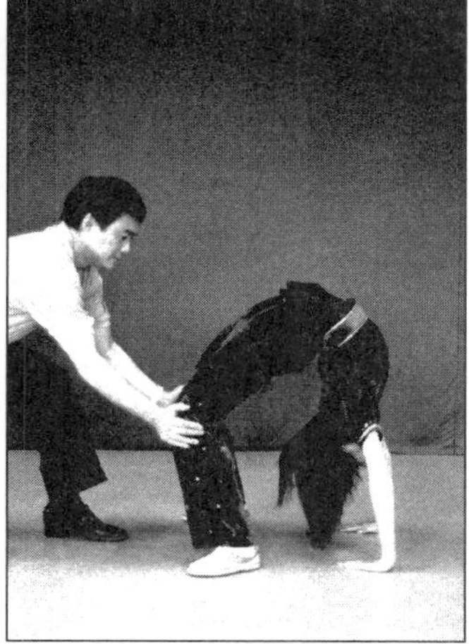
Figure 1-18

Bridge Bend (*xiayao* 下腰): Stand with your feet shoulder width apart, and stretch your arms over your head. Lower your arms slowly behind your body to form a bridge or a back bend (Figure 1-17). Hold this position for about 30 seconds.

Do this stretch gradually so you don't injure your back. An assistant may be used to help hold your legs in place to prevent your feet from slipping under you (Figure 1-18).

Figure 1-19

Figure 1-20

Figure 1-21

Figure 1-22

Swinging the Waist (*shuaiyao* 甩腰): Stand with your feet shoulder width apart and stretch your arms over your head. Use the waist and hips as the pivot, swing your upper body forward and backward. Allowing the upper body to wave forward and back (Figures 1-19 and 1-20).

Circling the Waist (*shuayao* 涮腰): Stand with your feet shoulder width apart, bend your upper body from your waist and hips, and stretch your arms. Use your waist and hips as the pivot, circle your upper body and your arms horizontally (Figures 1-21 and 1-22). Gradually speed up the circles. Do 10 to 20 times in each direction.

After this exercise, you may wish to squat down or bend from your waist and keep your head down for a while to prevent dizziness.

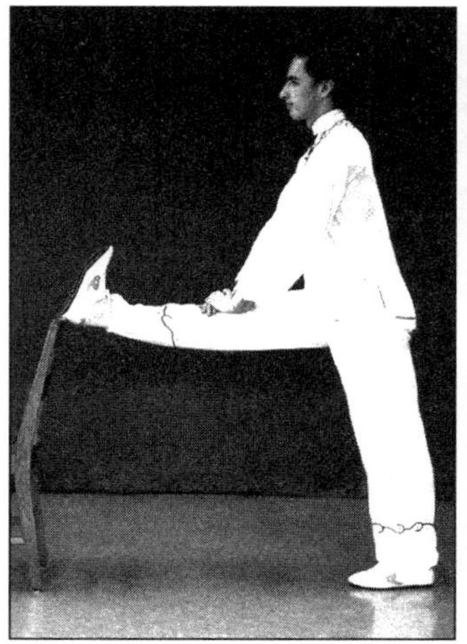
Figure 1-23

Figure 1-24

Stretch Your Legs for Powerful Kicks

Leg stretches are for developing the flexibility, agility, and power of the legs.

4. Front Pressing Leg Stretch (*zhengnyatui* 正壓腿):

Stand in front of a supporting structure about the height of your waist. Stand with your feet together and toes pointing forward. Place one foot on the support with your toes pointing upward. Keep your legs straight and hips square facing the supporting structure.

Drill 1: Place your palm over your knee (Figure 1-23). Gently and rhythmically lean forward, then back up. Gradually increase the depth of the lean. Do as many times as you like, then change legs and do the other side. Gradually over time, increase your flexibility until your forehead, nose, and chin are able to touch the tip of the toes (Figure 1-24).

Drill 2: After you have done the stretch, bend your knee and hold your knee up with your arms in front of your chest for about 10 seconds. Next, extend your leg straight and hold it above the supporting structure for about 10 seconds. This training will strengthen your legs and improve your ability to control your legs.

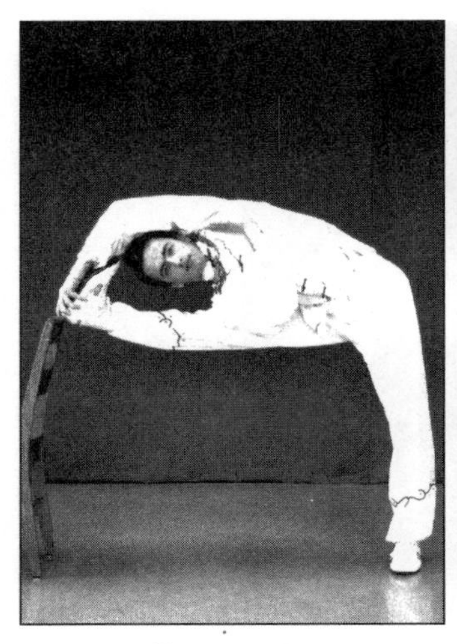
Figure 1-25

Figure 1-26

Figure 1-27

5. Side Pressing Leg Stretch (*ceyatui* 側壓腿):

Drill: Stand sideways in front of a supporting structure about the height of your waist. Stand with the support to your side. Place one foot on the support with toes pointing upward. Keep the other foot on the floor with your toes turned out slightly. Gently and rhythmically lean sideways, then up, with your upper body. Gradually increase the depth of the lean.

Do this stretch as many times as you like, then change legs and do the other side. Keep both legs straight during the stretch. Gradually over time, increase your flexibility until your upper body is parallel with the stretched leg (Figure 1-25).

6. Backward Pressing Leg Stretch (*houyatui* 後壓腿):

Drill: Stand facing away from the supporting structure with your feet together. Lift one leg up from behind you and place your foot on the support. Gently and rhythmically lean back, then up, with your upper body. Keep both legs straight and hips square during the stretch. Gradually increase the depth of the lean. Do this stretch as many times as you like, then change legs and do the other side. Gradually over time, increase your flexibility by stretching further back (Figure 1-26).

Figure 1-28

Figure 1-29

Figure 1-30

7. Half-Squat Stretch (*pubu yatui* 仆步壓腿):

Drill: Stand with your feet wide apart. Bend your right knee and squat down as low as you can, while keeping your left leg straight. Keep both feet flat on the floor and toes pointing forward. Then use your hands to hold on to the outer edge of your feet (Figure 1-27).

Hold this posture for about 30 seconds, then change sides by bending your left knee and straightening your right leg. You may also alternate from side to side without holding the posture for 30 seconds.

8. Leg Lifts:

Front Lift Stretch (*zhengbantui* 正搬腿): Bend your left knee and lift it up with your right hand (Figure 1-28). Then straighten your left leg by extending your left foot forward (Figure 1-29). As an alternative you may have an assistant help hold your leg up as high as your flexibility will allow (Figure 1-30). Hold the stretch for about 30 second, then change legs.

Figure 1-31

Figure 1-32

Figure 1-33

Side Lift Stretch (*cebantui* 側搬腿): Hold on to the back of your right leg with your right hand. Lift it up sideways as high as you can (Figure 1-31). As an alternative, you may have an assistant help hold your leg up, as high as your flexibility will allow (Figure 1-32). Hold the stretch for about 30 seconds, then change legs.

Back Lift Stretch (*houbantui* 後搬腿): Stand facing a supporting structure with your feet pointing forward. Place your hands on the support and have an assistant lift one of your legs up from behind you, as high as your flexibility will allow (Figure 1-33). Keep both legs straight and hips flat during the stretch.

Figure 1-34

Figure 1-35

9. Splits:

Regular Split Stretch (*qianhoupicha* 前後劈叉): Place your hands on the floor. Place your left leg in front and your right leg behind. Start by straighten your front leg, then gradually straighten your back leg. When you are able to do a complete split, keep your front foot pointing up and the inside edge of your back foot facing down, and extend your arms to your sides (Figure 1-34). Hold this stretch for about 30 seconds, then change sides. As your flexibility gets better, you may also lean forward and backward while holding this stretch.

Straddle Split Stretch (*zhengpicha* 正劈叉): Sit on the floor with your feet as wide apart as you can and lean forward. Gradually increase your flexibility until you are able to keep your legs 180 degrees apart. Then stretch your arms to your sides and put your feet flat on the floor (Figure 1-35).

1.2. Develop Stable Stances, Agility, and Proper Arm Movements

Stances

Stances are like the foundation of a house. When building a house, the foundation must be built properly to withstand the structural requirements of the house (your body weight), the occupants (your movements), and other natural and unnatural safety factors (your opponents). Stance training is for building strength and agility in your legs, so you can easily and instinctively switch from one movement to the next. Without strong stances and the agility to move with stability, your applications will not have a firm foundation to be executed properly. A poor foundation can render any good technique useless.

1. Horse Stance (*mabu* 馬步):

Posture: Stand with your feet apart about 3-4 times your own foot length. Face forward and keep your feet pointing forward. Squat down until your thighs are parallel to the floor. Keep your back straight and your fists at your waist, or extend one arm to the side as if you were punching (Figure 1-36).

Drill: Hold the stance for about 30 seconds. Gradually, increase the length of time. You may also alternate punching or palm striking forward while holding the stance; or jump up from the Horse Stance to standing with feet together, then jump back into Horse Stance again.

2. Bow Stance (*gongbu* 弓步):

Posture: Keep your feet apart about 4-5 times your own foot length. Face to your right and turn your foot in slightly, and bend your right knee so your right thigh is parallel to the floor. Keep your left leg straight and foot turned out about 45 degrees. An ideal Bow Stance is to have the heels lined up on an imaginary center line running from the front to the back. Keep your back straight and fists at your waist (Figure 1-37).

Drill: Hold the stance for about 30 seconds. Then change sides. Gradually, increase the length of time. You may also alternate punching or palm striking forward while holding the stance.

Figure 1-36

Figure 1-37

Figure 1-38

Figure 1-39

3. Empty Stance (*xubu* 虛步):

Posture: Stand with your feet one foot forward and one foot behind. Turn your back foot out about 45 degrees and squat down on your back leg. Raise your front heel off the floor with only your toes touching the floor and the top of your foot flat (Figure 1-38). You may place your hands around your waist or hook your back hand and extend your front palm.

Drill: Hold the stance for about 30 seconds. Then change sides. Gradually, increase the length of time and lower your posture. You may also alternate from side to side to practice both sides of the stance.

4. Half-Squat Stance (*pubu* 仆步):

Posture: Stand with your feet wide apart. Squat down as low as you can with your back straight and your feet flat on the floor. Keep your bent knee pointing in the same direction as your foot (Figure 1-39).

Figure 1-40

Figure 1-41

Figure 1-42

Drill: Hold the stance for about 30 seconds. Then change sides. Gradually, increase the length of time and lower your posture. You may also alternate from side to side to practice both sides of the stance.

5. Resting Stance (*xiebu* 歇步):

Posture: Place one foot in front of the other. Turn your front foot out and squat down until your back knee is next to your front ankle, while keeping your front foot flat and raising your back heel. Keep your back straight and go down as low as you can (Figure 1-40).

Drill: Hold the stance for about 30 seconds. Then change sides. Gradually, increase the length of time and lower your posture. You may also alternate from side to side to practice both sides of the stance.

6. T Stance (*dingbu* 丁步):

Posture: Stand with your feet together. Bend your knees as low as you can. Keep one foot flat on the floor while raising the other heel up (Figure 1-41).

Drill: Hold the stance for about 30 seconds. Then change sides. Gradually, increase the length of time and lower your posture. You may also alternate from side to side to practice both sides of the stance.

T resembles the Chinese character "丁", thereby the name T Stance was translated.

Figure 1-43

Figure 1-44

7. Crossed Legs Sitting Stance (*zuopanbu* 坐盤):

Posture: Sit all the way down on one leg with both the thigh and the leg on the floor. Cross the other leg over the lower leg (Figure 1-42).

Drill: From the standing position sit down into the Crossed Legs Sitting Stance. Then stand up and sit down again. Do 10 times, then change sides.

8. Half Horse Stance (*banmabu* 半馬步):

Posture: Start from a Horse Stance. Turn one foot out and shift a little more weight onto the other leg (Figure 1-43).

Dril: Hold the stance for about 30 seconds. Then change sides. Gradually, increase the length of time and lower your posture. You may also alternate from side to side to practice both sides of the stance.

9. Side Bow Stance (*hengdangbu* 橫襠步):

Posture: Start from a Bow Stance. Turn your back foot out and turn your upper body to face to the side (Figure 1-44).

Drill: Hold the stance for about 30 seconds. Then change sides. Gradually, increase the length of time and lower your posture. You may also alternate from side to side to practice both sides of the stance.

Figure 1-45

Figure 1-46

10. One Legged Stance (*dulibu* 獨立步):

Posture: Stand with your feet together. Turn one foot out about 45 degrees and raise the other knee up as high as you can, with the foot pointing down (Figure 1-45).

Drill: Hold the stance for about 30 seconds. Then change sides. Gradually, increase the length of time. You may also alternate from side to side to practice both sides of the stance to develop your balance and leg strength.

11. Ready Stance (*yubeibu* 預備步):

Posture: Stand at a comfortable height with one foot in front of the other with your front foot turned in slightly and back foot turned out. Keep about 60% of your weight on your back leg and 40% on your front leg (Figure 1-46).

There are many variations of the Ready Stance. The Ready Stance must allow you to move quickly into any other posture and in any direction. Usually, the weight distribution is about 60% on the back leg and 40% on the front leg.

12. Standing Stance with feet together (*libu* 立步):

Posture: Stand upright with your feet together (Figure 1-47).

13. Standing Stance with feet apart (*kailibu* 開立步):

Posture: Stand upright with your feet about shoulder width apart (Figure 1-48).

Figure 1-47

Figure 1-48

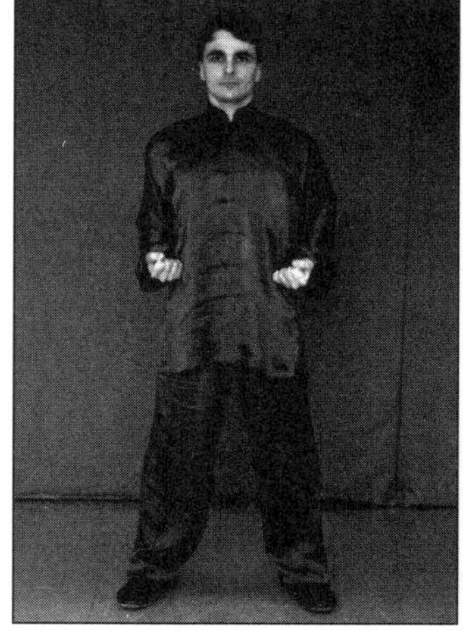

Figure 1-49

Figure 1-50

Stepping Patterns

1. Cross Over Step (*gaibu* 蓋步):

Drill: This is a stepping pattern that crosses one leg over the other leg. Start from Standing Stance with feet apart. Cross your right leg over your left leg (Figures 1-49 and 1-50). Then step forward with your left leg back into Standing Stance with feet apart. Keep repeating the stepping across the training area, then change sides.

Figure 1-51

Figure 1-52

2. Cross Behind Step (*chabu* 插步):

Drill: This is a stepping pattern that crosses one leg behind the other leg. Start from Standing Stance with feet apart. Cross your right leg behind your left leg (Figures 1-51 and 1-52). Then step forward with your left leg back into Standing Stance with feet apart. Keep repeating the stepping across the training area, then change sides.

3. Hit Step (*jibu* 擊步):

Drill: This is a stepping pattern that shuffles the back foot to the front foot while jumping up. Start by shifting your weight forward and raise your back foot up. Then push off the front foot and hit your back foot behind your front foot, as you bring your feet together in the air. Land on your right foot (Figures 1-53 to 1-56).

4. Switch Step (*dianbu* 墊步):

Drill: This is a stepping pattern that brings the back foot to the spot where the front foot was with a shuffle of your feet. Start by shifting your weight forward and raise your back foot. Then simultaneously raise your front foot up and stomp your back foot down (Figures 1-57 to 1-59).

Figure 1-53

Figure 1-54

Figure 1-55

Figure 1-56

Figure 1-57

Figure 1-58

Figure 1-59

Figure 1-60

Figure 1-61

Figure 1-62

5. Walking Step (*xingbu* 行步):

Drill: This is a stepping pattern that alternates feet stepping forward. Start with one foot in front of the next. Push off the back foot and raise your foot up behind you. Then step forward and do the same with the other foot by pushing off the back foot (Figures 1-60 to 1-62).

Arm Movements

In this section, we will introduce only the basic arm movements. We will introduce more specific uses of the arm in Chapter 3, when we introduce the fighting applications.

1. Fist:

Posture: A fist is accomplished by coiling all the fingers in towards the center of the palm with the thumb tightly pressed on the top of the index and the middle fingers. The different sections of the fist are described with different names. They are the *face, back, heart, eye, and wheel* of the fist (Drawing 1-1).

Drill 1: Alternate hands punching while in a Standing Stance with feet apart (*kailibu chongquan* 開立步沖拳). Start with your fists at your waist. When you punch, rotate your arm forward until the *heart* of the fist is facing down (Figures 1-63 and 1-64).

Drill 2: Alternate punching forward while in a Horse Stance (*mabu chongquan* 馬步沖拳). Start with your fists at your waist. When you punch, rotate your arm forward until the *heart* of the fist is facing down (Figures 1-65 and 1-66).

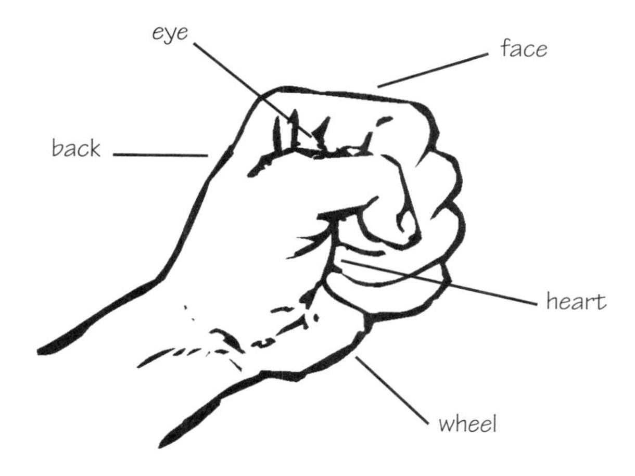

Drawing 1-1

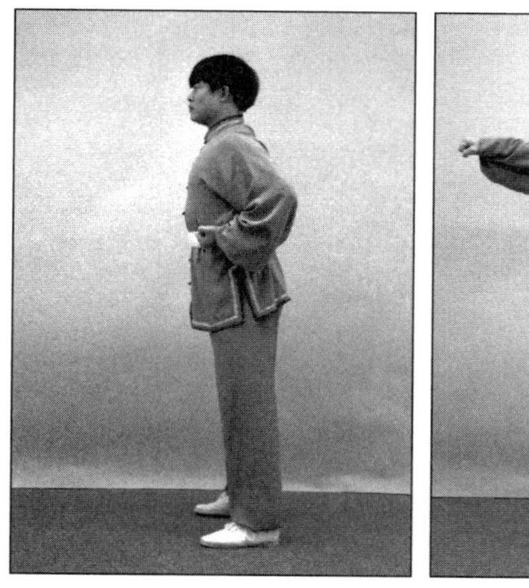

Figure 1-63

Figure 1-64

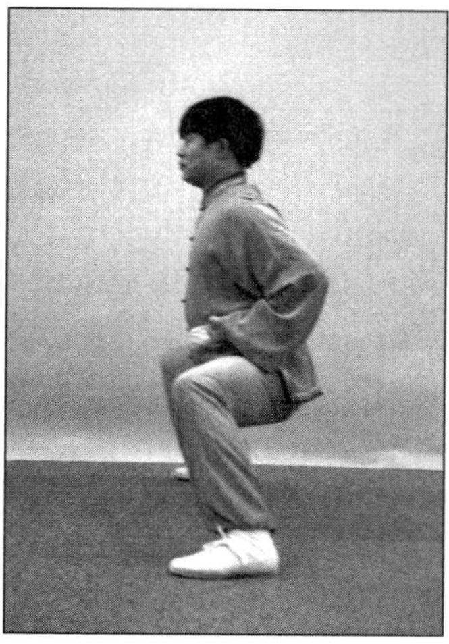

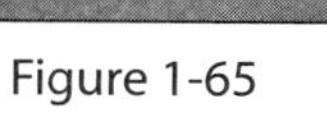

Figure 1-65

Figure 1-66

Figure 1-67

Figure 1-68 Figure 1-69

Drill 3: Alternate punching sideways while in a Horse Stance (*mabu hengchongquan* 馬步橫沖拳). Start with your fists at your waist. Punch sideways. When you punch, rotate your arm forward until the *heart* of the fist is facing down (Figure 1-67).

Drill 4: Alternate punching while in a Bow Stance (*gongbu chongquan* 弓步沖拳). Start with your fists at your waist. Punch with your left fist. Then pull your left fist back as you simultaneously punch forward with your right fist. When you punch rotate your arm in until the *heart* of the fist is facing down (Figures 1-68 and 1-69).

Drill 5: Alternate casting your fist up while in a Standing Stance with feet apart (*kailibu liangquan* 開立步亮拳). Start with your fists at your waist. Extend your right arm to your side, then up. At the same time, turn your head to look to your left. When you extend your arm up, rotate your fist until the *heart* of the fist is facing up (Figures 1-70 and 1-71).

Figure 1-70

Figure 1-71

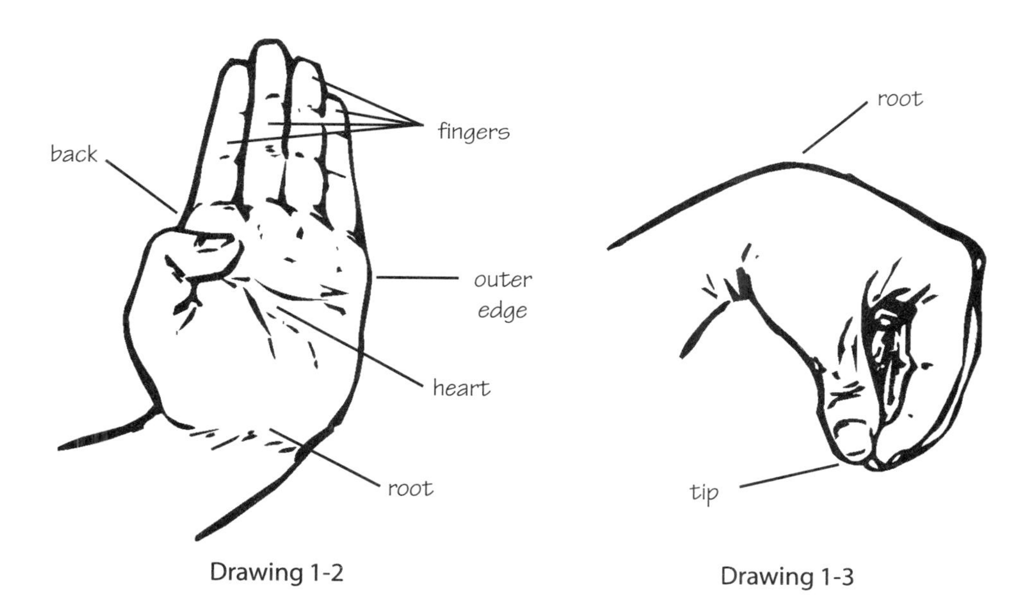

Drawing 1-2

Drawing 1-3

2. Palm and Hook:

Posture: A typical palm hand posture is accomplished by bending the thumb and tucking it tightly next to the edge of the palm, while keeping the other four fingers straight and tightly together. The different sections of the palm are described with different names. They are the *back*, *fingers*, *outer edge*, *heart*, and *root* of the palm (Drawing 1-2). A typical hook hand posture is accomplished by squeezing the fingers together and bending the wrist. The different sections of the hook are described with different names. They are the *root* and the *tip* of the hook (Drawing 1-3).

Figure 1-72

Figure 1-73

Figure 1-74

Drill 1: Alternate casting your palm up while in a Standing Stance with feet apart (*kailibu liangzhang* 開立步亮掌). Start with your fist at your waist. Extend your right arm to your side, then up. At the same time, turn your head to look to your left. When you extend your arm up, open your hand and rotate your palm to face up (Figures 1-72 and 1-73).

Drill 2: Alternate palm strikes while in a Standing Stance with feet apart (*kailibu tuizhang* 開立步推掌). Start with your fists at your waist. Open your right hand and push forward with your palm (Figure 1-74).

Drill 3: Alternate spearing and hooking while in a Standing Stance with feet together (*libu chuanshou liangzhang* 立步穿手亮掌). Start with your arms next to your sides (Figure 1-75). Extend your right hand up at an angle to your right (Figure 1-76). Spear your left hand up along your right arm. At the same time, bring your right hand down and move your left arm to your left (Figure 1-77). Cast your right hand down, then up, over your head, while hooking your left hand down behind you (Figures 1-78 and 1-78a).

Figure 1-75

Figure 1-76

Figure 1-77

Figure 1-78

Figure 1-78a

Figure 1-79

Figure 1-80

1.3. Integrate Your Body Movements

1. Slap the floor while in Half-Squat Stance (*pubu lunbi* 仆步掄臂):

Step 1. Start with your feet apart and arms stretched to your sides (Figure 1-79). Shift your weight to your right leg into a right Bow Stance. At the same time, swing your right arm down and back while swinging your left arm over your head and to your right (Figure 1-80).

Step 2. Shift your weight back and down to your left leg into Half-Squat Stance. At the same time, slap your right hand down next to your right foot and raise your left arm (Figures 1-81 and 1-82). Next stand up as in Figure 1-79 and repeat as many times as you wish.

2. Spear palm while in Bow Stance (*gongbu chuanzhang* 弓步穿掌):

Step1. Start with your feet apart and arms stretched to your sides (Figure 1-83). Shift your weight to your left leg into a left Bow Stance. At the same time, circle your right arm over your head and down in front of your face, while pulling your left hand next to your waist (Figure 1-84). Continue your right arm movement, bringing it down under your left armpit. At the same time, with your left hand spear up and forward above your right arm (Figure 1-85).

Figure 1-81

Figure 1-82

Figure 1-83

Figure 1-84

Figure 1-85

Step 2. Next, do the mirror image of the spear by turning your body to your right and shifting your weight to your right leg into a right Bow Stance. Alternate from side to side, as many times as you wish.

Figure 1-86

Figure 1-87

Figure 1-88

3. Spear palm while in Half-Squat Stance (*pubu chuanzhang* 仆步穿掌):

Step 1. Start in a right Half-Squat Stance with your left arm extended to your left foot and right arm extended back (Figure 1-86). Shift your weight forward into a left Bow Stance and raise your left arm (Figure 1-87). Turn your left foot out and step forward with your right foot. At the same time, swing your left arm over your head to your left side and swing your right arm down and up to your right side (Figure 1-88).

Step 2. Shift your weight onto your right foot and take another step with your left foot behind your right foot. At the same time, push your right hand down in front of your face and pull your left hand down to your waist (Figure 1-89). Shift your weight onto your left foot and bring your right knee up. At the same time, spear your left hand over your right arm (Figures 1-90 and 1-91).

Step 3. Step down with your right leg into a left Half-Squat Stance, and spear your right hand down towards your right foot (Figure 1-92). Repeat by doing the mirror image of the previous movements. Keep alternating sides as many times as you wish.

Figure 1-89

Figure 1-90

Figure 1-91

Figure 1-92

Figure 1-93

Figure 1-94

4. Turn body into Crossed Legs Sitting Stance (*fanyao zuopan* 翻腰坐盤):

Step 1. Start with your arms stretched to your sides with your feet apart (Figure 1-93). Step your left foot behind your right foot. At the same time, place your left hand next to your right shoulder (Figure 1-94).

Figure 1-95

Figure 1-96

Figure 1-97

Figure 1-98

Step 2. Pivot your body around 360 degrees to your left while swinging your arms counterclockwise. Finish the rotation by dropping down into a Crossed Legs Sitting Stance (Figures 1-95 to 1-98).

5. Lift palm while in Walking Step (*xingbu tiaozhang* 行步挑掌):

Drill 1: Start in a high Empty Stance with your left leg forward, and your right palm in front and left hook behind (Figure 1-99). Step forward with your right foot, while hooking back with the right hand and lifting the left palm up (Figure 1-100). Alternate from side to side as many times as you wish.

Drill 2: Start in a high Empty Stance with your right leg forward, and right palm in front and left hook behind (Figure 1-101). Step forward with your left leg, while hooking back with the right hand and lifting the left palm up from behind (Figure 1-102). Alternate from side to side as many times as you wish.

Figure 1-99 Figure 1-100 Figure 1-101

Figure 1-102 Figure 1-103 Figure 1-104

Drill 3: Start in a low Empty Stance with your left leg forward, and your left palm in front and right hook behind (Figure 1-103). Step forward with your right leg, while hooking back with the left hand and lifting the right palm up from behind (Figure 1-104). Alternate from side to side as many times as you wish.

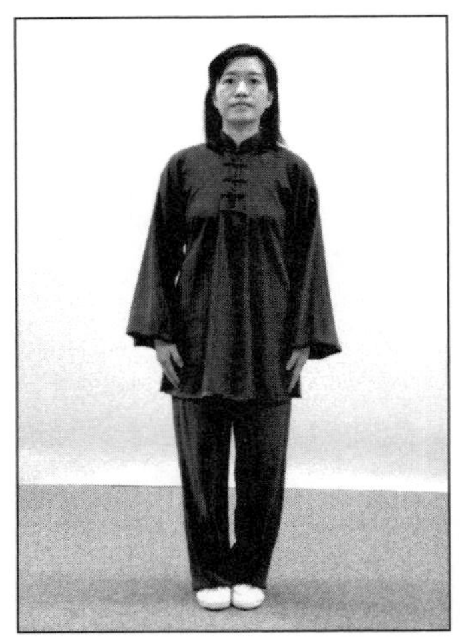

Figure 1-105

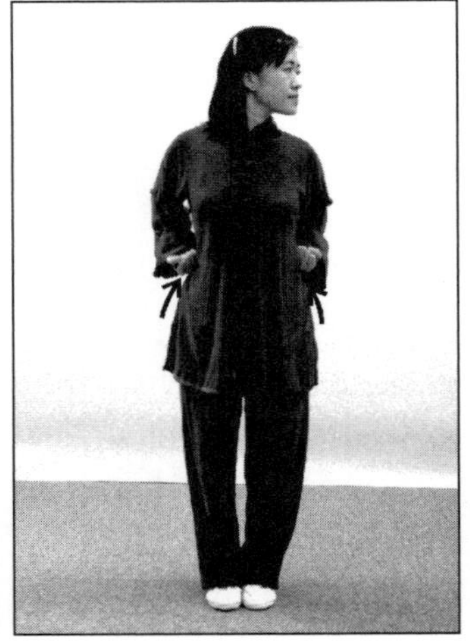

Figure 1-106

Figure 1-107

6. Five Stance Routine (*wubuquan* 五步拳):

Preparation 並步抱拳:

Step 1. Start with your feet together and your arms naturally down at your sides (Figure 1-105). Bring your fists up to your waist. At the same time, turn your head to look to your left (Figure 1-106).

Punch while in a Bow Stance 拗弓步沖拳:

Step 2. Bend both knees and shift your weight onto your right leg as you step to your left with your left foot into a left Gongbu (Bow Stance). At the same time, circle block with your left arm and punch forward with your right fist (Figure 1-107).

Punch While Spring Kicking Forward 彈踢沖拳:

Step 3. Stand up completely on your left leg and Spring Kick (Toe/Top of the Foot Kick) forward with your right leg. At the same time, pull your right fist back to your waist and punch forward with your left fist (Figure 1-108).

Block Up and Punch in Horse Stance 馬步架打:

Step 4. Step down with your right foot into a Mabu (Horse Stance) as you turn your body 90 degrees to your left. At the same time, lift your left arm up over your head and punch to your right side with your right fist (Figure 1-109).

Figure 1-108

Figure 1-109

Figure 1-110

Figure 1-111

Block Down and Punch while in a Resting Stance 歇步蓋打:

Step 5. Step to your right by crossing your left leg behind your right leg. At the same time, block down in front of your head with your right arm and pull your left hand back to your waist in a fist (Figure 1-110). Lower your body down into Xiebu (Resting Stance). At the same time, pull your right hand back to your waist in a fist, and punch forward with your left fist (Figure (1-111).

Figure 1-112

Figure 1-113

Figure 1-114

Lift Knee, Half-Squat Stance Down, and Spear Palm 提膝扑步穿掌:

Step 6. Turn your body 90 degrees to your left as you stand up, and open your left hand (Figure 1-112). Shift all your weight onto your right leg and bring your left knee up as high as you can. At the same time, pull your left hand down next to your right arm pit and spear up with your right hand over your left hand (Figure 1-113).

Step 7. Bend your right knee to lower your body and step to your left with your left foot into Pubu (Half-Squat Stance). At the same time, spear your left hand along your left leg until your toes (Figure 1-114).

Lift Palm While in Empty Stance 虚步挑掌:

Step 8. Shift your weight forward and lift your left arm up (Figure 1-115). Turn your left foot out and step forward with your right foot into a right Xubu (Empty Stance). At the same time, change your left hand into a hook as you pull it back to your back left corner; and scoop your right hand up until your fingers are pointing up (Figures 1-116 and 1-116a, back view).

Closing 收式:

Step 9. Turn your body 90 degrees to your left and bring your left foot next to your right foot. At the same time, change both hands into fists and bring them back to your waist (Figure 1-117).

Figure 1-115

Figure 1-116

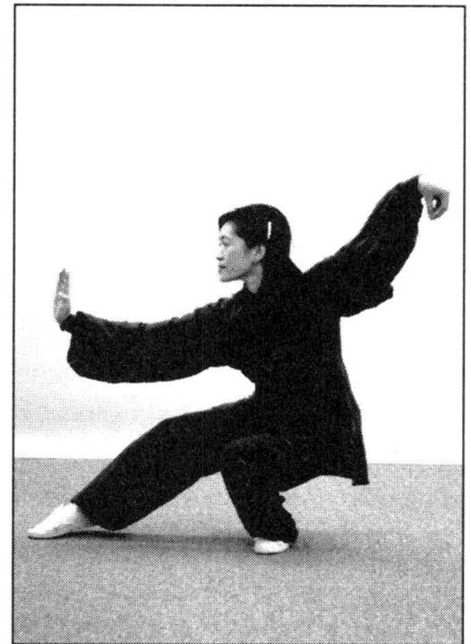
Figure 1-116a

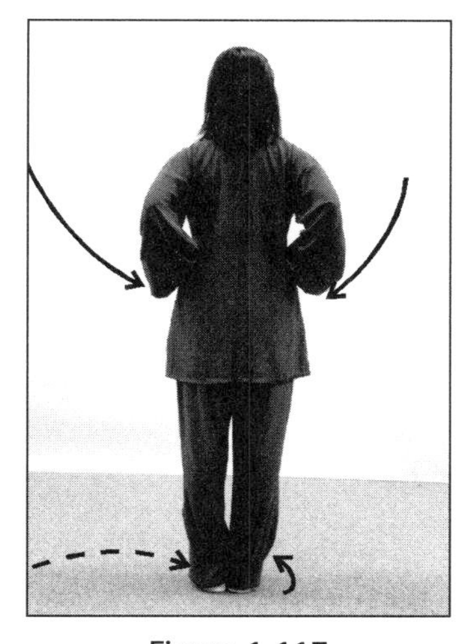
Figure 1-117

Step 10. Turn your head to look to your left and repeat Steps 2 through 9. This will bring you back to the starting position.

When you have returned to the starting position, you may repeat the exercise or do the mirror image. That is, instead of stepping to your left and punching with your right fist, step to your right and punch with your left fist. Do the mirror image of Steps 2 through 9. When you get to the end, do the mirror image again, which will bring you back to the starting position. Keep alternating from side to side by doing the left side twice and the right side twice, as many times as you wish.

Figure 1-118

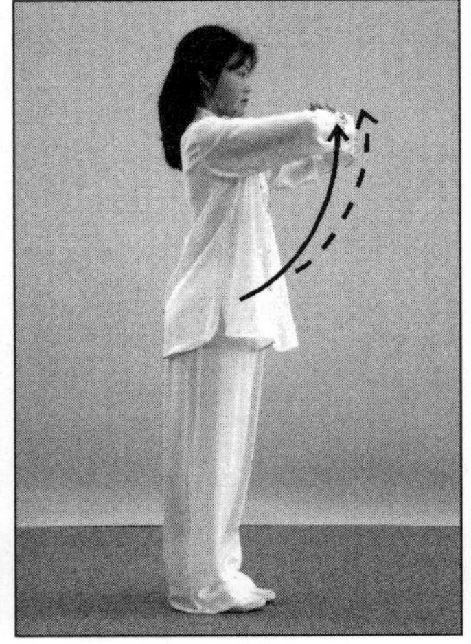

Figure 1-119

Figure 1-119a

7. Six Harmony Routine (*liuhequan* 六合拳):

Salutation:

Start with your feet together with your hands naturally down at your sides (Figure 1-118). Bring your hands together in a standard Wushu greeting (Figures 1-119 and 1-119a, front view).

This salutation is a standard greeting commonly used in the Chinese martial arts society. This greeting gesture is done by holding your right hand in a fist and keeping your left hand open with your thumb tucked in, and placing them next to each other in front of your chest. This greeting has been used since ancient China and has several implications. It implies righteousness, unity, and was a symbol for the defeated Ming Dynasty loyalists.

The shape made by the right fist resembles the ancient Chinese pictogram for the sun; and the shape made up by the left palm resembles the ancient pictogram for the moon. Both the sun and the moon are luminous objects. Luminescence implies righteousness and martial virtue. Making this symbol symbolizes the martial artist's willingness to work on the qualities of being a true martial artist.

The sun and the moon pictograms also make up the Chinese character *ming*. Ming was also the name of the Chinese dynasty before the Qing Dynasty took control of the empire. The defeated Ming loyalist revolted throughout the Qing Dynasty, trying to return the control of the empire back to the Ming emperor. This greeting symbol was their revolutionary code.

The land that we live on is either surrounded by a sea or is next to a lake. Water is an important way of transportation to the far reaches of the earth. It is also where most communities settled. These lakes and seas are represented by the greeting gesture. The right fist symbolizes the five major lakes in China, and the left hand with the thumb tucked in symbolizes the four seas surround-

Figure 1-120

Figure 1-121

Figure 1-122

Figure 1-123

ing the Central Kingdom (China). Martial artists used this greeting to symbolize brotherhood and unity everywhere under the heavens, when they traveled to the far corners of ancient China in quest of new knowledge. When this gesture is made, the person making the gesture is hoping that all martial artists will be united in brotherhood for the common good of the art and the society.

Routine:

Step 1. Bend your knees slightly. At the same time, move your hands apart in a clockwise pattern, left hand in front and right hand circles down, up, back, and down to your waist (Figures 1-120 and 1-121). Step forward with your left foot and follow up with your right foot until both feet are together. At the same time, punch forward with your right fist and pull your left hand back next to your right forearm (Figures 1-122 and 1-123).

Figure 1-124

Figure 1-125

Figure 1-126

Figure 1-127

Figure 1-128

Figure 1-129

Step 2. Step forward with your left foot into a left Gongbu. At the same time, bring your right fist back to your waist, and extend your left hand forward with your fingers pointing down and your palm facing to your right (Figure 1-124). Rotate your left palm to face down and strike upward with your right fist under your left palm (Figure 1-125).

Step 3. Turn your body 180 degrees around into a right Gongbu. As you turn, hit the inside of your right thigh with your right hand and hit the inside of your left thigh with your left hand (Figure 1-126). Quickly turn your body 180 degrees around again into a left Gongbu. At the same time, raise your right fist and hammer down in front of you into your left hand (Figures 1-127 and 1-128).

Figure 1-130

Figure 1-131

Figure 1-132

Figure 1-133

Figure 1-134

Figure 1-135

Step 4. Shift your weight back to your right leg and circular step with your left leg to your right. At the same time, extend your left hand forward and raise your right fist up (Figures 1-129 and 130).

Step around with your right leg into a right Gongbu. At the same time, hammer down with your right fist into your left hand (Figure 1-131). Quickly, punch with your left fist over your right fist (Figure 1-132). Back fist with your right fist and extend your left fist back (Figure 1-133).

Step 5. Do the mirror image of Step 4 by shifting your weight back to your left leg and circular step with your right leg to your left. At the same time, extend your right hand forward and raise your left fist up (Figures 1-134 and 135).

Figure 1-136 Figure 1-137 Figure 1-138

Figure 1-139 Figure 1-140 Figure 1-141

Step around with your left leg into a left Gongbu. At the same time, hammer down with your left fist into your right hand (Figure 1-136). Quickly, punch with your right fist over your left fist (Figure 1-137). Back fist with your left fist and extend your right fist back (Figure 1-138).

Step 6. Shift your weight back to your right leg and circular step with your left leg to your right. At the same time, extend your left hand forward and raise your right fist up (Figures 1-139 and 1-140).

Step around with your right leg and hammer down with your right fist (Figure 1-141). Continue the circular momentum of the previous movement and spin your body around on your right foot. As you turn, back fist with your left fist and raise your left knee up (Figure 1-142).

Figure 1-142 Figure 1-143 Figure 1-144

Figure 1-145 Figure 1-146 Figure 1-147

Step 7. Step down and forward with your left foot and bring your right foot next to your left. At the same time, pull your hands down to your left (Figure 1-143). Step forward with your right leg into a right Gongbu. At the same time, bring your hands back to your waist then push forward (Figures 1-144 and 1-145).

Step 8. Turn your body 180 degrees around into a left Gongbu. At the same time, bring your right fist back to your waist, and extend your left hand forward with your fingers pointing down and your palm facing to your right (Figure 1-146).

Repeat Steps 2 through 8. This will bring you back to the starting position facing the same direction as when you started (Figure 1-147). You can repeat as many times as you wish or finish.

Figure 1-148 Figure 1-149 Figure 1-150

Figure 1-151 Figure 1-152 Figure 1-153

Step 9. When you are ready to finish, rotate your left palm to face down and strike upward with your right fist under your left palm (Figure 1-148). Turn your body 180 degrees around into a right Gongbu. As you turn, hit the inside of your right thigh with your right hand and hit the inside of your left thigh with your left hand (Figure 1-149). Quickly turn your body 180 degrees around again into a left Gongbu. At the same time, raise your right fist and hammer down in front of you into your left hand (Figures 1-150 and 1-151).

Figure 1-154

Figure 1-155

Figure 1-156

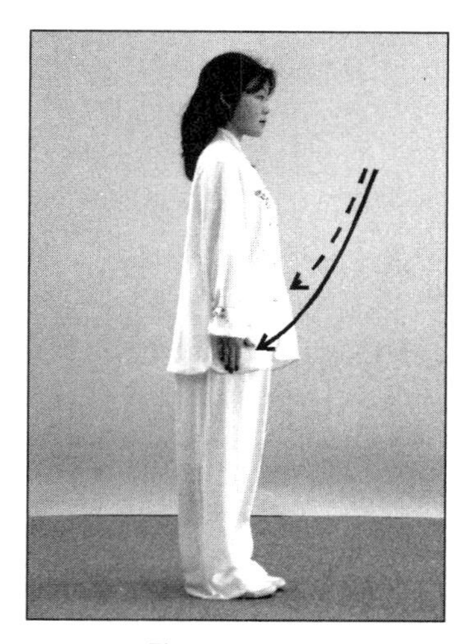

Figure 1-157

Step 10. Shift your weight back slightly to your right. At the same time, raise your right hand up and down to your waist, and extend your left hand forward (Figures 1-152 and 1-153). Bring your right foot forward and stomp down next to your left foot. At the same time, punch forward with your right fist, and pull your left hand back next to your right shoulder (Figure 1-154).

Step 11. Step back with your right foot, then bring your left foot next to your right foot. At the same time, lower both hands, then bring them together into a standard Wushu greeting (Figures 1-155 and 1-156).

Step 12. Lower both hands down to your sides (Figure 1-157).

Figure 1-158

Figure 1-159

Figure 1-160

1.4. Improve Your Balance

1. Balance with one knee up
   (*tixi pingheng* 提膝亮掌平衡):

   Drill: Start in a Standing Stance with feet apart and extend your right arm up to your right (Figure 1-158). Turn your body towards your right and spear your left hand over your right arm. At the same time, pull your right hand in towards your body (Figure 1-159). Lift your left knee up. At the same time, hook your left hand down and back, while casting your right palm over your head (Figure 1-160). Hold this posture for 10-30 seconds, then change sides.

2. Balance with one leg crossed over
   (*pantui pingheng* 盤腿平衡):

   Drill : Squat down as low as you can while keeping your back straight. Cross your left leg over your right thigh (Figure 1-161). Hold this posture for 10-30 seconds, then change sides.

Figure 1-161

Figure 1-162

Figure 1-163

Figure 1-164

3. Balance with one leg crossed behind (*goutui pingheng* 勾腿平衡):

Drill: Squat down as low as you can while keeping your back straight. Cross your left leg behind your right leg (Figure 1-162). Hold this posture for 10-30 seconds, then change sides.

4. Balance with one leg extended behind (*woyun pingheng* 臥雲平衡):

Drill: Squat down as low as you can while keeping your back straight. Extend your right leg straight out in front of you (Figure 1-163 or 1-164). Hold this posture for 10-30 seconds, then change sides.

Figure 1-165

Figure 1-166

5. Balance while leaning back and extending one leg forward (*yangshen pingheng* 仰身平衡):

Drill 1: Balance on your right leg while leaning your body back and extending your left leg forward. Keep your body and the extended leg straight. Stretch your arms to your sides to help with your balance (Figure 1-165). Hold this posture for 10-30 seconds, then change sides.

Drill 2: Same as Drill 1, except extend your leg up as high as you can. Hold this posture for a few seconds (Figure 1-166). Then bring the extended leg down and repeat a few more times. Next, repeat a few times on the other side.

6. Swallow Balancing Posture (*yanshi pingheng* 燕式平衡):

Drill: Start with your arms crossed in front of your chest and your left knee up (Figure 1-167). Lean your body forward and extend your left leg back and up behind you. Extend your arms to your sides to help with your balance (Figure 1-168). Hold this posture for 10-30 seconds, then change sides.

Figure 1-167

Figure 1-168

Figure 1-169

Figure 1-170

7. Balance while leaning forward and extending one leg back (*tanhai pingheng* 探海平衡):

Drill: Balance on your left leg while leaning your upper body forward and extending your right leg back and up. Extend your left arm forward and your right arm back (Figure 1-169). Hold this posture for 10-30 seconds, then change sides.

8. Balance while leaning sideways and extending one leg back (*ceshen pingheng* 側身平衡):

Drill: Balance on your left leg while leaning your upper body forward and extending your right leg back and up. Bend your arms and place your left fist next to your temple, and your right fist next to your hip (Figure 1-170). Hold this posture for 10-30 seconds, then change sides.

Figure 1-171

Figure 1-172

Figure 1-173

9. Balance with the back leg hooked up (*wangyu pingheng* 望月平衡):

Drill: Balance on your right leg and hook your left leg back and to the right. Extend your right arm to your right and left arm over your head, to help with your balance (Figure 1-171). Hold this posture for 10-30 seconds, then change sides.

10. Balance on your elbows (*zhoudaoli* 肘倒立):

Drill: Place your hands on the floor next to each other, and place your forearms on the floor. Then extend your legs up (Figure 1-172). Hold this posture for 10-30 seconds.

11. Balance on the shoulder and arms (*jiandaoli* 肩倒立):

Drill: Use your left arm, the side of your head, and your right hand to create a triangular foundation, and stretch your legs up (Figure 1-173). Hold this posture for 10-30 seconds.

12. Head Stand (*sanjiaodaoli* 三角倒立):

Drill: Use the top of your head and your hands to create a triangular foundation, and stretch your legs up (Figure 1-174). Hold this posture for 10-30 seconds.

13. Hand Stand (*shoudaoli* 手倒立):

Drill: Balance on your hands and extend your legs up (Figure 1-175). Hold this posture for 10-30 seconds.

Figure 1-174

Figure 1-175

Figure 1-176

Figure 1-177

Figure 1-178

14. Fist Hand Stand (*quandaoli* 拳倒立):

Drill: Balance on your fists and extend your legs up (Figure 1-176). Hold this posture for 10-30 seconds.

15. One Arm Stand with Hand (*danbidaoli* 單臂倒立):

Drill: Balance on your hands and extend your legs up. Then shift all your weight onto one hand and move the other hand off the floor (Figure 1-177). Hold this posture for 10-30 seconds.

16. One Arm Stand with Fist (*danbidaoli* 單臂倒立):

Drill: Balance on your fists and extend your legs up. Then shift all your weight onto one fist and move the other fist off the floor (Figure 1-178). Hold this posture for 10-30 seconds.

腿法

Chapter 2:

Developing Powerful Kicks

The legs are stronger than the arms. The proper application of the legs can be very devastating to an opponent. The legs are also longer than the arms, which allows for a longer distance application than the arms. Unfortunately, kicking requires that one or both legs be off the floor when executing the kick, making the body less stable. Therefore, the attempt in the kicking drills is to reduce the disadvantages, as much as possible, while enhancing the legs advantage over the arms.

There are many different ways that kicks can be accomplished. They can be accomplished by first bending the knee, then kicking, or keeping the kicking leg straight, then kicking. Kicks can be done with one leg on the floor or both legs off the floor. Kicks with one leg grounded may utilize the floor as a ground, and take advantage of the turning and pivoting momentum, to generate powerful kicks. Aerial kicks utilize the spinning and jumping momentum to deliver powerful kicks. Powerful kicks integrate the whole body in its execution.

Figure 2-1

Figure 2-2

Kicks are often combined with arm movements for coordinating the arms and the legs, as well as, for setting up simultaneous arm and leg attacks. Kicks may also involve the hitting of the hands on the foot. Besides training the coordination of your arms and legs and setting up a simultaneous offensive strategy with your arms and legs, it is also for conditioning your feet and hands for greater impact resistance. Hitting your palms on your feet is one of the best conditioning exercises for your hands and feet. Since you know how strong your hands and feet are, you can regulate how much force to put into the hit, and gradually increase the impact force as you get stronger.

In this chapter, we will start with the introduction of some basic jumping drills which can improve your kicking ability. We will then introduce kicks with one leg grounded on the floor, followed by aerial kicks. At the end of this chapter, we will also include additional drills that can enhance your overall kicking ability. To enhance your agility and jumping ability, you may also refer to Chapter 6, Section 8 for a description of Light-Body and Agility Training.

2.1. Jumping Drills

1. Light Jumps:

Drill: Stand with your feet about 6 inches apart. Keep your knees straight, but not locked. Use only your feet, bounce up and down as high as you can, 10 to 20 times.

2. Both Knees to Your Chest:

Drill: Stand in a high Horse Stance. Swing your arms as you jump up. When you jump, bring your knees up together as high as you

Figure 2-3

Figure 2-4

can. When you land, separate your legs and land lightly in a Horse Stance (Figure 2-1). Repeat 10 to 20 times.

3. Both Knees to Your Chest and Turn:

Drill: Stand in a high Horse Stance. Turn your upper body to your right with your arms also extending to your right. Swing your arms to your left as you turn your body to your left, and jump up and turn 360 degrees with your knees up. Land lightly in a Horse Stance. Repeat 10 to 20 times (Figure 2-2). Then do this drill on the other side.

4. One Knee to Your Chest:

Drill: Jump and bring one knee up to your chest while keeping the other leg straight. Keep doing the same leg or alternate legs (Figure 2-3). Repeat each leg, 10 to 20 times.

5. Jump and Reach Up:

Drill: Jump up as high as you can. As you reach up, stretch your body from your hands down to your toes and keep your body straight. Repeat 10 to 20 times.

6. Jump and Touch Toes:

Drill: Stand with your feet shoulder width apart. Bend your knees slightly, and lift your legs up at an angle to your sides. At the same time, slap your palms on top of your feet (Figure 2-4). Land lightly. Repeat 10 to 20 times.

Figure 2-5

Figure 2-6

Figure 2-7

2.2. Basic Kicks

1. Forward Front Kick (*zhengtitu* 正踢腿):

The kicking surface of a this kick is usually the heel. It can also be a kick with the ball of the foot or the back of the heel during the downward movement of the kick.

Drill: Stand with your feet together. Extend your arms out to your sides with your arms straight, palms facing to your sides, and fingers pointing up. Take a small step forward with your left foot (Figure 2-5). Shift your weight onto your left leg. Keep your body square facing forward and kick your right leg up as high as you can without leaning. Kick as close as possible to your forehead (Figure 2-6).

To continue on the other side, bring your leg down next to the standing leg, then take a transition step forward without moving your arms. Next, shift your weight forward and kick with your left leg. Alternate from one side to the next, taking a transition step in between kicks.

Figure 2-8

Figure 2-9

Figure 2-10

2. Angled Front Kick (*xietitui* 斜踢腿):

Drill: This kick is basically the same as the Forward Front Kick, but instead of bringing the kicking foot towards your forehead, you bring your kicking foot towards the opposite side of your head (Figures 2-7 and 2-8).

3. Side Front Kick (*cetitui* 側踢腿):

Drill: Start with your right foot forward and arms extended forward and back. Turn your right foot out about 30 degrees. Shift your weight onto your right foot and kick your left leg up as high as you can without bending your knee. At the same time, bring your left hand next to your right shoulder and extend your right arm up over your head (Figures 2-9 and 2-10).

4. Outside Crescent Kick (*waibaitui* 外擺腿):

This is a circular kick with the top of the foot sweeping across sideways. The kicking leg starts by circling in across the stationary leg, up, across, and down making a complete circle with your foot.

Drill: Start with your feet together and extend your arms to your sides (Figure 2-11). Take a small step at an angle towards your left with your left foot, turn your foot out about 30 degrees, and shift your weight onto your left leg, and bring your arms up with your palms overlapping over your head (Figure 2-12).

Figure 2-11

Figure 2-12

Figure 2-13

Swing your right foot next to your left leg, up, and down towards your right in a clockwise circle. As your leg moves in front of your face, pull your hands in the opposite direction of the kick, hitting the top of your right foot with the inside of both palms (Figure 2-13).

Complete the kick by placing your right foot down, gently touching the floor with the ball of your foot and your arms back to the starting position (Figure 2-14).

You may repeat the kick in place 10 to 20 times; then practice kicking with the other leg. You may also alternate kicking with one leg then the next across the training area, by stepping forward with the foot that has just completed the kick.

5. Inside Crescent Kick (*lihetui* 里和腿):

An Inside Crescent Kick is a circular kick with the sole of the foot. It is accomplished by swinging your kicking leg in from the outside, up and down to the opposite side.

Drill: From the starting position, take a small step forward with your left foot, turn your foot out about 30 degrees, and shift your weight onto your left leg (Figure 2-15). Swing your right leg from behind, to your right and up, in front of your body with your leg straight. At the same time, slap your left hand towards the oncoming foot, contacting the bottom of your right foot (Figures 2-16 and 2-17).

Figure 2-14

Figure 2-15

Figure 2-16

Figure 2-17

Figure 2-18

After the impact, continue the movement of your right leg towards your left and touch down lightly with the ball of your foot (Figure 2-18).

You may repeat the kick in place 10 to 20 times by moving your kicking foot back to the starting position. You may also alternate kicking with one leg then the next across the training area, by stepping forward with the foot that has just completed the kick, then kick with the back leg. Alternating from side to side.

Figure 2-19

Figure 2-20

Figure 2-21

6. Spring Kick (*tantui* 彈腿):

A left Spring Kick is accomplished by keeping your right foot on the floor, with your leg straight, but not locked. Lift your left knee up over your waist with your toes pointing down. Then snap your foot out until the power reaches to the tip of your toes (Figures 2-19 and 2-20). Your body is facing forward. This kick is also known as a Toe Kick. The kicking surface, however, is not the toes, but the top of the foot.

Drill: Start with your feet together and fists at your waist. Take a small step forward with your right foot and extend your left fist in front of you (Figure 2-21).

Shift all your weight onto your right foot, lift your left knee up over your waist and snap your left foot forward. At the same time, punch forward with your right fist, and pull your left fist back to your waist (Figure 2-22).

After completing the kick, bring your leg back down by bending your left knee, keeping your knee above your waist, and pointing your foot downward. This completes a left Spring Kick.

To do the other side, step down and forward with your left foot, shift your weight forward onto your left leg and kick with your right foot. At the same time, punch forward with your left fist and pull your right fist back to your waist. Alternate from side to side across the length of the training area.

Figure 2-22

Figure 2-23

Figure 2-24

7. Heel Kick (*dengtui* 蹬腿):

A Heel Kick is accomplished in a similar manner as a Spring Kick, by first lifting the kicking knee up over your waist, then extending the kicking foot forward. When you kick, point the foot up and kick with the heel.

Drill: Start with your feet together and fists at your waist. Take a small step forward with your right foot and extend your left fist in front of you (Figure 2-23).

Shift all your weight onto your right foot, lift your left knee up over your waist and extend your left foot forward. At the same time, punch forward with your right fist, and pull your left fist back to your waist (Figure 2-24).

After completing the kick, bring your leg back down by bending your left knee, keeping your knee above your waist, and pointing your foot down. This completes a left Heel Kick.

To do the other side, step down and forward with your left foot, shift your weight forward onto your left leg and kick with your right foot. At the same time, punch forward with your left fist and pull your right fist back to your waist. Alternate from side to side across the length of the training area.

Figure 2-25

Figure 2-26

Figure 2-27

Figure 2-28

8. Slap Toe Kick (*feijiao* 飛腳):

This kick is accomplished by kicking with the top of the foot while slapping your hand down on top of the kicking foot.

Drill: Stand with your left foot forward and your right foot behind. Bring your arms up over your head with your palms overlapping (Figure 2-25). Shift all your weight onto your left leg, bend your right knee slightly then kick up as high as you can. At the same time, slap down with your right hand on top of your right foot, and hook your left hand back (Figure 2-26). Put your right foot down and step forward and kick with the left foot in a similar manner across the length of the training area.

As an alternative, you may do the drill by slapping down with the opposite hand (Figures 2-27 and 2-28).

Figure 2-29

Figure 2-30

Figure 2-31

10. Turn Body Side Kick

(*zhuanshen cechuaitui* 轉身側踹腿):

Drill: Start in a ready position with your left leg in front and arms extended (Figure 2-29). Step forward with your right leg and turn your body 180 degrees around (Figure 2-30). Shift all your weight onto your right leg and side kick forward with your left leg (Figure 2-31).

Put your left leg down, back in the ready position. Repeat the kick across the length of the training area. Then do the right side in a similar manner.

Figure 2-32

Figure 2-33

11. Side Spring Kick (*cetantui* 側彈腿):

This is a kick with the top of the foot or the shin. As the name implies, it is a sideways Spring Kick. Instead of kicking vertically upward as in a Spring Kick, you spring kick sideways towards your target.

Drill: Start with your left leg forward in a ready position. Turn your left foot out, push off your right foot, lift your right knee up, then spring kick sideways in front of you (Figures 2-32 and 2-33). Put your right leg down and stand in a ready position with your right foot in front. Then do the kick with your left leg. Alternate legs across the length of the training area.

12. Reverse Arch Kick (*daoti* 倒踢):

This is a kick with the sole of your foot backward.

Drill: Start with your feet together. Bend your knees slightly and swing your arms behind you (Figure 2-34). Straighten your legs and swing your arms forward, up, then back. At the same time, lift your right leg up behind you as high as you can (Figure 2-35). Bring your arms and foot down and repeat a few more times. Then do the other side.

Figure 2-34

Figure 2-35

Figure 2-36

Figure 2-37

13. High Front Sweep Kick (*qiangaosaotui* 前高掃腿):

This is a kick with the tip of your foot. The intended target is usually the eyes.

Drill: Start with your left leg forward in a ready position (Figure 2-36). Turn your front foot out and kick forward. Just as you complete the extension of your leg, abruptly turn your body to your left and pull your right foot towards your left (Figure 2-37). Put your right leg down and stand in a ready position with your right foot in front. Then do the kick with your left leg. Alternate legs across the length of the training area.

Figure 2-38

Figure 2-39

Figure 2-40

14. High Back Sweep Kick (*hougaosaotui* 後高掃腿):

This is a kick either with the back of the heel or the sole of the foot.

Drill: Start with your left leg in front with your left arm extended in front of your chest (Figure 2-38). Turn your left foot out and step forward with your right foot. At the same time, swing your right fist around in front of you (Figure 2-39). Push off with your left foot, shift all your weight onto your right foot, and spin 180 degrees around to your left. At the same time, sweep your left leg up (Figure 2-40). Continue the momentum of your left foot and put it down behind your right leg and repeat the same kick across the length of the training area. Then do the kick with the other leg.

Figure 2-41

Figure 2-42

15. Lean Back Kick (*diantui* 點腿):

This is a kick with the top of the foot or the toes.

Drill: Start with your feet together and arms in front of your chest. Lean back as much as you can and kick forward with your right foot. At the same time, extend your arms to your sides (Figure 2-41). Straighten your body and bring your arms and leg back to the starting position and repeat the kick several times. Then do the kick with the other leg.

16. Lean Back Heel Kick (*yangshen dengtui* 仰身蹬腿):

This is a kick with the heel of the foot.

Drill: Start with your feet together and arms in front of your chest. Lean back as much as you can and kick forward with your right heel. At the same time, extend your arms to your sides (Figure 2-42). Straighten your body and bring your arms and leg back to the starting position and repeat the kick several times. Then do the kick with the other leg.

Figure 2-43

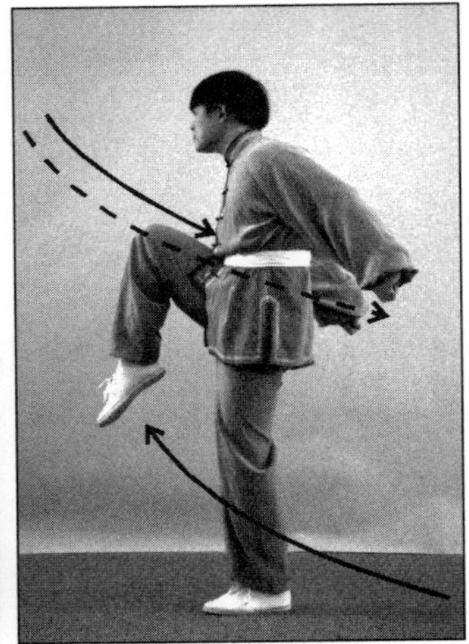

Figure 2-44

Figure 2-45

Figure 2-46

17. Knee Kick (*xiding* 膝頂):

This is a kick with the top of your knee while pulling your arms in the opposite direction of your kick.

Drill: Start with your left leg forward and arms extended in front of your body (Figure 2-43). Pull both arms back and lift your right knee up and forward as high as you can (Figure 2-44). Bring your right foot back down to the starting position and extend your arms forward. Repeat the kick several times. Then do the kick with the other knee.

18. Forward Low Sweep Kick-half circle (*qiansaotui* 前掃腿):

This is a kick with the front of your leg and foot, by pivoting on your front foot while sweeping your back leg forward. It is done with the body low to the ground and with the kicking foot touching the floor during the kick.

Figure 2-47

Figure 2-48

Figure 2-49

Drill: Start with your left leg forward and extend your left arm up (Figure 2-45). Push off with your right foot and pivot on the ball of your left foot. At the same time, sweep your right leg forward in a half circle (Figure 2-46). Shift your weight forward to your right leg and extend your right arm up. Then push off with your left foot, pivot on the ball of your right foot, and sweep your left leg forward in a half circle. Alternate from side to side across the training area.

19. Forward Floor Sweep Kick-full circle (*qiansaotangtui* 前掃搪腿):

This is a kick with the front of your leg, by pivoting on your front foot while sweeping the back leg forward, then backward in a circle.

Drill: Start with your left leg forward and extend your left arm up (Figure 2-47). Push off with your right foot and pivot on the ball of your left foot. At the same time, sweep your right leg forward 360 degrees around until you are facing the opposite direction (Figures 2-48 and 2-49). Turn to face the starting direction and repeat the drill several times. Then do the kick with the other leg.

Figure 2-50

Figure 2-51

Figure 2-52

Figure 2-53

Figure 2-54

20. Backward Floor Sweep Kick-full circle (*housaotui* 後掃搪腿):

This is a kick with the back of the leg by pivoting on the front foot while sweeping the back leg forward, then backward in a circle.

Drill: Start in a left Bow Stance and push forward with both palms (Figure 2-50). Squat down on your left leg and place your hands on the floor and sweep your right leg 360 degrees around (Figures 2-51 to 2-53). Stand up, hook your right hand back and extend your left hand forward (Figure 2-54). Bring your back

Figure 2-55

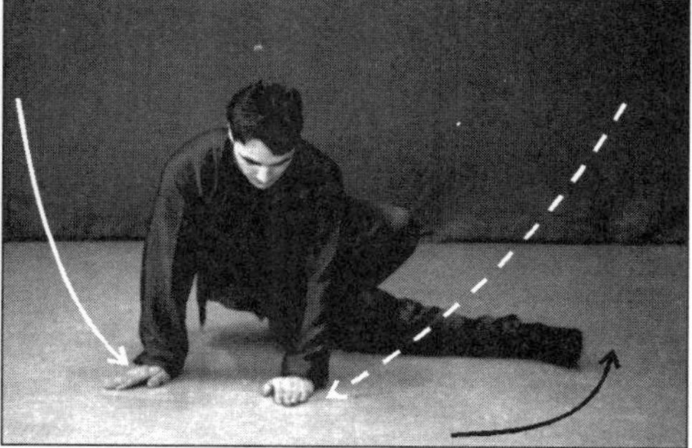

Figure 2-56

Figure 2-57

Figure 2-58

foot forward next to your front foot, stand up, and bring your fists next to your waist. Repeat the kick across the training area. Then do the kick with the other leg.

21. Grinder Kick (*mopantui* 磨盤腿):

This is a kick with the front of your leg by sweeping your kicking leg 360 degrees while keeping your body on the same spot.

Drill: Squat down on your left leg, straighten your right leg, and place your hands on the floor in front of you (Figure 2-55). Lift your arms up and sweep your right leg forward (Figure 2-56). Put your hands back down and lift your left foot off the floor as you continue to sweep your right leg in a circle. Then bring your legs back to the starting position (Figures 2-57 and 2-58). Repeat several times. Then do the kick with the other leg.

Figure 2-59

Figure 2-60

Figure 2-61

Figure 2-62

Figure 2-63

22. Step Kick (*caitui* 踩腿):

A Step Kick is a kick with the bottom of your foot at an angle downward. During the kick the foot is turned out at a 90 degrees angle.

Drill: Start in a ready position with your left leg forward (Figure 2-59). Turn your left foot out slightly and shift your weight onto your left leg. Then lift your right foot up and kick forward and down with the bottom of your foot (Figure 2-60). Put your right foot down and shift your weight onto your right leg. Then lift your left foot up and kick forward and down. Alternate from side to side across the training area.

Figure 2-64

Figure 2-65

Figure 2-66

23. Low Cut Kick (*xiachuaitui* 下踹腿):

A Low Cut Kick is a kick with the outside edge of the foot at an angle down.

Drill: Start in a ready position with your left leg forward. Take a step forward with your right foot and turn your foot out (Figure 2-61). Shift your weight onto your right leg and lift your left leg up (Figure 2-62). Kick forward and down with the outside edge of your left foot (Figure 2-63). Put your left foot down and turn your foot out. Then lift and kick with your right foot. Alternate from side to side across the training area.

24. Horse Kick (*juezitui* 撅子腿):

A Horse Kick is a kick with the heel or the bottom of the foot with the body turned sideways and leaning in the opposite direction of the kick.

Drill: Start in a ready position with your right leg forward (Figure 2-64). Hop forward and shift your weight back to your left leg and hook your right foot up (Figure 2-65). Stomp your right foot down contacting the floor with the ball of your right foot (Figure 2-66). Turn to face forward as in the starting position, and repeat the kick across the training area. Then do the kick with the other leg.

Figure 2-67

Figure 2-68

25. Low Hook Kick (*goutitui* 勾踢腿):

A Low Hook Kick utilizes the angle created by hooking the foot up. The kicking surface is the area between the foot and the shin.

Drill: Start in a ready position with your left leg forward (Figure 2-67). Turn your left foot out, shift your weight forward and hook kick forward with your right foot. At the same time, pull your right hand down in a hook and extend your left arm up (Figure 2-68). Put your right foot down and turn your foot out. Then repeat the kick with your left leg. Alternate from side to side across the training area.

Figure 2-69

Figure 2-70

Figure 2-71

26. Squat Kick (*dichuaitui* 低踹腿):

This is a kick with the outside edge of the foot while squatting down.

Drill: Start in a ready position with your right leg forward (Figure 2-69). Squat down quickly and shift all your weight onto your left leg. At the same time, kick forward with your right foot (Figures 2-70 and 2-71). Stand up and repeat the kick 10 to 20 times. Then do the kick with the other leg.

Figure 2-72

Figure 2-73

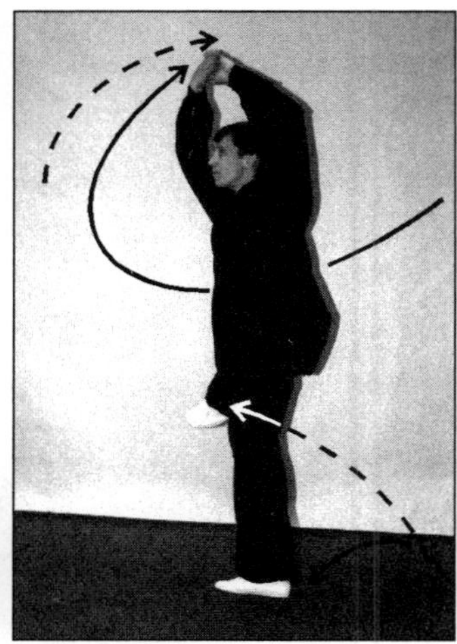

Figure 2-74

2.3. Jumping and Spinning Kicks

1. Jump Flying Kick

(*tengkong feijiao* 騰空飛腳, *erqitui* 二起腿):

This is a long range kick with the top of the foot. It is also referred to as Jump Slap Toe Kick. When the kicking foot is hit on the top by the opposite hand, it is referred to as tengkong xie feijiao, meaning angled Jump Flying Kick. To increase the challenge, the speed, and the difficulty of this kick, try to kick and land with the same leg.

Drill: Stand on your right leg with your left knee up, and your arms extended forward and back, left arm in front (Figure 2-72). Do a Hit Step, jibu, by stepping forward and down with your left, then push off with your left foot and hit your back foot behind your front foot. At the same time, bring your arms towards your chest, then extend them forward and back (Figure 2-73).

Land on your right foot, lift your left knee up as high as you can, and slap the back of your right hand with the front of your left hand over your head (Figure 2-74). Continue the momentum, kick up with the top of your right foot and hit down on the top of your foot with your right hand. At the same time, hook your left hand back (Figure 2-75). Continue down the training area, then change legs and do the other side.

Figure 2-75

Figure 2-76

Figure 2-77

2. Jump Spring Kick (*tiaotantui* 跳彈腿, *jiantantui* 箭彈腿):

This is basically the same as a Spring Kick, except that it is done with the addition of a skip forward or a jump forward. It can also be done with the non-kicking leg bent at the knee. Typically, the first leg lift or kick helps generate the lift for the second kick.

Drill: Start with your feet together and fists at your sides. Spring Kick with your left leg and punch with your right fist. Continue the lift of your left kick and kick with your right leg. At the same time, punch with your left fist. As you kick with your right leg, simultaneously bring your left knee up as high as you can and your right hand back to your waist (Figure 2-76). Continue down the training area, then change legs and do the other side.

3. Jump Heel Kick (*tiaodengtui*, 跳蹬腿):

This kick is done the same as Jump Spring Kick. The only difference is that the kicking surface is the heel and not the top of the foot (Figure 2-77).

Figure 2-78

Figure 2-79

4. Jump Both Legs Spring Kick Forward (*tengkong shuangda* 騰空雙打):

This is a kick with the top of both feet at the same time forward, while hitting both hands on top of the feet.

Drill: Start with your feet together. Swing your arms back, bend your knees and jump up as high as you can. At the same time, kick forward with your feet and hit the top of your feet with both hands (Figure 2-78). Land with both feet and repeat 10 to 20 times.

5. Jump Both Legs Spring Kick Sideways (*tengkong zuoyou huangda* 騰空左右雙打):

This is a kick with the top of both feet to the front corners simultaneously, while hitting one hand on top of each foot.

Drill: Start with your feet together. Swing your arms back, bend your knees and jump up as high as you can. At the same time, kick your feet to each front corner and hit the top of your feet with your hands (Figure 2-79). Land with both feet and repeat 10 to 20 times.

6. Jump Side Kick (*tengkong cechuaitui* 騰空側踹腿):

This is a long range kick typically done with a running start. The kicking surface can be the edge of the foot or the bottom of the foot.

Drill: From a running start, push off the ground with your left foot and kick forward with your right foot. Tuck your left knee up as

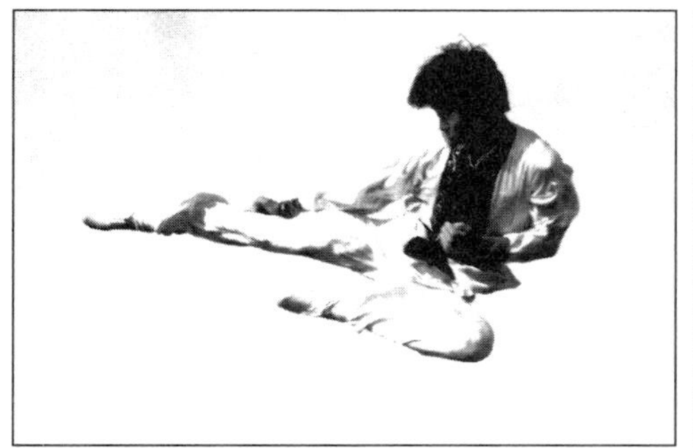

Figure 2-80

Figure 2-81

Figure 2-82

high as you can when you kick (Figure 2-80). Repeat 10 to 20 times, then do the other side.

7. Jump Both Legs Side Kick (*tengkong shuangjiao cechuaitui* 雙腳側踹腿):

This is similar to Jump Side Kick, except that when you kick, thrust both legs sideways instead of one leg (Figure 2-81).

8. Tornado Kick (*xuanfengtui* 旋風腿):

A Tornado Kick is a spinning kick with both feet off the floor during the kick. The kick resembles a tornado that spins around with a mighty force. A Tornado Kick is an Inside Crescent Kick with a spin and a jump (Figure 2-82).

Drill: Start with a high Empty Stance with your left leg forward. Extend your right arm over your head and left arm to your left (Figure 2-83). Circle your left arm and step to your left with your left foot (Figure 2-84). Take another step forward with

Figure 2-83

Figure 2-84

Figure 2-85

Figure 2-86

Figure 2-87

your right foot, bring your left hand towards your chest and lower your right arm (Figure 2-85).

Continue the momentum generated from your step, swing your arms to your left, push off with your feet, jump up, and spin to your left. When you are airborne, hit the bottom of your right foot with your left hand (Figure 2-86). Land and repeat 10 to 20 times, then change sides.

When you are able to do this kick easily and are able to do a full split, begin to land into a full split. In competition, both legs must land simultaneously and go into a full split to avoid deductions (Figure 2-87).

Figure 2-88

Figure 2-89

Figure 2-90

Figure 2-91

Figure 2-92

Figure 2-93

9. Spinning Outward Crescent Kick (*tengkong bailian* 騰空擺蓮):

This is kick is an Outside Crescent Kick with a spin and a jump.

Drill: Stand on your right leg with your left knee up. Extend your arms to your sides, right hand palm and left hand hook (Figure 2-88). Step down with your left foot, lower your right arm and extend your left arm in front of you (Figure 2-89). Take a circular step with your right foot and skip forward while lifting your left knee up (Figures 2-90 and 2-91).

Put your left foot down and take another step in an arc with your right foot (Figure 2-92). Swing your left foot up and quickly lift your left leg up and around and hit your hands together over your head (Figure 2-93).

Figure 2-94

Figure 2-95

Figure 2-96

Continue the momentum, and do a outward Crescent Kick in the air with your right leg (Figures 2-94 and 2-95). Land and repeat 10 to 20 times, then change sides.

As an alternative, you may land in a Bow Stance with your right arm extended and left arm bent (Figure 2-96).

10. Butterfly Kick (*xuanzi* 旋子):

This kick requires the first leg to swing up, and the second leg to jump off the floor. When the body is in the air, the upper body is horizontal to the floor. The kick requires that the body turn 360 degrees in mid air. When you land, you should face the same direction as when you started the kick (Figure 2-97).

Drill: Start with your left leg forward (Figure 2-98). Step forward with your right foot, then cross your left foot behind your right foot. Begin to swing your arms around to your left as you step (Figures 2-99 and 2-100).

Push off with your right foot and lift your right leg up, while continuing to swing your arms to your left (Figure 2-101). Before your right leg completes its lift, push off with your left foot and swing your body horizontally around (Figures 2-102 and 2-103).

Figure 2-97

Figure 2-98 Figure 2-99 Figure 2-100

Figure 2-101 Figure 2-102 Figure 2-103

Figure 2-104

Figure 2-105

Figure 2-106

Figure 2-107

11. Butterfly Kick with a Twist and Split (*xuanzi zhuanti sanbailiushidu jie picha* 旋子轉體三百六十度接劈叉):

To increase the challenge and the degree of difficulty, a midair twist is added to the Butterfly Kick. Landing in a split is often added to the kick to indicate the practitioner's jumping ability; flexibility; control of fast movements and stillness; and ability to jump high and land low quickly, and with stability. Don't attempt this kick, without first being able to do a regular Butterfly kick well or a full split. Like all challenging maneuvers, a qualified instructor's assistance and floor mat is recommended to learn this kick.

Figure 2-108

Figure 2-109

Drill: Continue from the regular Butterfly Kick. While you are airborne, pull your arms toward your chest and turn your body towards your right, bring your feet together, and twist 360 degrees around (Figures 2-104 to 2-106).

To further test the competitor's ability, in competitions, competitors must touch down with both legs extended and land in a full split to avoid deductions (Figure 2-107).

12. Jump Reverse Arch Kick with Both Feet (*tengkong shuangdaoda* 騰空雙倒打):

This kick is similar to the one legged Reverse Arch Kick, except that both legs are off the floor to do this kick.

Drill: Start with your feet together. Bend your knees slightly and swing your arms behind you (Figure 2-108). Jump off the floor with both feet and lift your feet up backward. At the same time, swing your arms forward, up, then back (Figure 2-109).

Figure 2-110 Figure 2-111

Figure 2-112 Figure 2-113

13. Inside Crescent Falling Kick (*pantuidie* 盤腿跌):

This is an intentional falling kick, utilizing the momentum of the kick, as well as, the body weight to increase the intensity of the kick. The falling kick is also done after a Jumping Side Kick. You will need to be able to do a Tornado kick well before attempting this kick. Also, use a floor mat when first learning this kick to prevent injury.

Drill: Start with your right leg forward (Figure 2-110). Swing your arms toward your left, push off with your feet and lift your left leg off the floor (Figure 2-111). From the momentum generated by your arms and your legs, bring your right leg up (Figure 2-112). Keep the body turning and land with your right leg straight

Figure 2-114

Figure 2-115

and left leg bent, and hands on the floor (Figure 2-113). When you land, the right foot, the outside of the left leg and thigh, and the hands touch down simultaneously.

14. Jump Double Forward Heel Kick

(*tengkong shuandengtui* 騰空雙蹬腿):

This is a kick with the heel of both feet while airborne (Figures 2-114 and 2-115). It is done by jumping up and shooting the legs out so that the body is parallel to the floor. Don't attempt this kick without a mat or the supervision of a qualified instructor.

Figure 2-116

Figure 2-117

Figure 2-118

2.4. Miscellaneous Drills to Enhance Your Physical Ability

The drills in this section can enhance your coordination and overall kicking ability. Many of the movements are also part of many Wushu style body conditioning, as well as, both offensive and defensive maneuvers. Practicing and learning these drills should be supervised by a qualified instructor.

1. Forward Walk Over (*qianshouruanfan* 前手軟翻):

Drill: Start with your right foot forward and extend your hands over your head (Figure 2-116). Put your hands on the floor and swing your left leg up, followed by your right leg (Figure 2-117). Put your left foot down, followed by your right foot next to your left (Figure 2-118). Repeat by stepping forward with your right foot.

To increase the challenge, practitioners can also work on a no handed forward flip (挺身前空翻, Figure 2-119).

2. Backward Walk Over (*houshouruanfan* 後手軟翻):

Drill: Start with your left foot forward and extend your arms over your head (Figure 2-120). Bend backward and place your hands on the floor, and swing your left leg up and towards the back (Figure 2-121). Continue the movement of the left leg backward, and swing your right leg off the floor (Figure 2-122). Put your left foot down, then your right foot (Figures 2-123 and 2-124). Repeat by bending back again.

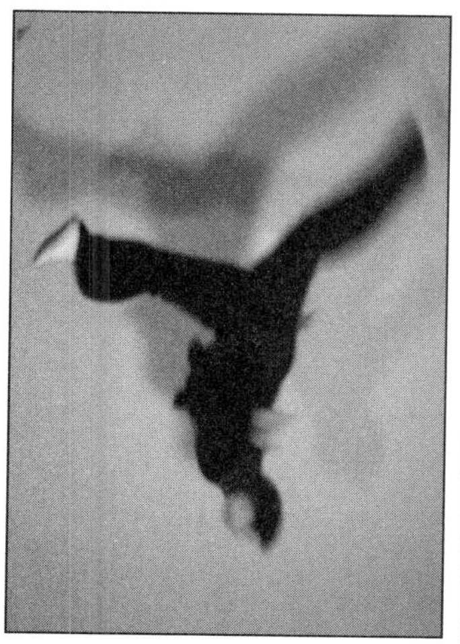

Figure 2-119

Figure 2-120

Figure 2-121

Figure 2-122

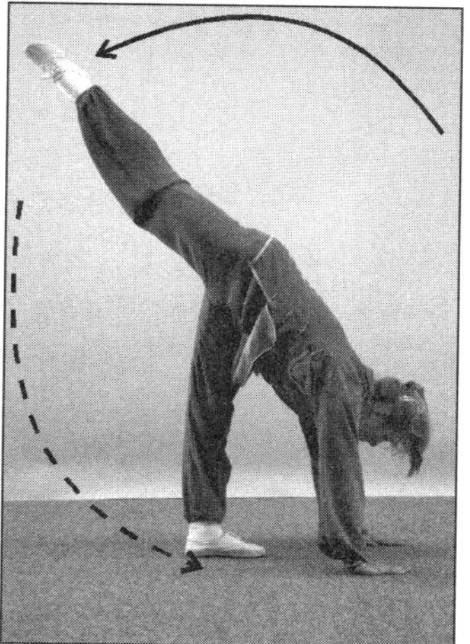

Figure 2-123

Figure 2-124

Figure 2-125

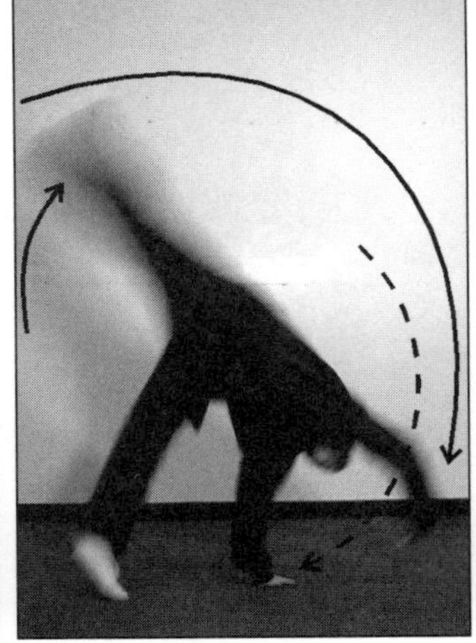
Figure 2-126

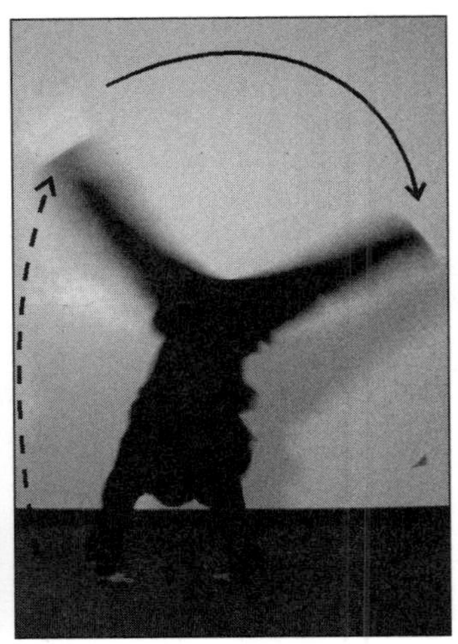
Figure 2-127

Figure 2-128

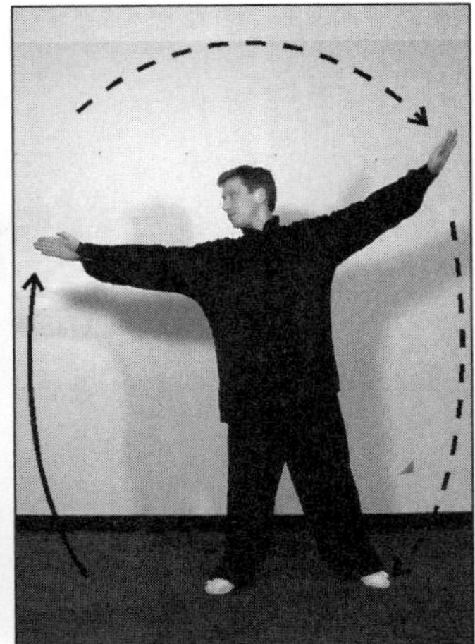
Figure 2-129

Figure 2-130

Figure 2-131

Figure 2-132

Figure 2-133

Figure 2-134

Figure 2-135

Figure 2-136

3. Cartwheel (*ceshoufan* 側手翻) and No Handed Cartwheel (*qiankongfan* 側空翻):

Cartwheels are done by pivoting the arms and legs around the center of the body. The arms and legs are like the outer rubber tires of a wheel rotating on its center. Start by doing a cartwheel with your hands supported on the floor (Figures 2-125 to 2-129). When you are able to do a cartwheel with hands, a qualified instructor can assist you in learning how to do a cartwheel without hands (Figures 2-130 to 2-133 or Figures 2-134 to 2-136).

To increase the challenge and degree of difficulty, some modern competition routines require that competitors be able to do a Jump Flying Kick followed by a no handed cartwheel (Figures 2-137 to 2-141).

Figure 2-137

Figure 2-138

Figure 2-139

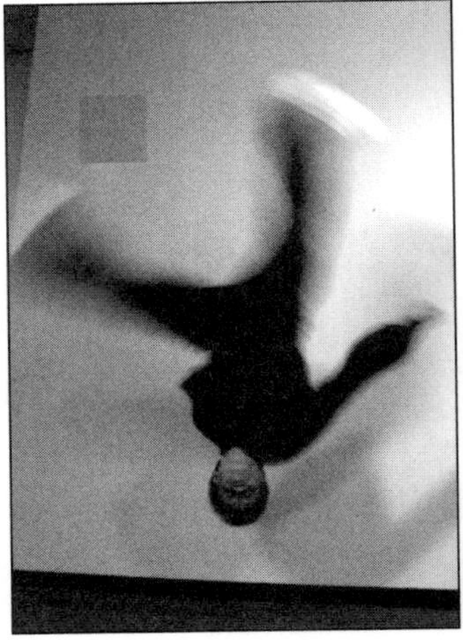

Figure 2-140

Figure 2-141

4. Shoulder Roll (*qiangbei* 搶背):

Drill: Start standing with your right leg forward. Bend your knees and push off your left foot as you place your right forearm on the ground (Figures 2-142 and 2-143). As your body begins to roll forward from your right shoulder to your left hip, tuck your knees toward your body, making your body like a ball and roll (Figure 2-144). Continue the roll and stand up (Figure 2-145).

5. Forward Drop (*zaibei* 栽碑):

Drill: Stand with your feet together and your hands to your sides (Figure 2-146). Raise your heels, keep your body straight, and allow your body to fall towards the floor. Right before your body

Figure 2-142

Figure 2-143

Figure 2-144

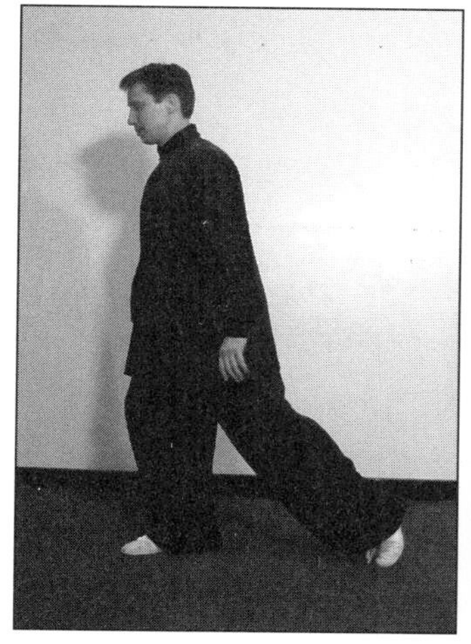
Figure 2-145

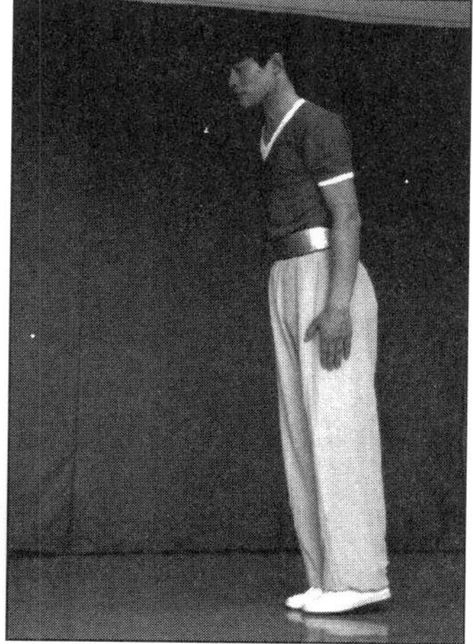
Figure 2-146

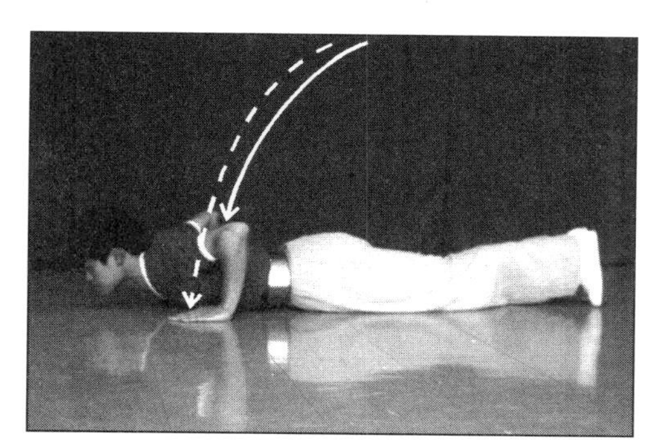
Figure 2-147

touches the floor, break the fall with your hands, but absorb the impact by bending your elbows (Figures 2-147).

Figure 2-148

Figure 2-149

Figure 2-150

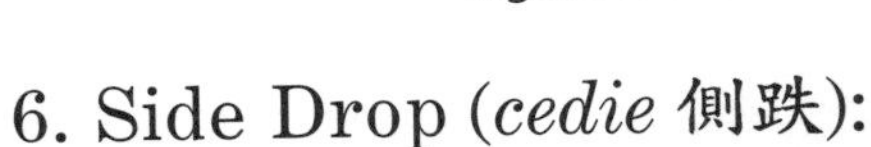

6. Side Drop (*cedie* 側跌):

Drill: Stand on your left leg with your right knee up, and hands facing out to your right side (Figure 2-148). Keep your body straight and allow your body to fall towards the ground, contacting the ground with the outside of your right leg and your hands (Figures 2-149 and 2-150).

Figure 2-151

7. Fish Jump (*yuyue* 魚躍):

Drill 1: Forward Jump: Start with your feet together, bend your knees and swing your arms backward (Figure 2-151). Swing your arms forward and jump up as high as you can. Land on your hands and extend your feet up and back (Figure 2-152). Gradually swing your body forward and place your legs lightly on the ground (Figure 2-153).

Drill 2: Backward Jump: Start with your feet together, bend your knees and swing your arms backward (Figure 2-154). Swing your arms up, jump up as high as you can, and turn your body around 180 degrees (Figure 2-155). Land on your hands and extend your feet up and back (Figures 2-156 and 2-157). Gradually swing your body forward and place your legs lightly on the ground (Figures 2-158 and 2-159).

Figure 2-152

Figure 2-153

Figure 2-154

Figure 2-155

Figure 2-156

Figure 2-157

Figure 2-158

Figure 2-159

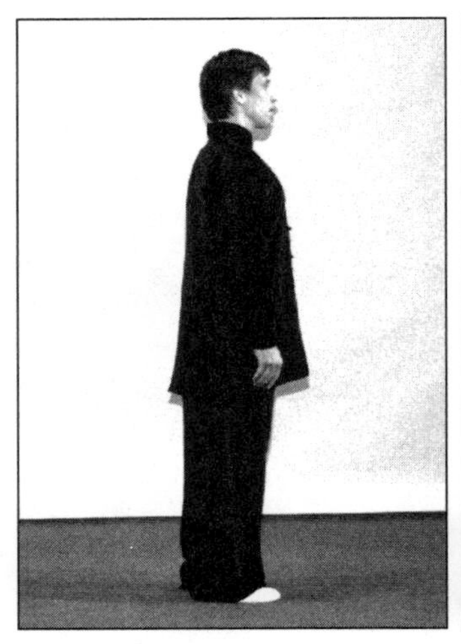
Figure 2-160

Figure 2-161

Figure 2-162

Figure 2-163

Drill 3: Back Flip Jump: Start with your feet together and hands naturally to your sides (Figure 2-160). Flip backward and touch down with our hands (Figures 2-161 and 2-162). Gradually swing your body forward and place your legs lightly on the floor (Figures 2-163 and 2-164).

8. Forward Head Flip (*toushoufan* 頭手翻, *toufan* 頭翻):

Drill: Flip with Hands: Start with your feet together. Bend down, place your hands on the floor about one shoulder width part, and place your head on the floor (Figure 2-165). Push off your feet and swing your legs up and over (Figure 2-166). When your legs pass vertical, push off with your hands and stand up (Figure 2-167). When you can do this drill easily with your hands, try it without your hands (Figures 2-168 to 2-170).

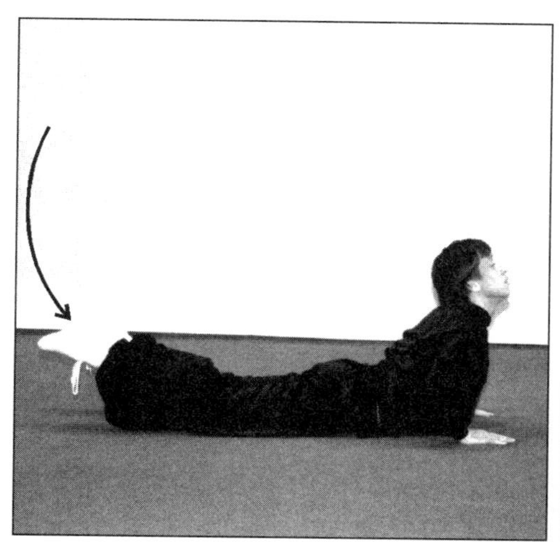

Figure 2-164

Figure 2-165

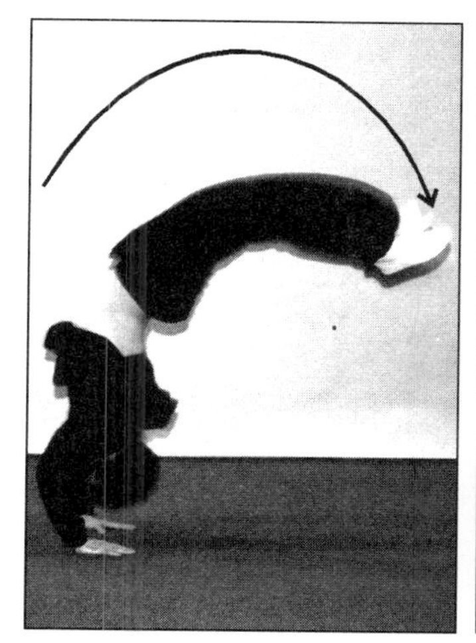

Figure 2-166

Figure 2-167

Figure 2-168

Figure 2-169

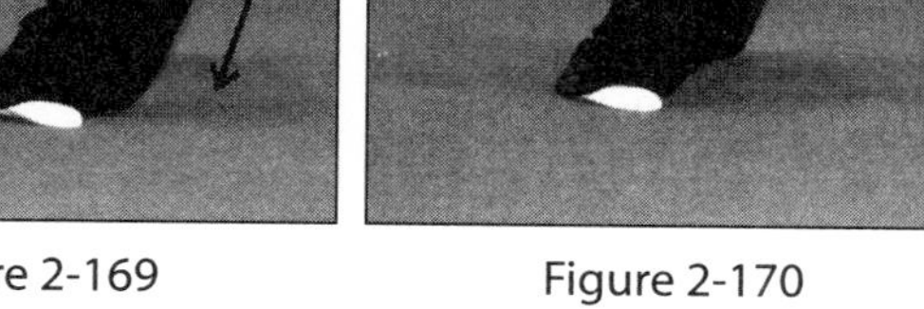

Figure 2-170

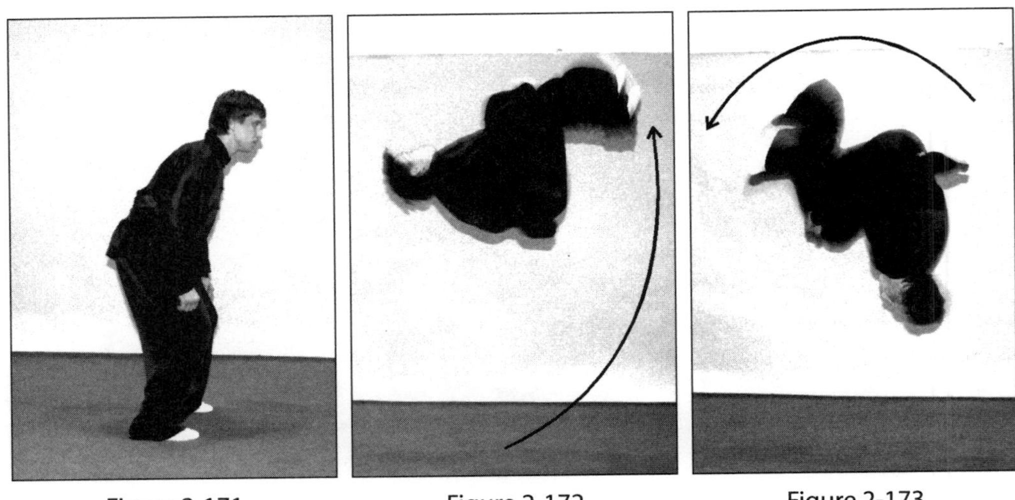

Figure 2-171 Figure 2-172 Figure 2-173

Figure 2-174

Figure 2-175

9. Back Flip without Hands (*houkongfan* 後空翻):

Drill: Start with your feet together and hands to your sides. Flip backward and land in Mabu (Figures 2-171 to 2-174). Take a step back with your right foot and place your knee on the floor. Lean back slightly and raise both hands up, as though you were drinking from a large container (Figure 2-175).

10. Jumping Extension (*yueqi xiapiquan* 躍起下劈拳):

Drill: From a running start, jump up as high as you can, extend your right arm forward and left arm back, and bring your right knee up and kick back with your left leg (Figure 2-176).

Figure 2-176

Figure 2-177

Figure 2-178

Figure 2-179

Figure 2-180

11. Back Roll Over (*jianjingfan* 挺身向後肩頸翻):

Drill: From a sitting position, extend your legs forward and place your hands on top of your feet (Figure 2-177). Swing your arms back and open to the sides, extend your legs straight up in the air and roll over your right shoulder. As you roll, turn your head sideways on the floor (Figures 2-178 and 2-179). Keep your back bent and gradually roll your body down to the floor (Figures 2-180 and 2-181).

Figure 2-181

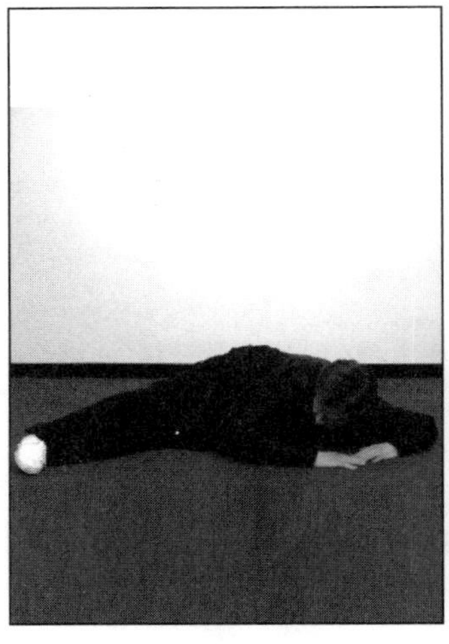
Figure 2-182

Figure 2-183

Figure 2-184

Figure 2-185

12. Black Dragon Wraps Around the Post (*wulongjiaozhu* 烏龍絞柱):

Drill: Start on the floor with your right leg straight and left leg bend, and hands on the floor (Figure 2-182). Swing your right leg from your right to your left (Figure 2-183). Roll over backward on your right shoulder, extend both feet up, and push upward with your hands (Figure 2-184). From the hand standing position, pull your feet down to the floor together and stand up (Figure 2-185).

Figure 2-186

Figure 2-187

13. Carp Flip (*liyudating* 鯉魚打挺):

Drill: Lay down on your back, place your hands over your head, palms down and fingers point towards your shoulders, and bring both legs towards your head with your legs straight (Figure 2-186). Spring up from the floor by kicking your legs up and forward while pushing off the floor with your hands (Figure 2-187).

實用踢打法

Chapter 3:

Free Fighting Applications

Wushu training is very extensive. A well-rounded Wushu practitioner must be proficient in many areas of Wushu, including Taolu (套路) and Sanshou (散手). Taolu is a term referring to Wushu routines, including bare-handed, weapon, and matching sets. Sanshou refers to free fighting skills. Sanshou literally means free hands, implying the free application of bare-handed techniques in Wushu fighting. A traditional Sanshou fighter is proficient in ti, da, shuai, and na; including the ability to strike vital points and use neutralization skills. For safety reasons, modern Sanshou competitions don't allow the use of na—joint controls. In this Chapter, we will focus on the ti and da applications. We will present 43 of the most commonly used fist, palm, and elbow striking methods; 32 of the most commonly used kicking methods; followed by 36 effective fighting combinations. The techniques can be used for self-defense training, as well as, for Sanshou competition training.

3.1. Mentally Prepare Yourself

There are many traditional fighting principles and key points that guide practitioners in their pursuit of greater skills. Here we will introduce the Mental and Physical Fighting Principle, the Five Keys of Combat, and Basic Sanshou Strategies. These are only general guidelines. Keep in mind that we are to, "Understand the martial principle, but not be restricted by the principle; and go beyond the principle, but not against the principle 明於術而不拘於術，脱規矩而不違規矩." In terms of Wushu, this phrase implies that martial artists should know how to apply the principles, but should not be restricted by the principles. If we restrict ourselves with general principles that do not fit the time, location, or situation; we will not be able to effectively apply our potential. We should be ingenious in applying our individual characteristics, with the principles as a guide.

Mental and Physical Fighting Principle (技擊中的內外)

This principle can be summarized into mental and physical components. The mental components are: make your opponent afraid of your presence (驚慌); be fearless and courageous in your offense (猛烈); be ruthless in your offense (狠毒); and be mentally alert to the various changing situations (神急). The physical components are: be able to see and strike an opponent's openings (封); be able to continue your advantageous offense without letting up (閉); be able to avoid, angle, and dodge attacks while staying in distance for counterattacks (閃); be able to use the hips for a close range strike (胯); be able to engage and apply neutralizing blocks and hooks with your arms and legs (鈎格); and be able to use pengda (挪打) with all of the strong parts of your body.

Make your opponent afraid of your presence. During combat, your presence, your charged up vitality of spirit can create a tremendous amount of pressure on your opponent. Make your opponent afraid of you, before engaging him. Your fearless and confident posture, your eyes, and vocal release, can scatter his concentration and spirit. His movement will be hindered and slowed, allowing your strikes to be more effective.

Be courageous in your offense. When engaging your opponent, express no fear, strike with speed and power. If you are able to avoid fighting, you would have already attained self-defense. If you must fight, the only reason to engage an attacker should be to strike back, otherwise, walk away.

Be ruthless in your offense. When you do strike, strike hard. In a life or death situation, let your attacker feel that you are ruthless and willing to die to protect yourself and your family! This type of expression will charge up your vitality of spirit and make your opponent think twice before attacking you or your family. It is said, "Ten thousand men can't stop a person that is not afraid to die (一人拼命萬夫莫擋)." In competition and training with your partners, this feeling must be restrained to avoid serious injury and to allow for a mutually beneficial learning experience.

Be mentally alert to the various changing situations. You need to be flexible in your mental and physical applications. Be mentally prepared for the many situations that may occur during combat. Stay calm so you will be able to react fast and vary your applications to the fast changing encounters. You don't need hundreds of techniques, but you do need to be able to apply enough techniques that allow you to vary from one situation to the next. In the presentation of the applications in this book, we will layout techniques in an order that will give you a clear idea of the possible variations to applying the techniques. When engaging your opponent, find his opening or create an opening for your strike. During training with a partner, observe his movements, and learn to set him up for an effective strike.

Be able to see and strike an opponent's openings and be able to continue your advantageous offense without letting up. When you are in an advantageous position, continue your advances so that your opponent is put in a constant defensive position, with no chance for him to apply his offensive moves.

Be able to avoid, angle, and dodge an attack while staying in distance for a counterattack. If you are in a disadvantageous position, you must be able to dodge your opponent's attack. You can, of course, move far away to avoid his attack. However, when you are far away, you also lose the option to counterattack. It is necessary to dodge your opponent's attack, yet maintain a striking distance to strike with an offensive application.

In actual combat, a *sense of distance*, your *timing*, and movement *angles* are keys to a successful application. A sense of distance is your ability to maintain a proper distance during defensive, as well as, offensive applications. The distance between you and your opponent is primarily adjusted with your stepping. It can also be adjusted with the forward, backward, sideways moving, and turning of your body. To avoid your opponent's attack, you will have to quickly move your body away from your opponent's effective striking distance.

Your timing is closely related to your sense of distance. If you are faster than your opponent, the distance between you and your opponent can be shorter before engaging. If you are slower than your opponent, you will have to take advantage of the longer distance between you and your opponent to account for the longer reaction time needed. Even if you are slower than your opponent, by taking advantage of the distance between you and your opponent, you can still become victorious over your opponent. Conversely, even if you are faster than your opponent, you may still be defeated if you don't understand your distance. When both fighters understand this principle, it becomes very difficult for either one to successfully strike the other without a good strategy.

The movement angling is set up by the body movements, including stepping, deflecting, and turning of the body. Basic angling can be seen in an evasive movement by dodging to your left or right to avoid being hit. You can also deflect the incoming attack, thus changing the angle of the strike and prevent being hit. Angling gives you the opportunity to counterattack by staying in range.

Be able to use the hips for a close range strike. When you are in very close range, learn to use your hips to deliver an effective offense. Since your hand and legs may be busy engaging your opponents arms and legs, utilizing your hips will provide an additional advantage for you. The hip strike can be like a powerful spring that shocks your opponent's balance and allows you to further strike with your legs or arms. Hip movements are also very important in takedown applications.

Be able to engage and apply neutralizing blocks and hooks with your arms and legs. The ability to engage and neutralize your opponent's attack is essential to counterattack. It is also a setup for taking your opponent down.

Be able to do pengda with all of the strong parts of your body. Pengda is a term referring to offensive-defense. Nearly all of the strong parts of your body can be used to strike your opponent. Typically there are thirteen areas that are utilized for applications. They are: your feet, knees, hips, shoulders, elbows, hands, and head. Peng (掤) refers to both defense, as well as, offense. Da (打) refers to offensive applications. The best defense is often an attack. This doesn't mean that you always attack first; it means that when you engage your opponent's attack, you immediately counterstrike as you avoid or neutralize his attack. Your strike is done when his offensive intention is still being initiated.

The Five Keys of Combat (技擊五要)

The five keys are sharp eyes (眼尖), fast hands (手快), steady courage (膽穩), firm stance and stepping (步堅), and solid power (力實). The eyes are trained to become like that of an eagle or an ape. Learn to be able to distinguish even the minute movements of your opponent, see through to his intentions, and be aware of all four directions. The hands are trained to be fast like wind gusting and thunder flashing. Fast hands can defeat slow hands. If the hands are not fast, even the most amazing hand techniques will not be effective. To be victorious one must be courageous enough to want to defeat an opponent during combat. When you are not afraid, then you can fully utilize and express your sharp eyes, fast hands, and power. It is said, "First there must be courage, then power, and then Kung Fu (一膽二力三功夫)." Stances and stepping must be trained to be firm, so that you will have a strong root. Therefore, before one learns how to fight, one must first practice one's stances. Your power must be sufficient to effectively apply your techniques. The more power you have, the better. Power is an attainment, that can only be gained with training.

To make your techniques effective, you not only need to have good techniques, you also need power. A smooth and accurate application of defensive and offensive techniques will allow you to deliver and express your power. Without power, you will restrict the effectiveness and the delivery of the techniques. Therefore, it is also important to work on strength building exercises in conjunction with technical drills.

Basic Sanshou Strategies

In free fighting competitions, in addition to having superb skills and courage, strategy is also very important. Based on Sunzi's guidelines, Sanshou fighting strategy will depend on the comparative strength and weaknesses between you and your opponent.

If your opponent's reactions are slower, his movements are not smooth, his endurance is not as good, or he is in a poor defensive position; attack directly. If your technical ability is not as good as your opponent, but your speed and power are greater than his; focus on your offense, put him in a constant defensive position, don't allow him to have a chance to apply his techniques. This strategy can be used when you are comparatively stronger, have better endurance, and are more courageous than your opponent. Even if your opponent has more experience than you, you can put him at a psychological disadvantage with your offense.

When engaging with an opponent that is good in defense, you will have to use fakes to mislead him into a disadvantageous position before you actually attack. Fake high to make him defend upward, but actually strike low; fake right, but actually strike to the left; or fake with a punch, but actually execute a takedown. You will have to make your opponent react to your fake attacks to make your strike effective.

When your opponent is stronger than you and is continuously attacking you; move around him, avoiding his attack, waiting and looking for an opportunity to strike back. It is said, "When you are stronger, attack the center; when you don't have the strength, go to the two sides (有力打正中，無力走兩旁)." Moving around your opponent will render his original attack ineffective and will cause him to have to readjust his posture and strategy, giving you more time to strike back. The agility of the feet and the understanding of timing, angles, and distance, are essential to make this strategy work for you.

A mentally less prepared opponent can be made afraid. You can put some fear in him by striking hard immediately as you engage. You can also hide your strength and pretend to be weak to bring his guard down. When he does, attack swiftly. Use methods to stir up his bad emotions to keep him off centered and leave him unable to apply his techniques effectively.

Every fighter has his own predominately used approaches. Whatever his approaches may be, find it, and prevent him from using it. Force him to use his less familiar approaches. If he is good with his arms, keep him at a distance and use your feet to attack his lower body. If he is good with his legs, use fast takedown techniques against him. If he is good with takedown techniques, keep him at a distance, attack and get out of range right away, don't let him grab a hold of you. If he is very good in many areas, use a hit and run approach so that he has no chance to apply his techniques.

Once you have discovered your opponent's weak points, focus your attacks on his weak points. Every fighter has his weak points. Some are poor in defending against kicks, punches, or takedowns. Some have a weak foundation. Some have major faults in their attacks.

If you are stronger with greater technical ability, but lack endurance or if you are stronger, but technically inferior, end the fight quickly. Find an opportunity to strike hard to reduce his fighting and winning spirit. If you have better endurance than your opponent, make him use up his energy. When your endurance is lacking, you must conserve your energy.

A well-rounded fighter can use constantly changing strategies and fighting approaches so that his opponent can't figure out what he will be doing next. This way you put your opponent into a passive and reactive position.

If your opponent is taller with a longer reach, use punches and takedown techniques to prevent him from being able to apply is longer range. If he is shorter and more agile, keep him at a distance and use long range punches and kicks against him.

There are many opportunities to strike at your opponent. However, the window of opportunity is very short during engagement. It is important to be able to capture the opportunity and use it to your advantage. When you notice that your opponent is not mentally or physically prepared, attack all of a sudden before he is able to react.

You can also attack when you notice your opponent set up, but before he is able to deliver his attack. There are certain small movements before one attacks. Learn to recognize these signals and avoid where the punch or kick is going to land, while striking his weak points. For example, many fighters will pull their shoulder back slightly before thrusting forward, and before they kick they will shift their weight back. After a fighter has missed his attack and in the process of retracting his arm or leg back, is a moment when his initial force has been delivered, but the new force is not yet ready to attack again. Take advantage of this situation by following his arm or leg in and striking to a weak point.

You can also set up an opportunity, by first attacking high to make your opponent defend up. When he defends up and leaves his lower body open, you immediately attack his lower body. You can also attack left, then right or down,

Figure 3-1

Figure 3-2

Figure 3-3

then up. Also, when your opponent loses balance and before he regains his balance, attack swiftly to take advantage of the opportunity.

3.2. Fist, Hand, and Elbow Applications

In the description of the applications, we will use the left hand and left foot forward as your starting position (Figure 3-1). We will refer to this starting position as the Ready Position throughout the description.

Fist:

1. Front Fist Jab (*Qianshou Chongquan* 前手沖拳): From the Ready Position, push off your right foot and shift your weight forward. Keep the ball of your right foot on the floor, but allow your heel to raise up. At the same time, turn your body to your right and jab forward with the *face* of your left fist. Keep your right fist next to your face to protect your head (Figure 3-2).

   The *face* of the fist is the front knuckle area of the hand when held in a fist. This strike is fast and effective for closing the distance, but not very powerful. It is usually used to set up for a more powerful punch or kick.

2. Rear Fist Jab (*Houshou Chongquan* 後手沖拳): From the Ready Position, push off your right foot and grind the ball of your foot counterclockwise, and shift your weight forward to your left foot. At the same time, turn your waist to your left and jab forward with the *face* of your right fist. Keep your left fist next to your face to protect your head (Figure 3-3).

Figure 3-4

Figure 3-5

Figure 3-6

This strike utilizes the push from the back leg and utilizes the turning of the waist to deliver a powerful jab.

3. Front Fist Side Hook (*Qianshou Guanquan* 前手貫拳): From the Ready Position, turn your upper body to your right. At the same time, circle your left fist out, forward, then hook in to your right. When you hook, keep your left arm bent and palm facing down. Keep your right fist next to your face to protect your head (Figure 3-4).

   This strike is a powerful attack to an opponent's head, ribs, chest, and abdomen with either the *face* of the fist or the *eye* of the fist. The *eye* of the fist is the area between the thumb and the index finger when the hand is held in a fist.

4. Rear Fist Side Hook (*Houshou Guanquan* 後手貫拳): From the Ready Position, push off your right foot and grind the ball of your foot counterclockwise, and shift your weight forward to your left foot. At the same time, circle your right fist out, forward, then hook into your left. When you hook, keep your right arm bent and palm facing down. The striking surface is your knuckles. Keep your left fist next to your face to protect your head (Figure 3-5).

5. Front Fist Upper Cut (*Qianshou Chaoquan* 前手抄拳): From the Ready Position, slide your left foot forward and follow up with your right foot to gain distance. At the same time, sink down slightly as you lower your left fist. Then rotate your left arm until your palm is facing in, and punch up to the upper right direction (Figure 3-6).

   This strike is used to attack an opponent's chin, head, chest, and abdomen.

Figure 3-7

Figure 3-8

Figure 3-9

6. Rear Fist Upper Cut (*Houshou chaoquan* 後手抄拳): From the Ready Position, take a circular step forward with your right foot to your right, and slide your left foot behind your right foot. At the same time, sink down slightly as you lower your right fist. Then rotate your right arm until your palm is facing in, and punch up to the upper left direction (Figure 3-7).

   When you punch, shift your weight forward slightly and turn your body to deliver a more powerful punch. Keep your left hand next to your face to protect your head.

7. Spinning Horizontal Back Fist (*Bianquan, Zhaunshen Fanbeichuai* 鞭拳，轉身反背鎚): From the Ready Position, bend your knees and squat down slightly. Arc your chest, bend your waist, and duck your head down slightly. Spring up quickly and pivot on your left foot and turn your body clockwise around to your right, back, then front. Lift up your right knee as you spin around, and use the spinning momentum to strike horizontally with the *back* of your right fist. Keep your left fist next to your face to protect your head (Figure 3-8).

   The *back* of the fist is the opposite side of the palm when the hand is held in a fist. This strike is used to attack an opponent's head, chest, and neck areas.

8. Springing Horizontal Back Fist (*Tanquan* 彈拳, *Bengquan* 崩拳): From the Ready Position, push off your right leg and shift your weight forward to your left leg. At the same time, coil your left arm in, then spring it horizontally forward with the back of your fist (Figure 3-9).

Figure 3-10

Figure 3-11

Figure 3-12

This strike is used for attacking an opponent's head, chest, abdomen; and an opponent's attacking hands and feet.

9. Hammer Fist (*Piquan* 劈拳): From the Ready Position, slide your left foot forward and follow up with your right foot. At the same time, strike down vertically with the *wheel* of the Fist (Figure 3-10).

   The *wheel* of the fist is the bottom edge of the palm when the hand is held in a fist. This strike is used to attack an opponent's face, shoulders, neck, and arms.

10. Horizontal Strike with the Heart of the Fist (*Hengkouquan* 横扣拳): From the Ready Position, move your left fist forward and in horizontally, striking with the *heart* side of the fist (Figure 3-11).

    The *heart* of the fist is the palm side of the fist when the hand is held in a fist. When striking with the *heart* of the fist, the thumb is pulled out to the side of the index finger instead of pressing on top of the index and the middle fingers. This strike is used to attack an opponent's head.

11. Vertical Strike with the Heart of the Fist (*Gaiquan* 盖拳): From the Ready Position, thrust your right arm forward, rotate your right fist until the palm side if facing down, then hammer down with the *heart* side of your fist (Figure 3-12).

    This strike is used to attack the top of an opponent's head and face.

Figure 3-13

Figure 3-14

Figure 3-15

12. Planting Fist (*Zaiquan* 栽拳): From the Ready Position, raise your right fist up to your ear height, with your elbow above your shoulder level. Punch forward and down slightly (Figures 3-13 and 3-14).

    This strike is used to attack the shoulders, neck, chest, and abdomen.

13. Inserting Fist (*Chaquan* 插拳): From the Ready Position, slide your left foot forward and follow up with your right foot. Shift your weight forward onto your left leg, drop your body down, and turn your body to your left. At the same time, raise your right fist up towards your ear level, rotate your arm in, and punch forward with your fist. The *eye* side of the fist is now facing down (Figure 3-15).

    This strike is used to attack the abdomen.

14. Lifting Fist (*Tiaoquan* 挑拳): From the Ready Position, step forward with your right leg and straighten your leg. At the same time, lower your right arm, then with the *eye* of the fist facing up, strike straight up (Figures 3-16 and 3-17).

    This strike is used to attack an opponent's chin.

Figure 3-16

Figure 3-17

Figure 3-18

Figure 3-19

Figure 3-20

Figure 3-21

15. Scooping Fist (*Liaoquan* 撩拳): A strike forward with the *back* of the fist as you scoop up is called a Front Scooping Fist (Figure 3-18). A strike backward with the *heart* of the fist or the *wheel* of the fist is called a Back Scooping Fist (Figure 3-19).

16. Spearing Fist (*Erhou Chuanchuai* 耳後穿鎚): From the Ready Position, lean your upper body forwards towards your left. At the same time, rotate your arm and punch forward with your right fist (Figure 3-20).

    The contact area is the *face* of the fist, with the *eye* of the fist pointing downward. This strike is used to as a surprise attack to an opponent's face.

Figure 3-22

Figure 3-23

Figure 3-24

17. Drilling Fist (*Zuanquan* 鑽拳): From the Ready Position, step forward with your right foot. At the same time, lower your left arm, rotate your right arm, and drill your right fist upward over your left arm (Figure 3-21)

    This strike is for attacking an opponent's chin and head. The left arm is used to deflect a punch while the right arm drills up to counterattack the opponent. The drilling punch by itself can also be used to simultaneously defect an opponent's punch and counterattack an opponent at the same time. The drilling motion of the forearm can deflect the opponent's punch to either side of your body, yet maintains the forward and upward momentum of the punch to deliver an effective counterattack.

18. Shearing Fist (*Hengquan* 橫拳): From the Ready Position, slide your left foot forward and follow up with your right foot. At the same time, lower your left arm, move your right fist under your left arm in a semicircle, then straighten your right arm and punch forward (Figure 3-22).

    The power for this punch is accomplished with the backward motion of the left arm and the forward motion of the right arm, creating a shearing force. This strike is used to attack an opponent's chest and abdomen.

19. Sideways Sweeping Fist (*Hengsaoquan* 橫掃拳): From the Ready Position, move your left fist out to your left slightly, then extend forward. As you complete the extension, pull your fist horizontally to your right (Figures 3-23 and 3-24)

    This strike is used to attack an opponent's head, neck, upper arm, and the side of the ribs.

Figure 3-25

Figure 3-26

Figure 3-27

Figure 3-28

20. Reverse Sideways Sweeping Fist (*Hou Hengsaoquan* 後橫掃拳): From the Ready Position, take a step forward with your right leg. At the same time, raise your right elbow, and horizontally move your right fist forward and to your right (Figures 3-25 and 3-26).

21. Jab-Hook Combination Fist (*Liquan* 秝拳): From the Ready Position, jab forward with your right fist. Continue the jabbing momentum and hook your fist to your left (Figures 3-27 and 3-28).

    This strike is used to attack an opponent's head, neck, chest, abdomen, and upper arm.

Figure 3-29

Figure 3-30

Figure 3-31

Hand and Palm:

22. Throwing Hand (*Shuaishou* 摔手): From the Ready Position, spring the back of your left hand forward (Figure 3-29).

    The movements of this attack are similar to the movements of the Springing Horizontal Back Fist. It is used to attack an opponent's face.

23. Slapping Hand (*Paishou* 拍手): From the Ready Position, move your left hand out slightly to your left, then slap forward and to your right (Figure 3-30).

    The movements of this attack are similar to the movements of the Horizontal Strike with the Heart of the Fist. Instead of using the *heart* of the fist, the Slapping Hand uses the palm and the fingers to attack an opponent, or to deflect an opponent's attack.

24. Inserting Palm (*Chazhang* 插掌): Keep all five fingers tightly together as an open hand and spear forward with your fingers (Figure 3-31).

    This strike is used to attack an opponent's throat, floating ribs, armpits, shoulder well, temples, solar plexus, and lower jaw. The shoulder well is the soft spot right in front of the collar bone.

Figure 3-32

Figure 3-33

Figure 3-34

25. Chopping Palm (*Kanzhang* 砍掌): Use the bottom edge of the palm and chop horizontally or at an angle (Figure 3-32)

    This strike is used to attack an opponent's shoulders, neck, face, upper arms; and the inside of the thighs and legs.

26. Splitting Palm (*Pizhang* 劈掌): Use the bottom edge of the palm and chop vertically downward (Figure 3-33).

    This strike is used to attack an opponent's shoulders, back, and the back of the head.

27. Facing Palm (*Pumianzhang* 扑面掌): Use the palm of the hand to slap down and forward (Figure 3-34).

    This strike is used to attack an opponent's face.

28. Cutting Palm (*Hengyezhang* 横掖掌): Use the bottom edge of the palm to cut horizontally forward with the fingers pointing sideways (Figure 3-35).

    This strike is used to attack an opponent's face, nose, throat, neck, abdomen, and ribs.

29. Scooping Palm (*Liaoyinzhang* 撩陰掌): Use the palm of the hand to scoop up towards the groin of an opponent (Figure 3-36).

30. Lifting Palm (*Tiaozhang* 挑掌): With the thumb side edge of the hand facing up, settle your palm and lift the fingers up (Figures 3-37 and 3-38).

Figure 3-35

Figure 3-36

Figure 3-37

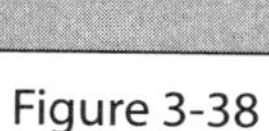

Figure 3-38

Figure 3-39

31. Spearing Palm (*Chuanzhang* 穿掌): Use one palm to push down while spearing the other palm over the palm that is pushing down.

    This is the same as the Inserting Palm (Figure 3-31) plus the downward pushing palm with the other hand.

32. Thumb Side of the Palm Strike (*Neicezhang* 内側掌): Tuck and line up your thumb under your index finger, and keep all other fingers straight and tightly together. Use the area created by the knuckles of the thumb and the edge of the index finger to strike in horizontally (Figure 3-39).

Figure 3-40

Figure 3-41

Figure 3-42

Elbow:

33. Sideways Elbow Strike (*Hengzhou* 横肘): From the Ready Position, bend your left arm, lower your fist, and strike horizontally forward with your left elbow (Figure 3-40).

34. Lifting Elbow Strike (*Tuozhou* 托肘): From the Ready Position, step forward with your right leg and strike up with your right elbow (Figure 3-41).

35. Horizontal Supported Elbow Strike (*Dingzhou* 頂肘): Line up your right hand with your left fist, and strike horizontally forward with your left elbow (Figure 3-42).

36. Sinking Elbow Strike (*Chenzhou* 沉肘): Bend your arm and drop down with your elbow. Striking with the upper part of the elbow (Figure 3-43).

37. Back Elbow Strike (*Huizhou* 回肘): Backward strike with your elbow (Figure 3-44).

38. Covering Elbow Strike (*Gaizhou* 蓋肘): Bend your arm and drop down with your right elbow. Striking with the lower part of your elbow (Figure 3-45).

39. Opening Elbow Strike (*Xianzhou* 掀肘): Striking back and up with your elbow (Figure 3-46).

40. Upward Supported Elbow Strike (*Shangdingzhou* 上頂肘): Line up your right hand with your left fist, and strike forward and up with your left elbow (Figure 3-47).

Figure 3-43

Figure 3-44

Figure 3-45

Figure 3-46

Figure 3-47

Figure 3-48

Figure 3-49

Figure 3-50

41. Downward Supported Elbow Strike (*Xiadingzhou* 下頂肘): Line up your right hand with your left fist, and strike forward and down with your left elbow (Figure 3-48).

42. Double Reverse Elbow Strike (*Xianghou Shuankaozhou* 向後雙靠肘): Strike back with both elbows (Figure 3-49). This strike is used to neutralize an opponent who is grabbing and holding you from the back.

43. Cutting Elbow Strike (*Jianzhou* 剪肘): Trap your opponent's arm between your arms and move your forearms in opposite directions to control or break an opponent's elbow (Figure 3-50).

3.3. Kicking Applications

1. Spring Kick (*Tantui* 彈腿): Kick with the tip of the toes and or the top of the foot (Figures 3-51 and 3-52).

2. Heel Kick (*Dengtui* 蹬腿): Kick with the heel first (Figure 3-53). Upon contact, push down with the ball of the foot.

3. Back Heel Kick (*Houdengtui* 後蹬腿): Kick with the heel towards the opponent while leaning your body in the opposite direction (Figure 3-54).

4. Side Kick (*Chuaitui* 踹腿): Kick sideways towards your opponent with the bottom or the outside edge of the foot (Figures 3-55 and 3-56).

Figure 3-51

Figure 3-52

Figure 3-53

Figure 3-54

Figure 3-55

Figure 3-56

Figure 3-57

Figure 3-58

Figure 3-59

5. Side Spring Kick (*Cetantui* 側彈腿): Kick with the top of the foot from the side towards your opponent (Figures 3-57 to 3-59).

6. Turn Body High Sweeping Kick (*Zhuanshen Hengsaotui* 轉身橫掃腿): Kick with the back of the heel or the back of the leg while spinning the body around (Figures 3-60 to 3-62).

7. Back Scoop Kick (*Houliaotui* 後撩腿): Kick with the back of the heel or the bottom of the foot by lifting it upward from the back (Figures 3-63 and 3-64).

Figure 3-60

Figure 3-61

Figure 3-62

Figure 3-63

Figure 3-64

Figure 3-65

Figure 3-66

Figure 3-67

Figure 3-68

8. Hook Kick (*Goutitui* 勾踢腿): Kick with the top of a flexed foot and the front part of the leg (Figure 3-65).

9. Intercepting Kick (*Jietui* 截腿, *Lanmenjiao* 攔門腳): A stepping downward kick with the foot turned out and using the bottom of the foot (Figure 3-66).

10. Shovel Kick (*Chantui* 鏟腿): Kick with the outside edge of the foot in an arc (Figures 3-67 to 3-69).

11. T Kick (*Cuntui* 寸腿): Kick with the tip of your foot or the ball of your foot towards your opponent's knee or shin (Figure 3-70).

12. Side Lift Kick (*Guaitui* 拐腿): Kick with the outer edge of the foot or the side of the leg towards your opponent's groin area (Figure 3-71).

Figure 3-69

Figure 3-70

Figure 3-71

Figure 3-72

Figure 3-73

Figure 3-74

Figure 3-75

13. Horse Kick (*Juetui* 蹶腿): Kick with the heel toward your opponent's groin area by lifting the leg up backward (Figure 3-72). Then drop the ball of your foot down towards your opponent's foot (Figure 3-73).

14. Stomp Kick (*Cuotui* 錯腿): Kick from the side towards your opponent's foot with the outer edge of the your foot (Figure 3-74).

15. Grind Kick (*Niantui* 碾腿): After stomping down towards your opponent's foot, grind your foot into your opponent's foot (Figures 3-75 and 3-76).

16. Back Hook Kick (*Guatui* 挂腿): Sweep your leg backward towards the back of your opponent's leg to make your opponent fall (Figure 3-77).

Figure 3-76

Figure 3-77

Figure 3-78

Figure 3-79

17. Outside Crescent Kick (*Bailiantui* 擺蓮腿): Lift your leg up high and sweep it from the inside out towards your opponent's rib, chest, back, or head (Figure 3-78).

18. Inside Crescent Kick (*Lihetui* 里合腿): Lift your leg up high and sweep it from outside in towards your opponent's face, head, back, chest, and abdomen (Figure 3-79).

Figure 3-80

Figure 3-81

Figure 3-82

Figure 3-83

19. Low Front Sweep Kick (*Saotangtui* 掃蹚腿): Squat down and sweep one leg forward with the front of your leg towards your opponent's ankle area (Figure 3-80).

20. Low Back Sweep Kick (*Housaotui* 後掃腿): Squat down and place both hands on the floor, while turning your body and sweeping backward with the back of your leg towards your opponent's leg (Figure 3-81 to 3-83).

Figure 3-84

Figure 3-85

Figure 3-86

Figure 3-87

21. Lean Back Heel Kick (*Yangshen Shangdengtui* 仰身上蹬腿): Grab a hold of your opponent's shirt and pull, while heel kicking towards your opponent's body, and throwing your opponent backward (Figures 3-84 to 3-86).

22. Axe Kick (*Chutoutui* 鋤頭腿): Kick your foot up, then down towards your opponent's face, chest, and abdomen (Figure 3-87).

Figure 3-88

Figure 3-89

Figure 3-90

Figure 3-91

23. Stepping Kick (*Caitui* 踩腿): Turn your foot in and kick down with your heel towards your opponent's thigh or leg (Figure 3-88).

24. Back Inserting Kick (*Houchatui, Toutui* 後插腿, 偷腿): Kick backward with your back leg towards your opponent's leg (Figure 3-89).

25. Jump Back Hook Kick (*Tiaobu Hougoutui* 跳步後勾腿): Jump forward then raise one leg and hook it back towards the back of your opponent's leg (Figures 3-90 to 3-92).

26. Black Dragon Wraps Around the Post Kick (*Wulong Jiaozhu* 烏龍絞柱): Use the legs like scissors moving them in opposite directions to take your opponent down (Figures 3-93 and 3-94 or 3-95 and 3-96).

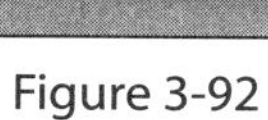

Figure 3-92

Figure 3-93

Figure 3-94

Figure 3-95

Figure 3-96

Figure 3-97

Figure 3-98

Figure 3-99

Figure 3-100

27. Back Stepping Kick (*Shajiaotui* 殺腳腿): Cross your back foot behind your front foot and sweep your front foot back towards the back of your opponent's leg (Figures 3-97 to 3-99).

28. Forward Knee Kick (*Zhengdingxi* 正頂膝): Kick with the knee forward and up (Figure 3-100).

29. Side Knee Kick (Cedingxi 側頂膝): Kick sideways with your knee (Figure 3-101).

30. Kneeling Kick (*Guixi* 跪膝): Kneel on your opponent while he is on the ground (Figure 3-102).

Figure 3-101

Figure 3-102

Figure 3-103

31. Jumping Knee Kick (*Tengkong Feidingxi* 騰空飛頂膝): Jump up and knee kick towards your opponent with one knee then the other knee (Figure 3-103).

32. Jumping Kneeling Kick (*Tengkong Guixi* 騰空跪膝): Chase after your opponent and follow up with a downward kneeling kick.

3.4. Sanshou Fighting Combinations

This section contains many effective fighting combinations. To make them useful to you, repetitive training is necessary to make the combinations part of your natural reactions. Train the combination by yourself to make the movements smooth and powerful. Then train with a partner to make the movements realistic. Alternate with your partner. One of you can be the attacker, the other can be the defender. Repeat as many times as you wish, then let the other person attack. Start from the Ready Position with your left hand and left foot forward. Common sense is also essential to prevent unnecessary injuries during your training.

The techniques presented in this section are to help you understand martial applications and give you *tools* to work with. To be able to use the techniques in an actual situation will require a lot of training. It is said that, "After repeating one hundred times, your body movement will become smooth; and after repeating one thousand times you will be able to understand the principles of the movements." This phrase implies that familiarity will make your movements natural and your techniques effective.

Even though the drills are demonstrated in a set pattern, keep in mind that there is more than one obvious application. In Chinese martial arts, many maneuvers are both defensive and offensive depending on the situation. Blocks can be used both as an offensive technique, as well as, a defensive technique that sets up for a counterattack. Your techniques can also have both consequential and inconsequential moves, this will prevent your opponent from knowing your intentions. For example, in an actual application, the punch could be used to distract your opponent - inconsequential movement, and the foot could be used as the actual attack - consequential movement. It could also be that the kick is inconsequential and the punch is consequential; or both consequential. Distinguish clearly what your intentions are during your training. This will train your heightened sense of awareness, as if you were in an actual combat.

Figure 3-104

Figure 3-105

Figure 3-106

Figure 3-107

1. Punches 冲拳:

   a. Suddenly shift your weight forward and jab towards your opponent's head or chest (Figure 3-104).

   b. Your opponent hooks with his left fist towards your head. You intercept with your right forearm and jab forward with your left fist (Figures 3-105 and 3-106).

   c. Your opponent punches to your head. You drop down quickly and punch with your left fist towards your opponent's rib area (Figure 3-107).

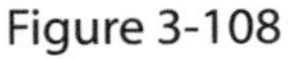

Figure 3-108

Figure 3-109

Figure 3-110

Figure 3-111

d. Your opponent hooks with his left hand towards your head. You drop down quickly and punch with your left fist towards your opponent's rib area (Figure 3-108).

e. As your opponent attempts to heel kick you, you quickly move forward to jam the opponent's kick, preventing the power to be delivered. At the same time, punch towards your opponent's head or chest with your left fist (Figure 3-109).

f. As your opponent's attempts to grab a hold of your leg to take you down, punch to his head with your left fist (Figure 3-110).

g. Your opponent punches towards your head. You drop down quickly and punch with your right fist towards your opponent's rib area (Figure 3-111).

Figure 3-112

Figure 3-113

Figure 3-114

Figure 3-115

h. Your opponent punches towards your chest. Use your left hand to push down the incoming punch. At the same time, punch forward with your right fist towards your opponent's head (Figure 3-112).

i. Your opponent hooks with his right fist towards your head. You intercept with your left arm and punch forward with your right fist towards your opponent's chest or head (Figure 3-113).

j. Your opponent kicks sideways with his right leg towards the side of your ribs. You intercept down with your left arm. At the same time, shift your weight forward with your left foot and punch with your right fist towards your opponent's head or chest (Figures 3-114 and 3-115).

Figure 3-116

Figure 3-117

Figure 3-118

Figure 3-119

k. Your opponent kicks sideways with his right leg towards your head. You intercept up with your left arm. At the same time, shift your weight forward and punch with your right fist towards your opponent's head or chest (Figures 3-116 and 3-117).

l. Punch to your opponent's head with your left fist, to make him defend up. Then punch down towards your opponent's abdomen with your right fist. Repeat one high punch and one low punch as fast as you can, and as many times as you wish (Figures 3-118 and 3-119).

Figure 3-120

Figure 3-121

Figure 3-122

Figure 3-123

2. Jab and Hook Combinations 左沖拳，右貫拳:

a. Jab to your opponent's head with your left fist to make him defend up. Then hook to your opponent's rib with your right fist (Figures 3-120 and 3-121).

b. Jab to your opponent's abdomen with your left fist to make him defend the midsection. Then hook to your opponent's head with your right fist (Figures 3-122 and 3-123).

Figure 3-124

Figure 3-125

Figure 3-126

Figure 3-127

3. Back Fist Combination 左彈拳，轉身右鞭拳: Back fist to your opponent's face with your left fist. Then spin around clockwise on the ball of your left foot, with your right knee up, and back fist to your opponent's face with your right fist (Figures 3-124 and 3-125).

4. Hook and Upper Cut Combination 左貫拳，右抄拳（勾拳): Hook to your opponent's face with your left fist. Then punch up with your right fist to your opponent's chin (Figures 3-126 and 3-127).

Figure 3-128

Figure 3-129

Figure 3-130

Figure 3-131

5. Strike with the *Heart* of the Fist Combination 左蓋拳，右橫扣拳: Strike forward and down with the heart of your left fist towards your opponent's nose. Then strike horizontally with the heart of your right fist towards your opponent's face (Figures 3-128 and 3-129).

6. Throwing and Slapping Hand Combination 右摔手，右橫扣拳（迎風擺柳）: Throw the back of your right hand towards the right side of your opponent's face. If the opponent blocks your right arm, pull your right arm back, then slap towards the left side of your opponent's face (Figures 3-130 and 3-131). You may hold your hand in a fist or keep it open.

Figure 3-132

Figure 3-133

Figure 3-134

7. Jab and Heel Kick Combination 右沖拳，跟步右蹬腿: Step forward with your right foot and jab with your right fist to make your opponent defend his head. As you jab, bring your left foot next to your right foot and lift your right knee up, and heel kick forward towards your opponent's abdomen. After making contact with your heel, push forward with the ball of your foot to knock your opponent down (Figures 3-132 to 3-134).

Figure 3-135

Figure 3-136

Figure 3-137

Figure 3-138

8. Jab and Side Spring Kick Combination 右沖拳，跟步右邊腿: Step forward with your right foot and jab forward with your right fist towards your opponent's head to make him defend his head. As you jab, bring your left foot next to your right foot and lift your right knee up, and side spring kick forward to your opponent's back, leg or head (Figures 3-135 to 3-138).

Figure 3-139

Figure 3-140

Figure 3-141

9. Jab, Jab-Hook, and Side Kick Combination 左沖拳，右秣拳，右踹腿: Jab with your left fist to your opponent's head (Figure 3-139). Turn your body to your right as you Jab-Hook with your right fist (Figure 3-140). If your opponent backs up, then side kick with your right foot to your opponent's abdomen (Figure 3-141).

Figure 3-142

Figure 3-143

Figure 3-144

10. Jab, Spinning Back Fist, and Side Springing Kick Combination 右沖拳，轉身左鞭拳，右邊腿: Step forward with your right foot and jab with your right fist towards your opponent's head (Figure 3-142). Spin around counterclockwise on the ball of your right foot, lift your left knee up, and back fist with your left fist (Figure 3-143). When your opponent retreats, step down with your left foot, and Side Spring Kick with the right foot to your opponent's leg or back (Figure 3-144).

Figure 3-145

Figure 3-146

Figure 3-147

Figure 3-148

11. Jab, Hook Kick, and Back Fist Combination 左沖拳，右勾踢，右彈拳: Jab with your left fist to make your opponent defend his head. Then hook kick with your right foot to your opponent's front leg (Figures 3-145 and 3-146). If your opponent is able to avoid the hook kick or is still standing after your kick, do a back fist with your right fist to your opponent's face (Figures 3-147 and 3-148).

Figure 3-149

Figure 3-150

Figure 3-151

12. Jab, Hook Kick, and Spinning Back Fist Combination 左沖拳，右勾踢，轉身左鞭拳: Jab with your left fist to make your opponent defend his head. Then hook kick with your right foot to your opponent's front leg (Figures 3-149 and 3-150). If your opponent is able to avoid the hook kick, continue your kicking momentum and do a spinning left back fist to his head or neck (Figure 3-151).

Figure 3-152

Figure 3-153

Figure 3-154

13. Jab, Hook Kick, and Low Back Sweep Kick Combination 右沖拳，墊步右勾踢，伏地后掃腿: Step forward with your right foot and jab with your right fist to your opponent's head to make him defend his head (Figure 3-152). As you jab, bring your left foot next to your right foot. Then hook kick with your right foot on the back of your opponent's leg (Figure 3-153). If the opponent lifts up his leg or is able to avoid the hook kick, continue the hook kick momentum by dropping your body down, and doing a back sweep with your left leg on the back of your opponent's leg (Figure 3-154).

Figure 3-155

Figure 3-156

14. Leg Intercept and Jab Combination 提膝格擋沖拳-防腿反擊法: Your opponent heel kicks to your waist or lower with his right foot. You raise your left knee up to intercept the kick. Then immediately step down and forward to punch with your left fist to his head (Figures 3-155 and 3-156).

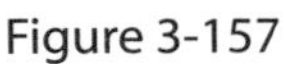

Figure 3-157

Figure 3-158

Figure 3-159

Figure 3-160

15. Countering a Heel or Side Kick 憋腿反擊: Your opponent attempts to heel or side kick.

    a. Turn your body to your right and lower your right forearm to intercept his kick (Figure 3-157).

    b. As he lifts his leg and before he completes his kick, move forward to prevent him from being able to complete the kick (Figure 3-158).

    Next, punch to his head with your right fist (Figure 3-159). As you punch, move your right leg next to your left leg, grab a hold of his leg, and sweep back with your left leg (Figure 3-160).

Figure 3-161

Figure 3-162

Figure 3-163

Figure 3-164

16. Countering a Low Kick Attack 防勾腿，掃腿反擊法: Your opponent hook kicks or sweep kicks towards your front leg.

a. Lift your front leg up and kick down towards his knee (Figures 3-161 and 3-162).

b. Lift your front leg up and side kick to his midsection (Figure 3-163).

c. Lift your front leg up and hook kick with your front leg on the back of his front leg (Figure 3-164).

Figure 3-165

Figure 3-166

Figure 3-167

Figure 3-168

d. Lift your front leg up, step forward behind his leg, and punch with your left fist to his face (Figure 3-165).

17. Countering a Side Spring Kick 十字防腿法還擊: Your opponent uses his right leg to side spring kick to your left side.

a. Turn your body to your left and block the kick by bending and pointing your left arm down, and placing your right arm next to your left arm pointing up. Once you have blocked the kick, step forward with your right foot and back fist with your right fist to his face (Figures 3-166 and 3-167).

Figure 3-169

Figure 3-170

Figure 3-171

Figure 3-172

b. Turn your body to your left and block the kick by bending and pointing your left arm up, and placing your right arm below your left arm pointing down. Once you have blocked the kick, punch with your right fist towards your opponent's head (Figures 3-168 and 3-169).

18. Countering a Punch with a Kick防沖拳以腿還擊: Your opponent punches to your head with his right fist.

a. Yield back and intercept the punch with your left arm to your right. Then heel or side kick to his midsection (Figures 3-170 and 3-171).

b. Shift your weight to your left and lean towards your left to avoid the punch. At the same time, Side Spring Kick to his abdomen or groin (Figure 3-172).

Figure 3-173

Figure 3-174

Figure 3-175

Figure 3-176

19. Countering a Hook Punch 防貫拳還擊法: Your opponent hook punches to your head with his right fist.

    a. Intercept up with your left arm and side kick to his midsection with your left foot (Figure 3-173).

    b. Intercept up with your left arm and hook kick with your right foot behind his front foot (Figures 3-174 and 3-175).

    c. Duck down to avoid the punch. Then move your head to your left and stand up. As you stand up, hook kick or front sweep kick with your right leg to the back of his front leg (Figures 3-176 and 3-177).

Figure 3-177

Figure 3-178

Figure 3-179

Figure 3-180

20. Countering a Spinning Back Fist 防鞭拳還擊法: Your opponent uses a spinning left back fist towards your head.

    a. Drop down and do a low front sweep kick or a low back sweep kick to your opponent's supporting leg (Figure 3-178).

    b. Step forward with your right leg as your opponent spins and block your opponent's elbow area with both of your hands (Figure 3-179). Then drop down and grab a hold of his legs, lift up and back to drop him (Figure 3-180).

Figure 3-181

Figure 3-182

Figure 3-183

Figure 3-184

c. If your opponent uses his right back fist towards your head, block or yield back to avoid the fist. Then Side Spring Kick to his abdomen with your right foot (Figures 3-181 and 3-182).

21. Countering an Upper Cut防勾拳還擊法: Your opponent punches to your abdomen with a right upper cut.

    a. Drop your left forearm down and hook your right fist towards his head (Figures 3-183 and 3-184).

Figure 3-185

Figure 3-186

Figure 3-187

Figure 3-188

b. Drop your left forearm down and punch with your right fist from over your head towards his head (Figures 3-185 and 3-186).

c. Drop your left forearm down, then punch forward towards his face (Figures 3-187 and 3-188).

Figure 3-189

Figure 3-190

Figure 3-191

Figure 3-192

22. Hook Kick and Back Step Combination 勾踢腿，殺腳腿: Hook kick to your opponent's front leg. If he is able to lift his leg to avoid being kicked, back step towards his leg and hook your right fist under his left arm or punch with your right fist to his face (Figures 3-189 and 3-190 or 3-191 and 3-192).

23. Throwing Hand, Intercepting Kick, and Side Kick Combination 摔手，截腿（攔門腳），踹腿: Throw your left hand towards your opponent's face to make him protect his head. Then kick down to his front shin with your right foot, and follow up with a side kick with your left foot to his abdomen (Figures 3-193 to 3-195).

24. Jab and Spinning Kick Combination 斜上步沖拳，轉身后高掃腿: Step to your left with your right foot and jab to your opponent's head with your right fist to make him defend his head

Figure 3-193

Figure 3-194

Figure 3-195

Figure 3-196

(Figure 3-196). Continue the stepping momentum, and heel kick or high sweep kick to his head (Figure 3-197).

Figure 3-197

Figure 3-198

Figure 3-199

Figure 3-200

Figure 3-201

25. Jab and Horse Kick Combination 斜上步沖拳，轉身勾襠: Step to your left with your right foot and jab to your opponent's head with your right fist to make him defend his head (Figure 3-198). Continue the stepping momentum and horse kick towards his groin with your left foot (Figure 3-199).

    This combination is illegal to use in Sanshou competitions. It is for self-defense use only.

26. Spring Kick, Inside Crescent Kick, and Back Low Sweep Kick 彈腿，里合腿，伏地后掃腿: Spring kick with your left foot towards your opponent's groin to make him defend and pay attention to his lower body (Figure 3-200). Then do a high inside crescent kick to his head with your right foot (Figure 3-201). If he

Figure 3-202

Figure 3-203

Figure 3-204

Figure 3-205

is able to avoid the high kick, put your foot down, and drop down to do a back sweep kick with your left leg (Figure 3-202).

This combination is illegal to use in Sanshou competitions. It is for self-defense use only.

27. Pull, Knee Kick, and Elbow Strike Combination 擒手正膝横肘: Your opponent punches to your head with his right fist. You turn your body to your left and intercept his punch with both of your hands (Figure 3-203). Grab a hold of his arm and pull back as you raise your knee towards his groin or abdomen (Figure 3-204). Put your right foot down and continue the momentum by elbowing to his head with your right elbow (Figure 3-205).

    This combination is illegal to use in Sanshou competitions. It is for self-defense use only.

Figure 3-206

Figure 3-207

Figure 3-208

28. Elbow Strikes Combination 格擋上步橫肘，插步掀肘，轉身回肘: Your opponent punches to your head with his right fist. You intercept with your left forearm. At the same time, step forward with your right foot and side elbow strike with your right elbow to his head (Figure 3-206). If he is able to avoid your side elbow strike, you continue the right elbow momentum, move it down then up towards his chin. At the same time, step with your left foot behind your right foot (Figure 3-207). Then spin your body around and back elbow strike to his head with your left elbow (Figure 3-208).

    This combination is illegal to use in Sanshou competitions. It is for self-defense use only.

Figure 3-209

Figure 3-210

Figure 3-211

Figure 3-212

29. Elbow Strikes and Jumping Knee Kick Combination 上頂肘，騰空頂膝，橫肘: Both you and your opponent are standing with your right foot and right arm forward. Your opponent hooks toward your head with his left fist. You intercept the hook by raising your right arm, step forward, and strike up with your left elbow towards his chin (Figures 3-209 and 3-210).

    If your opponent is able to avoid your elbow strike by moving back, maintain the same distance by skipping forward with your left leg and knee kick with your right knee to his chest or abdomen (Figure 3-211). If your opponent blocks your kick by pushing down on your knee, you then side elbow to his head with your right elbow (Figure 3-212).

    This combination is illegal to use in Sanshou competitions. It is for self-defense use only.

Figure 3-213

Figure 3-214

Figure 3-215

Figure 3-216

30. Spring Kick and Elbow Strike Combination 彈腿挑肘: Kick to your opponent's groin with your right foot to bring his attention down. Then step down with your right foot and strike up with your right elbow (Figures 3-213 and 3-214).

    This combination is illegal to use in Sanshou competitions. It is for self-defense use only.

31. Reverse Elbow and Horse Kick Combination回肘，厥子腿: Your opponent punches to your head with his right fist. You pretend to retreat by stepping back with your left foot. At the same time, duck your head down and strike up with your right elbow towards his head (Figure 3-215). Then horse kick to his groin (Figure 3-216).

Figure 3-217

Figure 3-218

Figure 3-219

This combination is illegal to use in Sanshou competitions. It is for self-defense use only.

32. T Kick, Elbow Strike, and Spring Kick Combination 丁腿，挑肘，彈腿: Kick to your opponent's front shin or knee with the ball of your right foot to bring his attention down (Figure 3-217). Step down and shift your weight forward, and strike up with your right elbow towards his chin (Figure 3-218). If your opponent is able to move back and avoid your strike, skip forward and Spring Kick to his groin with your right foot (Figure 3-219).

    This combination is illegal to use in Sanshou competitions. It is for self-defense use only.

Figure 3-220

Figure 3-221

Figure 3-222

33. Side Lift Kick, Horse Kick, and Back Scoop Kick Combination 拐腿，蹶腿，后撩腿: Kick to your opponent's groin with the outside edge of your foot (Figure 3-220). If he moves back, put your foot down then kick up with a horse kick to his groin (Figure 3-221). If he is still able to move away, put your foot down, then scoop up with your right foot to his groin again (Figure 3-222).

    This combination is illegal to use in Sanshou competitions. It is for self-defense use only.

Figure 3-223

Figure 3-224

Figure 3-225

34. Shovel Kick, Horse Kick, and Back Fist Combination 鏟腿，轉身后勾腿撩陰，反背鞭拳: Kick to your opponent's shin with a shovel kick across his shin (Figure 3-223). Put your foot down to your right, then turn your body and horse kick to his groin with your right foot (Figure 3-224). Then step down and do a back fist to his head with your right fist (Figure 3-225).

    This combination is illegal to use in Sanshou competitions. It is for self-defense use only.

Figure 3-226

Figure 3-227

Figure 3-228

35. Slapping Hand, Knee Kick, and Back Sweep Combination 拍手閃身膝頂-轉身后掃腿: Your opponent steps forward and punches to your head with his right fist. Turn your body to your right and slap his arm to your right and kick to his chest or abdomen with your right knee (Figures 3-226 and 3-227). If he is able to avoid your kick, you continue your turning momentum to your left and step down with your right foot. Immediately drop down and back sweep to his leg with your left leg (Figure 3-228).

    This combination is illegal to use in Sanshou competitions. It is for self-defense use only.

Figure 3-229

Figure 3-230

Figure 3-231

36. Stomp Kick, Knee Kick, and Elbow Strike Combination 錯腳，膝頂，橫肘: During a very close range situation, stomp down on the top of your opponent's foot with your front foot (Figure 3-229). While he is distracted by the pain of his foot, skip forward and knee kick with your right knee to his abdomen (Figure 3-230). Step down and follow through with a right side elbow strike to his head (Figure 3-231).

    This combination is illegal to use in Sanshou competitions. It is for self-defense use only.

實用快跤法

Chapter 4:

Practical Takedown Applications

In the previous chapters, we have presented many ti and da methods. In this chapter, we will focus on takedown or Shuaijiao methods. Takedown methods are a component of all Wushu styles and are referred to by many different names. It is also known as Jiaodi (角抵), Jiaoli (角力), Xianpu (相撲), etc. Shuaijiao has also been a popular competition event since ancient times. It's objective is to skillfully utilize the body's leverage to take down the opponent or distress the opponent. In free fighting applications, a more specific takedown approach is used. It is called Kuaijiao (快跤), meaning quick or fast takedown. In a quick takedown, the practitioner refrains from struggling with their opponent. Kuaijiao techniques are generally done as a follow up to a kick or a punch. After the takedown, they continue to strike until the opponent is completely subdued. Once they engage, the takedown is accomplished right away. If a takedown can't be accomplished; further kicks, punches, or Qinna must be applied.

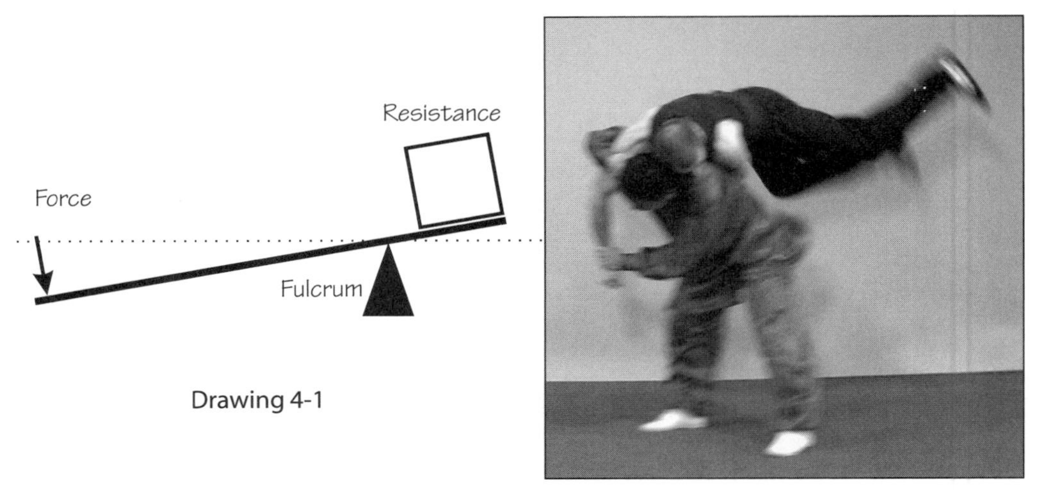

Drawing 4-1

Figure 4-1

4.1. Use Leverage to Your Advantage

In the applications, kicking, hooking, locking, and tripping with the leg; striking, grabbing, and pushing with the arms; or leaning and striking with the upper body, are often combined to accomplish an effective and devastating takedown. The shoulders, elbows, hips, palms, and/or the knees are often used as the pivot point to take down the opponent. With the proper use of the body's leverage, a practitioner is able to easily takedown their opponent with a shrugging of the shoulders, a turning of the waist, a twisting of the hips, a dropping of the elbow, a dropping of the knee, or a hooking of the leg. The use of angles opposite to the normal movements of the joints and the use of leverage to off set the opponent's balance are also essential for a successful takedown technique.

Proper body mechanics not only help to conserve energy, it also helps to move your opponent with the least amount of effort and allows you to move heavier objects. Improper body mechanics can cause physical damage to your body from strain and fatigue. The human body is very complex and is filled with many physical potentials when it has been properly conditioned. In applying takedown techniques, the proper use of the lever principle is essential to an effective takedown.

A lever is a device that consists of a rigid bar that moves on a fulcrum, using force applied at a second point to lift up resistance at a third point. A fulcrum is the point of support on which a solid bar turns in raising or moving something. There are generally three different types of levers that differ only in the location of the fulcrum, the effort or force, and the weight or the resistance.

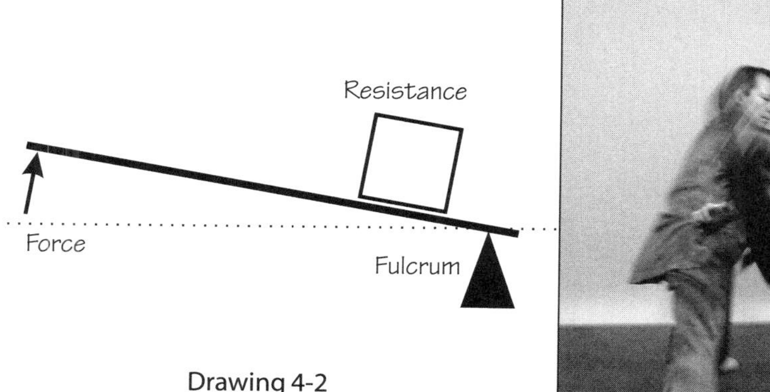

Drawing 4-2

Figure 4-2

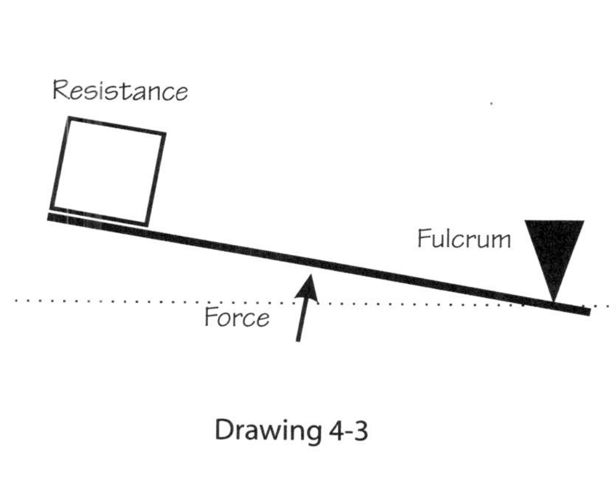

Drawing 4-3

Figure 4-3

The first type of lever has the fulcrum between the resistance and the force (Drawing 4-1). This type of lever is best applied to throw your opponent over your back (Figure 4-1). In this type of takedown, your back becomes the pivot point, and the force is primarily applied from your arms. His weight is the resistance. The second type of lever has the resistance between the fulcrum and the force (Drawing 4-2). This type of lever is best applied to trip your opponent with one leg or arm, while pushing in the opposite direction with the other arm (Figure 4-2). The third type of lever has the force between the fulcrum and the resistance (Drawing 4-3). This type of lever is best applied to lift your opponent up from under their center of gravity, then throwing them forward, backward, or sideways (Figure 4-3).

In a simple lever, the first type is the most effective means of moving the resistance or weight, then the second, and the third. During the application of a takedown technique, both you and your opponent are in constant motion and changing postures, so that the most effective application of the lever principle will depend on the situation. You don't need to know hundreds of takedowns, but you do need to understand and be able to apply enough techniques so that you can improvise those techniques to varying situations. For more takedown techniques, please refer to the book, *Xiaoyaoshuai*, by the authors. It focuses primarily on takedown techniques.

An effective takedown application, is an effective utilization of the lever principle. It also depends on your ability to take advantage of your opponent's body momentum against them, utilizing their physical misalignment and bad balance against them. Without proper alignment or balance, they will not be able to successfully apply their offensive attack; and they will be more vulnerable to your offensive maneuvers. You can simply push or ram your opponent from an advantageous position.

Before you start practicing with your partner, make sure that you have plenty of room to practice. Be careful with the throws during practice, so you don't injure each other. Make sure that both of you are familiar with the rolls and falls introduced in Chapter 1. A safety mat and common sense are needed to have a productive practice.

4.2. Fast Takedown Techniques

Takedown 1. Announce to the East but Attack to the West (聲東擊西-勾踢腿)

Step 1. Start in a ready position with your left foot forward (Figure 4-4). Your opponent steps forward with his right foot and punches to your head with his right fist. You yield back and intercept with your left forearm and deflect his punch to your left (Figure 4-5).

Step 2. Shift your weight forward and punch to his head with your right fist. Your opponent intercepts your punch to his right with his left forearm (Figure 4-6). Grab a hold of his right wrist with your left hand, hook your right hand back on his upper arm or shoulder, and kick to his front leg with a right hook kick, to take him down (Figure 4-7).

Figure 4-4

Figure 4-5

Figure 4-6

Figure 4-7

Notes:

A. Your initial intercept and the punch must be done as close together as you can. This way your opponent will have less chance to initiate another attack because you are forcing him to defend upward which provides an opportunity for you to effectively kick his leg.

B. Keep in mind that the only reason to engage your opponent is to counterattack, otherwise, just yield back and avoid the attack.

C. The hook back with your right hand and the kick are done simultaneously in opposite directions. If he is too close for you to kick effectively, use the following technique to take him down.

Figure 4-8

Figure 4-9

Takedown 2. An Autumn Wind Blows the Falling Leaves (秋風掃落葉-橫肘撞跌)

Figure 4-10

Step 1. From a ready position, your opponent steps forward with his right foot and punches to your head with his right fist. You yield back and intercept with your left arm and deflect his punch to your left (Figure 4-8).

Step 2. Push his arm down and hold it tight under your left arm as you step in with your right foot and punch to his head with your right fist. He intercepts your punch with his left arm. You step in further with your right foot, follow through with a right elbow to his head, and swing your left foot around to your right (Figure 4-9).

Step 3. Turn your body to your left, pull his right arm towards you and continue the pressure one his head or shoulder with your right elbow, to take him down (Figure 4-10).

Notes:

A. When you return the punch with your right fist you should already be aware that your opponent can intercept your punch with his left forearm. Follow through immediately with a right elbow strike

Figure 4-11

Figure 4-12

towards his head or shoulder. This will give you a chance to set up for the takedown.

B. If your opponent is very strong, sweep your right leg back on his left leg as you turn your body to your left.

Figure 4-13

Takedown 3. The Clever Girl Threads the Needle (巧女穿針–抱腿跌)

Step 1. From a ready position, your opponent steps forward with his right foot and punches to your head with his right fist. You yield back and intercept with your left arm and deflect his punch to your left (Figure 4-11).

Step 2. Step in with your right foot and punch with your right fist to his head to make him block inward with his left forearm (Figure 4-12). Drop down quickly and grab a hold of his front leg, step back with your left foot and pull back, to take him down (Figure 4-13).

Note:

A. This takedown works best when your opponent is pushing forward as you attempt to punch him. If he is leaning back as he intercepts your punch, use the following takedown technique.

Figure 4-14

Figure 4-15

Takedown 4. Yellow Dragon Stirs the Water
(黃龍三攪水-抱腿按胸跌)

Figure 4-16

Step 1. From a ready position, your opponent steps forward with his right foot and punches to your head with his right fist. You yield back and intercept with your left arm and deflect his punch to your left (Figure 4-14).

Step 2. Step in with your right foot and punch with your right fist to his head to make him block inward with his left forearm (Figure 4-15). Press forward with your right arm, and grab a hold of his right leg with your left hand and lift up, as you slide forward with your right foot, to take him down (Figure 4-16).

Notes:

A. This takedown works best when your opponent is leaning backward. If he is very strong in pushing back, use the previous technique to take him down.

Figure 4-17

Figure 4-18

Figure 4-19

Figure 4-20

Takedown 5. The Heavenly Lord Embraces the Golden Vase (天官抱金瓶-抱雙腿跌)

Step 1. From a ready position, your opponent steps forward with his right foot and punches to your head with his right fist. You yield back and intercept with your left arm and deflect his punch to your left (Figure 4-17). He follows up with another punch with his left fist. You deflect the punch to your right with your right forearm (Figure 4-18).

Step 2. Strike to his head and chest area with both palms to make him yield back. Then drop down quickly and grab a hold of both legs and lift up, to take him down (Figures 4-19 and 4-20).

Figure 4-21

Figure 4-22

Note:

A. If you are unable to make your opponent lean backward, continue with the next technique and throw him over your shoulder.

Takedown 6. The Lion Plays with the Ball

(獅子戲球-挑襠跌)

Step 1. From a ready position, your opponent steps forward with his right foot and punches to your head with his right fist. You yield back and intercept with your left arm and deflect his punch to your left (Figure 4-21).

Step 2. You counter his punch by stepping in with your right foot and punching to his midsection with your right fist to make him block your arm down (Figure 4-22). Continue your forward momentum, hitting his chest with your right shoulder while lowering your right arm between his legs and throwing him back over your right shoulder (Figures 4-23 and 4-24).

Figure 4-23

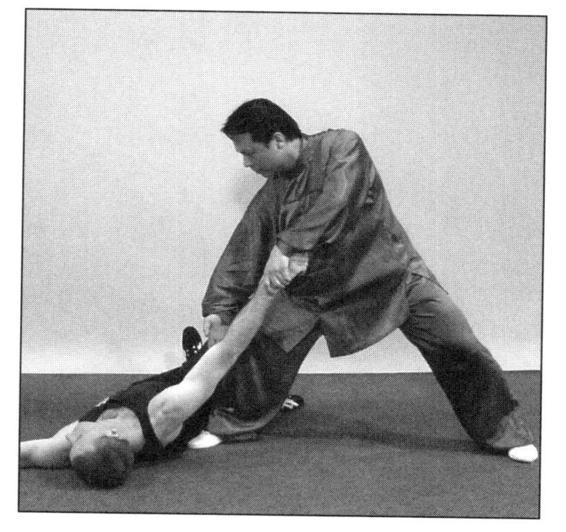

Figure 4-24

Note:

A. Bend your knees, not your back to get under your opponent's center of gravity and lift him up with your legs. When you throw him over your shoulder, pull with your left hand, lift with your right arm, pivot on your right shoulder, and lift with your legs.

B. If you don't have the opportunity to lower your right arm between your opponent's legs, continue with the next technique.

Figure 4-25

Figure 4-26

Figure 4-27

Figure 4-28

Takedown 7. Change the Scenery to Move the Mountain (換景移山-過肩跌)

Step 1. From a ready position, your opponent steps forward with his right foot and punches to your head with his right fist. You yield back and intercept with your left arm and deflect his punch to your left (Figure 4-25).

Step 2. You counter his punch by stepping in with your right foot and punching to his midsection with your right fist to make him block your arm down (Figure 4-26).

Figure 4-29

Figure 4-30

Step 3. Continue your forward momentum, hitting his chest with your right shoulder while hooking your right arm under his right arm (Figure 4-27). Pull his right arm down while wedging your back tightly against his body; as you take another step with your left foot, and throw him over your right shoulder (Figures 4-28 to 4-30).

Note:

A. Keep your body tight against your opponent's body as you throw him over your shoulder.

Figure 4-31

Figure 4-32

Takedown 8. Dapeng Spreads Its Wings (大鵬展翅-提腿搬)

Figure 4-33

Step 1. From a ready position, your opponent steps forward with his right foot and punches to your head with his right fist. You yield back and circle both forearms clockwise to intercept his punch to your right (Figure 4-31).

Step 2. Slide your left foot in and chop to his neck with your left hand to make him intercept with his left arm (Figure 4-31). Keep the pressure on his left arm with your left arm, pressing forward and down. At the same time, grab a hold of his right leg with your right hand and lift up, to take him down (Figure 4-33).

Note:

A. When you chop in with your left hand, push off with your right foot and step in with your left foot as deep as you can. The upward lift with your right hand, and the forward and downward press with your left arm, must be accomplished at the same time, to make the takedown more effective.

Figure 4-34

Figure 4-35

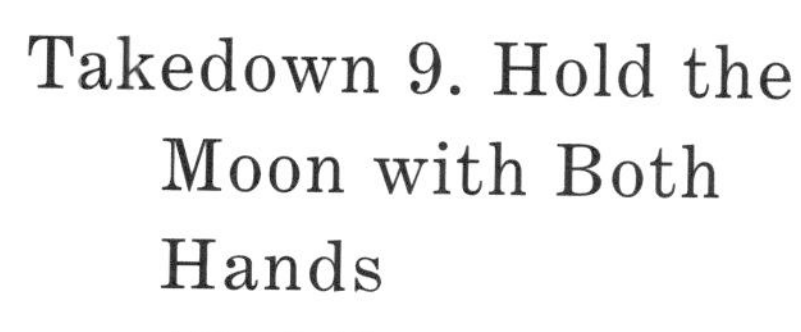

Takedown 9. Hold the Moon with Both Hands (雙手捧月-挫頭跌)

Figure 4-36

Step 1. From a ready position, your opponent steps forward with his right foot and punches to your head with his right fist. You yield back and circle both forearms clockwise to intercept his punch to your right (Figure 4-34).

Step 2. Step in with your left foot and strike to his head with your right palm, and grab a hold of the back of his head with your left hand (Figure 3-35). Push down to your left with your right hand and take him down over your left thigh (Figure 3-36).

Note:

A. Keep the momentum of your right palm moving forward until your opponent is leaning back, before turning to your left to take him down.

B. If your opponent prevents you from exerting enough pressure on his upper body to take him down, continue with the next technique.

Figure 4-37

Figure 4-38

Takedown 10. The Lion Wags Its Tail
(獅子擺尾-跘腿跌)

Figure 4-39

Step 1. From a ready position, your opponent steps forward with his right foot and punches to your head with his right fist. You yield back and circle both forearms clockwise to intercept his punch to your right (Figure 4-37).

Step 2. Step in with your left foot and strike to his head with your right palm. He intercepts with his left arm (Figure 4-38). Bring your right leg up and sweep back on his leg as you continue the pressure with your right hand to your left, to take him down (Figure 3-39).

Note:

A. The backward sweep with your right leg and the pressure you exert on your opponent's upper body must be in opposite directions to make the takedown more effective.

Takedown 11. An Old Oxen Turns Its Head
(老牛擺頭-穿頸切)

Step 1. From a ready position, your opponent steps forward with his

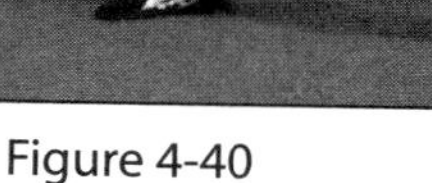

Figure 4-40

Figure 4-41

Figure 4-42

Figure 4-43

right foot and punches to your head with his right fist. You yield back and intercept with your left forearm to your right (Figure 4-40).

Step 2. Keep your left hand on his right arm as you step in with your right foot and strike to his chest with your right arm. He intercepts down with his right arm (Figure 4-41). Slip your right arm up towards his neck and turn your body around 180 degrees, to take him down (Figures 4-42 and 4-43).

Note:

A. Keep the swinging strike with your right arm continuous. When your opponent intercepts your strike, immediately move your right arm up to his neck and turn your body to take him down.

Figure 4-44

Figure 4-45

Takedown 12. A Heavenly Horse Falls to the Earth (天馬落地-轉身捌)

Figure 4-46

Step 1. From a ready position, your opponent steps forward with his right foot and punches to your head with his right fist. You yield back and circle both forearms clockwise to intercept his punch to your right (Figure 4-44).

Step 2. Grab a hold of his right wrist with your right hand, press on his elbow with your left arm . At the same time, turn and step with your right foot until you are facing the same direction as him (Figure 4-45). Pull with your right hand and push with your left hand, while turning your body to your right, to take him down (Figure 4-46).

Note:

A. Before you turn your body to take your opponent down, first lock his elbow and pull him in the direction that he was facing. This will get him off balance and make the takedown more effective.

Figure 4-47

Figure 4-48

Takedown 13. The Leopard Cat Climbs Up the Tree (狸貓上樹-粘腿跌)

Figure 4-49

Step 1. From a ready position, your opponent steps forward with his right foot and punches to your head with his right fist. You yield back and circle both forearms clockwise to intercept his punch to your right (Figure 4-47).

Step 2. Grab a hold of his right wrist with your right hand, press on his elbow with your left arm. At the same time, step kick down on his left knee with your right foot, to take him down (Figures 4-48 and 4-49).

Note:

A. The pressure on your opponent's arm is in the opposite direction of the pressure you exert on his knee. The opposite forces make it easier to take him down.

Figure 4-50

Figure 4-51

Takedown 14. The Feudal Lord Stretches the Bow (霸王開弓-左勾跌)

Figure 4-52

Step 1. From a ready position, your opponent steps forward with his right foot and punches to your head with his right fist. You yield back and circle both forearms clockwise to intercept his punch to your right (Figure 4-50).

Step 2. Grab a hold of his right wrist with your right hand, press on his elbow with your left arm. Chop to his neck with your left hand and hook your left foot behind his right leg, to take him down (Figures 4-51 and 4-52).

Note:

A. Even if your opponent is able to intercept your chop to his neck with his left arm, you should still be able to take him down with the hook kick, by maintaining constant pressure on his right arm while kicking.

Figure 4-53

Figure 4-54

Figure 4-55

Figure 4-56

Takedown 15. A Gust of Wind in the Prairie (平地刮風-勾腿跌)

Step 1. From a ready position, your opponent steps forward with his left foot and punches to your head with his right fist. You intercept his punch with your left arm to your right (Figure 4-53).

Step 2. He continues his attack with a kick with his right leg to the side of your ribs. You hook your left arm down and around his leg and block inward with your right forearm (Figure 4-54).

Step 3. Strike in with your right fist to your opponent's head to make him block, while kicking and hooking his back leg, to take him down (Figures 4-55 and 4-56).

Figure 4-57

Figure 4-58

Note:

A. Your opponent's high punch is a fake punch to make you intercept upward which exposes the left side of your ribs to his kick. You lower your left arm and allow him to contact your left upper arm with his leg. You then lock his leg tightly with your left arm by hooking your left arm upward. Your right forearm block assists your arm lock. It also prepares you in case his kick was to your head.

B. If you don't get the chance to kick, do the following technique.

Takedown 16. The Purple Swallow Flys Diagonally (紫燕斜飛-大擬跌)

Step 1. From a ready position, your opponent steps forward with his left foot and punches to your head with his right fist. You intercept his punch with your left arm to your right (Figure 4-57).

Step 2. He continues his attack with a kick with his right leg to the side of your ribs. You hook your left arm down and around his leg and block inward with your right forearm (Figure 4-58).

Step 3. Pull back with your left arm while pressing in towards his thigh with your right forearm. At the same time, step in with your right leg then left leg and spin 180 degrees around to your left, to take him down (Figures 4-59 and 4-60).

Figure 4-59

Figure 4-60

Note:

A. The more you are able to utilize your opponent's kicking momentum, the easier the takedown will be. If he is very strong, you may also sweep your right leg back on his left leg to make the takedown even more effective.

Figure 4-61

Figure 4-62

Figure 4-63

Figure 4-64

Takedown 17. The Fisherman Rows the Boat

(魚公划船-別腿跌)

Step 1. From a ready position, your opponent steps forward with his left foot and punches to your head with his right fist. You intercept his punch with your left arm to your right (Figure 4-61).

Step 2. He continues his attack with a kick with his right leg to the side of your ribs. You hook your left arm down and around his leg and block inward with your right forearm (Figure 4-62).

Step 3. Strike in with your right hand to his head, while stepping in with your right leg behind his left leg, and sweeping your leg backward (Figures 4-63 and 4-64).

Figure 4-65

Figure 4-66

Note:

A. Keep the pressure with your right arm in the opposite direction of the back sweep with your right leg, while maintaining the hold on his right leg with your left arm.

Figure 4-67

Takedown 18. Plant the Willow Tree Upside Down (倒插楊柳-抱腿旋)

Step 1. From a ready position, your opponent step forward with his left foot and punches to your head with his right fist. You intercept his punch with your left arm to your right (Figure 4-65).

Step 2. He continues his attack with a kick with his right leg to the side of your ribs. You hook your left arm down and around his leg and block inward with your right forearm (Figure 4-66).

Step 3. Clamp both hands down and hold on to your left wrist with your right hand. Step in with your left foot and twist your arms down clockwise, to take him down (Figure 4-67).

Note:

A. This takedown is also a joint control on his knee.

Figure 4-68

Figure 4-69

Takedown 19. The Phoenix Spreads Its Wings (單鳳展翅-上搬腿)

Figure 4-70

Step 1. From a ready position, your opponent steps forward with his left foot and punches to your head with his right fist. You intercept his punch with your left arm to your left (Figure 4-68).

Step 2. He continues his attack with a kick with his right leg to the side of your ribs. You turn your body to your left slightly while lowering your left arm down to receive the kick with your upper arm (Figure 4-69).

Step 3. Lift your left elbow up from under his leg and push forward, while stepping forward with your left leg and punching to his head with your right fist (Figure 4-70).

Note:

A. When you receive his kick with your left upper arm, keep your arm tight against your body so that your ribs are protected by your arm. If your arm is away from your body, your own elbow may impact your ribs.

Figure 4-71

Figure 4-72

Figure 4-73

Figure 4-74

Takedown 20. The Unicorn Strikes the Bell (獨角撞鐘-肘撞胸)

Step 1. From a ready position, your opponent steps forward with his left foot and punches to your head with his right fist. You intercept his punch with your left arm to your left (Figure 4-71).

Step 2. He continues his attack with a heel kick to your chest. Move slightly to your left, turn your body to your right, and lower your left forearm to intercept his kick (Figure 4-72).

Step 3. As he brings his leg down, punch to his head with your right fist to make him block (Figure 4-73). Step in with your right foot and ram him with your forearms, to knock him down (Figure 4-74).

Figure 4-75

Figure 4-76

Note:

A. Minimize the time difference between your left arm intercepting his kick and punching with your right fist, by punching over your left arm.

Figure 4-77

Takedown 21. Golden Dragon Closes Its Mouth (金龍合口-拉腿跌)

Step 1. From a ready position, your opponent steps forward with his left foot and punches to your head with his right fist. You intercept his punch with your left arm to your left (Figure 4-75).

Step 2. He continues his attack with a heel kick to your chest. Move slightly to your left, turn your body to your right, and lower your right forearm to intercept his kick (Figure 4-76).

Step 3. Grab a hold of his right leg, step back with your right leg, and pull his leg toward you (Figure 4-77).

Note:

A. Keep your left arm movement minimal by only lowering your arm. The deflection of the kick is primarily done by the turning of your body and rotating your left forearm.

Figure 4-78

Figure 4-79

B. Keep your opponent's kicking momentum forward while you pull his leg back.

Takedown 22. The Mountain Goat Lifts Its Leg (羚羊提腿-踭腿跌)

Figure 4-80

Step 1. From a ready position, your opponent steps forward with his left foot and punches to your head with his right fist. You intercept his punch with your left arm to your left (Figure 4-78).

Step 2. He continues his attack with a heel kick to your chest. Move slightly to your left to block his kick (Figure 4-79).

Step 3. Lower your right forearm and grab a hold of his right leg, punch to his head with your left fist, and sweep your right leg back from behind his left leg (Figure 4-80).

Note:

A. This technique is a follow up to the previous technique when he attempts to pull his leg back as you grab it. When he attempts to pull his leg back, you punch to his head to make him defend upward, while sweeping back with your right leg from behind his left leg. If your leg is unable to reach behind his leg, continue with the next technique.

Figure 4-81

Figure 4-82

Takedown 23. Plant the Flower at the Sea Bottom (海底插花-踩腿跌)

Figure 4-83

Step 1. From a ready position, your opponent steps forward with his left foot and punches to your head with his right fist. You intercept his punch with your left arm to your left (Figure 4-81).

Step 2. He continues his attack with a heel kick to your chest. Move slightly to your left, turn your body to your right, and lower your left forearm to intercept his kick (Figure 4-82).

Step 3. Grab a hold of his right leg with your right arm, chop your left hand towards him and press forward (Figure 4-83). Step kick with your right foot to his knee, to take him down (Figure 4-84).

Note:

A. Kick the inside of your opponent's knee while continuing to press forward and to your right with your left arm, to make the takedown more effective.

Figure 4-84

Figure 4-85

Figure 4-86

Figure 4-87

Takedown 24. Golden Rooster Announces the Dawn (金雞報曉-撿腿跌)

Step 1. From a ready position, your opponent steps forward with his left foot and punches to your head with his right fist. You step back with your left foot and intercept his punch to your right with your right arm (Figure 4-85).

Step 2. He continues his attack with a right toe kick to your groin (Figure 4-86). You lift your right leg up to deflect his kick to your left (Figure 4-86). Grab a hold of his leg with your left hand and lift upward, while punching to his head with your right fist (Figure 4-87).

Figure 4-88

Figure 4-89

Note:

A. The lifting of your right leg and the grabbing with your left hand must be done simultaneously to accomplish an effective takedown.

Figure 4-90

Takedown 25. Pick Up the Treasure from the Sea Bottom (海底取寶-靠提翻)

Step 1. From a ready position, your opponent steps in with his right foot and punches to your head with his right fist. You step back with your left foot and intercept his punch with your right arm to your left (Figure 4-88).

Step 2. Bring your left arm up from under your right arm and strike to his face. At the same time, sink down and step in with your left foot, and hook your right hand under his right thigh (Figure 4-89). Press your left arm down on his chest and lift his leg up with your right arm, to take him down (Figure 4-90).

Note:

A. When you take your opponent down, the motion of your hands are in a circular arc. If you attempt to lift your oppenent's leg straight up, it will require more effort.

實用擒拿法

Chapter 5:

Practical Joint Control Applications

In the previous chapters we have presented many ti, da, and shuai methods. In this chapter, we will focus on na, an abbreviation for qinna. Qinna also utilizes the principle of leverage like in a take down technique, by neutralizing and controlling a seemingly stronger opponent. By aligning yourself properly, while taking your opponent off his or her alignment, you will be able to apply a successful Qinna technique. Refer to Chapter 4 for a description of levers and its effects in applications.

It is usually faster to kick and punch, than it is to apply Qinna or a take down technique on your opponent. However, sometimes a kick or punch are ineffective for close range applications. In this situation, if you are able to apply a takedown or Qinna technique you will have an advantage over your opponent. Keep in mind that effective kicking and punching may be used instead of a Qinna technique. Conversely, Qinna techniques may also set up for futher kicks and punches. In this chapter, we will introduce Qinna techniques from different grabbing and punching attacks. These techniques are designed to help you understand the basic applications of joint controls used in Wushu. The techniques are presented in a preset situation. Many possible variations could exist in a real life situation. To be able to successfully use the technique you must be flexible in the applications of different techniques. When one technique can't be executed, you must immediately vary it or go to another technique. The various techniques will also give you many options in the applications of the Qinna techniques. When one technique doesn't work, or if your opponent is aware of the technique you are trying to do, you may need to change the technique or distract your opponent to continue with the intended technique.

It is recommended that you have mastered the technique from the grab as presented in this chapter before attempting to apply the technique in other situations. The techniques are designed to introduce various common situations. When you are able to execute all the techniques successfully in a preset manner like in this chapter, you will have enough knowledge and techniques to freely apply one technique to the next to make your Qinna effective. The proper application of Qinna in these techniques will give you a good understanding of what works and what doesn't work. The more people you practice with the more you will be able to feel how the techniques should be applied to different body types and levels of strength. Once you have mastered the Qinna techniques in this chapter, you will be able to vary these techniques and come up with many new techniques to fit the various situations during a real life confrontation.

The first step in learning Qinna is to understand how to neutralize a grabbing attack. It is difficult to use force against force to get away from a stronger opponent. Instead of going against your opponent's strength, find the weaker part of your opponent's body and use your entire body against that part. Once you are successful in neutralizing your opponent's grab, you can follow up with a Qinna to control your opponent. You will not be able to apply your Qinna technique if you are unable to first neutralize your opponent's attack. The best Qinna techniques are the ones that neutralize your opponent's attack while setting up a Qinna. This way your opponent will have less chance of realizing your intention before you complete your technique.

Neutralization practice is for learning to create an angle which is disadvantageous for your opponent, as well as, reducing your own exposure to further attack. By locating the weak points on your opponent, you can effectively neutralize your opponent's grabs. By the turning of your body or moving the opponent's arms to obstruct their own arm, you will reduce the opponent's options to continue with their attack. After you have neutralized the attack, you can then follow up with a Qinna technique.

Unless your opponent already has you in a Qinna control, they usually won't use two hands to grab a hold of your arm. If they do, they will leave themselves vulnerable to an attack with your free hand. Therefore, there are typically four likely grabs to the arms that can be used. Either, they will grab

Figure 5-1

Figure 5-2

you with the same side hand or cross over and grab with the other hand. They can also grab you either from the top or from the bottom. We will first introduce neutralization drills for these four types of grabs.

Neutralization is done similarly when the grabs are on your forearm, upper arms, shoulders, and many other parts of your body. Once you understand how the structure of the body works or doesn't work, then you will be able to apply techniques that place your opponent's body in positions that the body is not meant to be in, to accomplish proper Qinna controls.

Before you begin practicing with your partner, make sure that you have a mutually agreed upon signal to let each other know when the technique is working. Excessive pressure during practice can cause permanent damage to your partner. Usually a slap with the other hand on your body or on the floor, or simply saying stop, is a good signal to your partner to ease the pressure.

5.1. Neutralization Drills

1. Neutralizing a Grab from the Top — Cross Grab:

Step 1. Your partner grabs a hold of your right wrist with his right hand (Figure 5-1). Drop your right elbow slightly, rotate your palm to face you, then circle your forearm up clockwise (Figure 5-2). Rotate your right forearm and press the edge of your right palm on his wrist and cut down to neutralize the grab (Figure 5-3). Repeat 10 times, then grab your partner's wrist, and let your partner practice this exercise.

Figure 5-3

Figure 5-4

Figure 5-5

Figure 5-6

Step 2. Your partner grabs a hold of your right wrist with his right hand (Figure 5-4). Drop your right elbow slightly and press your forearm into his hand, while pulling your fist in, to neutralize the grab (Figure 5-5). Repeat 10 times, then grab your partner's wrist, and let your partner practice this exercise.

Step 3. Repeat Steps 1 and 2. Instead of your partner grabbing a hold of your right wrist with his right hand, your partner grabs a hold of your left wrist with his left hand.

Figure 5-7

Figure 5-8

Figure 5-9

Figure 5-10

2. Neutralizing a Grab from the Top — Same Side Grab:

Step 1. Your partner grabs a hold of your right wrist with his left hand (Figure 5-6). Drop your right elbow slightly, rotate your palm to face you, then circle your forearm up counterclockwise (Figure 5-7). Rotate your right forearm and press the edge of your right palm on his wrist and cut down to neutralize the grab (Figure 5-8). Repeat 10 times, then grab your partner's wrist and let your partner practice this exercise.

Step 2. Your partner grabs a hold of your right wrist with his left hand (Figure 5-9). Bend your elbow and press your forearm into his hand, while pulling your arm away, to neutralize the grab (Figure 5-10). Repeat 10 times, then grab your partner's wrist and let your partner practice this exercise.

Figure 5-11

Figure 5-12

Figure 5-13

Figure 5-14

Step 3. Your partner grabs a hold of your right wrist with his left hand (Figure 5-11). Circle your arm up counterclockwise up (Figure 5-12). Open your hand and press the space between your index finger and thumb into his forearm as you turn your body to your left, to neutralize the grab (Figure 5-13). Repeat 10 times, then grab your partner's wrist and let your partner practice this exercise.

Step 4. Repeat Steps 1 to 3. Instead of your partner grabbing your right wrist with his left hand, your partner grabs a hold of your left wrist with his right hand.

Figure 5-15

Figure 5-16

3. Neutralizing a Grab from the Bottom — Cross Grab

Step 1. Your partner grabs a hold of your right wrist with his right hand from the bottom (Figure 5-14). Press your forearm down on his hand and push down, to neutralize the grab (Figure 5-15). Repeat 10 times, then grab your partner's wrist and let your partner practice this exercise.

Figure 5-17

Step 2. Your partner grabs a hold of your right wrist with his right hand from the bottom (Figure 5-16). Circle your right arm down counterclockwise to your right and press into his hand with your forearm, to neutralize the grab (Figure 5-17). Repeat 10 times then grab your partner's wrist and let your partner practice this exercise.

Step 3. Repeat Steps 1 and 2. Instead of your partner grabbing your right wrist with his right hand, your partner grabs a hold of your left wrist with his left hand.

Figure 5-18

Figure 5-19

Figure 5-20

Figure 5-21

4. Neutralizing a Grab from the Bottom — Same Side Grab

Step 1. Your partner grabs a hold of your right wrist with his left hand from the bottom (Figure 5-18). Rotate your right arm down clockwise to your right to neutralize the grab (Figure 5-19). Repeat 10 times, then grab your partner's wrist and let your partner practice this exercise.

Step 2. Your partner grabs a hold of your right wrist with his left hand from the bottom (Figure 5-20). Press your right forearm down on his hand to neutralize the grab (Figure 5-21). Repeat 10 times, then grab your partner's wrist and let your partner practice this exercise.

Figure 5-22

Figure 5-23

Figure 5-24

Figure 5-25

5.2. Qinna Techniques

Qinna 1: Wrap Silk Around the Hand (蠶絲手)

Step 1. Your opponent grabs a hold of your right wrist from the top with his right hand (Figure 5-22). Place your left hand on top of his right hand and cinch your thumb down on his index finger (Figure 5-23). Raise your right arm up clockwise up to neutralize his grab (Figure 5-24).

Step 2. Push your left hand towards your right hand, while hooking the fingers of your right hand onto his wrist and begin extending your arms toward his body (Figure 5-25). As he begins to go down, take a step back with your right foot, maintain the pressure on his wrist, and control him down to the floor (Figure 5-26).

Figure 5-26

Notes:

A. When you rotate your forearm up, let the pivoting point of the clockwise circle be as close to the location of the grab as possible. This will allow you to use minimal force to neutralize the grab. Next, while keeping your elbow pointing down, extend your arm forward and down towards your opponent.

B. In executing this technique, you are creating a Z angle with your opponent's arm, and twisting while bending your opponent's forearm and wrist. When you extend your arms forward, extend at a 90 degree angle towards the plane of your opponent's body. When executing the technique, maintain constant pressure on your opponent's wrist. By holding onto your opponent's fingers, you prevent your opponent from escaping from your Qinna.

C. When you step back you lower your opponent to the floor and move your body away from your opponent's reach. The technique is completed when you move back into a Half-Squat Stance. However, the movement of your arms should be continuously forward and slightly to the side on the way down. This will maintain the pressure on your opponent's arm.

D. There are three common mistakes in executing this technique. First, if your left hand fails to hold onto your opponent's hand when you extend your arms. In this case, you will only be neutralizing and not be able to control your opponent. Second, if your right elbow is raised up to the side instead of maintaining it on the same plane. When this happens your opponent can rotate his body around and hit you with his left arm. Third, if your opponent's arm is not in a Z angle with the edge of his palm facing up. To create the Z angle in this situation, hook the fingers of your right hand back as you extend your arms perpendicular to the plane of your opponent's body.

Figure 5-27

Figure 5-28

Figure 5-29

Figure 5-30

Qinna 2. Shoot the Rocket to the Sky (冲天炮)

Step 1. Your opponent grabs a hold of your right wrist from the top with his right hand (Figure 5-27). Raise your right arm up clockwise to neutralize his grab and press the edge of your right palm down on his wrist (Figures 5-28 and 5-29).

Step 2. Grab a hold of his right palm with your left hand from the bottom and grab a hold of his wrist with your right hand. Twist his arm clockwise and push it up (Figure 30).

Notes:

A. This technique can be used as an alternative to Qinna 1 when the opponent's arm remains straight and you are unable to create the Z angle required to execute the technique.

Figure 5-31

Figure 5-32

B. The neutralization by your right arm sets up the initial rotation on your opponent's arm. In a flexible person, the rotation of your left hand may not be sufficient enough to create pain. In this case, you will have to take advantage and continue the pressure started by your right hand and twist more with your left hand. Your left hand may also grab his fingers instead, which will create even more pressure on him.

C. If your opponent does not feel any pain, it is probably because you did not provide enough rotation with your right arm, and the left hand was not able to create enough torsion to cause the necessary pressure. Retry this technique and make sure you settle your right palm while neutralizing and maintaining the pressure with your left hand.

D. If your opponent is able to turn around as you torque his hand, he will be able to do a back fist with his left fist. This is usually the result of not enough torque on your opponent's arm and not lifting up enough. You will have to lift his arm up while maintaining pressure with his arm at the side of him, not behind him.

Figure 5-33

Figure 5-34

Qinna 3. Dragonfly Touches the Water (蜻蜓點水)

Step 1. Your opponent grabs a hold of your right wrist from the top with his right hand (Figure 5-31). Rotate your right arm up clockwise and counter grab his wrist, while striking to his elbow with your left palm (Figures 5-32 and 5-33).

Step 2. Lock his elbow by pushing down with your left hand and pulling in the opposite direction with your right hand. Then take a step back with your right foot and pull him down to the floor (Figure 5-34).

Note:

A. The pressure on your opponent's elbow is downward while the pressure on his wrist is upward. It is important that in the final control, the forces are applied in opposite directions between your left and right hands.

Figure 5-35

Figure 5-36

Qinna 4. Rhino Looks at the Moon (犀牛望月)

Step 1. Your opponent grabs a hold of your right wrist from the top with his right hand (Figure 5-35). Step forward with your left foot and turn your body to your right. At the same time, rotate your right hand counterclockwise to your right to make his arm face up. Hit his elbow with your left forearm to assist the right arm rotation. Then clamp your left hand on top of his hand (Figure 5-36).

Step 2. Lift up with your left arm, push down with your left hand, and press down with your right forearm (Figure 5-37).

Notes:

A. The deflection with your left forearm creates a rolling pressure that assists the right hand in turning your opponent's arm. Maintain a constant torque on your opponent's arm. This technique uses a seesaw like movement with your opponent's arm. The pressure you exert down with both hands is balanced by the weight of your opponent's body, and the pivoting point is his elbow.

B. If your opponent is able to hit you with his other hand, you probably did not turn his arm enough, or you did not step far enough to his side. It is important that his arm is facing upward so that his arm can't bend at the elbow.

C. If your opponent does not feel the pain, make certain that your left arm is pressing directly on the base of his elbow. Also, make certain that you are pushing up at an angle into his body, while maintaining the torque and pressure on his arm.

Figure 5-37

Figure 5-38

Figure 5-39

Figure 5-40

Qinna 5. Erlang Carries the Firewood (二郎扛材)

Step 1. Your opponent grabs a hold of your right wrist from the top with his right hand (Figure 5-38). Step forward with your left foot and turn your body to your right. At the same time, rotate your right arm counterclockwise to your right to make his arm face up. Hit his elbow with your left forearm to assist the right hand rotation. Then strike to his ribs with your left elbow (Figure 5-39).

Step 2. Take another step back with your right foot and move his arm over your shoulder. Clamp both of your hands on his wrist and pull down while standing up (Figure 5-40).

Figure 5-41

Figure 5-42

Notes:

A. When you rotate your opponent's hand to your right, you prevent his left hand from reaching you. Keep constant pressure on the rotation of your right hand. This will keep his arm straight and make the technique more effective.

B. If your opponent does not feel any pressure and can still hit you with his left hand, wedge your shoulder up and forward a little more. This will lift his shoulder up to create the control.

Figure 5-43

Figure 5-44

Qinna 6. Dragon Lowers Its Body (龍形下勢)

Step 1. Your opponent grabs a hold of your right wrist from the top with his right hand (Figure 5-41). Circle your right arm up clockwise to neutralize the grab (Figure 5-42).

Step 2. Cut your right hand down on his wrist and counter grab his wrist, while pressing your left forearm on his elbow; and kick to his knee with your right foot and lean into him (Figures 5-43 and 5-44).

Note:

A. Maintain the pressure on his arm, by pulling and pushing with your hands in opposite directions, as you lower your body.

Figure 5-45

Figure 5-46

Figure 5-47

Figure 5-47R

Qinna 7. Irrefusable Dinner Engagement (霸王請客)

Step 1. Your opponent grabs a hold of your right wrist from the bottom with his right hand (Figure 5-45). Circle your arm down clockwise and push his elbow to your right with your left hand (Figure 5-46).

Step 2. Push his arm behind his back with his fist pointing up and squeeze his arm between your hands and chest (Figures 5-47 and 5-47R).

Note:

A. As you push your opponent's arm back, rotate your right wrist up slightly to make his fist point up. When you squeeze his arm, lift up slightly with your hands.

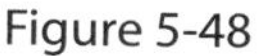

Figure 5-48

Figure 5-49

Figure 5-50

Figure 5-51

Qinna 8. Pull the Bow to Shoot the Tiger (彎弓射虎)

Step 1. Your opponent grabs a hold of your right wrist from the bottom with his right hand (Figure 5-48). Circle your arm down clockwise to neutralize his grab (Figure 5-49).

Step 2. Rotate your right wrist up and grab a hold of his thumb with your left hand (Figure 5-50). Rotate your left hand in, as you hold onto his thumb, and lift up. At the same time push forward with your right hand towards his body so that he can't move (Figures 5-51 and 5-51R).

Notes:

A. Grab your opponent's thumb as you cicle your arm down before he lets go completely.

Figure 5-51R

B. Keep your right hand anchored on your opponent's body to prevent him from moving around. You can also grab his shirt or skin to keep him locked.

Qinna 9. Green Dragon Turns Its Head (青龍返首)

Step 1. Your opponent grabs a hold of your right wrist from the bottom with his right hand (Figure 5-52). Circle your arm down counterclockwise as you step forward with your left foot, and hit his elbow with your left arm and raise it up (Figure 5-53).

Step 2. Clamp your left hand on top of his wrist and pull down, while wedging your left shoulder up towards his shoulder (Figure 5-54).

Figure 5-52

Figure 5-53

Figure 5-54

Note:

A. Keep rotating your opponent's right arm while keeping his arm rounded to maintain the lock on his shoulder. The raising of your shoulder and the pulling with your hands are in opposite directions to maintain maximum pressure on your opponent's shoulder.

Figure 5-55

Figure 5-56

Figure 5-57

Figure 5-58

Qinna 10. White Ape Offers the Fruit (白猿獻果)

Step 1. Your opponent grabs a hold of your right wrist from the bottom with his right hand (Figure 5-55). Push your right arm towards his head, while grabbing his hand with your left hand and circling your hands down counterclockwise (Figures 5-56 and 5-57).

Step 2. Push down and rotate your right arm to face up, while lifting your forearm up from under his upper arm. At the same time, step in with your left foot behind him (Figure 5-58).

Note:

A. When you grab your opponent's right hand with your left hand, clamp your fingers on the inside of his palm and dig your thumb on the back of his hand. Then rotate counterclockwise. When you lift your right

Figure 5-59

Figure 5-60

hand up, slip your right arm in while rotating your right arm to face up.

Qinna 11. Reverse Wrap Hand (反纏手)

Figure 5-61

Step 1. Your opponent grabs a hold of your right wrist from the top with his left hand (Figure 5-59). Place your left hand on top of his hand, cinch your thumb down on his index finger, and circle your right arm counter-clockwise up (Figure 5-60).

Step 2. Hook your right hand on his wrist and push your left hand forward, while extending both hands forward. At the same time, take a step back with your right foot and pull him down (Figure 5-61).

Note:

A. The overall movement is backward, however, when you step back, maintain pressure forward on his wrist. The pressure as you step back, is important to balance the forward movement as your opponent goes down to the floor.

Figure 5-62

Figure 5-63

Qinna 12. Bow and Beg for Forgiveness (磕頭求情)

Step 1. Your opponent grabs a hold of your right wrist from the top with his left hand (Figure 5-62). Circle your right hand counterclockwise, open your hand and press the *tiger's mouth* on his wrist (Figure 5-63). The tiger's mouth is the space between your thumb and index finger when they are stretched apart.

Step 2. Grab a hold of his wrist with your right hand, grab a hold of his right hand with your left hand, and press your armpit area down on his elbow (Figure 5-64). Pull his wrist and press down on his elbow with your armpit as you lower your body down (Figure 5-65).

Figure 5-64

Figure 5-65

Notes:

A. The pressure is on your opponent's left elbow. By placing your arm pit directly on his elbow, you make his elbow the pivoting point of the arm, and make it bend in an unnatural direction. As you lower your body to exert pressure on his arm, make certain that his elbow continues to be the pivoting point by pulling your hands up and pushing his body down, creating pressure in opposite directions.

B. If you should over rotate his arm, the pressure may not be sufficient to control him. You need to maintain the pull by your hands and the push with your armpit in opposite directions. If you over rotate, you will have to change the direction of the pull and the pressure exerted by your armpit. You will have to exert your armpit pressure slightly back instead of down and pull his hand in the opposite direction to the pressure exerted by your armpit.

Figure 5-66

Figure 5-67

Figure 5-68

Figure 5-69

Qinna 13. Push the Boat Along the Current (順水推舟)

Step 1. Your opponent grabs a hold of your right wrist from the top with his left hand (Figure 5-66). Bend your elbow and circle up clockwise, at the same time, grab a hold of his hand from underneath with your left hand (Figure 5-67).

Step 2. Slip your right wrist from his grasp and rotate your palm to grab his fingers (Figure 5-68). Rotate his arm and circle down to your left (Figure 5-69).

Notes:

A. Keep the circular momentum of your right arm when executing this technique. When you grab a hold of your opponent's hand, make certain that your fingers are hooked on the inside of his palm. This

Figure 5-70

Figure 5-71

will give you a better grab and more rotation to create more pressure. If your left thumb is strong enough you should press your left thumb on the back of his palm at the metacarpal of the pinkie. This will give you even more leverage.

Figure 5-72

B. When you grab the fingers of your opponent's hand with your right hand, line up your pinkie with his pinkie and torque his hand clockwise. If your opponent's elbow raises up too much and he is able to turn his body around, check the angle of your push when you bring him down. Make sure that you are pushing him down at an angle to your left.

Qinna 14. Large Python Turns Its Body (大蟒翻身)

Step 1. Your opponent grabs a hold of your right wrist from the bottom with his left hand (Figure 5-70). Lower your right arm and bend your elbow over his forearm; at the same time, place your left hand over his left hand (Figure 5-71).

Step 2. Grab a hold of his left hand with your left hand, press your forearm down on his wrist, and take him down (Figure 5-72).

Figure 5-73

Figure 5-74

Notes:

A. When you bend your elbow, press your forearm into your opponent's wrist to neutralize the grab.

B. Your left hand holds onto your opponent's left hand tightly, so that it can't slip off. Your right elbow circles in a counterclockwise direction over his arm. Once your elbow is over his arm, circle back and down on his forearm to lock his wrist. This is a wrist control, so you want to make his elbow bend. If his elbow won't bend, it becomes an elbow control.

Figure 5-75

Qinna 15. Immortal Points the Way (仙人指路)

Step 1. Your opponent grabs a hold of your right wrist from the bottom with his left hand (Figure 5-73). Circle your right arm clockwise to your right; at the same time, hook your left arm under his left arm (Figure 5-74).

Step 2. Place your left hand on top of your right wrist and push both hands down, while raising your left elbow up (Figure 5-75).

Note:

A. When you circle your right arm, rotate and point your fist towards your opponent before moving your arm to your right. This will set it

Figure 5-76

Figure 5-77

up for your left arm to hook under his arm. When you complete the circle to your right, rotate your right arm until your arm is facing down.

Figure 5-78

Qinna 16. Send the Bird to the Forest (送鳥入林)

Step 1. Your opponent grabs a hold of your right wrist from the bottom with his left hand (Figure 5-76). Circle your right arm counterclockwise to your right and grab a hold of his hand with your left hand from underneath (Figure 5-77).

Step 2. Twist his fingers counterclockwise with your left hand, push up with your right hand on his fingers, and lift his arm up (Figure 5-78).

Note:

A. Maintain a constant rotation on your opponent's arm. Before you push up, lower his left hand slightly until it is lower than his elbow to create better control. This is especially important if your opponent is much taller than you.

Figure 5-79

Figure 5-80

Qinna 17. Child Worships the Buddha (童子拜佛)

Figure 5-81

Step 1. Your opponent grabs a hold of your right shoulder with his left hand (Figure 5-79). Lock his hand in place with your left hand and swing your right arm over his forearm (Figure 5-80).

Step 2. Hook back slightly with your elbow and press your upper arm down on his wrist (Figure 5-81).

Notes:

A. Keep a strong lock on your opponent's hand, but don't try to pull his hand off your shirt. His hold on your shirt becomes part of your lock on his wrist.

B. When you swing your arm over your opponent's arm, raise your arm slightly to rotate the edge of his palm to face upward. This will create a painful wrist lock.

C. If you are unable to create enough pressure for your opponent to go down, it is probabaly because the inside edge of his palm is not facing up. You may need to raise your right arm higher to lift the edge of his palm upward before hooking your elbow down.

Figure 5-82

Figure 5-83

Figure 5-84

Figure 5-85

D. Make sure when you execute this technique that your opponent's arm is in a Z shape. When you bow towards him, turn your body slightly from your left back to your right, as though you were looking for something on the floor.

Qinna 18. Carp Jumps Up from the Water (鯉魚打挺)

Step 1. Your opponent grabs a hold of your right shoulder with his left hand (Figure 5-82). Grab a hold of his hand with your left hand and push up on his elbow with your right hand (Figures 5-83 and 5-84).

Step 2. Move in closer and place your right leg in front of his left leg and sweep back. At the same time, push up then down on his arm to lock his shoulder (Figure 5-85).

Figure 5-86

Figure 5-87

Note:

A. Execute the leg sweep and the arm movement at the same time to achieve the best control.

Figure 5-88

Qinna 19. White Elephant Lifts Its Trunk (白象撅鼻)

Step 1. Your opponent grabs a hold of your right shoulder with his left hand (Figure 5-86). Swing your right hand up clockwise towards his head to distract him (Figure 5-87).

Step 2. Continue the circular movement of your right arm around his left arm and lift up while turning your body to your left (Figure 5-88).

Notes:

A. When you lower your arm, press down on your opponent's arm to make his elbow bend.

B. When you turn your body, shift your weight to your left leg and use your legs to help lift your opponent's arm up. When you lift the arm, execute the arm movement as though you were doing an upper cut, without raising your shoulder. If your opponent is very strong, use your left hand to help lift up your right fist.

Figure 5-89

Figure 5-90

Figure 5-91

Figure 5-92

Qinna 20. Turn Over the River and Empty the Sea (翻江倒海)

Step 1. Your opponent grabs a hold of your right shoulder with his right hand (Figure 5-89). Swing your right hand up counterclockwise towards his head to distract him, while grabbing his right hand with your left hand (Figure 5-90).

Step 2. Continue the circular movement of your right arm down on his right arm to make it bend (Figure 5-91). Turn your body to your right and hook your right arm up from under his right arm, while pushing down on his face with your left hand (Figure 5-92).

Figure 5-93

Figure 5-94

Note:

A. When you swing your right arm counterclockwise, use your waist to move the arm. Your right arm should move more than one revolution before lifting up to create a good lock on his shoulder.

Figure 5-95

Qinna 21. Embrace the Tiger and Return to the Mountain (抱虎歸山)

Step 1. Your opponent grabs a hold of your right shoulder with his right hand (Figure 5-93). Swing both arms to your right and move his right arm down. Circle your right arm down until you neutralize his grab (Figure 5-94).

Step 2. Step in with your right foot behind his front leg. Strike to his chin with your right hand, grab the back of his head and turn your body to your left, as you twist his neck to your left (Figure 5-95).

Notes:

A. Be very careful not to injure your partner's neck. During training, don't actually hit your partner's chin with your right hand.

B. Press your hip into his lower back as you turn his neck to your left.

Figure 5-96

Figure 5-97

Qinna 22. Comet Chases the Moon (流星趕月)

Step 1. Your opponent grabs a hold of your right shoulder with his right hand (Figure 5-96). Raise your arms up and lock his arm between your arms, with your left forearm on his upper arm and your right forearm on his forearm (Figure 5-97).

Step 2. Turn to your right and lower your body. At the same time, pull your right arm in and press out with your left arm (Figure 5-98).

Figure 5-98

Note:

A. Keep constant pressure on your opponent's elbow by pulling and pushing your arms in opposite directions. A slight rotation of your arms inward will keep his arm straight and his elbow locked as you control him.

Figure 5-99

Figure 5-100

Figure 5-101

Figure 5-102

Qinna 23. Mantis Catches the Cicada (螳螂捕蠶)

Step 1. Your opponent grabs a hold of your right shoulder from the back with his left hand (Figure 5-99). Turn around and grab a hold of his left hand with your left hand and begin to swing your right arm up counterclockwise (Figure 5-100).

Step 2. Continue raising your right arm until it is over his his left arm. Hook your right hand down on his left elbow (Figure 5-101). Grab and turn his left wrist to your left, while hooking down and to the right with your right hand on his elbow, and step back with your left foot (Figure 5-102).

Notes:

A. If your opponent tries to punch you with his right hand, use your left hand to intercept his punch, then grab his left hand.

Figure 5-103

Figure 5-104

B. When you raise your right arm turn the edge of your opponent's left hand to face up and keep it facing up with your left hand. This will make the lock on his wrist more effective.

C. The pressure exerted on your opponent's arm with your hands are in opposite directions.

Figure 5-105

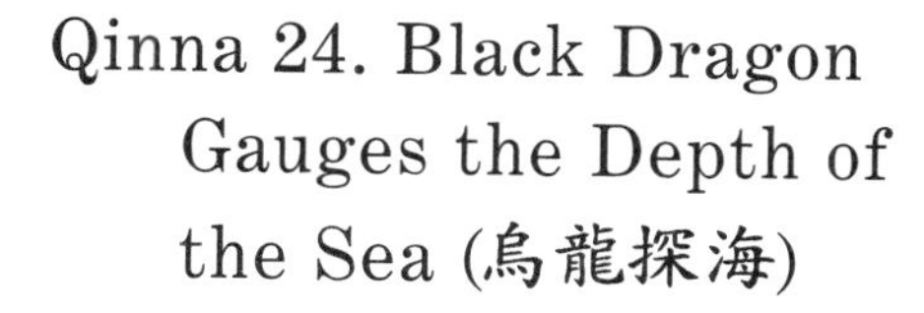

Qinna 24. Black Dragon Gauges the Depth of the Sea (烏龍探海)

Step 1. Your opponent chokes your neck with both hands (Figure 5-103). Turn to your left, swing your right arm across his left arm, and grab a hold of his left hand with your left hand (Figure 5-104).

Step 2. Press down on his wrist with your right upper arm. Maintain the pressure and turn to face him (Figure 5-105).

Notes:

A. Keep your opponent's left hand tight on your shoulder, by hooking your fingers on the inside of his left palm and pressing it towards your body. The turning of your body and the raising of your elbow create the proper angle for the control. The circling of your elbow creates the torsion required for the control.

Figure 5-106

Figure 5-107

B. When you swing your right arm to your left, turn until the edge of your opponent's left palm is facing upward and keep the edge facing up with your left hand. If you are unable to create enough pressure on his wrist, turn your body further to your left to make the edge of his left palm face up, then circle your elbow down to your right.

C. The movement of your right elbow is counterclockwise and down to your right, while pressing on his forearm.

Figure 5-108

Qinna 25. Take the Goat Along the Way (順手牽羊)

Step 1. Your opponent chokes your neck with both hands and is pushing in (Figure 5-106). Step back with your right foot, swing your left arm across his right arm, and grab a hold of his left wrist with both hands (Figure 5-107).

Step 2. Press down on his elbow with your left armpit and pull his left wrist up with your hands (Figure 5-108).

Note:

A. The pull upward with your hands and the press down with your armpit are in opposite directions to create the best control

Figure 5-109

Figure 5-110

Figure 5-111

Qinna 26. Ride the Horse Down the Mountain (騎馬下山)

Step 1. Your opponent chokes your neck with both hands (Figure 5-109). Shuffle step forward with your left foot and bring your right foot back, swing your left arm across his right arm, and grab a hold of his left wrist with your right hand (Figure 5-110).

Step 2. Swing your left arm across his neck and press down (Figure 5-111).

Note:

A. Keep your opponent's lower back tight on your body as you press down with your left arm.

Figure 5-112

Figure 5-113

Qinna 27. Guangong Restrains the Horse (關公勒馬)

Step 1. From a ready position, your opponent steps forward with his right foot and punches to your head with his right fist. You yield back and intercept his punch with your left forearm to your right (Figures 5-112 and 5-113).

Step 2. Counter punch with your right fist to his face to make him block outward (Figure 5-114). Pull your right arm back and lock his arm between your arms and take him down to the floor (Figures 5-115 and 5-116).

Figure 5-114

Figure 5-115

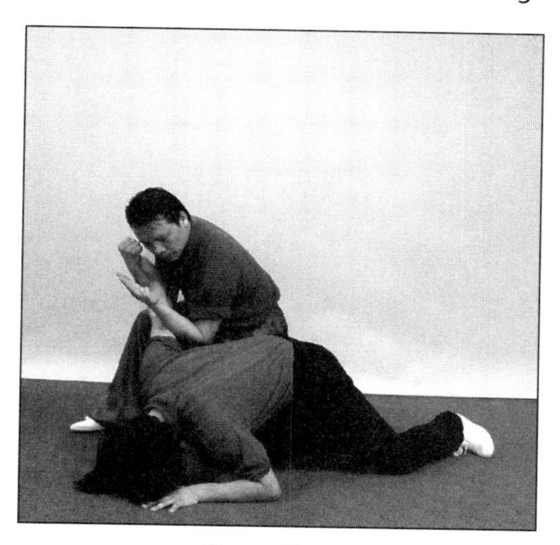

Figure 5-116

Notes:

A. This Qinna can be applied when your opponent's punching arm is straight.

B. The intercept and punch must be applied simultaneously to catch your opponent's arm by surprise.

C. If your opponent's arm bends during the attack, use the following technique instead.

Figure 5-117

Figure 5-118

Figure 5-119

Figure 5-120

Qinna 28. Reverse Rotate the Elbow (回手轉肘)

Step 1. From a ready position, your opponent steps forward with his right foot and punches to your head with his right fist. You yield back and intercept his punch with your left forearm to your right (Figure 5-117).

Step 2. Counter punch with your right fist to his face to make him block inward (Figure 5-118). Chop your right arm down on his arm to make his arm bend (Figure 5-119). Slide your left foot forward behind him and lift your right arm up from under his arm (Figure 5-120).

Note:

A. This technique can be used when your opponent's arm is bent. If his arm is straight, use the previous technique.

Figure 5-121

Figure 5-122

Qinna 29. The Cloud Moves with the Wind (雲順風動)

Figure 5-123

Step 1. From a ready position, your opponent steps forward with his right foot and punches to your head with his right fist. You yield back and intercept his punch with your left forearm to your right (Figure 5-121).

Step 2. Grab a hold of his right hand with both hands as he attempts to pull his fist back (Figure 5-122). Circle his arm to your left, then down to the floor to your right (Figure 5-123).

Notes:

A. This technique is accomplished as your opponent attempts to pull his punching arm back. You continue his backward movement then redirect the arm down into an elbow control.

B. Your right hand can be used as an attack to your opponent's face if you are unable to grab a hold of his right hand. Your right arm could also be used as a defensive block if he should attempt to punch you with his left fist.

Figure 5-124

Figure 5-125

Qinna 30: The Fierce Tiger Descends the Mountain (猛虎下山)

Step 1. From a ready position, your opponent steps forward with his right foot and punches to your head with his right fist. You yield back and intercept his punch with your left forearm to your right (Figure 5-124).

Step 2. Push his arm down and grab a hold of his right wrist with your left hand and step in with your right foot. At the same time, upper cut towards his chin with your right fist. He intercepts your upper cut by lowering his left forearm (Figure 5-125).

Step 3. You follow the downward movement of his block and hook your right arm under his left arm and lift it up (Figure 5-126). Turn your body to your right as you continue to raise his arm up, then down to the floor (Figure 5-127).

Figure 5-126

Figure 5-127

Notes:

A. When you lift your opponent's arm, make sure that your opponent's wrist and elbow are in a vertical plane. This creates an initial control. As you attempt to bring his body down, continue the upward momentum a little more before reversing the direction. This will make the movement smoother and more circular, and makes the control more effective. As you bring your opponent down, adjust your legs accordingly to maintain constant pressure on his elbow.

B. If you are unable to create enough pressure on your opponent's arm, check to make sure that your right hand is on or close to your opponent's elbow. If your right hand is on his shoulder, it will require more power to take him down. The further away your hand is from his shoulder, the more leverage you will have to create pressure on his shoulder. The movement is as though you were trying to take off a chicken wing by rotating the wing.

C. This technique may also be applied with an initial outward intercept with your left arm instead of an inward intercept.

Figure 5-128

Figure 5-129

Qinna 31. Ride the Tiger and Lock the Shoulder (胯虎挫肩)

Step 1. From a ready position, your opponent steps forward with his right foot and punches to your head with his right fist. You yield back and intercept his punch with your left forearm to your right (Figure 5-128).

Step 2. Push his arm down and grab a hold of his wrist with your left hand and step in with your left foot. At the same time, punch to his head with your right fist. He intercepts your punch to his right with his left arm (Figure 5-129).

Step 3. Hook your right hand on his right shoulder and yank it down. At the same time, twist his right arm and push it forward with your left hand (Figure 5-130). Continue the previous movement and take him down to the floor. Kneel down on the side of his chest with your left knee and continue the pressure with your arms (Figure 5-131).

Figure 5-130

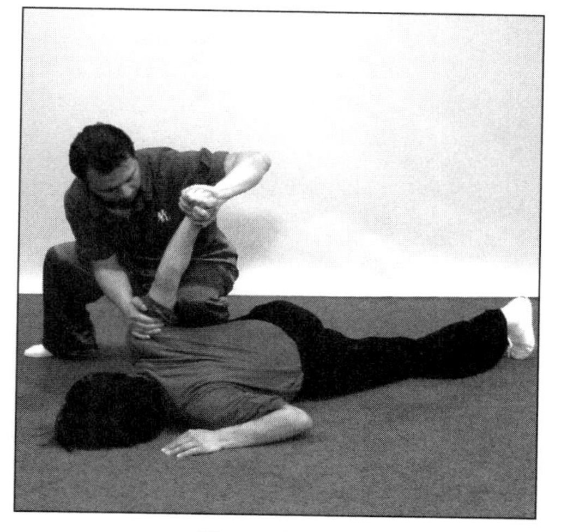

Figure 5-131

Notes:

A. When you take your opponent down, keep a constant torque on his right arm.

B. This technique may also be applied with an initial outward intercept with your left arm, instead of an inward intercept.

Figure 5-132

Figure 5-133

Qinna 32. Chase the Snake Back to Its Hole (追蛇入洞)

Figure 5-134

Step 1. From a ready position, your opponent steps forward with his right foot and punches to your head with his right fist. You yield back and intercept his punch with your left forearm to your left (Figure 5-132). You counter punch to his chest with your right fist. He intercepts your punch by lowering his left arm (Figure 5-133).

Step 2. Push his right arm forward and down, while hooking your left arm up. Place your right hand on top of your left hand and continue to push down, while lifting up with your right arm (Figure 5-134).

Notes:

A. Hook your right arm back on your opponent's right arm and press forward with your left arm to make his right arm bend.

B. Use your right hand to help push your left hand down on your opponent's arm while lifting your right elbow up to contol him.

Figure 5-135

Figure 5-136

Qinna 33. Turn Your Body and Carry the Firewood (轉身揹柴)

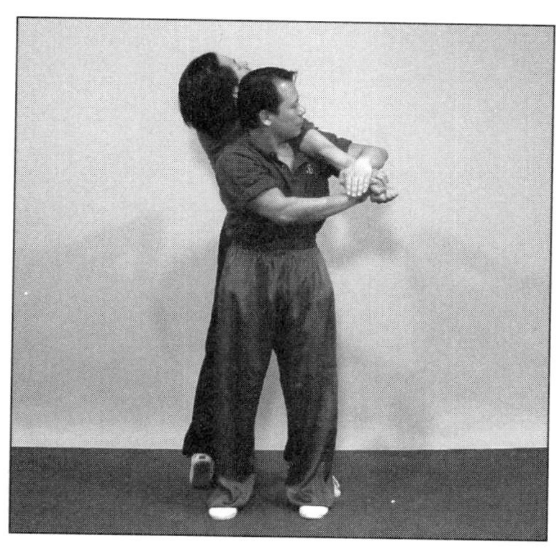

Figure 5-137

Step 1. From a ready position, your opponent steps forward with his right foot and punches to your head with his right fist. You drop down, block up with your right forearm and grab a hold of his wrist with your right hand. At the same time, punch to his ribs with your left fist. Your opponent intercepts your left punch to his left with his left hand (Figure 5-135).

Step 2. Bend your left arm and strike to his ribs with your left elbow as you take a cross step with your right foot behind your left foot (Figure 5-136). Turn to your right and pull his arm over your left shoulder and down, and stand up (Figure 5-137).

Note:

A. Press up with your shoulder tight against the back of your opponent's shoulder and rotate his arm until it is facing upward, when applying this technique.

Figure 5-138

Figure 5-139

Figure 5-140

Figure 5-141

Qinna 34. Caihe Carries the Basket (采和挎籃)

Step 1. From a ready position, your opponent steps forward with his right foot and punches to your head with his right fist. You yield back and slap his arm to your left with your right hand (Figure 5-138).

Step 2. Strike to his head with your left palm from under his right arm (Figure 5-139). Hook your left arm down and back around his right arm and strike forward with your right palm (Figure 5-140). Turn your body around and lift his elbow up (Figure 5-141).

Notes:

A. When you initially strike forward with your left palm, contact your opponent's right arm and follow his arm in towards his head to distract

Figure 5-142

Figure 5-143

him. When you hook your left arm back, first hook down then back up.

Figure 5-144

Qinna 35. Golden Boy Presents the Painting (金童獻圖)

Step 1. From a ready position, your opponent steps forward with his right foot and punches to your head with his right fist. You yield back and circle both arms clockwise to intercept his punch. Then grab a hold of his right wrist with your right hand and press your left forearm tight on his right arm (Figure 5-142).

Step 2. Pull and twist with your right hand and press down on his elbow with your left forearm. At the same time, step kick to his knee with your right foot and take him down (Figures 5-143 and 5-144).

Notes:

A. Keep the pressure on your opponent's elbow, by applying pressure from each hand in opposite directions.

B. Apply the initial lock on your opponent's arm, continue the circular motion of your block to twist his arm until his elbow is facing upward.

Figure 5-145

Figure 5-146

Figure 5-147

Figure 5-148

C. The kick to the knee distracts your opponent and makes it easier to control his arm.

Qinna 36. Imperial Cat Catches the Mouse (御貓捕鼠)

Step 1. From a ready position, your opponent steps forward with his right foot and punches to your head with his right fist. You yield back and intercept his punch to your right with your right forearm (Figure 5-145).

Step 2. Grab a hold of his right wrist with your right hand and pull down. At the same time, palm strike to his head with your left hand to make him block (Figure 5-146). Slide your right foot back and continue to pull, while twisting his arm with your right

Figure 5-149

Figure 5-150

hand. At the same time, push down with your left hand on top of his elbow until he is on the floor (Figures 5-147 and 5-148).

Notes:

A. The more you are able to continue your opponent's momentum as you apply the technique, the more effective the technique will be.

B. When you strike forward with your left palm, press on your opponent's arm with your forearm at the same time.

Qinna 37. Lift Up Your Head and Extend Your Chest (抬頭挺胸)

Step 1. From a ready position, your opponent steps forward with his right foot and punches to your head with his right fist. You yield back and circle both arms clockwise to intercept his punch. Then grab a hold of his right wrist with your right hand and press your left forearm tight on his right arm (Figure 5-149).

Step 2. Strike towards his neck with your left arm, while pulling his right arm and locking his elbow on your chest (Figure 5-150). Turn your body towards your left (Figures 5-151 and 5-151R).

Notes:

A. Keep constant pressure on your opponent's arm to lock his elbow, when you strike towards his neck.

B. If your opponent prevents you from locking his neck, use the following technique.

Figure 5-151

Figure 5-151R

Qinna 38. Luohan Takes a Nap (羅漢睡覺)

Step 1. From a ready position, your opponent steps forward with his right foot and punches to your head with his right fist. You yield back and circle both arms clockwise to intercept his punch. Then grab a hold of his right wrist with your right hand and press your left forearm tight on his right arm (Figure 5-152).

Step 2. Pull his arm down, bring your left elbow over his arm, and strike towards his head with your left elbow (Figure 5-153). Pull his wrist up and press down on his arm with your armpit and lean on him to take him down. When he is one the floor, continue to keep the pressure on his arm while placing your body weight on his back (Figure 5-154 and 5-155).

Figure 5-152

Figure 5-153

Figure 5-154

Figure 5-155

Note:

A. The initial lock is on your opponent's elbow. When you complete the control, both his shoulder and his elbow are locked.

Figure 5-156

Figure 5-157

Qinna 39. Flying Eagle Catches the Rabbit (飛鷹捕兔)

Step 1. From a ready position, your opponent steps forward with his right foot and punches to your head with his right fist. You yield back and circle both arms clockwise to intercept his punch. Then grab a hold of his right wrist with your right hand and press your left forearm tight on his right arm (Figure 5-156).

Step 2. Push his right arm down and strike to his head with your right palm (Figure 5-157). If he intercepts your right arm to your left, continue the momentum by striking your right palm on his right shoulder, and elbow him to his head. At the same time, bring your left arm up from under his arm and lock his right shoulder with both arms (Figure 5-158).

Step 3. Raise your left elbow up as you pull back and down with your hands to control him on the floor (Figures 5-159 and 5-160).

Figure 5-158

Figure 5-159

Figure 5-160

Notes:

A. The action of the right arm must be continuous. If the strike to the face fails, continue the pressure on your opponent by striking or pressing your arm towards his body.

B. As you pull your opponent's shoulder down, first raise your left elbow up to weaken his arm alignment and set up the initial lock on his shoulder, so that he will not be able to resist when you pull down.

Figure 5-161

Figure 5-162

Qinna 40. Iron Ox Plows the Field (鐵牛耕地)

Step 1. From a ready position, your opponent steps forward with his right foot and punches to your head with his right fist. You yield back and circle both arms clockwise to intercept his punch. Then grab a hold of his right wrist with your right hand and press your left forearm tight on his right arm (Figure 5-161).

Step 2. Strike with your left arm towards his neck (Figure 5-162). If he is able to intercept your arm, strike to his body with your right knee (Figure 5-163). If he is able to push your knee down, follow his push and lock his elbow under your armpit as you pull his wrist upward (Figures 5-164 and 5-165).

Figure 5-163

Figure 5-164

Figure 5-165

Notes:

A. The strike to the neck distracts your opponent and sets up for the knee attack.

B. Your right knee attack forces your opponent to intercept down, which starts his forward motion which you can use against him in this qinna.

武術功夫訓練

Chapter 6:

Wushu Kung Fu Attainment Training

As we mentioned in the Introduction, the term Kung Fu or gongfu is more than just a term referring to Chinese martial arts. It is also a term meaning the attainment of a skill or an ability through a steady input of time and effort. When we use the term Wushu Kung Fu, it means the lasting ability or skill attained in Wushu training. In Wushu, a practitioner's level of Kung Fu is the attainment of many different types of skills, including the ability to apply hard and subtle skills, Wushu Qigong, light and agile movements, etc.

A well-known saying in the Wushu community states, "When one practices Wushu without the Kung Fu attainment training, it will all be lost when one gets old (練武不練功，到老一場空)." This statement implies that if a martial artist only trains the routines and the techniques of Wushu movements without Kung Fu attainment training, their ability will be limited and won't withstand the test of time and age. Wushu technical skills without Kung Fu attainment are only useful against people without martial arts or fighting training.

There are people that have learned many Wushu routines, but don't understand the applications of the movements or have the ability to apply the techniques. These individuals are technically not training Wushu as a martial art. Their Wushu training is considered a sport and performing art, not martial art. A martial artist must do Kung Fu attainment training. Each and every style of Wushu, has their unique system of Kung Fu attainment training methods. The training methods we will be introducing in this chapter are all practical, efficient, and effective.

In the book, *Qigong Empowerment*, we already introduced the Intensive Iron Shirt training; plus many conditioning methods to withstand impact for the solar plexus, throat, armpits, head, legs, muscles, and groin. Please refer to it for additional training methods not included in this book. In the future, we will also introduce the rare Emei Dapeng Qigong training, an important training for increasing a person's strength and power by increasing their internal energy. Dapeng Qigong is also a method of attaining the Golden Bell Cover ability to withstand impact to the body.

Our objective in this chapter is to familiarize you with the vast content of Wushu training, giving you a greater understanding of the extensive and long history of traditional Wushu Kung Fu attainment training. Much of the training we have presented in this chapter, provides direct challenges to the physical body, as well as, to the human psyche. The training is passed down from ancient times, yet concurs with modern scientific understanding, for fostering the development of the underlying potential of the practitioner.

6.1. Iron Arm Training (金鋼鐵臂功)

In free fighting applications, the arms have many functions. With proper training, they can express an incredible amount of power. The arms can be trained to be like an iron whip, which can break thick sticks and shatter rocks, not to mention your opponent's bones and tendons. To achieve steel-like arms, practitioners must go through a lot of hard work.

1. Stance Training (樁功)

Posture: Place 5 to 10 metal rings on each of your forearms and extend your arms forward while standing in a Horse Stance. Point the index finger and thumb of both hands towards each other while coiling the other fingers in towards the palm (Figure 6-1).

Figure 6-1

Figure 6-2

Figure 6-2a

Figure 6-3

Figure 6-4

Intention: Visualize that your feet are immersed into the earth like the roots of a strong tree. All your cells are shielding you from the pressure bombarding you from around you. You are unmoved by the strong wind and the thunderstorm. Gradually, forget about your body and stand for as long as you can.

2. Explosive Power Drill (金剛爆發勁功)

Step 1. Continue from Part 1. Inhale and bring your hands back next to your waist (Figures 6-2 and 6-2a). Hold your breath, hold up your huiyin (the perineum area), slowly push your hands forward. When your arms have extended halfway, all of a sudden, strike forward as fast and powerful as you can (Figures 6-3 and 6-4). Then exhale, relax your huiyin and your body. Repeat 9 times.

Figure 6-5

Figure 6-6

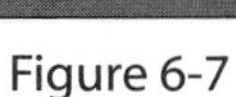

Figure 6-7

Figure 6-8

Step 2. Move your arms to your sides (Figure 6-5). Inhale and bring your hands back next to your waist (Figure 6-6). Hold your breath, hold up your huiyin, slowly push your hands to your sides. When your arms have extended halfway, all of a sudden, strike sideways as fast and powerful as you can (Figures 6-7 and 6-8). Then exhale, relax your huiyin and your body. Repeat 9 times.

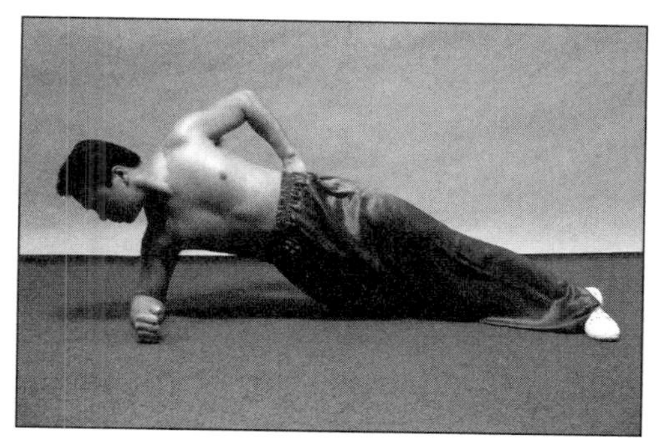

Figure 6-9

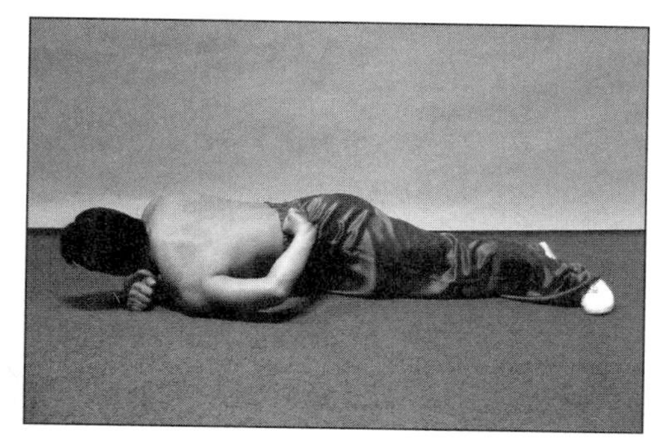

Figure 6-10

Figure 6-11

3. Sleeping Luohan Rotates Its Arm Drill (睡羅漢轉臂功)

Step 1. Lie down on your right side. Elevate your body with your right forearm, the outer edge of your right foot, and the sole of your left foot. Place your right fist on your back (Figure 6-9).

Step 2. Inhale, turn your body towards the floor, and touch your left shoulder down to the floor (Figure 6-10). Exhale and bring your body back up to the starting position (Figure 6-11). Repeat 18 times.

Step 3. Change sides and repeat 18 times.

Figure 6-12

Figure 6-13

Figure 6-14

Figure 6-15

Figure 6-16

4. Dapeng Flaps Its Wings Drills (大鵬翅功)

Step 1. Stand in a Horse Stance with your arms raised at shoulder level and bent. Support weight bags on your arms (Figure 6-12). Start with weight bags that are about 10 pounds each. Fan your arms up and down 18 times (Figures 6-13 and 6-14).

Step 2. Continue from the previous step. Toss the weight bags up and catch them with your arms 18 times (Figure 6-15). You may toss the weight bags together or alternate from one side to the next.

Figure 6-17

Figure 6-18

Figure 6-19

Step 3. Stand in a Horse Stance, side to side with a partner. One of you presses down with one arm while the other person supports the arm up with his arm (Figure 6-16). Hold the posture for 10 to 30 seconds. Change sides, then change arm positions with your partner on both sides.

Figure 6-20

5. Arm Conditioning Drills (撞臂功)

Step 1. Stand upright with your palms facing down at your sides (Figure 6-17). Relax your body and pay attention to your laogong point on your palms for a few breaths. The laogong point can be located by coiling your fingers in as if your were making a fist. The point between your middle and index fingers is the laogong point. It is between the third and the fourth metacarpal bones.

Step 2. Inhale and raise your arms up to shoulder level (Figure 6-18). Exhale and rotate your arms until your palms are facing up (Figure 6-19). As you exhale, lead your qi to your arms.

Step 3. Hit your arms against each other until all the surfaces on both arms are covered (Figure 6-20). Gradually increase the strength of the strike.

Figure 6-21

Figure 6-22

Figure 6-23

Figure 6-24

Step 4. Hit your index and middle fingers against each other until all the surfaces on both index and middle fingers are covered (Figure 6-21). Gradually increase the strength of the strike.

Step 5. Stand facing a partner and condition each other's arms. Swing your right forearms down toward each other (Figure 6-22). Pull your arm back slightly, then swing your arms up toward each other (Figure 6-23). Then swing your arms down toward each other (Figure 6-24). Cover as much surface of the lower arm as you can, and with increasing force. Then condition the other arm. Condition each arm for 5 to 10 minutes each session.

Step 6. If you don't have a partner, you can condition your arms on a tree or a post following the same guidelines as if you were training with a partner (Figures 6-25, 6-26, and 6-27).

Figure 6-25

Figure 6-26

Figure 6-27

Figure 6-28

Figure 6-29

6. Brick Drill (磚功)

Step 1. Stand in a Horse Stance. Hold one brick in each hand and alternate pushing one brick forward and pulling one brick back in front of your chest (Figures 6-28 and 6-29). Repeat 50 to 100 times or more gradually.

Figure 6-30

Figure 6-31

Figure 6-32

Step 2. Hold two bricks together with both hands (Figure 6-30). Use your shanzhong (mid point between nipples) and dantian (four fingers width down from your navel) as the diameter to move the bricks in a circular path. Inhale and circle the bricks up to your shanzhong level and bring your mind to your shanzhong (Figure 6-31). Exhale and circle the bricks down to your dantian level and bring your mind to your dantian. Repeat 9 to 18 times or more in a clockwise direction, then in a counterclockwise direction.

Figure 6-33

Step 3. Make the circle bigger. Use the baihui (on the top of the head) and the huiyin (groin level) as the diameter to move the bricks in a circular path (Figures 6-32 and 6-33). Repeat 9 to 18 times or more in a clockwise direction, then in a counterclockwise direction.

7. Rolling the Cylinder on Your Arms (滾筒功)

Step 1. Find a cylindrical container about 3 to 5 feet long and fill it with sand. The weight could be 30 to 100 pounds depending on your condition. Stand in a Horse Stance and place the cylinder on your hands with your palms facing up.

Figure 6-34

Figure 6-35

Step 2. Raise your arms up and allow the cylinder to roll up your arms. Then lower your arms and allow the cylinder to roll back down to your hands.

Step 3. Toss the cylinder up in the air. Rotate your arms until your palms are facing down and catch the cylinder with the back of your forearms.

Step 4. Raise your arms up and allow the cylinder to roll up your arms. Then lower your arms and allow the cylinder to roll back down to your hands.

Step 5. Toss the cylinder up in the air. Rotate your arms until your palms are facing up and catch the cylinder with your hands.

Step 6. Repeat rolling the cylinder up and down your arms, and tossing and catching the cylinder, 9 to 18 times or more.

6.2. Iron Leg Training (鐵腿功)

1. Stance Training (樁功):

Step 1. Stand in a Horse Stance (Figure 6-34). Gradually build up your leg strength to 10 to 30 minutes or more. When you can easily hold your Horse Stance for 10 minutes or more, add weight to your stance to further strengthen your legs (Figure 6-35). Gradually increase the weight.

Figure 6-36

Figure 6-37

Step 2. Stand in a Empty Stance (Figure 6-36). Gradually build up your leg strength to 10 to 30 minutes or more on each side. When you are able to hold your Empty Stance for 10 minutes or more, add weight to your stance to further strengthen your legs (Figure 6-37). Gradually increase the weight.

2. Squatting Drill (下蹲功)

Step 1. Place your palms together in front of your chest. Stand on your right leg and extend your left leg straight in front of you. Squat down with your right leg while maintaining the left leg straight (Figure 6-38). Then stand up (Figure 6-39). Repeat 10 to 50 times. Then do the other side.

Step 2. Squat down as low as you can and walk forward without raising your head up and down (Figures 6-40 and 6-41). Do as many steps as you can and gradually increase the amount of steps over time from 50 to 100 to 1000, or more.

3. Strengthening Your Toes (腳趾功)

Step 1. Use your toes to support your body (Figure 6-42). You may hold onto a table or any support to keep your balance. Hold for as long as you can and gradually increase to 30 seconds, then to 1 minute or more over time. When you can easily stand on the toes of both feet for 1 minute, then stand on the toes of one foot.

Figure 6-38

Figure 6-39

Figure 6-40

Figure 6-41

Figure 6-42

Figure 6-43

Step 2. Stand on one leg and use the big toe to write letters on the ground or floor (Figure 6-43). Press your toe into the ground or floor as hard as you can and write the letters A to Z. Then change legs and repeat the step.

Step 3. Raise one leg up and write the letters in the air (Figure 6-44). Write the letters A to Z or any inspirational and encouraging words that you would like. Then change legs and repeat the step.

Figure 6-44

Figure 6-45

Figure 6-46

Figure 6-47

4. Stretch Your Legs (壓腿)

Use the same basic leg stretching exercises introduced in Chapter 1. Elasticity and the ability for your leg muscles to contract and relax are important factors for developing powerful and fast kicks.

5. Kicking Power Training

Step 1. Resistance Kicking (橡皮筋功): Tie a piece of elastic band on a solid and stable object, and tie the other end around your ankle. Practice kicking with different forward, backward, and sideway kicks (Figure 6-45). Gradually increase the amount of each kick and the tightness of the elastic band.

Step 2. Kicking Sand Bags (踢沙袋功): Hang a sandbag at about chest height. Use different forward, backward, sideway, knee, and spinning kicks to kick the sandbag (Figure 6-46). Gradually increase the amount of each kick and strength of each kick.

Step 3. Have a few sandbags weighing 10 to 20 pounds ready. Lift one sandbag up at a time with your foot or toss it up in the air with your hands. As the bag falls, kick it with your feet, with different types of kicks (Figure 6-47). Gradually increase the amount of each kick and the weight of the sandbags.

Step 4. Stand in front of a solid wall and do heel kicks and side kicks. Gradually increase the amount of each kick and the strength of each kick.

Figure 6-48

Figure 6-49

Step 5. Stand in front of a wooden dummy or a tree. Put some markings of different colors on the wooden dummy or tree indicating the different vital parts of the body. Use different kicks to hit the color coded points (Figure 6-48).

Gradually speed up your kicks and the combination of kicks, as well as, the strength of each kick. Initially, you may wrap thick layers of padding on the wooden dummy or tree to prevent injuries to your feet. When your feet get stronger, remove or reduce the padding.

Step 6. Bury an 8 foot long post about 3 feet into the ground outside, or find a strong healthy tree in your yard, or stabilize a wooden dummy indoors. Use a back sweep kick and a front sweep kick to hit the post, tree, or wooden dummy (Figure 6-49). Gradually increase the amount of each kick and the strength of the kick.

Figure 6-50

Figure 6-51

6.3. Iron Sand Palm Training (鐵沙掌)

Iron Sand Palm is also known as Dali Jingangzhang (大力金剛掌) or Zhenshanzhang (震山掌). When properly conditioned, the practitioner's palm becomes a powerful and deadly weapon. It is, therefore, also known as Life Ending Palm (絕命掌) and Destroying the Heart Palm (摧心掌). The training is very physically demanding, therefore this type of palm training is referred to as Yanggang Zhangfa (陽剛掌法), meaning the Yang and hard palm training method. With proper and dedicated training, a practitioner will be able to attain powerful palm strength in one to two years.

1. Arm Strength Building

Since the arms are the direct connection to your palms, it is important that the arms are strong enough to support what the palms are about to do. If the arm is not strong or conditioned properly, the stronger palm will become ineffective because the support will not allow the powerful palm to carry out its force. If the palm does exert its force outward and the support is not strong or conditioned enough, the joints in the arm may become injuried. Therefore, Iron Sand Palm training must also include some arm strength building training.

Step 1. Stand in a Horse Stance with both palms extended in front of you (Figure 6-50). Inhale bring your intention to your dantian (about 4 fingers width below your navel). Exhale bring your intention to your palms. Repeat 18 to 36 times.

Figure 6-52

Figure 6-53

Figure 6-54

Step 2. Golden Dragon Turns Its Body (金龍翻身): From a push up position, keep your feet as close together as you can, place one palm on the floor and extend the other arm up (Figure 6-51). Inhale, bend your supporting arm and bring your body down close to the floor, without touching the floor (Figure 6-52). Exhale, straighten your supporting arm and go back to the starting position (Figures 6-53 and 6-54). Repeat 9 to 27 times, then do the other arm.

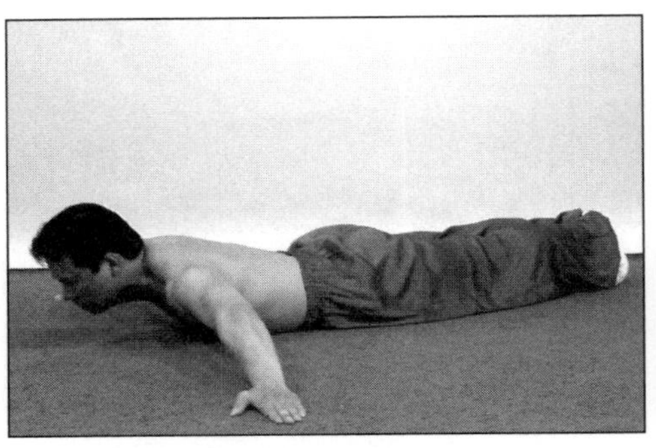

Figure 6-55

Figure 6-56

Figure 6-57

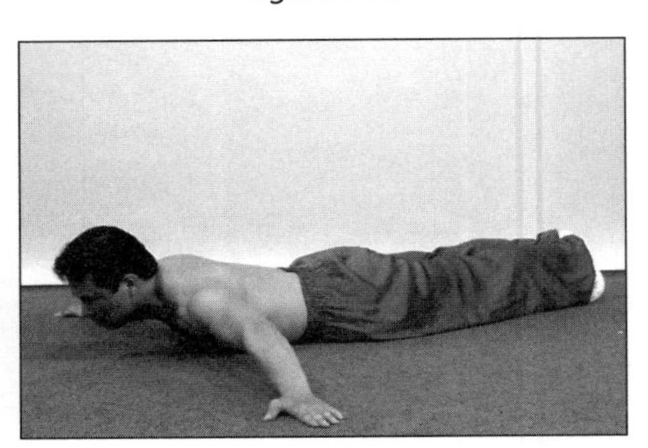

Figure 6-58

Step 3. Support the Ground with Spiritual Strength (神力撑地): Lie down with your face down and arms stretched to the sides, palms down, and feet together (Figure 6-55). Inhale and bring your mind to your dantian. Exhale, use your arms, abdomen, and feet to create a closing in force to lift your body off the floor. Bring your hands as close together as you can (Figures 6-56 and 6-57). Again inhale, bring your intention to your dantian and lower your body down to the starting position (Figure 6-58). Repeat 9 to 27 times.

Step 4. Stand upside down next to a wall. Inhale, bend your arms and lower your body down. Exhale and straighten your arms to lift your body upward. Repeat as many times as you can. Build up to 36 times or more.

Step 5. Support a weight on both hands in front of your chest. Push the weight up by straightening your arms. Find a weight that will allow you to extend it up and lower it for 36 to 50 times. Gradually increase the weight as you get stronger.

2. Hit a Hanging Sandbag

The following drills require that you use your palms to hit a sandbag. You will need to use a bruise liniment to massage your hands before and after the training, to prevent blood stasis and to improve the energy circulation to your hands. Prolonged training with blood stasis (bruises) can cause an arthritic condition in your hands. It is imperative that you use a proper bruise or training liniment to prevent long term injuries or problems to your hands. Many liniments are now readily available in the martial arts community. You can also make your own. We have listed several liniment formulas in Appendix B.

Step 1. Stand in front of a hanging sandbag that is at about chest level. Use different palm strikes to hit the sandbag, making the bag swing back and forth. Start with a bag that is filled with about 30 pounds of sand.

Step 2. Push the bag and make is swing forward. When the bag swings back, hit it with a filing movement of the palm to make the bag spin. Gradually increase the weight of the sand bag.

3. Hit a Flat Sandbag

Step 1. Prepare a flat sandbag and place it on a stable surface. Warm up some liniment and place it in a container that both hands can fit into. There should be enough liniment to immerse both hands completely up to the wrist.

Step 2. Use the front, back, and edge of both palms to hit the sandbag. Start gently and gradually increase the force. Inhale and raise one hand up over your head. Exhale and hit the sandbag with your palm. Concentrate your intent on the training. Relax your arm and allow the weight of the arm to slap the palm down. Tighten your palm as you contact the bag; then relax your palm immediately. Your palm should hit the bag like a whip snapping down. Hit the sandbag until the hands are hot and begin to turn red.

Step 3. Immerse your hands in the warm liniment for 5 to 10 minutes. Gently massage the hands while the hands are immersed in the liniment. Practice daily to strengthen the palms and to increase your power.

4. Bricks and Roofing Tile Training

Step 1. Lay two bricks on a stable surface and place a third brick over the two lower ones, making a bridge. Then place a thick old book on top of the top brick.

Step 2. Use the same training method described in Steps 2 and 3 of Part 3. to hit the book. Your intention is to break the brick as your hand contacts the book. Hit the book daily. Reduce the thickness of the book by removing one page everyday after your training. By the time you reach the bare brick, your palm will be strengthened significantly. Your palms should be able to withstand the force of the impact and eventually be able to break the brick. Note: Properly made concrete bricks will be much more challenging to break than bricks made of clay material.

Step 3. Periodically, test your progress by attempting to break roofing tiles. Start bricking one tile, two tiles, and so on and so forth, until you are able to break 20 to 30 one inch roofing tiles with your palm. When you attempt to break the tiles or strike at an opponent, tense your hand on contact. After the break, relax immediately.

5. Traditional Mountain Moving Palm Training (排山掌法)

Step 1. Prepare a flat stable table with a smooth and durable top. Place a heavy concrete brick on the table. The brick should be heavy enough that you can barely move it by pushing it.

Step 2. Stand in a Bow Stance in front of the table. Place one or both palms on the brick with your arms bent. Push the brick forward by exerting a quick push from your legs, waist, back, and arms, without leaning forward. Practice daily until you are able to easily push the brick forward about a foot. Then add 20 to 30 pounds more on top of the brick and keep training. Train until you are able to move over 300 pounds with a powerful push of your palms.

6.4. Red Sand Palm Training (紅沙掌)

Red Sand Palm is also known as Zhusazhang (硃沙掌) or Yinrouzhang (陰柔掌). The focus of this training is on the internal energy development as opposed to the more physically intensive training of the Iron Sand Palm. There-

Figure 6-59

Figure 6-60

Figure 6-61

fore, Red Sand Palm is referred to as Yinrou Zhangfa (陰柔掌法). The *yin* in *yinrou* is used in contrast to the *Yang* in *Yanggang Zhangfa* of the Iron Sand Palm. The devastating power is from internal strength developed through continuous training. This training is also good for smoothing your energy channels, regulating internal energy, and strengthening bones and tendons. The ability attained from this training can be very deadly. It is not suitable for individuals without compassion and individuals that get enraged too easily. Because of this, we will only introduce the general training concepts.

Part 1. Internal Energy Development (內功練習)

1. Lift Up the Mountain (托山功)

Step 1. Stand with your feet shoulder width apart, with your arms bent, and palms facing up (Figure 6-59).

Step 2. Inhale and visualize that all the righteous-qi (good energy) of the universe is entering your entire body from everywhere and gathering at your dantian.

Step 3. Exhale, use your mind, don't tense your muscles, extend your arms up slowly and visualize that you are lifting a huge mountain (Figure 6-60). As you exhale, bring the qi from your dantian through your three yin and three yang channels in your arms, to your laogong points on your palms, and pay attention to the heavy weighted sensation as you extend your arms.

Step 4. Inhale, lower your arms down to the starting position, and feel the heavy weight pressing down on your hands (Figure 6-61). Repeat Steps 3 and 4, 18 to 36 times.

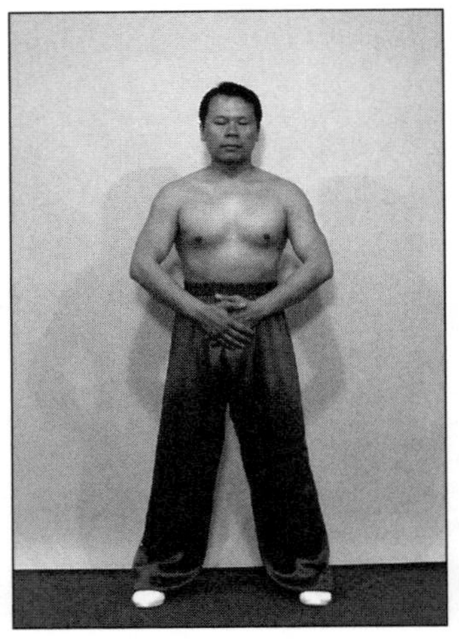
Figure 6-62

Figure 6-63

Figure 6-64

Figure 6-65

Figure 6-66

Step 5. Lower your arms and overlap your hands on your dantian. Inhale and exhale naturally, and pay attention to our dantian for 30 seconds (Figure 6-62).

2. Push the Mountains Apart (撑山功)

Step 1. Stand with your feet shoulder width apart, with your arms extended to your sides, and palms facing down (Figure 6-63).

Step 2. Inhale, bend your arms and bring you hands towards your chest, and visualize that the righteous-qi of the universe is entering your entire body from everywhere and gathering at your dantian (Figure 6-64).

Figure 6-67

Figure 6-68

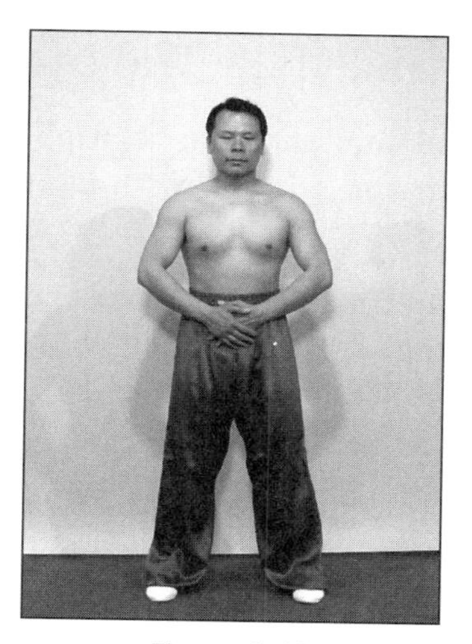
Figure 6-69

Step 3. Exhale drop your elbows and push your palms to your sides (Figures 6-65, 6-66, and 6-67). When you exhale, bring your intention to your laogong points on your palms, don't tense your muscles, and visualize that you are separating two mountains apart.

Step 4. Point your fingers to your sides with your palms facing down (Figure 6-68). Repeat Steps 2, 3, and 4, 18 to 36 times.

Step 5. Lower your arms and overlap your hands on your dantian. Inhale and exhale naturally, and pay attention to our dantian for 30 seconds (Figure 6-69).

Figure 6-70

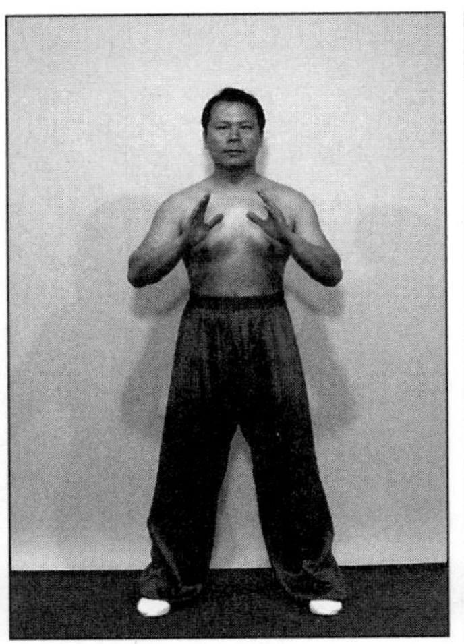

Figure 6-71

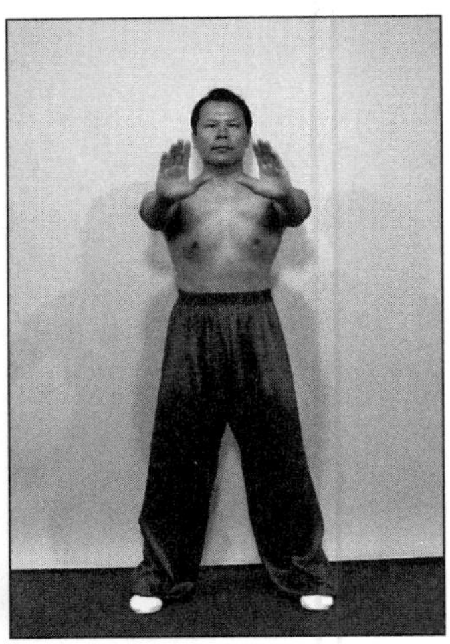

Figure 6-72

3. Push the Water and Make Waves (推波作浪)

Step 1. Stand with your feet shoulder width apart and visualize that you are standing on a beach with your feet immersed in the water.

Step 2. Inhale, bring your hands up to your chest (Figures 6-70 and 6-71). Visualize that the righteous-qi of the universe is entering your entire body from everywhere and gathering at your dantian.

Step 3. Exhale, push your palms forward (Figure 6-72). When you exhale, bring your intention to your laogong points on your palms, don't tense your muscles, and visualize that you are pushing at the water.

Step 4. Inhale, bring your hands back towards your chest (Figure 6-73). When you bring your hands back, visualize and feel the pressure of the wave crashing down on your palms. Then, again, exhale and push your palms forward (Figure 6-74). Repeat Steps 3 and 4, 18 to 36 times.

Step 5. Lower your arms and overlap your hands on your dantian. Inhale and exhale naturally, and pay attention to your dantian for 30 seconds (Figure 6-75).

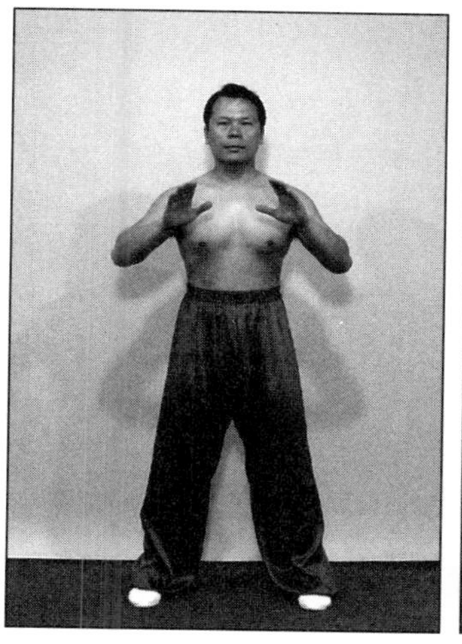
Figure 6-73

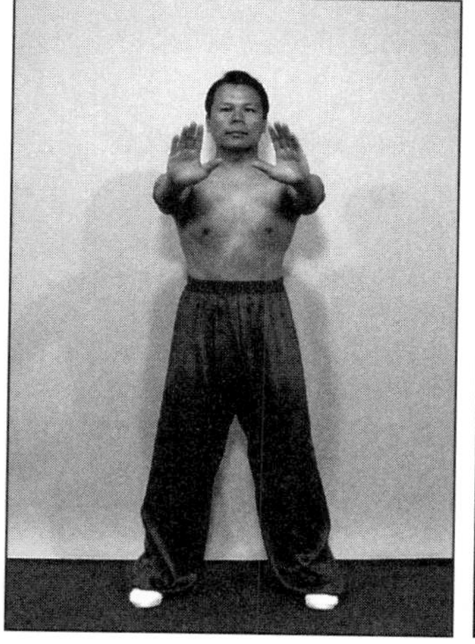
Figure 6-74

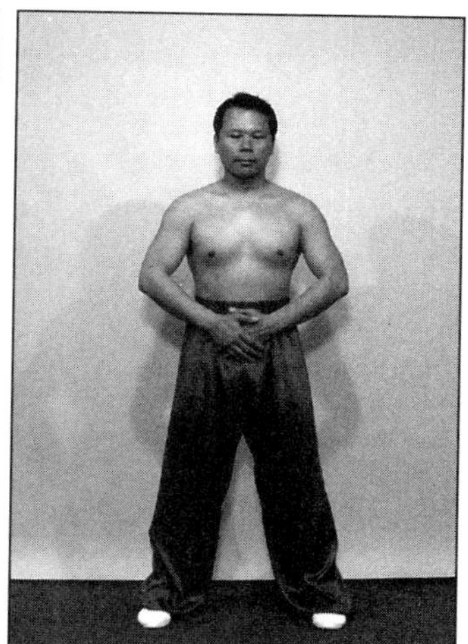
Figure 6-75

Part 2. Power Emitting Training

4. Striking at Water Training (擊水功)

Prepare a large bucket of water. Stand in a high Horse Stance in front of the bucket. Focus on your dantian for a few breaths, then focus on the water. Alternate striking at the water your palms without touching the water. When you strike down, send your intention all the way down to the bottom of the bucket. Inhale when your palm is up and exhale when you strike down with your palm. Train 100 to 1000 strikes a day until you are able to displace the water without actually contacting the water with your palms.

5. Striking a Piece of Hanging Paper Training (擊紙功)

Hang a rectangular piece of paper about shoulder level. Lead your qi to your palms and alternate striking the free hanging paper with your palms. Strike at the paper 100 to 1000 times everyday. Initially, you may only be able to make the paper swing back and forth. Keep training until you are able to break the paper with your palms.

6. Displacing the Sand Immersed in Water Training (擊水分沙功)

Find a 2 to 3 feet in diameter shallow bucket, place about a one inch thick layer of sand in the bucket, then fill the bucket with a few inches of water. Stand in front of the bucket and focus on your dantian for a few breaths, then focus on the sand in the bucket. Lead your qi to your palms and alternate hitting the surface of the water with each palm. Train 100 to 1000 strikes a day until you are able to displace the sand in the bottom of the bucket with each strike.

7. Rubbing Sand Training (搓沙功)

Find a bucket and fill it with thick clean sand. Put your hands in the sand and rub the sand. Practice daily until you are tired. Keep training and gradually raise your hands above the sand over time. The goal is to be able to make the sand below your hands move without touching the sand. This training can strengthen your hands and train your mind to send energy to your palms on demand.

Legend has it, that ancient practitioners also trained with iron sand and iron balls after training with the sand. Martial arts novels have also written about masters that were able to move the iron balls without touching them. These practitioners were able to strike at their opponents and injury them without touching their opponents. The authors have met many legendary practitioners and have heard a lot of these stories, but have not personally witnessed practitioners with these abilities.

8. Sun, Moon, and Well Training (日，月，井掌功)

Stand and face the sun or the moon. Focus your intention and lead your qi to your palms. Alternate striking with your palms at the sun or the moon. Every time you strike, visualize that the sun or the moon has been shaken and is vibrating. Train 100 times or more everyday with each palm.

Stand in front of a well in a Horse Stance. Use your palms to strike at the water in the well. Inhale, when you raise your palm and exhale when you strike down. Train 360 times with each palm. Within one to two years, you may be able to hear the sound reflecting back from the bottom well due to your palm strikes. Keep training until you are able to make the water in the well splash.

Different objects in our environment contain different qualities of qi. Striking at the sun, moon, and well are also means to absorb the energy of the sun, moon, and well.

9. Striking at Fire Training (擊火功)

Light a candle or an old lamp in a room without a breeze. Focus your mind on the fire. Alternate using your palms to strike at the fire, without touching it. Inhale when you bring your palm away from the fire and exhale when you strike towards the fire. Don't lock your elbow when you strike at the fire.

Start with your palm a few inches from the fire when you strike. When you are able to consistently extinguish the fire, then move half a step back and continue the training. Train 100 to 1000 times each day until you are able to extinguish the fire a few feet away from the fire.

Figure 6-76

6.5. Cavity Press Finger Training (點穴手)

This finger conditioning training is also referred to as Jingang Two Finger Chan (金剛二指禪), Jingangzhi (金剛指), or Dianshigong (點石功). There is a saying in Wushu that states, "Three punches are not as powerful as an elbow strike, three elbows are not as powerful as a palm strike, and three palm strikes are not as powerful as a finger strike." Another saying states, "A palm strikes at an area and a finger focuses on one point." The power of the fingers have been well valued and trained. Before you begin your training, warm up your fingers and rub them with the other hand for a few minutes. Cover every joint of your fingers. After you are done with each session of your training, massage your fingers and wash your hands with moderately warm water for a few minutes to prevent your fingers from stiffening. Dry your hands and apply bruise liniment to your hands and massage for a few minutes. (See Appendix B for training liniment information).

1. Dapeng Stretches Its Claws (大鵬探爪)

Step 1. Stand with your feet shoulder width apart and extend your arms to your sides with your palms facing down (Figure 6-76).

Step 2. Inhale, visualize that the vital-qi of the universe is entering your body through your baihui and laogong points, and gathering at your dantian. Exhale, gently hold up your huiyin and draw in your abdomen. Lead qi from your dantian up your spine (Governing Vessel), to your shoulders, and along the top of your arms, to your fingers.

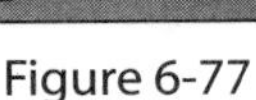

Figure 6-77

Figure 6-78

Figure 6-79

Figure 6-80

Step 3. Hold your breath, squeeze your fingers inward and visualize that your are crushing a steel ball in each hand (Figures 6-77 and 6-78). Then complete your exhalation.

Step 4. Do Steps 1 to 3, 9 times.

2. Hungry Tiger Catches Its Prey (餓虎仆食)

Step 1. Lie down on the floor in a push up position. Start supporting your body up with five fingers, then gradually reduce the amount of fingers you use to support your body (Figure 6-79).

Step 2. Inhale and raise your hips up into a reversed V shape (Figure 6-80).

Step 3. Exhale, bend your arms and swing your body back down past the starting position, and arch your back (Figure 6-81).

Step 3. Repeat Steps 2 and 3, 10 to 20 or more times. Gradually increase the number of repetitions as you get stronger.

Figure 6-81

Figure 6-82

3. Supporting your body with your fingers

Step 1. Support your body in a one arm push up position. Start supporting your body with five fingers. Gradually reduce the support as your fingers get stronger (Figure 6-82). Start with 30 seconds, one minute, five minutes, or more; gradually build up your finger strength.

Step 2. Sit on a chair or a bench. Start with all ten fingers supporting your body off the bench. Gradually reduce the amount of fingers you need to support your body. Start with 30 seconds, one minute, five minutes, or more; gradually build up your finger strength.

4. Striking at the Sun and Moon Training (指點日月功)

In the early morning strike at the sun and in the evening when there is a moon, strike at the moon, with your fingers. Train everyday until you can feel a qi sensation emitting from your fingers.

5. Striking Fire Training (擊火功)

Light a candle or an old lamp in a room without a breeze. Focus your mind on the fire. Alternate using your fingers to strike at the fire without touching it. Inhale when you bring your fingers away from the fire and exhale when you strike towards the fire. Don't lock your elbow when you strike at the fire.

6. Spearing Training (插截功)

Step 1. Cut your nails. Find a large container and fill it with rice. Stand in front of the container in a Horse Stance. Hold your fingers tightly together and alternate spearing your fingers into the rice. Train 100 to 1000 times a day with each hand.

When the rice in the container has been ground to a powder, replace the rice with moon beans and continue your training. When the moon beans have been ground to a powder, replace the moon beans with steel pellets. (Traditionally, iron sand and iron ore were used. To reduce the chances of infection, use steel pellets which are rust proof).

Step 2. Steel Finger Training (金剛指): Have a consistent location or an object that you can strike regularly, such as the ground, a rock, a tree trunk, a wooden board, or a metal board. Strike the ground or the object anytime you have a chance, until your fingers are sore and you are tired.

In the past, practitioners used to hang a heavy object such as an old stone grinder or a heavy metal plate near the entrance to their home. They would strike the hanging object with their fingers every time they walked past it.

6.6. Sound, Eyes, and Ear Training

Sound training is also referred to as Thunder Sound Training (雷嘯功，雷聲功). It is an internal strength training. Sound training can enhance the emitting of the dantian qi, as well as, sound expression from the abdomen. Internal qi can be greatly strengthened with proper sound training. Letting out the Lion's Roar Sound can be devastating to your opponent.

During the Three Kingdom era in China, General Zhang Fei (張飛) was chased by several hundred thousand enemy troops to a bridge. He stood alone on the bridge and let out a Lion's Roar Sound that vibrated throughout the battlefield. The enemy troops were halted in their chase, fearing that there may be an ambush waiting for them. One of the enemy generals was so frightened that he fell off his horse and died.

The training focuses on the "ah (啊)" and the "ha (哈)" sounds. This sound training can develop your Yang qi for internal energy. When accomplished, the emitted sound will be like thunder and a lion's roar, penetrating through the opponents' ear drum to their nerve centers. The sound may have different pitches. It can be a short and piercing sound to the opponents' ears. It can be a shock wave like pitch such as a crashing tidal wave. It can also be like the explosion of a bomb that shocks through the nervous system. These sounds can make your opponent very uncomfortable, make them lose the will to continue fighting, make them faint, or frighten them.

In any style of martial arts, the eyes are considered the most important. In the Long Fist styles, it is stated, "Punch like a shooting star, and eyes flash like an electric current (拳似流星眼似電)." The eyes express your vitality of spirit. In combat, your vitality of spirit expressed through your eyes can place a tremendous amount of pressure on your opponent. The eyes are also very important in Light Body and in Cavity Press. When your eyes are sharp, you will have an advantage over your opponent.

The ears are also an important component of martial arts training. A common phrase states, "The eyes see six paths and the ears listen to eight directions (眼觀六路，耳聽八方)." The ears can hear from the directions that the eyes can't see. In combat situations that involve more than one opponent, it is imperative that you are aware of opponents from any direction.

Sharp eyes and sensitive ears are both important qualities to become a highly skilled martial artist.

1. Lion's Roar Training (獅吼功)

Step 1. Go into a wooded area or to the mountains. Breath deeply 36 times, to regulate your breathing.

Step 2. Inhale slowly and fill your lungs. Exhale, let out an "ah" or "ha" sound. When you exhale, tighten your dantian and visualize that energy has been emitted from your dantian through the sound of your voice. Start with 20 or 30 times. Gradually build up the number of repetitions without hurting your throat.

Step 3. Massage your dantian until it feels warm.

2. Wisdom Eye Training (慧眼功)

Step 1. When you wake up in the morning, before you open your eyes, warm up your thumbnails by rubbing them next to each other. Gently press and massage over your eyelids, 18 times.

Step 2. Keep your eyes closed. Circle your eyes 9 times in each direction.

Step 3. Massage the zanzhu point, 72 times. The zanzhu point is located at the inside corners of the eyebrows.

Step 4. With both hands, massage from your eyebrows, past the top of your ears, to the back of your neck, seven times.

Step 5. Massage from the midpoint of your eyebrows up to your hairline, 72 times. When you feel saliva filling up in your mouth during your massage, swallow it, and bring your mind to your dantian.

3. Night Vision Training

Step 1. Recite the Grand Golden Light mantra, "Dao dao jin guang tong lian tian, yu zhou wan wu jie wei wo (道道金光通連天，宇宙萬物皆爲我)." Recite 7 times. This is a Daoist mantra for developing your intention, concentration, and your light-qi.

Step 2. Practice during the night under very low light. Distinguish the shapes and locations of surrounding objects. Then turn off the lights and try to locate the objects.

3. Sun and Moon Focusing Training (日月明目功)

Step 1. Early in the morning just before the sun rises, stand facing east and wait for the sun to rise. Keep your eyes closed until you feel the warmth of the sun's rays on your eyelids. With your eyes closed, circle your eyeballs 36 times in each direction.

Step 2. Open your eyes and look at the red sun for 2-3 minutes. Note: don't look at the sun when it has risen too high above the horizon and has changed to a golden color.

Step 3. Close your eyes and again circle your eyeballs 36 times in each direction.

Step 4. At night, look at the moon without blinking. Start with a few minutes, to 10 minutes, to 30 minutes, or more. When there is no moon, light a piece of incense and focus on the burning incense.

4. Counting Training (靈目功)

Step 1. Count inanimate objects, such as the bricks on a wall, tiles on a roof, as fast as you can.

Step 2. Count live animals such as fish or birds. Start counting them when they are still. Then make them swim or fly and count them again as fast as you can.

5. Ear Sensitivity Training (順耳功)

Step 1. Warm up your palms by rubbing them together. Gently press your palms over your ears. Place your index fingers over your middle fingers. Tap your index fingers down on the back of your head, 24 times. You will hear the "tong, tong..." sound. This exercise can improve your hearing, regulate the central nervous system, and eliminate some minor headaches.

Step 2. Sit in a quiet place. Calm your mind and listen to the different low sounds around you to develop the sensitivity of your hearing.

Step 3. String two ancient coins with a hole in the middle (or two washers) and suspend them from the ceiling. Swing the coins like a pendulum and listen to the sound they make as they cut through the air. When you can hear the pendulum sound easily, start listening to the sound of the wind under various conditions, both light and heavy.

6.7. Emitting Neijin—Internal Strength Releasing Training

Emitting Internal Strength is a term which describes the delivery of force from less visible parts of the body. Unlike external muscular force which when being applied, has obvious muscular contraction to exert the force. Internal strength is more subtle during its set up. The force is generated from all over the body, including the internal organs. It is often undetectable until the release of the force. Therefore, it was referred to as Neijin (內勁), Internal Strength. Neijin is further distinguished into Gangjin (剛勁) and Roujin (柔勁). Gangjin refers to the focused, powerful, and rapid release of force. Roujin refers to the steady, continuous, and gradual release of force. There are many terms and training methods used to develop Neijin.

Zhaojin (找勁) — Looking for Jin: Zhaojin is an attempt to understand yourself and what your capabilities are. When you move, pay attention to the mechanics of your body, locate the best alignment for releasing force, know where your body is in an advantageous or disadvantageous position. Feel the flexible joint connections, yet integrated with the other joints in your body. Feel the connections from your feet to your waist and to your hands. Learn to emit power from the whole body.

Jiejin (接勁) — Intercepting and Connecting Jin: Jiejin is the ability to intercept and neutralize your opponent's jin. Then utilize his jin against him and add on to your jin for an even more devastating counterattack. The ability to reestablish your jin, when it has been disconnected as you engage with your opponent, is also referred to as Jiejin. Jiejin is the prerequisite for being able to have Listening Jin and Utilizing Jin.

Tingjin (聽勁) — Listening Jin: Through the engagement and contact with your opponent, you decipher the strength of his force, direction, and angle on you, which provides you with the information you need to apply a successful offense.

Yongjin (用勁) — Utilizing Jin: Yongjin stresses four key words. They are, yin (引) — luring, hua (化) — neutralizing, na (拿) — controlling, and fa (發) — emitting. Yin is to lead your opponent into an advantageous position for you and awkward position for him, making him unable to effectively apply his offensive technique or defend himself. Hua is to neutralize his attack and render it ineffective. Na is to control the direction of his jin and prevent him from being able to apply his jin on you. Fa is to emit your jin towards his weak points and where he can easily be taken off balance to defeat him. Successful Yongjin is the ability to lead, neutralize, control, and emit jin during combat.

As it is with all fields of study, it is important to have a qualified teacher to guide you in the proper training approaches. The opportunity to observe and study from an experienced teacher can't be replaced with any book. Their experiences and abilities can enlighten and speed up your progress. In jin training, words and photos can't express fully the intricacies of jin. In this section, we can only point out some key points in jin training.

1. Cunjin (寸勁) — Inch Jin and Anjin (暗勁) — Hidden Jin Training

Cunjin implies emitting jin into your opponent from a very close range. Typically, it is emitted from within an inch of your opponent's body, thereby the term Cunjin. Cunjin is also referred to as toujin (透勁) — penetraing jin because the power can penetrate into the organs from a strike on the surface of the body. A powerful cunjin applied to the chest can be felt on the back of the body.

Cunjin is a powerful destructive force that can be devastating to the opponent's internal organs. Because a sudden delivery of power is applied to an opponent from a close range, it is very hard for an opponent to defend. Both the Internal and External Styles of Wushu include cunjin. Internal Styles especially focus on this training. Due to the shocking vibration to the internal organs, people being hit with cunjin may become confused, may throw up food and blood, and lose the will to continue fighting. Extreme care should be used when training with a partner, and cunjin ability should not be used unless your are under an extreme threat from an attacker.

The correct integration of yi (意) — intent, qi (氣) — breathing and energy, shen (神) — vitality of spirit, and li (力) — physical strength must be coordinated to achieve the most powerful effect. When your hands or feet are almost touching your attacker, a sudden vibratory power is emitted to one small area on your attacker's body.

The effect of anjin is similar to cunjin. Anjin implies that jin is emitted when you are already in contact with your opponent. Anjin is considered roujin (柔勁), implying that it is so subtle that it is nearly impossible to detect. A practitioner that has a high level of anjin ability can emit jin anytime and at any point of contact. They can reach the point where the posture becomes insignificant to issuing power and only the yi is focused. At this point, opponents are unable to figure out whether or not you have jin or not. Thereby, the saying, "Have force or no force, have intention or no intention; it's from no intention that the true intention is derived (拳無拳，意無意，無意之中是眞意).

Cunjin and anjin training requires long term dedicated effort. Below are descriptions of some training methods to assist in your training:

Step 1. Stand in front of a sandbag. The distance between your body and the bag is a little shorter than the length of your arm from your shoulder to your wrist. Place one of your palms about one inch from the bag with your arm bent. When you exhale, turn your waist and straighten your arm rapidly as you thrust your palm against the sandbag. Practice 100 or more times with each palm, then practice 100 or more times with each fist.

Step 2. Stand in front of a sandbag. Place one of your palms on the bag with your arm bent. When you exhale, turn your waist and straighten your arm as you send a vibratory shock through the sandbag. Practice 100 or more times with each palm, then practice 100 or more times with each fist.

Step 3. Have a partner hold a solid object such as a board in front of them with their arms straight. Place one of your fists about one inch from the board or on the board. Inhale bring your mind to your dantian. Hold your breath slightly and lead your qi from your dantian up to your shanzhong point (midpoint between the nipples), to your armpit, along the lower part of your arm. When you exhale, send your qi to your fist, let out a "Ha" sound, turn your waist, and straighten your arm, to send your partner backward. Practice with each arm, then alternate with your partner.

Step 4. When you are able to send one person back easily, have another one push on the back of the person holding the board. When you are able to send both people backward easily, have more and more people line up and support the person's back in front of them.

2. Tanpaojin (彈爆勁) — Spring Explosive JinTraining

This type of jin requires that you have abundant Internal Strength. It is an emission of power from the whole body. In an instant, all the corresponding muscle and qi are activated to release the power. The whole body becomes like a coiled spring that has just been released. An opponent is bounced far away on contact and it is almost like they have been hit by a shock wave.

The power is achieved by the rapid contraction and releasing of the muscles compounded with the relaxed and sudden release of the heightened vitality of spirit. During combat, the mind and body must be in a relaxed and alert state. In a relaxed state, power is conserved and being gathered, and ready for action. This is referred to as song (鬆). During the moment of releasing power, the body tightens and the vitality of spirit is elevated and expressed. This is referred to as jin (緊). Jin (緊) which means tightening is not to be confused with jin (勁) which means an expression of power.

Once the power is released, the mind and body immediately return to a song state. If your body is immediately put into tension as you engage with your opponent, your vitality of spirit will also be put into tension, which will prevent you from moving agilely and your delivery of power will be hindered.

The root of Tanpaojin is at the feet, directed by the waist, past the shoulders, and expressed through the hands. Tanpaojin can have penetrating power like Cunjin. It can also be expressed like a forceful shock making the opponent lose balance and knocking the opponent to the ground.

Step 1. Standing Training: Stand in a high ready stance with about 70% of the weight on the back leg and 30% on the front leg. Keep the back foot solid on the ground and slightly shift the weight off the front heel. Feel the opposing force between the hips and the knees. Raise your arms up as though you were embracing a tree, with your palms facing in and your arms about shoulder level. Feel the expanding, yet embracing inward force of the arms. Stand in this posture for 10 minutes or more, and gradually increase to 60 minutes to develop more internal energy.

Step 2. Emitting Power Forward: Stand like in the Standing Training, gently hold your hands in loose fists by coiling your pinkie, fourth, and middle fingers towards your palm, and making a ring shape with your index finger and thumb. Visualize that your elbows to your hands are like two nails. The rest of your body is like a giant hammer.

With a sudden push off the back leg, shift from a 70% back weight distribution to a 70% front weight distribution. As your weight shifts forward, the *giant hammer* hits the two *nails* and sends them rapidly forward. As your forearm moves forward, rotate your palms to face down and release the power outward through your fingers. At the point of power release, the fingers are sprung straight. Do 20 to 100 times each session.

Notes:

A. Before you release the power, the body is relaxed, not tense. As the fingers straighten, halt the hands and pull back as though you were touching a hot plate.

B. At the instant of power release, the light weighted front heel thrusts down to the ground, as you push forward with the back leg. As the power moves up your legs to your arms, immediately shift your weight back to the starting position with 70% of your weight on the back leg and slightly shift the weight off the front heel.

C. At the instant of power release, gently lift up your head and have a forward feeling with your forehead.

D. When the hands have extended completely, the arms should have a sideways expanding feeling, as though you were breaking a rope that was binding your arms together tightly.

E. Your intention is to release your power as far as you can.

F. After the power has been released, allow the recoil to make your body bounce slightly, like a spring after it has released its potential power.

Step 3. Emitting Power Downward: Stand like in the Standing Training. Visualize that there is a pulley with one end of the rope supporting a heavy weight and the other end tied to a short rod. Your hands are holding the rod. With a sudden push off the front foot, shift your weight backward and squat down on the back leg. At the same time, change your hands to fists and pull the imaginary rod down to pull up the heavy weight on the other end. When you pull down, tug your chin towards your chest. As you complete the pull downward, push off your back foot and bounce back to the starting position. Do 20 to 100 times each session.

Step 4. Emitting Power Sideways: Hold your arms up as if your were embracing a huge ball, with your arms at shoulder level, hands facing in, and middle fingers pointing at each other. Visualize that there is a dam of water pushing against your right arm. As water is suddenly released, turn your body to your left. Imagine that your right arm is being pushed by the powerful force of the water, and the ball between your arms is being compressed. As your left arm is being pushed to your left, rotate your left hand to face down and release the power from your left arm to your left. Do 20 to 100 times each session.

Practice releasing sideways power with both arms, while in a high Horse Stance, and with left and right foot forward stances.

Step 5. Emitting Power to Opposite Directions: Stand like in the Standing Training. Hold your hands in loose fists with your arms bent. Keep your lead fist higher than your back fist. From a relaxed state, all of a sudden, punch forward with both fists, while rapidly rounding and leaning your back towards your rear. This will create an explosive power forward with your hands and backward with your back. Train in a stationary stance, as well as, in moving stances. Do each side both stationary and moving, 20 to 100 times each session.

Stand as above. Thrust your elbows to either side of your body simultaneously. Practice with one leg forward then the other. Do each side 20 to 100 times each session.

Step 6. Emitting Touch and Releasing Power: This type of power requires a high level of integration of the vitality of spirit, intention, and physical movement. It is a high level power release that is not restricted by any posture, time, or location. This ability typically requires that the practitioner has already attained the Iron Shirt or Golden Bell ability. A strong physical body combined with the ability to instinctively tighten the body on contact with an opponent's body or weapon, can bounce the opponent or his weapon away.

This type of power release must be trained regularly with focused intention and a highly charged vitality of spirit, until it becomes a natural reflex. Usually the arms are the easiest to train for this ability. An arm conditioning exercise is a good way to start this training. When you do arm conditioning, as your arm comes into contact with your partner's arm, tighten at the point of contact to bounce his arm away. You can also have your partner kick towards your chest with the bottom of his foot. As his foot comes into contact with your chest, tighten your chest and push forward slightly to bounce him away. You can come up with your own training regiment, but train carefully. Be sensible about how hard you train. Train regularly, gradually increase the force, and use common sense to prevent injuries to yourself or your training partner.

Over ninety years ago, Shou-Yu Liang's grandfather, Liang Zhixiang, was forcefully blind sided on his back by an eight men carriage carrying a high position government official in the narrow Chongqing City street. He instinctively tightened his body to the ground and protected himself from the impact. His reaction knocked the eight men carriage to the ground, throwing the official out of the carriage. Liang Zhixiang knew he was in trouble. He had to flee and hide for several days before venturing out in the city. The power and ability he expressed was a type of touch and release of power, he developed with his Dapeng Qigong and years of power training.

Step 7. Closing Exercise: After training, it is always advisable to do a closing exercise. This is especially important in exercises that express power, spirit, and intention. After each session of training, bring your mind back to your dantian. It is said that when your spirit of vitality returns to your body, your energy will automatically return also. You will feel physically and mentally at ease with a proper closing.

Inhale, raise your arms over your head, breath deep down to your dantian (bring your mind to your dantian) and visualize the universe's energy is entering your dantian. When you exhale, lower your hands to your dantian and keep your mind at your dantian, and store qi into your dantian. Hold this position for one minute or more. Then warm up your hands and massage your face, sides of your nose, ears, neck, around your eyes, your dantian, kidney area, your arms, etc. for a few minutes.

6.8. Light Body and Agility Training (輕功)

Qinggong (輕功), or Qingshenfa (輕身法) is an agility training to make the body move fast like the wind and light as a feather. Ancient great Wushu masters all had amazing Qinggong. High level qigong is a dying art because it requires decades of extremely hard training. We will introduce both the Qigong and the physical training that are used to develop Qinggong abilities. Many of the training methods are dangerous and require a high level of concentration and focus. Train with care, and use common sense and good judgment. Focus on one or two exercises at a time, start slowly and gradually increase your training intensity.

There are many types of training methods from the past. Some were actual training methods and some were legendary training methods which produced legendary abilities. Some of the training is as common as walking on a balance beam, bamboo sticks, ropes, etc., while at the highest levels the training becomes nearly magical. Legend has it, that some practitioners were able to create enough buoyancy from their dantian qi to be able to walk on the rising smoke and heat of candles or incense. Legend also has it, that practitioners of old were able to seemingly walk on top of water and walk on sand without leaving footprints.

Part 1: Internal Energy Development

1. Qigong

Step 1. Qi Permeating Technique (百會貫氣法): This is a Qigong method to fill your body with qi through your baihui point, and to purify your body of impurities. Please refer to the book, *Qigong Empowerment* for a description.

Step 2. Sink Qi to Your Dantian (沉氣丹田法): Use the same arm movements as in Qi Permeating Technique. When you bring the qi into your body, instead of going through your body, to your feet, and to the ground; keep it in your dantian. Do nine times. Then overlap your palms on your dantian for one minute.

Step 3. Spiral Dantian Qi (丹田螺旋上升功): Visualize that you are standing on top of water. Inhale, visualize the qi in your dantian is spiraling clockwise upward (looking up at the clock) and creating a spiraling energy field all around your body. As the qi spirals clockwise, it lifts the body off the ground to the sky. Exhale, visualize that the qi field begins to spiral counter-clockwise, and slowly lowers your body back to the ground. Do 9 to 18 times.

When you visualize elevating and lowering your body, also keep your mind on the word, “qing”, meaning very light, as in nearly weightless. When you visualize that your body is being elevated and lowered, it is gently supported at the feet and over your baihui with a floating cloud.

Step 4. Fill Qi from Your Yongquan Upward (湧泉貫氣上升功): Continue from Step 3. Visualize that you are standing on top of water. Inhale, absorb qi from the yongquan points on the bottom of your feet up to your baihui on top of your head. When the qi reaches your weizhong points (back of the knees), visualize that your body begins to float upward off the floor to the sky. At the same time, rotate your palms to face upward. When the qi reaches your baihui point, think of the word “qing” and visualize that you are floating weightlessly in the sky.

Exhale, lead the universe's qi into your baihui and your entire body. Turn your palms to face down and overlap them on your dantian. When the qi reaches your yongquan points, visualize that your body is lightly lowered down until your are standing on top of water. Do 9 to 18 times.

Step 5. Light Stepping Training (輕靈步法練習): Inhale and raise your left knee up with your toes pointing down. Use the muscles around your knee to extend your left foot forward and touch down with the ball of your foot. Exhale and shift your weight forward and raise your right heel off the floor.

When you step, visualize that you are walking weightlessly on a cloud, and think of the word "qing". Alternate feet as you walk forward 50 to 100 steps. Keep your body straight. When your foot touches down, keep it stable without wobbling around. Move your arms naturally and coordinated with your stepping.

Step 6. Sitting Meditation (坐功): This meditation is for nourishing your qi. To attain a high level qinggong ability, it is imperative that your dantian qi is full, your qi and blood are flowing smoothly, and with sufficient internal energy all over your body. We are listing a few qigong meditation techniques that you can practice. If you are not familiar with sitting meditation, please refer to the *Seven Keys for Sitting Meditation* in the book, *Qigong Empowerment.*

A. Sit in a comfortable crossed leg position or on a chair, overlap your palms over your dantian, and practice Reverse Abdominal Breathing. When you inhale, gently draw in your abdomen and hold up your anus area. When you exhale, relax your abdomen and anus. This type of breathing is one of the most simple and effective ways to train and increase your dantian qi.

B. Microcosmic Circulation (小周天功法): Please refer to the book, *Qigong Empowerment*, for a description.

C. Achieving Through Spiritual Flame (靈熱法): Please refer to the book, *Qigong Empowerment*, for a description.

D. Dantian Qi Ball Rotation (丹田內轉球功): Sit cross legged. Visualize that there is a qi ball spinning and rotating inside your abdomen at your dantian. Inhale and absorb the pure qi of the universe into your body from all points on your body. When you inhale, gently hold up your anus area, and gather qi to your dantian. Exhale and visualize the qi that you absorbed into your dantian is moving around the qi ball, making it spin and rotate more actively. Pay attention to the sensation of the qi and qi ball at your dantian. Repeat 18 to 36 times each session.

Part 2. External Training

The training methods introduced below are traditional methods used by practitioners. Today, the training is typically not taken to the same extent as in the past. The reason being, is that spending all your available time training to move as light as a feather, doesn't guarantee that you will be victorious when engaging with an opponent. Training time must also be allocated to other areas of your Kung Fu attainment training.

Be careful and use good judgment so as not to injure yourself. An injury could set your advancement back many months or even years.

1. Jumping Training

Step 1. Keep your feet together, legs straight, tighten your thighs, but don't lock your knees. Relax your arms with a slight bend and keep your eyes looking forward. Jump off the floor with a push of your feet. Keep your torso and legs straight as you jump up and land. Jump up immediately as you land, as though you have just landed on a trampoline. Do three sets of 50 jumps each session. Rest in between sets. Practice twice a day. When you can do three sets easily, gradually add weight to your ankles and do the jumps. You can also begin to practice jumping on sand to increase the difficulty.

Step 2. From a standing position, bend your knees and swing your arms to jump forward. When you jump, push off your feet, lift your knees up as high as you can, and jump as far as you can. Do three sets of 20 to 50 times. Rest in between sets.

Step 3. Suspend a pole on two ends at a height which you can jump over easily. Stand in front of the pole and jump over with both feet together. After you land, jump backwards over the pole. Do three sets of 20 to 50 times. Rest in between sets. Gradually elevate the height of the poles as you are able to jump higher.

Step 4. Find a stable flat elevated surface at a height which you can jump up to. Jump up and down, landing softly. When you land, catch your balance on the ball of your feet before jumping down or up again. Do three sets of 20 to 50 times. Rest in between sets.

Step 5. Dig a hole about 3 feet in diameter and one foot deep. Jump out of the hole, then from where you land, jump back into the hole. Do three sets of 20 to 50 jumps, in and out. Rest in between sets. Train twice a day. Every two weeks, deepen the hole by an inch and continue to jump in and out of the hole.

To increase the challenge, you may also wear a weighted jacket and tie weights to your ankles to increase the intensity of your workout. If you do, also increase the weight on the jacket and weight on your ankles every two weeks. Increase the weight by a few ounces at a time.

In the past, practitioners were known to be able to jump on and off the houses in Northern China. Some practitioners could even carry another person on their back and jump up to the roof of a house. The training involved is so demanding, that it would take nearly all day to do the training, leaving little or no time to do other types of training or have a life. Today's practitioners are no longer training to the extent that the practitioners of the past did.

2. Running Training

Practitioners of the past were also known to be able to jog and sprint easily for 30 kilometers with 40 pounds of weight or more. Their abilities were referred to as Flying on the Ground (陸地飛行術), and Flying Hair Legs (飛毛腿).

Step 1. Start jogging a few miles at a time to gradually build up your endurance. Sprint to build up your speed. You may also wear a weighted jacket and tie weights on your ankles to increase the intensity. When moving without weights, you will feel much lighter in your steps. Start with only a few pounds and gradually increase the weight over time.

Step 2. Instead of jogging and sprinting on level surfaces, run on uneven surfaces.

3. Precision Walking Training

Traditionally, there are many types of precision and Light Body walking training. You can choose one or more to practice.

A. Set up 5 to 9 posts in the ground. If you are setting up five posts, the pattern would like the 5 dots on a game dice. Keep the posts about one shoulder width apart from the center post. If you are setting up 9 posts, place eight posts in a circle and one in the middle of the circle. Place the posts in a circle about one shoulder width apart from each other. Bury the posts deep into the ground, so that they are stable. Practice walking on the posts everyday in different patterns.

From the previously described post training, replace the thick posts with thin bamboo sticks. Legend has it, that practitioners of the past were able to walk on bamboo sticks that had been sharpened. The authors have not personally witnessed anyone doing this.

B. Set up some clay roofing tiles on the ground, with the rounded surface facing up. Everyday walk gently on the tiles, as quickly and as lightly as possible, without breaking them.

C. Set up a huge round container of water and fill it with water. Stand on the edge of the container and walk on the edge with the balls of your feet. Walk every day. Every two weeks, remove one bowl of water from the container and continue walking daily. You can also increase the intensity of your training by wearing a weighted jacket.

D. Set up bricks in a circle or in a line about one foot apart from each other. Walk on the bricks everyday, as quickly and lightly as possible. Start with the bricks laying flat. When you are able to walk easily on the bricks, turn the bricks on their sides. Gradually, turn the bricks on their ends.

E. Find a large round wicker basket. Fill it with rocks. Practice walking on the edge of the basket. Every month remove a few rocks from the basket and continue your practice. Remove as many rocks as you can and still be able to walk on the edge of the basket without tipping it over.

4. Running Up the Wall Training

Firmly attach a large 10 to 12 foot long board, one end on a stable support and the other end on the ground. Start with about a 25 degree incline. Run up and down the incline. Every month increase the incline by an inch.

You can also prop the large board on a solid wall. Firmly stabilize the board on both ends. From a running start, run up the board. Start with a small incline and build it up to a steeper incline; eventually remove the board and run up the wall.

5. Other Training

Each and every style of Wushu has many unique Qinggong training methods. Below are some other training methods that are commonly used by practitioners.

A. Practice climbing up a wall with knives. Alternate piercing one knife at a time into the gaps between the bricks and climb up the wall with the assistance of your feet.

B. In the narrow gap between two walls, press your back on one wall and your feet on the other wall, and climb up the wall.

C. In the narrow gap between two walls, press one foot and one hand on each wall, and climb up the wall.

D. On the inside corner of a building with rough surfaces. Lean your back towards the corner and climb up the wall. Some special shoes may also be worn to do this training.

E. Run in a thick forest as fast as you can. Try not to contact the tree trunks or branches with your body. Jump over branches when they are in your way. As you run, practice defensive and offensive maneuvers.

F. Practice jumping into a shoulder roll. Start by jumping over an elevated staff like a fish jumping out of the water. When you land, roll and stand up quickly. Gradually begin to jump over a long table, windows, etc.

G. Grab a hold of a high bar and swing your body up over the bar. Hook your feet on the bar and suspend your body upside down until you are tired. Then pull your body up and grab a hold of the bar with your hands and lower your body.

H. Grab a hold of a thick rope and climb up and down the rope with your hands and feet. When you can do this easily, climb up and down with only your hands.

I. Run up a high fence, place your hands on the top of the fence and flip your body on top or over the fence.

點穴法

Chapter 7:

Cavity Press

Dianxue (點穴, Cavity Press), also known as Dim Mak, contains a thick layer of mystery. Martial arts practitioners and non-practitioners alike, are intrigued and curious about dianxue. In Chinese novels and movies, Wushu masters have been portrayed with lightning fast hands. With a strike on the appropriate vital point at the right time, they were able to immobilize their opponents, freeze, or kill them on the spot. Dianxue is an amazing and effective technique in martial arts, however, many novels and movies have over exaggerated it. Dianxue is the ingenious combination of Wushu, Qigong, and Traditional Chinese Medicine (TCM). The person that has the dianxue applied on them may lose their fighting ability, lose their mobility, get seriously injured, pass out, or even die. Dianxue is also used in healing and is a valuable method used in TCM and by Qigong healers for treating illnesses.

In a fighting application, with focused power and speed, a strike with the fingers, palm, fist, elbow, knee, or toes, to the proper points on the body can restrict and cause qi, as well as, blood to scatter in the opponent's energy pathways. This can cause a restriction and/or loss of qi and blood to the area being struck which can result in numbness, temporary paralysis, dizziness, passing out, or even death. Many of these points are located on the weak or sensitive spots of the body, and/or are located near sensitive nerve centers. The sensitivity of these locations can be explained with today's scientific reasoning and medical understanding. However, there are many other vital points that have not been explained by Traditional Western Medical theories. One of the wishes of the authors is to promote further research by presenting some of the information that they have.

7.1. The Cavity Press Concept

The human body is a complex network of interrelated systems. The head, the limbs, and the internal organs are all connected and supported by muscles, sinews, and tendons. They are nourished by the irrigation pathways we call blood vessels. According to TCM, blood and qi are interrelated. In fact, the term qixue (氣血), meaning qi-blood is often used together to refer to the nutrient and energy supply in the body. If the muscles or tendons were to break or be restricted, the body would lose mobility to the affected areas. If the blood supply is cut off, the body would eventually lose sensation to the affected area. From the experiences of the Wushu practitioners of old, many areas were discovered in the body that could be struck or grabbed to put an opponent in submission. Many of these points correspond to the standard acupuncture points and some are specific points used in Wushu dianxue.

According to TCM, there are twelve energy channels that correspond to the organs in the body. They are:

1. Hand Maximum Yin Lung Channel
2. Hand Yang Equilibrium Large Intestine Channel
3. Foot Yang Equilibrium Stomach Channel
4. Foot Maximum Yin Spleen Channel
5. Hand Minimum Yin Heart Channel
6. Hand Maximum Yang Small Intestine Channel
7. Foot Maximum Yang Urinary Bladder Channel
8. Foot Minimum Yin Kidney Channel
9. Hand Equilibrium Yin Pericardium Channel
10. Hand Minimum Yang Triple Burner Channel

11. Foot Minimum Yang Gall Bladder Channel
12. Foot Equilibrium Yin Liver Channel.

There are also eight extraordinary vessels. They are:

1. Governing Vessel
2. Conception Vessel
3. Thrusting Vessel
4. Girdle Vessel
5. Yang-Activation Vessel
6. Yin-Activation Vessel
7. Yang-Maintenance Vessel
8. Yin Maintenance Vessel.

The twelve channels connect to their respective organs and have accessible acupuncture points on the surface of the body. The eight extraordinary vessels don't pertain to any particular organs, but they supplement the twelve channels. Two of the eight extraordinary vessels have accessible acupuncture points of their own. They are the Governing Vessel and the Conception Vessel. These energy pathways are the connectors between the organs and the limbs, they link the upper and lower body, and are the regulator and the balancer for the entire body; making the human body an integrated whole.

Within the twelve channels and eight vessels, only fourteen of them have accessible acupuncture points on the surface of the body. These fourteen energy pathways are often lumped together, and are referred to as the Fourteen Meridians. They include all twelve channels, plus the Governing Vessel and the Conception Vessel.

The acupuncture points or qi cavities are locations on the surface of the skin which connect to the channels or vessels. These locations either have a great accumulation of qi, or are points for draining or nourishing qi, or are important passages for the energy pathways. Since these points connect with the energy pathways which in turn connect directly or indirectly to the organs, they can affect the flow of qi through and from the organs. Through the stimulation of these points, the energy system in a person's body can be affected either positively or negatively. The main function of the energy pathways is to conduct the regular physiological activities of the body when it is functioning in a normal state. They also systematically reflect symptoms of disease when the body is ill.

In the earliest TCM written record, the *Yellow Emperor's Internal Classics* (黃帝內經), there are 365 acupuncture points, corresponding to the number of days in a year. The points used in dianxue are mostly derived from these

365 points. Generally, there are 108 points used for martial arts applications. When applied properly, 36 of the 108 points are considered major points that can cause death when properly applied; and 72 of them are considered minor points that can cause serious injuries.

The qi flow pattern in the channels follows a set pattern similar to the sun rising at dawn and setting in the evening. It is also similar to the changing of the seasons from one to the next in a cyclic pattern. If we were to use Greenwich Mean Time (GMT) as a reference, the sun rises at a different GMT in different regions of the world. This is like the *apex* of the qi flow in the body. In a 24 hour day, the apex of the qi, flows from one channel to the next in a specific cyclic pattern. This cyclic pattern assists in transporting energy and nutrients all over the body, as well as, regulating and integrating all the systems of the body. Whenever the apex of the qi flow reaches a specific channel, the points on that channel will subsequently be *opened.*

In ancient China, the day was divided into 12 time units, each unit consisted of two hours. At each time unit, the apex of the qi flows from one channel to the next. For example, from about 7:00-9:00 A.M., the apex of the qi flows into the Stomach Channel. The points on the channel gradually open starting with the first point moving toward the last point on the channel. The points that are opened are referred to as *shixue* (實穴), meaning genuine point. The points that are closed are referred to as *kongxue* (空穴), meaning empty point. When the apex of qi flow is in the Stomach Channel, the points on the other 11 channels are considered empty points, only the points on the Stomach Channel are considered genuine points or opened points.

If a point on the apex channel is a shixue, and that point is one of the 36 major points or one of the 72 minor points, striking that point would cause a major restriction of the energy. This would cause the apex of the qi flow to come to an abrupt pause or stop, sending a ripple effect back to all the other channels. This could result in a numbing and/or paralysis of the entire body or sections of the body. Therefore, striking these points at the right time would cause more severe damage than at other times. When the point is not a shixue point it will still cause injury when struck with enough force, although the injury would not be as severe as if it were a shixue point.

The basic framework of the human body's skeletal system consists of 200 distinct bones. The bones and joints collectively are known as a skeleton. The bones are attached together by skeletal muscle tissue. Skeletal muscle is also known as voluntary muscle which is consciously controlled by our will. Muscles move parts of our body through contractions. The attachment of the muscles on the skeleton generally have at least two points. One point is referred to as the origin, where the body part is less moveable. The other point is the insertion point, where the muscles are put into motion through their contractions.

From a dianxue point of view, if the circulation of qi and blood is restricted at the origin and/or the insertion points of the muscle attachment, then the mobility of the muscle would be impaired. Many of these areas are very sensitive to pain. When struck or grabbed with sufficient force, the whole body could be debilitated. Generally, the accessible muscle origins are close to the surface of the body and right over the attached bones. They include the back of the hands and feet, the wrists, ankles, elbows, knees, shoulders, shoulder blades, armpits, face, neck, chest, back, and waist.

Many skeletal muscles work in pairs. One muscle is used to move the body in one direction and the other muscle is used to move the body in the other direction. The active muscle of the pair is referred to as the prime mover, the other muscle is referred to as the antagonist. When the prime mover contracts, the antagonist muscle must relax to achieve smooth, coordinated movement. From a dianxue point of view, if the antagonist muscle were forced to contract, then the prime mover would be unable to function properly.

When certain vital areas of the body are struck with enough force, a physiological reaction occurs and can cause the body to over react. In some cases, excessive muscle would be forced to contract and would reduce the diameter of the blood vessels, which would increase the blood pressure of the person being struck. If the blood pressure is not lowered quickly, damage would occur. In other cases, the body would be forced to release excess chemicals as the local changes in the tissue occur. Some of these chemicals could increase the diameter of the blood vessels which would decrease the blood pressure of the person being struck. If the blood pressure were to drop too quickly, it could cause the person to pass out. And, if the blood pressure is not restored quickly, damage will occur. Many of the effects of dianxue are not yet explainable. Some effects can be explained with modern medical and scientific reasoning, but there are still many unexplainable areas that need further research to understand how and why it works.

Dianxue ability comes only with years of dedicated hard work and training. A practitioner needs to train their internal energy, and have an abundance of qi to make dianxue work. Physical conditioning is also required to allow the internal strength to radiate through your arms and fingers (or toes and legs) to your opponent. In general, there are four areas a practitioner must work on intensively to apply dianxue effectively.

First, a practitioner must be totally familiar with the locations of the acupuncture points. One must be able to locate these points with their eyes closed. One must also be familiar with the pattern, the direction, and apex time of energy flow in the body. Even with a very powerful strike, if the timing and location of the strike is not correct, the dianxue will not be as effective. Traditionally, the training included making a wooden man with points marked on it. Practitioners practiced striking the points during the day and at night until they were able to hit the points at will. They would memorize which points belonged to which channel and organ, what technique and herb to use, what the signs are when dianxue is applied properly, and how to revive a person.

Secondly, a practitioner must be able to strike with enough jin backed with internal energy. A practitioner must train two or three sessions a day leading qi from their dantian to the fingers or other striking surface. During each session, a practitioner must also strike each point hundreds of times. After training, the striking surface must be massaged with appropriate herbal liniments. Common sense is essential during training to prevent injuries because injuries can set a practitioner's training back significantly.

Thirdly, a practitioner must also train their eyes. Sharp eyes are a prerequisite of dianxue (眼力爲點穴法之魁). Finally, a practitioner must be able to apply the appropriate technique to the point of focus because different points require different striking methods.

Just as there are many different styles of Wushu, there are also many styles of dianxue training. Each style may have its own striking techniques and striking points to focus on. Some styles are similar. Some styles use different names for the same point. Some also use the same name, but refer to different points. Some styles follow the acupuncture convention. Some styles follow the regional preference to name the points.

There are many similarities in the timing and points used in different styles. There are also many differences between styles in terms of the timing and points used. These are due to differences in their approaches, the techniques used, the power required, and the understanding of the qi flow. These differences also exist in TCM where one doctor may use a different approach and technique to treat a similar illness. To the unfamiliar eye, they may seem contradictory. However, if we look deeper into their approaches, they are all valid.

Dianxue techniques in the past have been very secretive. They were only taught verbally, one on one, from the master to the most virtuous disciple. In this chapter, we will introduce many non-vital and vital dianxue points. We have refrained from introducing the specific methods used in striking the vital points. The information we have presented in this chapter is the essence passed down from the ancestors of Wushu.

The timing of vital point strikes is very involved. Each time unit is further divided into four upper, four middle, and four lower periods. The apex time on a specific person is also affected by the location, sleeping habit, emotional state, biological time, etc. The authors' purpose of introducing dianxue, is to make people aware of the profound and extensive nature of Wushu, as well as, the intricate and complex nature of the human body. The authors also hope to clarify some of the dianxue concepts; hoping that practitioners will continue to do research into these amazing dianxue methods; and will not use these methods to maliciously hurt others; and will use them only for self-defense during a life or death situation. Keep in mind that the purpose of learning Wushu is to strengthen the body, use it for self-defense when necessary, and to discipline ourselves.

In this chapter, we will use the customary terms to describe the location of the points as much as possible. Many of the descriptions require that the reader be familiar with the medical terms for the different parts of the body. It can be confusing for individuals that are not familiar with medical terms. Therefore, we have simplified the descriptions with terms that are commonly used. The simplified descriptions, however, will only describe the approximate location of the point. In locating the points for acupuncture needle insertion, please refer to a detailed description of the point locations in an acupuncture reference book.

There are some terms we have used in locating the points that you will need to be familiar with to understand the description of the locations. Dorsal refers to the back of the body. Ventral refers to the front of the body. Medial refers to the part of the body that is near the centerline of the body. Lateral refers to the part of the body that is the furthest away from the centerline of the body. A cun is a unit of measure based on the relative size of an individual. There are three commonly used methods for locating points on the body: 1. Use the specified cun units that have been assigned to the different parts of the body. Then divide the specific parts of the body into the units assigned to locate the point. 2. Use the distance between the crease of the middle joint of the middle finger, when the tips of the middle finger and the thumb are touching, as one cun. 3. Use common body points as a reference to locate the points. Refer to acupuncture books or study from a qualified teacher. In our future Qigong book, we will also present the points in more detail.

7.2. Numbing Points (麻筋，麻穴)

1. Twenty-Four Numbing and Controlling Points (二十四麻穴)

Point 1: On the back of the hand between the second and the third metacarpal bones. Metacarpals are bones in the palm which connect to the finger bones. The second metacarpal bone connects to the index finger, and the third metacarpal bone connects to the middle finger.

Point 2: On the back of the hand between the third and the fourth metacarpal bones.

Point 3: On the back of the hand between the fourth and the fifth metacarpal bones.

Point 4: The Hegu (合谷) point is on the midpoint between the first and the second metacarpal bones.

Point 5: The Quchi (曲池) point is at the lateral side of the elbow crease.

Point 6: The Shousali (手三里) point is on the front lateral side of the forearm, 2 cun below the elbow crease. There are 12 -1/2 cun between the crease of the elbow and the wrist.

Point 7: The tendon at the elbow.

Point 8: The Jianjing (肩井) point is located at the highest point of the shoulder.

Point 9: The Fengwei (鳳尾) point is right under the shoulder blade.

Point 10: The Jianfeng (肩峰) point is at the junction between the shoulder blade, clavicle, and humerus.

Point 11: The tendon at the armpit.

Point 12: The Adam's Apple.

Point 13: The throat.

Point 14: The sternocleidomastoid muscle that connects from behind the ears to the sternum.

Point 15: The Yaoyan (腰眼) point, also known as the laughing point (笑腰穴), is located on either side of the waist below the last rib. This is considered a vital point. Serious injury can result when applied with excessive force.

Point 16: The muscles on the inner thighs.

Point 17: The Xuehai (血海) point is on the inner thigh above the knee. This point can be located by placing the palm on the opponent's kneecap with the fingers pointing up. Where the thumb touches is the xuehai point.

Point 18: The Weizhong (委中) point is on middle of the back of the knee.

Point 19: The tendons on either side of the knee.

Point 20: The Chengshan (承山) point is on the back of the leg, on the lower part of the gastrocnemius muscle.

Point 21: The Zuwan (足腕) point is on the Achilles tendon behind the ankle.

Point 22: The Jiexi (解谿) point is on the front of the leg and at the junction between the tibia and foot bones.

Point 23: The Yongquan (湧泉) point is on the bottom of the foot where there is an indentation between the second and third metatarsal bones of the foot. If this point is applied at the apex of its energy flow with sufficient force, it could be life threatening.

Point 24: The Taichong (太衝) point is on top of the foot between the first and second metatarsal bones.

7.3. Knockout Points (閉氣，致暈穴)

Knockout points include points that can cause oxygen deprivation and points that cause so much pain to the body that the body passes out to save itself from the shock. The brain has the ability to "short circuit" itself by passing out when external stimuli is too great. The act of passing out relaxes the body and stops the involuntary reaction which causes damage to the body. When the flow of blood throughout the body suddenly decreases, the body is in a state of shock due to a lack of oxygen to the brain. Applying pressure to the arteries to the brain, will reduce the blood supply and cause the brain to pass out. Applying pressure to the breathing system, will cause the oxygen supply to diminish and will also cause the brain to pass out. The points listed in this section can cause serious injury or death when being applied to another person. Don't apply these techniques unless you are in grave danger. By knowing these vital areas, you can also protect these areas from your opponent's attack.

1. Nine Oxygen Deprivation Knockout Methods from the Wudang System (武當閉氣法)

Method 1: Squeeze the sides of your attacker's neck with your arms, from the side of your opponent, to stop the blood supply from the carotid artery to the brain.

Method 2: Squeeze your attacker's throat with your hands from the back to seal the breathing passageway to the lungs.

Method 3: Squeeze your attacker's larynx with your thumb and index finger from the front, pressing on the Adam's Apple with the knuckle of your middle finger to seal the breathing passageway to the lungs.

Method 4: Squeeze the side of your attacker's neck and throat simultaneously from the back to stop the blood supply to the brain and oxygen supply to the lungs.

Method 5: Chop to the side of your attacker's neck to stop the blood supply to the brain.

Method 6: Control your attacker's arm to his back and strike with your palm to the fengwei (鳳尾) point on the bottom of the shoulder blade. With enough force, this will shock your attacker's lungs and cause your opponent to spit up blood and pass out.

Method 7: Strike the side and bottom of your attacker's rib cage to shock your opponent's lungs.

Method 8: Strike with your fist to your attacker's solar plexus or press into the solar plexus to prevent your attacker from breathing.

Method 9: Squeeze your attacker's dantian to prevent your attacker from breathing.

2. Eleven Vital Knockout Points (致暈十一穴)

Point 1: The Naohu (腦戶) point is on the back of the head, at the protrusion and base of the occipital bone.

Point 2: The Xinmen (囟門) point is on the centerline on the top of the head, 3 cun in front of the baihui. It is at the junction between the skull bones on the top of the head, also called the fontanelle. There are 12 cun from the hairline on the forehead to the hairline on the back of the head. The baihui point is located at the intersection of the centerline of the head and the line connecting the tip of the ears.

Point 3: The Shangxing (上星，神堂) point is on the centerline on the top of the head, 1 cun above the hairline.

Point 4: The Qianding (前頂) point is on the centerline on the top of the head, 1-1/2 cun in front of the baihui.

Point 5: The Houding (後頂) point is on the centerline on the top of the head, 1-1/2 cun behind the baihui.

Point 6: The Fengfu (風府，天星) point is on the back of the head, on the indentation under the protrusion and the base of the occipital bone.

Point 7: The Touwei (頭維) point is on the corner of the forehead, 1/2 cun above the hairline.

Point 8: The Erhou (耳後) point is on the back of the ear over the jugular vein.

Point 9: The Yamen (啞門) point is on the back of the neck between the first and second cervical vertebrae, a 1/2 cun above the hairline.

Point 10: The Tongtian (通天) point is on either side of the centerline on the top of the head, about 1 cun in front of the baihui and 1 cun to the side.

Point 11: The Yuzhen (玉枕) point is on the back of the head, and 1-1/3 cun on either side of the naohu point.

3. Emergency Reviving Method (緊急解穴術)

Sometimes in training or competitions, accidents occur. In cases when an individual has been knocked out, you can apply a basic technique to revive them. To heal a vital point injury, it is important to know how the qi flows in the body, tuina, acupuncture, herbal usage, and the specifics of relieving the vital point injury. The ability to use specific techniques in an emergency can prevent a more serious or prolonged disorder to the injured person. After the injured person is no longer in a critical state, follow up with medical treatment immediately and/or herbal remedies to speed up the recovery.

There are many specific reviving methods which can be used when vital points have been hit with a dianxue technique. We will introduce the specific vital point reviving methods in our future qigong book for interested readers. Here we will only introduce general treatment methods. In a situation when the injured person's qi flow has been interrupted, the traditional treatment method is described below:

Method 1. Keep the injured person calm. Sit them upright, but don't move them unnecessarily.

Method 2. Place your hand on the front of their chest and gently massage for about one minute in a clockwise direction. Then massage the back for another minute in a clockwise direction. Next, gently tap on the chest and back to get the qi circulating smoothly.

Method 3. Press on the injured person's renzhong (人中) point below the nose, and press the hegu (合谷) point between the metacarpal bones of the thumb and the index finger, to revive them.

Method 4. If the injured person has lost a lot of energy (very weak), or has lost bowel control, hold on to his baihui (百會) point, and press the huiyin (會陰) point with an object (such as his shoe), to prevent his original qi from depleting completely out of his body.

Method 5. Have a qualified healer or medical person take care of the injured person. Also use a herbal formula to speed up the recovery.

7.4. Common Striking Points Used in Fighting

1. Shaolin 18 Points (少林點打十八穴)

Point 1: The Shenmen (神門) point is on the ventral and medial side of the wrist.

Point 2: The Waiguan (外關) point is on the dorsal side of the forearm between the ulna and radius bones, and 2 cun above the wrist.

Point 3: The Shousanli (手三里) point is on the ventral and lateral side of the forearm, 2 cun below the elbow. There are 12-1/2 cun between the elbow and the wrist.

Point 4: The Zhizheng (支正) point is on the dorsal and medial side of the forearm, 5 cun above the wrist.

Point 5: The Laogong (勞宮) point is on the front of the palm between the third and the forth metacarpal bones. It is between the tip of the middle and forth fingers when the hand is held in a fist.

Point 6: The Daling (大陵) point is on the middle of the ventral side of the wrist.

Point 7: The Fengshi (風市) point is on the lateral side of the thigh, even with the tip of the middle finger when the arms are relaxed next to the thighs.

Point 8: The Huantiao (環跳) point is on the buttock, midway between the tip and lateral side of the femur and the tailbone.

Point 9: The Xiyan (膝眼) point is on the indentation on either side of the kneecap.

Point 10: The Sanyinjiao (三陰交) point is on the inside of the leg, 3 cun above the ankle.

Point 11: The Zusanli (足三里) point is on the lateral side of the leg, 3 cun below the "eye of the knee", about one finger width from the shin bone.

Point 12: The Weizhong (委中) point on the middle of the back of the knee.

Point 13: The Chengshan (承山) point is on the back of the leg, on the lower part of the gastrocnemius muscle.

Point 14: The Neihuaijian (内踝尖) point is on the inner side of the ankle bone.

Point 15: The Waihuaijian (外踝尖) point is on the outer side of the ankle bone.

Point 16: The Xuehai (血海) point is on the inner thigh above the knee. The point can be located by placing the palm on the opponent's kneecap with the fingers pointing up. Where the thumb touches is the xuehai point.

Point 17: The Heding (鶴頂) point is 1 cun above the middle of the kneecap.

Point 18: The Weigongshangxue (尾宮上穴) point is slightly above the weigong (tailbone).

7.5. Examples of Vital Points Used in Different Styles

There are numerous vital points used by different Wushu styles. We have listed a few here for your reference.

1. Emei Seventy-Two Points (峨嵋七十二穴)

Point 1: On the back of the hand between the second and third metacarpal bones. Causes numbness and pain when this area is grabbed or struck with a dianxue technique.

Point 2: On the back of the hand, between the knuckles of the second and the third metacarpal bones. Causes numbness and pain when this point is grabbed or struck with a dianxue technique.

Point 3: On the back of the hand between the third and fourth metacarpal bones. Causes numbness and pain when this point is grabbed or struck with a dianxue technique.

Point 4: On the back of the hand, between the knuckles of the third and fourth metacarpal bones. Causes numbness and pain when this point is grabbed or struck with a dianxue technique.

Point 5: On the back of the hand between the fourth and fifth metacarpal bones. Causes numbness and pain when this point is grabbed or struck with a dianxue technique.

Point 6: On the back of the hand, between the knuckles of the fourth and fifth metacarpal bones. Causes numbness and pain when this point is grabbed or struck with a dianxue technique.

Point 7: Hegu (合谷) point. Causes numbness, pain, and/or loss of consciousness when this point is grabbed or struck with a dianxue technique.

Point 8: Yangchi (陽池) point. Causes numbness and pain when this point is grabbed or struck with a dianxue technique.

Point 9: Yanggu (陽骨) point. Causes numbness when this point is grabbed.

Point 10: Wanmai (腕脈) point. Causes numbness and/or loss of consciousness when this point is grabbed.

Point 11: Neiguan (内關) point. Causes soreness, numbness, pain, and/or loss of consciousness when this point is grabbed.

Point 12: Shousanli (手三里) point. Causes soreness, pain, and/or loss of muscle control when this point is grabbed, or this area is hit or struck with a dianxue technique.

Point 13: Quchi (曲池) point. Causes soreness, pain, and/or a loss of muscle control when this point is grabbed or this area is hit.

Point 14: Tendon at the elbow (肘下麻穴). Causes numbness and/or loss of muscle control when this point is grabbed, or this area is hit or struck with a dianxue technique.

Point 15: Tendon at the inner side of the upper arm (大臂内側筋). Causes soreness and/or pain when this point is grabbed or this area is hit or struck with a dianxue technique.

Point 16: Binao (臂臑) point. Causes numbness and pain when this point is grabbed, or this area is hit or struck with a dianxue technique.

Point 17: Jianjing (肩井) point. Causes pain, a loss of consciousness, and/or paralysis when this point is grabbed or chopped with the edge of the palm.

Point 18: Jianfeng (肩峰) is the junction between the shoulder blade, clavicle, and the humerus. Causes the arm to lose mobility when this area is hit with the palm or fist.

Point 19: The tendon at the armpit. Causes extreme pain and/or loss of consciousness when this point is grabbed.

Point 20: Suoguwo (鎖骨窩) is at the indentation at the clavicle. Causes extreme pain when this point is struck or grabbed.

Point 21: Jianjin (肩筋), the trapezius muscle at the shoulder. Causes soreness, pain, numbness, and/or loss of consciousness when this point is grabbed or chopped with the edge of the palm.

Point 22: Jingdajin (頸大筋) is the sternocleidomastoid muscle at the sides of the neck. Causes numbness and/or loss of consciousness when this point is grabbed or chopped with the edge of the palm.

Point 23: Lower part of the throat. Causes oxygen deprivation when this area is grabbed, chopped with the edge of the palm, or struck with a dianxue technique.

Point 24: Middle part of the throat. Causes serious injury or internal bleeding when this area is grabbed, chopped with the edge of the palm or punched.

Point 25: Top part of the throat. Causes serious injury when this area is grabbed, poked, or hit with a Tiger's Mouth strike (the area between the thumb and the index finger).

Point 26: Taiyang (太陽) point. Causes a loss of consciousness when this area is hit or this point is struck with a dianxue technique.

Point 27: Erqiao (耳竅) point. Causes a loss of consciousness when this point grabbed or struck with a dianxue technique.

Point 28: Burong (不容) point. Causes a loss of consciousness when this point is grabbed or struck with a dianxue technique.

Point 29: Yasaixue (牙腮穴). Causes pain and/or loss of consciousness when this point is grabbed, hit with the palm or fist, or struck with a dianxue technique.

Point 30: Eyes. Causes serious injury when this point is struck with a dianxue technique.

Point 31: Shangen (山根) point. Causes serious injury and/or a loss of consciousness when this area is hit or chopped with the edge of the palm, or this point is struck with a dianxue technique.

Point 32: Renzhong (人中) point. Causes serious injury when this point is struck with a dianxue technique.

Point 33: Tiantu (天突) point. Causes serious injury and/or a loss of consciousness when this point is grabbed or struck with a dianxue technique.

Point 34: Jiangtai (將台) point. Causes serious injury or internal bleeding when this area is hit, chopped with the edge of the palm, or punched; or this point is struck with a dianxue technique.

Point 35: Xinkan (心坎) point. Causes serious injury, vomiting, and/or a loss of consciousness when this point is pressed with the palms, elbowed, or struck with a dianxue technique.

Point 36: Xuanji (璇璣) point. Causes serious injury when this point is pressed with the palms, elbowed, or struck with a dianxue technique.

Point 37: Qimen (期門) point. Causes serious injury when this point hit with the palm, fist, elbow, or struck with a dianxue technique.

Point 38: Zhangmen (章門) point. Causes serious injury when this point is grabbed; hit with the palm, fist, or elbow; or struck with a dianxue technique.

Point 39: Shuifen (水分) point. Causes pain, vomiting, and/or a loss of consciousness when this area is hit or struck with the knee, elbow, or heavy impact; or this point is struck with a dianxue technique.

Point 40: Xiawan (下脘) point. Causes pain, vomiting, and/or a loss of consciousness when this area is hit or struck with the knee, punched, or elbowed; or this point is struck with a dianxue technique.

Point 41: Belly Button. Cause pain, vomiting, and/or a loss of consciousness when this point is grabbed or struck with a dianxue technique.

Point 42: Chigushangxue (恥骨上穴). Causes pain and/or serious injury when this area is hit or kicked with the heel; or this point is struck with a dianxue technique.

Point 43: Groin. Causes pain, serious injury, and/or a loss of consciousness when this point is kicked with top of the foot or hit with a scooping palm attack.

Point 44: Baihai (白海) point. Causes pain and/or numbness when this point is hit with the palm or foot.

Point 45: Yamen (啞門) point. Causes serious injury and/or a loss of consciousness when this point is chopped with the edge of the palm, punched, or struck with a dianxue technique.

Point 46: Tianzhu (天柱) point. Causes serious injury when this area is hit or chopped with the edge of the palm; or this point is grabbed or struck with a dianxue technique.

Point 47: Fengyan (鳳眼) point. Causes serious injury when this area is hit, or this point is struck with a dianxue technique.

Point 48: Fenghuangrudong (鳳凰入洞) point. Causes serious injury when this area is hit or this point is struck with a dianxue technique.

Point 49: Fengwei (鳳尾) point. Causes serious injury when this area is hit or this point is struck with a dianxue technique.

Point 50: Beiliang (背樑) point. Causes serious injury and/or paralysis when this area is hit or elbowed; or this point is struck with a dianxue technique.

Point 51: Jizhong (脊中) point. Causes serious injury and/or paralysis when this area is hit, punched, elbowed, or hit with the palm.

Point 52: Xiaoyaoxue (笑腰穴) point. Causes serious injury and/or uncontrollable laughing when area hit; or this point is grabbed or struck with a dianxue technique.

Point 53: Jingcu (精促) point. Causes serious injury when this area is hit, elbowed; or this point is struck with a dianxue technique.

Point 54: Weilong (尾龍穴，督脈穴) point. Causes serious injury when this point is kicked, or struck with a dianxue technique.

Point 55: Huantiao (環跳) point. Causes soreness, numbness, and/or pain when this area is hit, elbowed, or kicked with the knee.

Point 56: Weizhong (委中) point. Causes soreness, numbness, pain, and/or a loss of leg control when this point is grabbed or kicked.

Point 57: Tendons on the back of the knee (委中旁大筋). Causes soreness, numbness, and/or pain when this area is grabbed.

Point 58: Chengshan (承山) point. Causes soreness, numbness, and/or pain when this area is grabbed or kicked.

Point 59: Zhubin (築賓) point. Causes soreness, numbness, and/or pain when this point is grabbed; or this area is hit or heel kicked.

Point 60: Gongsun (公孫) point. Causes soreness, numbness, and/or pain when this point is grabbed.

Point 61: Taiqi (太汒) point. Causes soreness, numbness, and/or pain when this point is grabbed.

Point 62: Zuqianwo (足前窩) point. Causes soreness, numbness, pain, and/or a loss of foot control when this point is grabbed or stepped on.

Point 63: Taichong (太衝) point. Causes soreness, numbness, pain, and/or a loss of consciousness when this point is grabbed or stepped on.

Point 64: Yongquan (湧泉) point. Causes serious injury when this point is grabbed or the area is hit.

Point 65: Baihui (百會) point. Causes serious injury, vomiting, and /or a loss of consciousness when this area is hit, punched, or struck with the palm.

Point 66: Yintang (印堂) point. Causes serious injury when this point is punched, elbowed, or struck with a dianxue technique.

Point 67: Xuehai (血海) point. Causes serious injury when this area is hit or punched; or this point is grabbed or struck with the palm.

Point 68: Quze (曲澤) point. Causes soreness, numbness, and/or pain when this point is grabbed.

Point 69: Shaohai (少海) point. Causes soreness, numbness, pain, and/or a loss of arm control when this point is grabbed or this area is hit.

Point 70: Rugen (乳根) point. Causes soreness, numbness, pain, and/or serious injury when this area is hit or punched, hit by the palm; or this point is struck with a dianxue technique.

Point 71: Zusanli (足三里) point. Causes the leg to be numb when this point is kicked.

Point 72: Sanyinjiao (三陰交) point. Causes the leg to be numb and injures the dantian qi when this point is kicked, grabbed, or struck with a dianxue technique.

2. Shushan Thirty-Six Points (蜀山三十六穴)

Baihui (百會), taiyang (太陽), yintang (印堂), naohu (腦户), yamen (啞門), zangxue (藏血), huagai (華蓋), juque (巨闕), qihai (氣海), zhishi (志室), changqiang (長強), guanyuan (關元), zhongji (中極), youmen (幽門), qixuenang (氣血囊), mingmen (命門), xinjingxue (心經穴), rugen (乳根), qimen (期門), yingchuang (膺窗), zhangmen (章門), lingtai (靈台), qihaishu (氣海俞), jiuwei (鳩尾), shangqu (商曲), shuifen (水分), huiyin (會陰), hekou (鶴口), yongquan (湧泉), zangxin (攢心), jianwo (肩窩), wanxin (腕心), shijie (食結), xuechi (穴池), suoyao (鎖腰), qishi (氣食).

3. Shaolin Striking Points as They Relate to the Twelve Time Units (少林寺按時辰打穴法)

11:00 P.M. to 1:00 A.M. — Zi (子) time, is at the renzhong (人中) point.

1:00 A.M. to 3:00 A.M. — Chou (丑) time, is at the tianting (天庭) point.

3:00 A.M. to 5:00 A.M. — Yin (寅) time, is at the qiaokong (喬空，鼻樑) point.

5:00 A.M. to 7:00 A.M. — Mao (卯) time, is at the yasai (牙腮) point.

7:00 A.M. to 9:00 A.M. — Chen (辰) time, is at the taiyang-taiyin (太陽太陰) point.

9:00 A.M. to 11:00 A.M. — Si (巳) time, is at the jiangtai (將台) point.

11:00 A.M. to 1:00 P.M. — Wu (午) time, is at the maiwan (脈腕) point.

1:00 P.M. to 3:00 P.M. — Wei (未) time, is at the qikan (七坎) point.

3:00 P.M. to 5:00 P.M. — Shen (申) time, is at the dantian (丹田) point.

5:00 P.M. to 7:00 P.M. — You (酉) time, is at the baihai (白海) point.

7:00 P.M. to 9:00 P.M. — Xu (戌) time, is at the donghudilou (洞壺滴漏) point.

9:00 P.M. to 11:00 P.M. — Hai (亥) time, is at the yongquan (湧泉) point.

4. The Song of Qi-Blood Circulation in the Channels (十二時辰氣血流注歌)

3:00 A.M. to 5:00 A.M. — Yin (寅) time, the apex of qi-blood circulation enters the Lung Channel.

5:00 A.M. to 7:00 A.M. — Mao (卯) time, the apex of qi-blood circulation enters the Large Intestine Channel.

7:00 A.M. to 9:00 A.M. — Chen (辰) time, the apex of qi-blood circulation enters the Stomach Channel.

9:00 A.M. to 11:00 A.M. — Si (巳) time, the apex of qi-blood circulation enters the Spleen Channel.

11:00 A.M. to 1:00 P.M. — Wu (午) time, the apex of qi-blood circulation enters the Heart Channel.

1:00 P.M. to 3:00 P.M. — Wei (未) time, the apex of qi-blood circulation enters the Small Intestine Channel.

3:00 P.M. to 5:00 P.M. — Shen (申) time, the apex of qi-blood circulation enters the Urinary Bladder Channel.

5:00 P.M. to 7:00 P.M. — You (酉) time, the apex of qi-blood circulation enters the Kidney Channel.

7:00 P.M. to 9:00 P.M. — Xu (戌) time, the apex of qi-blood circulation enters the Pericardium Channel.

9:00 P.M. to 11:00 P.M. — Hai (亥) time, the apex of qi-blood circulation enters the Triple Burner Channel.

11:00 P.M. to 1:00 A.M. — Zi (子) time, the apex of qi-blood circulation enters the Gall Bladder Channel.

1:00 A.M. to 3:00 A.M. — Chou (丑) time, the apex of qi-blood circulation enters the Liver Channel.

5. The Song of Dianxue (點穴歌訣)

The circulation of qi-blood in the body has an apex at different points throughout the day. If injury were to occur at the right time and at the passing point, life would end in 3 to 7 days. Remember each and every name clearly in your mind.

11:00 P.M. to 1:00 A.M. — Zi (子) time, the apex is at the xinwo (心窩) point.

1:00 A.M. to 3:00 A.M. — Chou (丑) time, the apex moves up to the shanzhong (膻中) point.

3:00 A.M. to 5:00 A.M. — Yin (寅) time, the apex is at the lianquan (廉泉) point.

5:00 A.M. to 7:00 A.M. — Mao (卯) time, the apex is at the yintang (印堂) point.

7:00 A.M. to 9:00 A.M. — Chen (辰) time, the apex is at the baihui (百會) point.

9:00 A.M. to 11:00 A.M. — Si (巳) time, the apex is at the fengfu (風府) point.

11:00 A.M. to 1:00 P.M. — Wu (午) time, the apex is at the jizhong (脊中) point.

1:00 P.M. to 3:00 P.M. — Wei (未) time, the apex is at the left and right shenshu (腎俞) point.

3:00 P.M. to 5:00 P.M. — Shen (申) time, the apex is at the weidi (尾骶) or the last lumbar.

5:00 P.M. to 7:00 P.M. — You (酉) time, the apex is at the huiyin (會陰) point.

7:00 P.M. to 9:00 P.M. — Xu (戌) time, the apex is at the guanyuan (關元) point.

9:00 P.M. to 11:00 P.M. — Hai (亥) time, the apex is at the navel.

6. Qingjing Buqimen Thirty-Six Points (清淨布氣門三十六穴)

Baihui (百會), tiangong (天宮), meixin (眉心), taiyang (太陽), renzhong (人中), ermen (耳門), tiantu (天突), lianquan (廉泉), hugai (華蓋), rugen (乳根), renying (人迎), ruzhong (乳中), shanzhong (膻中), zhongting (中庭), jiuwei (鳩尾), shenque (神闕), dantian (丹田), zhongwan (中脘), qimen (期門), zhangmen (章門), guanyuan (關元), queyun (曲暈), jianjing (肩井), huiyin (會陰), huantiao (環跳), changqiang (長強), mingmen (命門), beizhong (背中), lingtai (靈台), yongquan (湧泉), shenxshu (腎俞), feishu (肺俞), dazhui (大椎), fengchi (風池), yamen (啞門), zhishi (志室).

Appendix A: Glossary

This glossary includes many Wushu styles, Wushu practitioners, Wushu weapons, and Wushu terms that practitioners of Chinese martial arts can refer to. It is by no means a complete list of all the possible terms in Wushu, but we believe we have compiled the most inclusive list of Wushu styles in one book. Next to the description of the styles and weapons we have included many photos of practitioners of these styles and weapons. All styles and weapons are described under the Chinese pinyin romanization and cross referenced with the English equivalent.

It is not our intent, nor is it possible, to fully describe each and every style in one book. Our intent in this glossary is to present the rich variety of Wushu styles that are available. There are even more styles that have not been included in this glossary. To learn the specifics of each Wushu style we have presented in this glossary, you will need to study from an instructor of that particular style and or other resource. Hopefully, the information given in this book will stir your curiosity to learn more about the different styles out there.

In the list of the known routines named under each style, we have selected some representative routines. It is by no means a complete list of the routines of that style. Also, in our research we found some discrepancies in the information from different sources. We have presented what is available to us. Again, to learn more knowledge about a specific style, please study with a qualified practitioner of the style.

The practitioners whose photos appear in this glossary are introduced under the practitioners' name. We have included many of the most outstanding Wushu practitioners and instructors today. With their photos, we hope you will gain a better understanding of the characteristics of the style they represent. Many of these practitioners are prominent figures in multiple Wushu styles. Due to a limitation of typesetting space, we were only able to include some photo demonstrations and a short biography (125 words) of the practitioners. If you would like to know more details and accomplishments about the practitioners, please contact them directly.

The authors have put a lot of effort into compiling the biographies and photographs of the many practitioners. It is their hope that their efforts will help promote not only these practitioners, but Wushu in general, and to help prospective students of Wushu find teachers that suit their particular needs. No payment was received from the practitioners included in this glossary. The authors believe and wish that these practitioners will continue to be pillars of Wushu and our society.

At the end of this glossary are two addendums listing many other practitioners not included in the main section of the glossary. Next to their names we have included the last known location of these practitioners. The authors hope that with these lists and the descriptions in the main section of the glossary you will have a good starting point for locating a practitioner in your area.

There are several different standards used in the romanization of Chinese characters to the Roman alphabet. They include pinyin, Wade-Giles, Yale, Gouyu, and Hong Kong. The romanization system used in this volume is the pinyin system. Pinyin is the official romanization system of the People's Republic of China which was adopted in the 1950's. It is now widely adopted and accepted in China and abroad. The pinyin system of romanization is generally spelled more phonetically than other romanization systems.

China is a vast country with over fifty ethnic groups. Each ethnic group has their unique dialect of Chinese. Even though the dialects may differ from one region of China to the next, the written language is the same. In the pinyin romanization of the Chinese characters, we have used the official dialect, Mandarin — *putonghua* or *guoyu*.

If there is any confusion regarding the romanization of the Chinese characters using other systems, look up the term in this glossary. We have cross referenced many terms with other romanizations. For individuals that can read Chinese characters, we have included most of the Chinese characters in this glossary. The characters are placed next to the translated term or the pinyin, in alphabetical order.

Unlike the common English way of writing or addressing people by their first name, Chinese surnames are placed ahead of the given name. This sometimes causes confusion to readers. Many people are unable to tell which is the first name and which is the surname. Most Chinese names are three syllables long, one for the surname and two for the first name. There are, of course, exceptions. The given name (first name) is often romanized with a hyphen (-) with each of the syllables in the given name capitalized or is lumped together in a romanized form with only the first letter capitalized. Chinese names all have a significant meaning to the individual, each syllable in the name can be a word. The combination of syllables can add to the meaning of an individual word, or can have a totally different meaning if written separately or in a different context. In this glossary, all names are listed in alphabetical order with the last name first.

A

Alamudeen, Saleem He began his Wushu training in the early 1970's. He is a prominent practitioner of Hongjiaquan in the U.S. He is also a practitioner of Taijiquan, Baguazhang, Xingyiquan, and Qigong. He currently teaches at the Lam Tang Kung Fu Academay and the Circle Center Tai Chi School *See* his photo demonstration under Hongjiaquan.

Anhui Province 安徽省 A Chinese province located on the eastern part of China. The Yangtze River runs right through this province. It borders Jiangsu Province to its east and covers over 139 thousand square kilometers with a population of over 61 million people as of 1999.

Arsenalt, Al One of the founding members of the International Wushu Sanshou Dao Association (IWSD); and a martial arts instructor and a police officer for the Vancouver Police. He is currently the President of the IWSD. He is well-known for his ground control techniques, Karate, Judo, Jujitsu, Taijiquan, Shuaijiao, Qinna, and Qigong abilities. He received a gold medal for his performance in the 1994 Shanghai International Wushu Festival. He is a sixth level black belt in Wushu Sanshou Dao. *See* his photo demonstration under Wushu Sanshou Dao.

Ax *see* Fu

B

Drawing B-1

Ba 鈀 A rake (Drawing B-1). It evolved from a farming tool into an ancient military and Wushu weapon.

Figure B-1

Baguazhang 八卦掌 An Internal Style Wushu also romanized as Pa Kua Chang, and translated as Eight Trigram Palm. This style originated from the Emei Mountains. One of the major branches of Baguazhang came from Dong Haichuan (1813-1882), a Qing Dynasty's royal bodyguard from Heibei Province who traveled to the Emei Mountains and learned Baguazhang. He received his inspiration from Daoist teachings and derived the Baguazhang Style. Dong's students had already studied other martial arts before learning from him. Therefore, Baguazhang has developed many different characteristics since Dong himself.

Figure B-3

There are other sources of Baguazhang other than from Dong Haichuan. Some believe that the Priest Gao Xian (高仙) of the Hebei Province also learned it in the Emei Mountains. His Baguazhang was known as the Hard Eight Palm (硬八掌). Also, in Hebei Province, Wang Zhaoxian

Figure B-2

(王沼先) and Tian Hui (田回) from Beijing both practiced variations of Baguazhang from the Emei Mountains. Their Baguazhang is over 300 years old, and is not directly related to Dong Haichuan. However, the most influential development of Baguazhang is from the Dong Haichuan lineage.

The theoretic foundation of Baguazhang is based on the *Yijing* (易經, Book of Changes). Bagua or the eight trigrams are the basic elements of the *Yijing*. This style integrates circular stepping and energy circulation with martial arts movements. The movements are always changing, spinning and turning, while rapidly moving in curvilinear patterns. Its movements are described as, "Walk like a dragon, retrieve and spin like an ape, change momentum like an eagle, and calm and steady like a still tiger". In its applications, Baguazhang uses motion against an opponent's stillness, and stresses the use of rapid stepping and turning movements to evade an opponent's frontal attacks. One of the most predominant characteristics of Baguazhang is the use of palms (zhang) for its applications, thus the style is named Baguazhang.

Figure B-1: Bagua Zhuanzhang (八卦轉掌)/Zhao Ziqiu
Figure B-2: Bagua Sanshou Saber/Wang Shutian
Figure B-3: Baguazhang Application/Liang Shou-Yu and Wu Wen-Ching
Figure B-4: Baguazhang Application/Jerry Alan Johnson
Figure B-5: Swimming Body Baguazhang (游身八卦掌)/Helen Liang
Figure B-6: Jiulong Baguazhang/John Painter
Figure B-7: Bagua Low Stance Training/Sam Masich
Figure B-8: Bagua Deer Hooks/Wu Wen-Ching
Figure B-9: Bagua Saber/Yang Fukui
Figure B-10: Baguazhang/Robert Ross

Figure B-11: Baguazhang/Zhang Li
Figure B-12: Baguazhang/Zhang Hong Mei
Figure B-13: Bagua Saber/Thomas Uva, Robert Ross, Denise Breiter-Wu, Jeffrey Lykins, Howard Means, Ryan May, Frank Whitsitt-Lynch

Baihequan 白鶴拳 Translated as White Crane Style. This is a Southern Style. The characteristics of the White Crane style include light and agile movements; short, but ever changing, hand movements; and a whiplike manifestation of power from the waist. The origin of Baihequan is believed to have been passed down from Fang Huishi (方慧石) who learned his martial arts from the Southern Shaolin Temple and later taught it to his daughter, Fang Qiniang (方七娘). The time period was between 1662 and 1735.

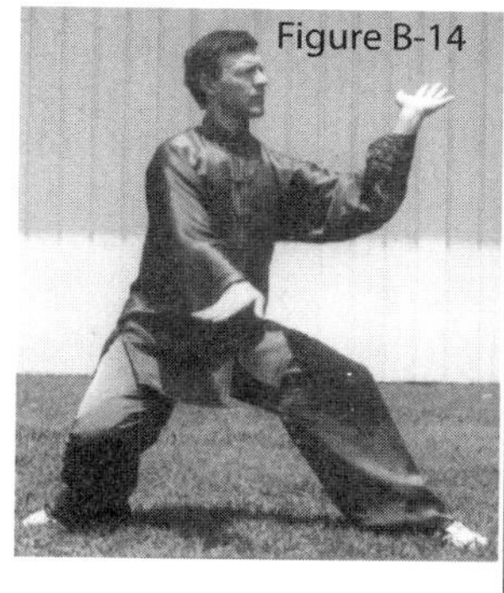

Legend has it, that Fang Qiniang was on her way home from washing clothes one day and observed a great white crane on the roof of her home. Driven by curiosity and apprehension that the crane would damage the clothes she hung out to dry, she took a stick and attempted to scare the crane away. When she tried to hit the head of the crane, the crane moved its head and extended its wings to defend against the strike. When she tried to hit the wings of the crane, the crane agilely jumped away and used its claws to deflect the stick. When she tried to spear to the crane's body, the crane shook its wings, while retreating and striking forward with its beak.

Fang Qiniang was amazed and impressed with the crane's ability and studied the crane movements. From then on, the crane rested on the roof of her home everyday, and she attacked the crane to study its movements. She then combined her Southern Shaolin martial arts training with the crane movements and created Baihequan.

Also see Fujian Hequan and Wuzuquan.

Figure B-14: Baihequan/Jeff Bolt
Figure B-15: Fujian Hequan/Augustine Ngu

Baimeiquan 白眉拳 Translated as White Eyebrow Style. This is an Emei Style. Legend has it, that it was created by a Taoist priest named Baimei. The known routines include: Xiaoshizi (小十字), Dashizi (大十字), Sanmenbagua (三門八卦), Shibamoqiao (十八摩橋), and Menghuchulin (猛虎出林). This style is popular in Guandong Province, Hong Kong, and many Southeastern Asian nations.

Figure B-16: Baimeiquan/Ken Low

Bajiquan 八極拳 Translated as the Eight Extreme Fist. It is commonly believed that Bajiquan was known as Baziquan (八子拳) as recorded in the Ming Dynasty Wushu classic, the *New Book of Effective Disciplines* (紀效新書). The modern version of Bajiquan is believed to have been passed down from Wu Zhong (吳鐘) (1712-1802). According to legend, Wu Zhong learned his Bajiquan from a wandering Daoist. Its characteristics include explosive power, stomping the foot, and utilizes close range movements in its applications.

Figure B-17: Old Bajiquan/Adam Hsu (photo by Marie Anthony)
Figure B-18: Big Frame Bajiquan/Michael Li
Figure B-19: Bajiquan/Tony Chen

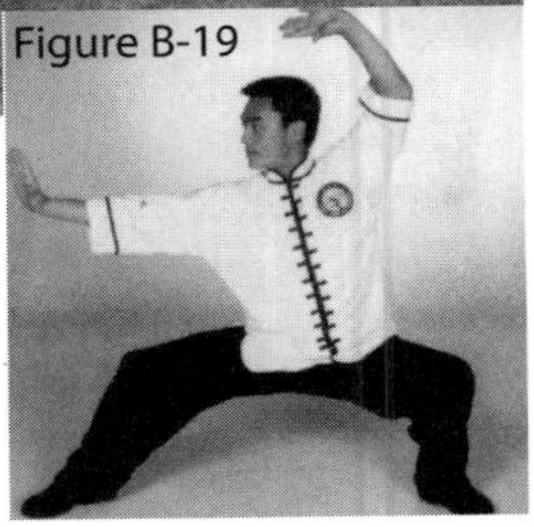

Barbosa, Fred He began his Wushu training from Wu Wen-Ching in 1999. He is a Way of the Dragon School assistant instructor, and a Systems Engineer for Fleet Bank Boston. *See* his photo demonstration under Wushu Bingqi.

Batuo 跋陀 The first Abbot of the Shaolin Temple. Legend has it, that Emperor Xiaowen (孝文帝) built the Shaolin Temple for Batuo to teach Buddhism in 495 A.D. He was there for over thirty years before Damo.

Beijing City 北京市 The capital of China and one of China's four municipalities that is under the direct jurisdiction of the central government. It is a political, economic, transportation, science, and cultural center. Bejing is located in the Northeastern part of China, about 150 kilometers from the Bohai Sea. It covers over 16 thousand square kilometers, with a population of over 12 million people as of 1999.

Beipai 北派 Beipai is used as opposed to Nanquan. This term refers to Wushu styles originating in the areas above the Yangtze River in China.

Benglong Wushu 崩龍武術 This term refers to the Wushu developed by the Benglong ethnic people living in the Yunnan Province. The Benglong people are known for their bravery and love of Wushu. Their Wushu is known as Zuoquan (左拳), meaning Left Fist. When engaged in combat or competition, their winning blow often comes from their left fist, thereby, the term Zuoquan. Benglong Wushu has high stances. They have a weapon routine known as Benglongdao (崩龍刀).

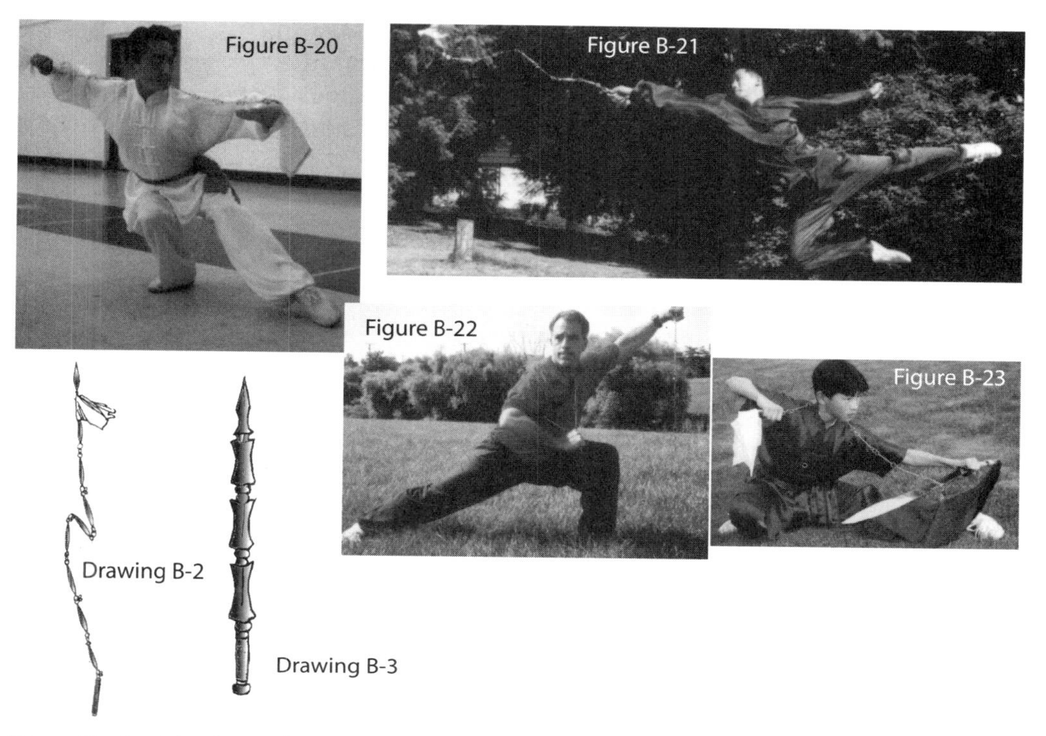

Bian 鞭 A whip. It can be one piece or chain linked. This term refers to weapons with whip-like characteristics. Chain linked bian include the Seven, Nine (Drawing B-2), or Thirteen Sectioned Chain. A one piece bian is a hard whip. Zhujieganbian (竹節剛鞭, Drawing B-3) is a hard whip with the body carved into bamboo-like sections with sharp protrusions.

Figure B-20: Nine Sectioned Chain/Hansen Lee

Figure B-21: Nine Sectioned Chain/Hui Mo

Figure B-22: Double Chain/Joel Timons

Figure B-23: Saber and Chain/Sam Li

Biangan *see* Gun

Bishil, Hassan (1968-) Born in the city of Makkah, Saudi Arabia. In 1987, Mr. Bishil started Wushu training in his home country. Three years later, he began traveling around the world seeking out Wushu and Qigong teachers. He has studied on a one-to-one basis with several prominent Wushu and Qigong teachers in China, Hong Kong, and North America. Since 1992 he has been teaching and holding workshops in Saudi Arabia and the U.S. He is a member of the International Wushu Sanshou Dao Association. *See* his photo demonstration under Tanglangquan.

Bishou 匕首 Refers to a double edged dagger (Drawing B-4). It is also referred to as duanjian (短劍) or short sword. It is classified as a small weapon, used for close range applications. Bishou is used singularly or in a pair.

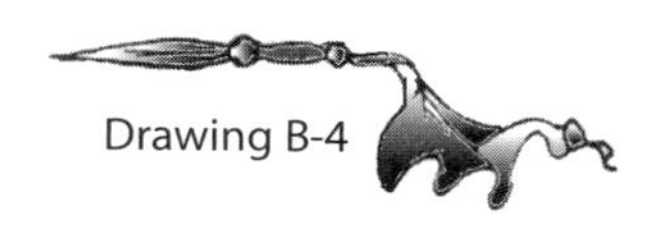

Bodhidharma *see* Damo

Bolt, Jeff One of most significant contributors to the promotion of Wushu in the United States. He was one of the first to organize national Wushu competitions in the United States. He has been the director of U.S. National Chinese Martial Arts tournaments since 1986. He was instrumental in forming a national Wushu federation and has served as an administrator for several organizations. He was the Vice President of U.S.A.W.K.F. and was the Sanshou coach of the U.S. National Wushu Team. He currently teaches in Texas, USA. *See* his photo demonstrations under Changquan and Baihequan.

Boziquan 跛子拳 Cripple Style. This style was created by a Chan Buddhist priest, Jinyun (淨雲禪師). It imitates the characteristics of a handicapped or injured person in its movements. There is only one known routine with over 80 movements.

Breiter-Wu, Denise She is the editor of this book and many others. She is a former elementary school teacher and movement therapist. She is the cofounder, and now works as the director, an instructor, and an editor at The Way of the Dragon School and Publication Company. She has been practicing Wushu, Taijiquan, and Qigong for over 20 years. She is the wife of Wu Wen-Ching and the mother of Andrew Wu. *See* her photo demonstrations under Baguazhang, Chaquan, and Wangshi Wushu.

Bujas, Tony Also known as Ante Bujas. He is a Third Level Black Belt in Wushu Sanshou Dao. He is also an instructor of Xingyiquan, Baguazhang, and Sanshou at the S.Y.L. Wushu Institute. He studied Hongjiaquan for ten years, and has been studying Internal Style Wushu and qigong from Shou-Yu Liang for more than ten years. *See* his photo demonstrations under Huheshunxingquan, Guai, and Wushu Sanshou Dao.

C

Cailifoquan 蔡李佛拳 One of the Southern Styles of Guangdong Province. This style was created by Chen Heng (陳亨). Chen first learned Fojiaquan (佛家拳) from his father. Later, he also studied Liquan (李拳) from Li Youshan (李友山) and Caiquan (蔡拳) from Cai Fu (蔡福). Chen combined the essence of the three styles and created Cailifoquan. This style is popular in Guangdong, Foshan (佛山), Hong Kong, Europe, and America. There are numerous routines in this style. Its movements are described as "Still like static water when on guard, and attack like a hungry leopard catching its prey."

Figure C-1

Figure C-2

Figure C-3

Figure C-1: Hongsheng Cailifoquan (鴻勝蔡李佛拳)/Wong Tat-Mau
Figure C-2: Cailifoquan/Mak Hin Fai
Figure C-3: Xiongsheng Cailifoquan (雄勝蔡李佛拳)/Sam Ng
Figure C-4: Liuyedao (柳葉刀)/Hilbert T.S. Yiu
Figure C-5: Panlonggun (盤龍棍)/Hilbert T.S. Yiu

Caiquan 蔡拳 Translated as Cai Family Fist. This style was created by Cai Boda (蔡伯達) and Cai Jiuyi (蔡九儀). They were monks from Fujian Shaolin Temple. Later, it was spread to Guangdong Province by the monk Cai Fu (蔡福). It is one of the major Southern Styles in Guangdong today. Some of the known routines include: Shiziquan (十字拳), Dayuntian (大運天), Xiaoyuntian (小運天), Tianbianyan (天邊雁), Lusuimei (柳碎梅), and Liangyisixiangquan (兩儀四象拳).

Canbimen 蠶閉門，蠶門，蠶絲門 Translated as Silk Reeling Style. This style originated from Huang Yichuan (黃益川) of Jiangxi Province. Canbimen focuses on coiling and neutralizing. Its movements are continuous like the reeling of silk, thus the term Can, meaning silk or silk worm. There are over seventy known barehanded routines, thirteen weapon routines, and thirteen Sanshou training methods.

Figure C-6: Inviting Hand/Zhao Ziqiu

Cangzhou Wushu 滄州武術 This term refers to the Wushu styles known in the Canzhou area. Cangzhou is located in Hebei Province. Historically, Cangzhou was poor. To make matters worse, the government officials were corrupt and took advantage of the people. To defend themselves, the Cangzhou people had to train Wushu.

There were many other factors which made Cangzhou a gathering place for Wushu practitioners. Many Wushu practitioners were exiled to Cangzhou. Some were sent there as prisoners and some were there to hide from government persecution. Because of the many talented Wushu practitioners in Cangzhou, ancient armed guards would humble themselves when passing through Cangzhou, so as not to anger them.

There have been many Wushu styles which have originated from Cangzhou. In the recent past, many patriots from Cangzhou successfully defeated many foreign challengers. These prominent Wushu practitioners include Wang Ziping (王子平), Li Guanming (李冠銘), Ding Faxiang (丁發祥), and Zhang Zhankui (張占魁). They all left behind many exciting stories.

Carroll, Sam He began his martial arts training in 1982, and has been studying Wushu from Wu Wen-Ching since 1993. He is an instructor at The Way of the Dragon School and is currently pursuing a graduate degree in Ocean Engineering. *See* his photo demonstration under Shaolin Wushu.

Case, Ron He is a First Degree Black Belt in Nisei Karate and a Wushu practicitioner. He is the leader of the S.Y.L. Wushu Institute Hard Qigong Performance team. *See* his photo demonstration under Wushu Sanshou Dao.

Central Guoshu Institute 中央國術館 The national martial arts organization founded in Nanjing (南京) in 1928 by Zhang Zhijiang (張之江). It was responsible for organizing national competitions, training Wushu instructors, testing, and promoting Wushu. It was later relocated in Sichuan and closed in 1949. Many graduates of the Central Guoshu Institute are currently leading Wushu professors, coaches, and Wushu leaders in China. *Also see* Guoshu.

Cha 叉 A fork like weapon. There are many types of cha. Cha were used for hunting and fishing, and gradually evolved to become Wushu weapons. Long cha usually consist of three prongs with a pole extension (Drawing C-1). Short cha are also referred to as Nancha (南叉, Drawings C-2 and C-3). Nancha are typically used in pairs and practiced mostly in Southern Styles.

Figure C-7: Southern Cha/Ayron Howey

Figure C-8: Cailifo Cha/Hilbert T.S. Yiu

Chain *see* Bian

Chan 禪 A Buddhist practice following the Sutrayana practices of the Mahayana Vehicle. It is also romanized as Zen from the Japanese pronunciation. The original word came from the Sanskrit word, "dhyana".

Chan 鏟 A shovel. It evolved from a farming tool into a weapon. Ancient monks living outside of the temples often used this weapon. It was used to carry heavy weight, make paths when traveling in the mountains, and as a self-defense weapon. Well-known chans include: Fangbianchan (方便鏟, Drawing C-4) and Yueyachan (月牙鏟, Drawing C-5).

Figure C-9: Yueyachan/Wang Ziping

Chan, Paul 陳郁 He began his Wushu training in 1942. He is the disciple of Chen Dou (陳斗), a prominent practitioner of Daopai. He is also well-known for his Hongjiaquan and Cailifoquan. He is the first president of the Confederation of Canadian Wushu Organizations and the president of the Canadian National Chinese Martial Arts Federation. See his photo demonstration under Daopai.

Chang, Chung-Jen 張仲仁 He is a prominent practitioner of Taijiquan. He was a consultant for the highly acclaimed movie, *Pushing Hands*. He has produced several instructional Taiji videos and hosted a Taijiquan cable TV program. He was a grandchampion at a national Taiji tournament and has judged competitions in various localities. He is especially well-known for his remarkable fluidity and flexibility. During his 20 plus years of teaching, he has developed his own successful system of increasing the flexibility of the body. His wide range of studies include: Taiji Daoyin, Chen Style Taijiquan, Yang Style Taijiquan, Taiji Sword, and Push Hands. He currently teaches in Maryland, USA, and gives workshops throughout North America. *See* his photo demonstration under Taijiquan.

Changjiang *see* Yangtze River

Changquan 長拳 Long Fist. This is a term referring to the many Northern Style Wushu including: Chaquan, Huaquan, Paoquan, Hongquan, Liuhequan, Yanqingquan, etc. Changquan movements are usually long, open, and extended. It includes many fast and agile maneuvers, as well as, high jumps and aerial kicks.

Modern competition Changquan routines have absorbed the characteristics of Chaquan, Hongquan, Huaquan, Paoquan, Hongquan, in its routines. Changquan is suited for youngsters learning Wushu because it sets a solid foundation for studying other styles of Wushu. In Modern Wushu competitions, Changquan routines must include a proper fist, palm, and hand hook; and the five basic stances, gongbu (弓步), mabu (馬步), pubu (仆步), xubu (虛步), and xiebu (歇步). The routines must also contain a definite amount of punching, palm striking, elbow striking, spring kicking, high sweep kicking, low sweep kicking, and slap kicking techniques. They must also contain a definite amount of balancing, jumping, and tumbling techniques.

Figure C-10: Lift Knee and Flash Palms/Liang Shou-Yu
Figure C-11: Changquan Closing Posture/Zou Yinghui
Figure C-12: Block Up in Empty Stance/Liang Shou-Yu
Figure C-13: Changquan/Liu Yu

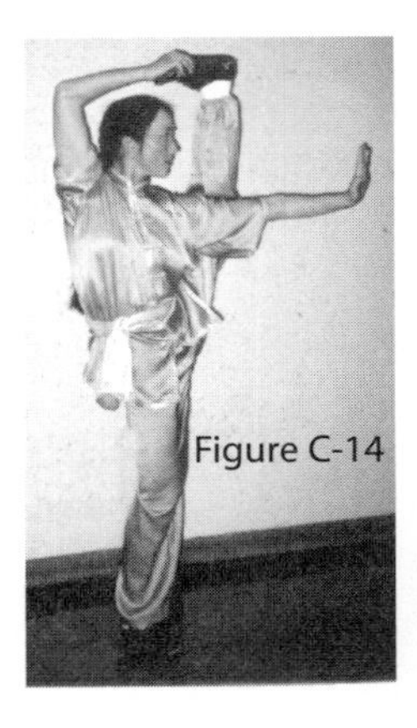

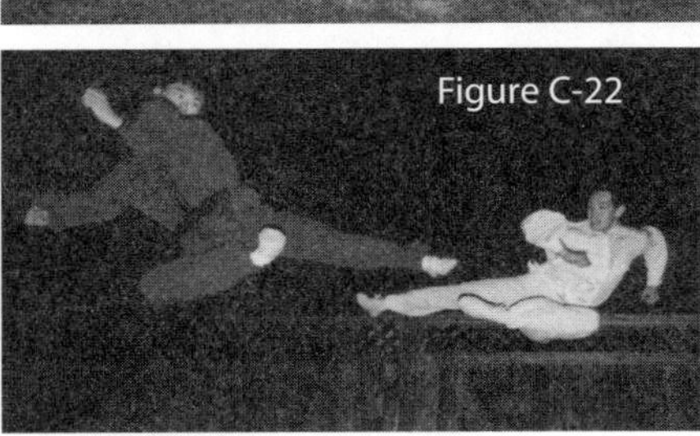

Figure C-14: Changquan/Liu Yu

Figure C-15: Gongliquan (功力拳)/Jeff Bolt

Figure C-16: Changquan/Sanford Lee

Figure C-17: Changquan/Katrina Leung

Figures C-18 and C-20: Wushu Basics/Derek Cheng, Fremont Woo, Tjhie Wei Tjong, William Lai, Michael Holmes, Mo Hui, Yang Chen-Han, Perry Lo, and Fred Ho

Figure C-19: Changquan/Tadeusz Gacki

Figure C-21: Changquan/Henry Gong

Figure C-22: Jumping Side Kick/ Yang Chen-Han and William Lai

Figure C-23: Changquan/Ivan Wong

Chaquan 查拳 A major Wushu style. Its training content is both systematic and complete. Chaquan, Huaquan, Hongquan, Paoquan, and Tantuimen are from the same origin. It has traditionally been very popular among the Hui ethnic Chinese. The Hui people are predominately of the Muslin faith giving the Chaquan style a very close tie to the Chinese Muslin community. It is not surprising that the practitioners of Chaquan in the past have mostly been the Hui ethnic Chinese. In 1928, when the Central Guoshu Institute was founded, Chaquan became one of the primary required studies at the institute. The teachers were all Hui ethnic Chinese.

There are many legends concerning the origin of Chaquan. There are inconsistent records indicating the origination period of Chaquan. There are records that indicate it originated during the Tang Dynasty, Ming Dynasty, and the Qing Dynasty. Despite the inconsistency in the date of origin, these records all consistently indicate that this style was founded by a practitioner with the last name Cha. Cha began teaching his martial arts in the Shandong area. Later, the martial arts that Cha taught, spread all over China and became known as Chaquan. The exact origin still needs to be verified with more research.

One legend has it, that during the Tang Dynasty (618-907), General Cha Gelu (查格魯) led five thousand Hui (回) soldiers to stop the largest revolt during the Tang Dynasty. The revolt was known as Anshizhiluan (安史之亂). General Cha was successful in stopping the revolt, but he was also injured during the engagement. Cha recuperated in Guanxian (冠縣) County of Shandong Province. While he was there, he taught his Wushu to the Hui ethnic Chinese. To remember and honor him, practitioners named their Wushu, Chaquan.

Another legend has it, that Cha Mier (查密爾) created Chaquan in the beginning of the Ming Dynasty. Yet, another legend, believes it was created by Cha Shangyi (查尚義), an Hui ethnic Chinese from the northeastern part of China.

There are ten bare-handed Chaquan routines. Each routine is made up of 30 to 60 techniques. Each application can be practiced individually or with a partner. The movements start from the very basic to the more advanced, containing lively and intricate maneuvers. Each routine has its training key words and phrases that go with the techniques to assist the practitioner in memorizing and understanding the applications. Each routine, also has its particular emphasis and focus. The ten routines are: Yilu Muzi (一路母子), Erlu Xingshou (二路行手), Sanlu Feijiao (三路飛腳), Silu Shengping (四路升平), Wulu Guandong (五路關東), Liulu Maifu (六路埋伏), Qilu Meihua (七路梅花), Balu Lianhuan (八路連環), Jiaolu Longbaiwei (九路龍擺尾), and Shilu Chuanquan (十路串拳).

Chaquan is a major representation of Changquan styles. Modern Changquan routines are all based on Chaquan and Huaquan foundations. Well-known representatives of Chaquan in the recent past include: Wang Ziping (王子平) and Zhang Yingzheng (張英掙).

Figure C-24: Suohouqiang (鎖喉槍)/Wang Jurong

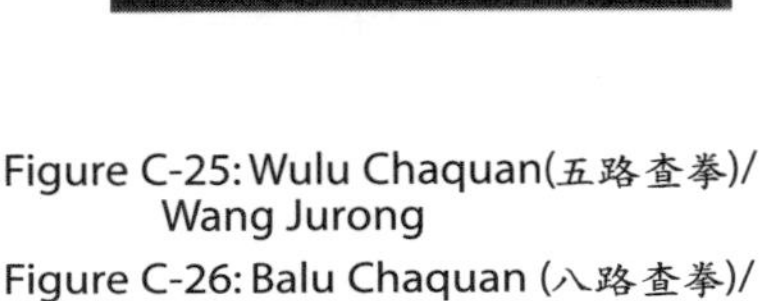

Figure C-25: Wulu Chaquan(五路查拳)/ Wang Jurong
Figure C-26: Balu Chaquan (八路查拳)/ Wu Wen-Ching
Figure C-27: Wulu Chaquan (五路查拳)/Grace Wu
Figure C-28: Silu Chaquan(四路查拳)/Wang Jurong
Figure C-29: Simendao (四門刀)/Wu Wen-Ching
Figure C-30: Chaquan/Denise Breiter-Wu
Figure C-31: Chaquan/Betty Lew-Watson

Chau, William 巢金超 President of the Chinese Wushu Association (安大略中國武術總會會長) in Ontario, Canada and a lifetime member of the Hong Kong Chinese Medicine Association (香港中醫師公會永遠會員). He is a prominent practitioner in Tantuimen, Piguaquan, Fanzi Yingzhuamen, Cailifoquan, Mizongquan, Dachengquan, and traumatology. *See* his photo demonstration under Dachengquan.

Chen, Bill 陳子榆 He is a prominent Wushu practitioner in Texas. He was a Wushu instructor at the University of Washington. He was a judge at many U.S. National Wushu competitions. He is one of Liang Shou-Yu's students. In the early 1980's, he was responsible for inviting Liang Shou-Yu to teach Wushu at the University of Washington. *See* his photo demonstration under Liuhemen.

Chen, Irene 陳仲瑜 A member of the Canadian Wushu team. She was a gold medalist many times in U.S. and Canadian international Wushu competitions in the compulsory Nanquan and other categories. She is a S.Y.L. Wushu Institute instructor and is included in the book, the *China's Contemporary Wushu Masters* (中國當代武林名人志). *See* her photo demonstration under Dao.

Chen, Jian 陳堅 Also known as Chen Dingfu (陳定富) and nicknamed Luyadaoren (綠鴉道人). He is the 23rd generation head instructor of the O-Mei Qigong and Sword School (峨嵋氣功劍派). In his youth, he was a member of the Sichuan Wushu team winning numerous gold medals. He was a Wushu instructor at Chengdu Physical Education College and a head instructor at Chengdu City Police Academy. He is also a prominent practitioner of traumatology. Currently, he teaches and does his healing practice in San Francisco, California, U.S.A. *See* his photo demonstrations under Emei Shierzhuang and Emei Wushu.

Chen, Tony 陳朝輝 Also known as Chen Zhaohui. He learned Wushu from his father, Chen Jian, since age six. He has been a gold medalist in numerous national championships in China, and received his Wuyin (武英) title in 1991. He was the U.S.A. Kickboxing Champion and International Kung Fu Champion in 1997. He is the founder of the O-Mei Kung Fu Academy in San Francisco, California, USA. He is also the Chairman of the California Affiliate of the International Wushu Sanshou Dao Association. He is a Sixth Level Black Belt in Sanshou Dao. In 2000, he appeared on the cover of Kung Fu Qigong Magazine. He has demonstrated in several instructional videos. The instructors at his school include many prominent Wushu practitioners. *See* his photo demonstrations under Bajiquan and Tanglangquan.

Chen, Xiaowang 陳小旺 (1946-) A prominent representative of the 19th generation Chen Style Taijiquan. He has been a Taijiquan gold medalist and a recipient of Outstanding Performance awards many times in China national Wushu championships. He has written two books on Chen Style Taijiquan. He currently teaches in Australia and gives workshops around the world. *See* his photo demonstration under Taijiquan.

Cheng, Aiping 程愛萍 A former member and later became a coach of the Zhejiang Wushu team. She attained gold medals in both double sword and Sun Style Taijiquan, and a silver medal in Yang Style Taijiquan in a National Wushu competition in China. She is the demonstrator in the official Sun Style instructional video produced by the China Sports Committee. In the 1970's, she was a member of the Wushu Delegation to the United States and performed at the White House. Since her immigration to the U.S., she has been active as a judge in U.S. national and international Wushu competitions. She currently teaches in Connecticut, U.S.A. See her photo demonstrations under Taijiquan and Mulanquan.

Cheng, Derek 鄭子樂 A S.Y.L. Wushu Institute instructor. He is a Canadian national Sanshou competition silver medalist in the 75-80 kilogram category. He is also included in the book, *China's Contemporary Wushu Masters* (中國當代武林名人志). He is a Third Level Black Belt in Wushu Sanshou Dao. In 2001, he was the gold medalist in the 70 to 75 Kg Canadian National Sanshou competition in 1999. He was selected to represent Canada at the 6th World Wushu Championships. In 2001, he was also certified by the International Wushu Federation as an International Sanshou Fighting Judge. He is a member of the Board of Directors of Wushu B.C. *See* his photo demonstrations under Yingzhuaquan, Huanglinpai, Emei Shaolin, Gun, and Wushu Sanshou Dao.

Cheng, Kexin 程克欣 A prominent Yijing and Bagua prediction practitioner. A Sichuan native, also known for his Qigong and Sanshou ability. He is the founder and chairman of the *China Kexingzhang Association (中國克星掌協會)*, an International Wushu Sanshou Dao Association affiliate. In his youth, he studied Wushu and Sanshou from Liang Shou-Yu. He was also selected as one of the top ten Qigong practitioners in China, in *Who's Who in the World* (世界名人錄), and *China's Con-*

temporary Wushu Masters (中國當代武林名人志). He has written several books about Bagua, Qigong, and healing. His students have received gold medals for their Qigong and Sanshou abilities. He gives workshops all over China and has been well received by both Chinese and foreign students. Many magazines and newspapers have dedicated articles about him. *See* his photo demonstration under Kexingzhang.

Cheng, Shaoming 程紹銘 (1969-)He started his Wushu training when he was six. He has won first place in several martial arts tournaments both in China and in the U.S.; subsequently he has been invited to be a judge at numerous martial arts tournaments. He was a student of Sha Guozheng (沙國政, 1904-1993), a prominent practitioner of Baguazhang, Xingyiquan, Taijiquan, and Tongbiquan. He currently teaches Taijiquan, Xingyiquan, and Baguazhang in Athens, Georgia; and is the chief coach of the U.G.A. martial arts team. He is also pursuing his Ph.D. degree at the University of Georgia. *See* his photo demonstration under Xingyiquan.

Cheung, Kerry He began his Hongjiaquan training when he was five with his father, Raymond Cheung. He is now an instructor of Hongjiaquan and a practitioner of Lion Dancing. Through the introduction of his father, he has also been training at the S.Y.L. Wushu Institute since 2000. He has competed in many West Coast North American Wushu competitions and attained many gold medals and all-around championships. *See* his photo demonstration under Hongjiaquan.

Cheung, Purdy She began her Hongjiaquan training at age five with her father Raymond Cheung. She is now an instructor of Hongjiaquan and the drummer for the Lion Dancing team. Through the introduction of her father, she has also been training at the S.Y.L. Wushu Institute since 2000. She has competed in many Wushu competitions and attained many gold medals. *See* her photo demonstration under Hongjiaquan.

Cheung, Raymond 張煒焜 A prominent practitioner of Shaolin Hongjiaquan. He was the Vice President of the West Coast Martial Arts Association, Vice President of Wushu B.C., and the Vice President of the Confederation of Canadian Wushu Organizations. He was instrumental in the organization of several west coast international Wushu championships and the Canadian Wushu team selections. *See* his photo demonstration under Nanquan.

Chi Kung *see* Qigong

Chiang, Che Cheng 江志成 A native of Taiwan, he started his Wushu training when he was a child. He is a prominent practitioner of TCM traumatology and a prominent promoter of Wushu. He was the director and head coach of the Taipei City Guoshu. He attained over twenty gold medals in all Taiwan and international Sanshou competitions. In 1968, he was invited to Japan and Korea to teach Wushu. He was awarded a ninth degree black belt. He has a Master's and a Ph.D. degree in Oriental Medicine, and received a professor certificate from the state of California. He is currently the President of the U.S.A. Chinese Kung Fu Association, President of the International Wushu Federation, and president and chairman of many other organizations. He has organized eight World Cup International Wushu Championships. *See* his photo demonstration under Dao.

Chin, Chris A member of the Canadian Wushu team. He has been a gold and silver medalists many times in U.S. and Canadian national Wushu competitions. He studied at the S.Y.L. Wushu Institute from 1992 to 1997. Later, he also trained under Li Wenqi, Bruce Fontaine, and Fred Whitting. *See* his photo demonstration under Xiandai Wushu.

Chin, Douglas A member of the Canadian Wushu team. He has been a U.S. and Canadian national gold medalist and all-around champion many times in international competition routines. In the 1995 World Wushu Championships held in the U.S. he attained a silver medal in the compulsory saber category, and in the 1999 World Wushu Championships held in Hong Kong, he attained fourth place in the compulsory spear category. He studied at the S.Y.L. Wushu Institute from 1992 to 1997. Later, he also trained under Li Wenqi, Bruce Fountaine, and Fred Whitting. *See* his photo demonstration under Xiandai Wushu.

Chongqing City 重慶市 One of China's four municipalities that is under the direct jurisdiction of the central government. Chongqing is located next to the Yangtze River within Sichuan Province. It is the newest of the four Chinese cities that are under the direct jurisdiction of the central government. It has a population of over 30 million people as of 1999.

Choy Lay Fut *see* Cailifoquan

Chuanquan 船拳 Translated as Boat Fist. In the Wuxing area of Zhejiang Province, people often tie two boats together and set up a platform for a fighting competition. Chuanquan was the result of these competitions. There are many barehanded and weapon routines in this style.

Drawing C-6

Chui 錘 A hammer like weapon (Drawing C-6). The hammer head can be shaped like a cube, sphere, or melon. It can have long handles or short handles. Long handled chui are usually used as one weapon, where as short handled chui are often used in a pair. Traditional chui were made of bronze or iron. They can weigh up to 20 Kg each.

Figure C-32

Figure C-32: Tiangangchui (天罡錘)/ Wu Wen-Ching

Chung, Andrew He began his martial arts training in 1969. His teachers include: Chang Yuan-Wei, Huang Wei-Lun, Lee Kwong Ming. His foundation training comprised of the Hakka Tanglangquan (Southern Praying Mantis), Baimeiquan, and Yongchunquan. He later studied the Internal Styles of Taijiquan, Baguazhang, Xingyiquan, and Liuhebafa. In the 1980's he was the gold medalist in numerous competitions in the United States. For the past decade, he has served as a judge and an advisor for numerous national competitions in the U.S. He is also an active promoter of martial arts competitions within the state of Florida where he resides and has been teaching since 1979. *See* his photo demonstration under Nanquan.

Chuojiao 戳腳 Translated as Piercing Feet. This is a style that focuses primarily on the applications of the feet. It is classified as Changquan. Legend has it, that Wu Song (武松), a hero of the Song Dynasty (960-1126) used Chuojiao to defeat his adversary. Wu Song was also known for his heroic feat in killing a man-eating tiger with his bare hands. "Wu Song Strikes the Tiger (武松打虎)" is a very well-known story in Chinese folklore. Wu Song is credited as the founder of this style.

Figure C-33

Figure C-33: Chuojiao/Michael Li

Cohen, Kenneth S. 高漢 The Executive Director and founder of the Qigong Research and Practice Center. He is a world renowned health educator, China scholar, and Qigong practitioner with more than thirty years experience. He is the author of the internationally acclaimed book, *The Way of Qigong*. He currently teaches Qigong, Taijiquan, Baguazhang, and Xingyiquan in Nederland, Colorado, U.S.A. More about him and his school can be found at *www.qigonghealing.com*. *See* his photo demonstrations under Wudang Wushu and Xingyiquan.

Comet Hammer *see* Liuxingchui

Cane *see* Guai

Concealed Weapons *see* Wushu Anqi

Contemporary Wushu *see* Xiandai Wushu

Cotton Fist *see* Mianquan

Cotton Palm *see* Mianzhang

Figure D-1

D

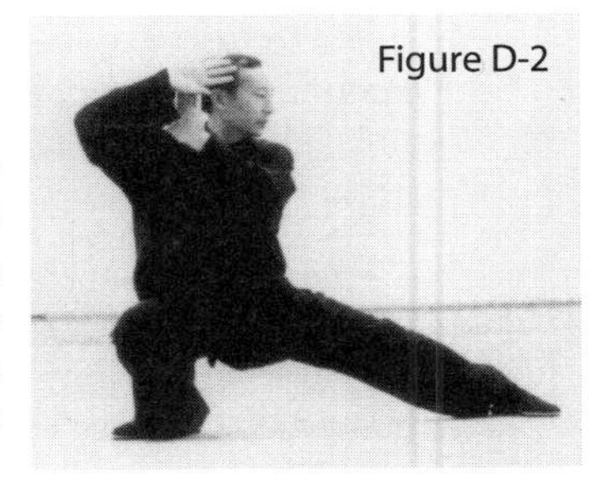
Figure D-2

Dabeiquan 大悲拳 Legend has it, that it originated during the Ming Dynasty. It was a style practiced by the monks at the Henan Shaolin Temple and at Wutaishan (五台山). Dabeiquan is based on the teachings of the Buddhist Dabeizhou (大悲咒). In the 1960's, a high priest, Qiyun Fashi (奇雲法師), taught this style in Beijing.

Practitioners of Dabeiquan are required to recite a phrase from the sutra along with each posture. Its characteristics include that of Taijiquan, Xingyiquan, and Baguazhang. There are two routines in this style. They are Bashiliushi (八十六勢) and Yibaiershiliushi (一百二十八勢).

Information provided by Yuan Shaoliang.

Figures D-1 and D-2: Dabeiquan/Yuan Shaoliang

Dachengquan 大成拳 Also known as Yiquan (意拳) and translated as the Great Accomplishment Fist. It was created by Wang Xiangzhai (王薌齋, 1885-1963). Wang learned Xingyiquan from Guo Yunshen (郭雲深). Later, Wang focused on the yi component, discarded the xing component of Xingyiquan, and focused on standing postures to develop internal strength, and created Yiquan. Wang traveled extensively all over China and exchanged techniques with Wushu practitioners throughout China.

Figure D-3
Figure D-4

Because Wang was also good in Taijiquan, Baguazhang, and Shaolin Wushu, and had a high level of attainments, people later referred to his creation of Yiquan, as Dachengquan, meaning the great achievement style. This was because he was able to integrate the essence of different Wushu styles into Yiquan.

Figure D-3: Dachengquan/Zhang Shu-Fang
Figure D-4: Dachengquan/William Chau

Dagger *see* Bishou

Damo 達摩 (?-536) Damo or Bodhidharma was the 28th generation successor of Chan Buddhism from Southern India. He came to China in the 520's. According to legend, he traveled from Guangdong, then to Henan Shaolin Temple. He is regarded as the father of Chan Buddhism in China. For lack of a better choice and lack of definite information, and also to honor him, many Shaolin Wushu and Qigong methods were credited to him.

Dang 鎲 It is a long weapon with a spear head and a moon shaped piece below the spear. Around the moon shaped piece are sharp ring blades (Drawing D-1). Dang are usually over 8 feet long and may weigh up to 200 pounds.

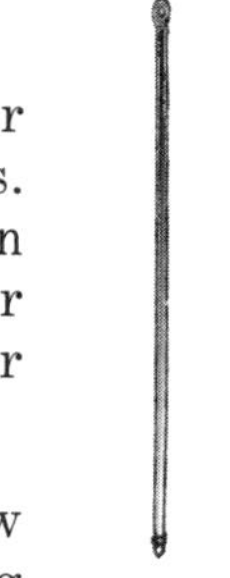

Drawing D-1

Dao 刀 It is to a curved and bladed weapon with a short or long handle, such as a saber. Dao is known as *baibingzhidan* (白兵之膽) or the *spirit of all weapons*. Dao movements are described as a fierce tiger. Dao has many different types including: Dandao (單刀), Shuandao (雙刀), Dadao (大刀), Guangongdadao (關公大刀), Chunqiudada (春秋大刀), Qinglongdadao (青龍大刀), Jiuhuandadao (九環大刀), Pudao (朴刀), Duandao (短刀), Yaodao (腰刀), Miaodao (苗刀), and Xiaoshuangshou (小雙手). In the ancient military and Wushu, the commonly used dao were: Dandao, a single saber; Shuangdao, a double saber; Dadao; and Pudao.

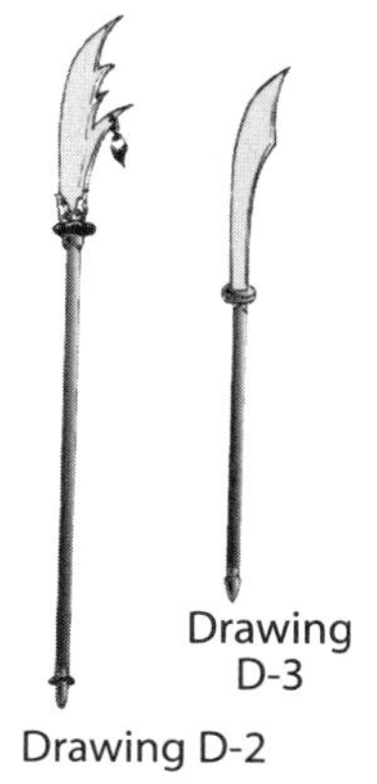

Drawing D-3

Drawing D-2

Dadao (Drawing D-2) is known as the *baibinzhishuai* (白兵之帥) or the *commander of all weapons*. Pudao (Drawing D-3), also referred to as *Shuangshoudai* (雙手帶) is shorter and lighter than the Dadao, but longer than a single saber. It was the choice weapon for many legendary generals in ancient China.

Figure D-5

Figure D-6

Figure D-7

Figures D-5 and D-6: Qinglongdadao (100 plus pounds)/Liang Shou-Yu
Figure D-7: Pudao/Wu Wen-Ching

Figure D-8: Butterfly Knives/Sunny Tang
Figure D-9: Zhanhuadao (戰花刀)/Maria Liang
Figure D-10: Dadao/Mike Sigman
Figure D-11: Dadao/He Tao
Figure D-12: Dadao vs. Saber/Chiang Che Cheng
Figure D-13: Double Sabers/Malee Khow
Figure D-14: Saber/Irene Chen
Figure D-15: Pudao/Zhang Peng
Figure D-16: Saber/Rafael De La Cruz

Daopai 道派 This style originated from Shaolin Wushu. It was taught by a monk named Ruilong (瑞龍). Many of the Shaolin Buddhist monks were counterrevolutionary against the Qing Dynasty. The Qing Emperor persecuted the Shaolin monks everywhere they went. To disguise himself and his teachings, monk Ruilong named his Wushu, Daopai, so as to mislead his persecutors.

The notable practitioners of this style include: Yu Yunlong (余雲龍), Yu Mei (余妹), and Chen Dou (陳斗). The known routines include: Yingtouquan (硬頭拳), Zhongweiquan (重圍拳), Sijinggangquan (四金剛拳), Damoquan (達摩拳), Shiba Luohanquan (十八羅漢拳), Dianluohanquan (癲羅漢拳), Zhifawhenlu (指法問路), and Rouqiao (柔橋). Daopai also has many different weapon routines and sparring sets.

Figure D-17: Daopai Quangong (道派拳功)/Paul Chen

Dashaozigun *see* Gun

Dashengmen *see* Houquan

Deer Hook *see* Yuanyangyue

De La Cruz, Rafael He began his martial arts training in 1969 and has continued his Wushu training with Wu Wen-Ching since 1999. He is a Way of the Dragon School assistant instructor; and he is the Vice President of the Latin American Operations for the GTECH Corp. *See* his photo demonstration under Wushu Bingqi.

Diaojiaquan刁家拳 Translated as Diao Family Fist. Legend has it, that it originated in Jiangxi Province and spread to Meixian (梅縣) and Xingning (興寧) in Guangdong Province.

Dishuquanfa地術犬法 Translated as Ground Dog Style. It is also known as Digongquan (地功拳) and Gouquan (狗拳). Known for kicking techniques executed after intentionally falling to the ground, and other ground fighting techniques. There are over ten known routines in this style.

Ditangquan 地趟拳 Translated as Ground Style. This style was recorded in the Ming Dynasty *Martial Classic* (拳經) of *Jixiaoxinshu* by Qi Jiguang (戚繼光). Qi indicated the existence of ground fighting methods of Qiandie Zhang (千跌張之跌). Other known ground fighting information includes the Internal Family Fist's 72 Ground Fighting techniques (内家拳七十二跌). Ditangquan uses offensive ground fighting techniques to engage their opponents. Some known traditional barehanded routines include: Jiugunshibadie (九滾十八跌), and Jiudishibagun (就地十八滾); weapon routines include: Guntangdao (滾趟刀) and Gunlongqiang (滾龍槍).

Figure D-18: Splits Breakfall/Dianne Naughton

Figure D-19: Ditangquan/Joel Timons

Du Cane, John (1949-) One of the prominent figures in the promotion of healing and martial arts in the United States. He was born in South Africa and was educated in England where he earned a Masters Degree in English Literature from Cambridge University. He began his Qigong and Taijiquan practice in 1975 with many prominent practitioners from China, England, and North America; including the practitioners: Chiu, Choi, Liang Shou-Yu, Wu Wen-Ching, Chen, Terry Dunn, Paul Dillon, and Ken Cohen. Since 1990, he has owned Dragon Door Publications, a mail order house and publisher for resources on Qigong, healing, fitness, and internal martial arts. He is the author of four instructional videos on Qigong and a form guide for animal Frolic Qigong. *See* his photo demonstration under Qigong.

Drunken Style *see* Zuiquan

Duanbang *see* Gun

Duanbin Boji 短兵搏擊 Short weapon sparring. This is a fighting competition category in Wushu. In this competition, competitors must follow the specific rules and guidelines for the use of short weapons.

Figures D-20: Short Weapon Sparring/Zhang Shu-Fang and Zhao Li-Ying

Figure D-21 Short Weapon/Zhao Li-Ying

Dumen 杜門 Translated as Du Family Style. In the 1600's, Du Guanyin (杜官印) of Sichuan taught many students in Chengdu (成都). Dumen uses the Zijiqishen (知機其神) philosophy from Yijing (易經). The known routines of this style includes: Simenquan (四門拳) and Baiheizhuang (白鶴樁). Its fighting training includes: Yinyangshou (陰陽手), Taijishou (太極手), Wuxingshou (五行手), and many types of weapon training.

Dunhuangquan 敦煌拳 A Wushu style based on the drawing, Dunhuang Bihua (敦煌壁畫). Its movenents are graceful and firm, containing both defensive and offensive applications. The movements of the fist, palm, hook, claw, fingers, and the entire arm are closely associated with the energy channels in the body. Dunhuangquan is a physical exercise that is good for toning the body, weight loss, and illness prevention. It is also entertaining to watch and enjoyable to perform. The known routines include: Dunhuangquan and Dunhuang Rings (敦煌圈).

Information provided by Zang Lijuan.

Figure D-22: Dunhuangquan/Zang Lijuan

Figure D-23: Dunhuang Rings/Zang Lijuan

E

Eagle Claw Style *see* Yingzhuaquan

Eight Trigram Palm *see* Baguazhang

Emei Piercer *see* Emeici

Emei Shaolin 峨嵋少林 Translated as Shaolin Wushu of the Emei Mountains. It inherited its training from the Shaolin Temple. The Emei Shaolin routines are, however, no longer available in the Henan Shaolin Temple. This style contains both hard and intricate neutralizing techniques. It is a style with routines containing only practical Sanshou applications. The known routines include: Tiangan (天罡), Qixing (七星), Heihu (黑虎), Tianhe (天河), Feilong (飛龍), and Bafa (八法).

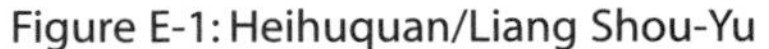

Figure E-1: Heihuquan/Liang Shou-Yu

Figure E-2: Heihuquan/Wu Wen-Ching
Figure E-3: Huweitui (虎尾腿)/Andrew Wu
Figure E-4: Tianganquan/Derek Cheng

Emei Shierzhuang 峨嵋十二樁 Translated as Emei Twelve Postures. Legend has it, that the Chan Buddhist priest, Baiyun (白雲禪師), created this style in the Emei Mountains. He combined Taoist, Medical, and Buddhist philosophy with Qigong, and created this style during the Southern Song Dynasty (1127-1279). There are twelve steps in their training. Thereby, the name, Shierzhuang.

Figure E-5: Emei Shierzhuang/Chen Jian

Emei Wudang Neijiaquan 峨嵋武當內家拳 Translated as Internal Style of Emei and Wudang. According to legend, a wandering Taoist from Emei named Wang Loadao (王老道) went to the Wudang Mountains to study Neijiaquan which was created by Zhang Sanfeng (張三丰). Wang further developed what he learned and it became known as Emei Wudang Neijiaquan. There are five known barehanded routines and one staff routine.

Emei Wushu 峨嵋武術 This is a term referring to all the styles that originated from the Emei Mountains. Emei Wushu is one of the three major groups of Wushu styles in China. The others are Shaolin and Wudang Wushu. The Emei Mountains are considered one of the four major Buddhist mountains in China, as well as, one of the famous Daoist mountains. The Emei Mountains are located at the southwestern part of Sichuan Province. The peak of the Emei Mountains reaches an elevation of 3,099 meters above sea level, making it the highest peak in the Sichuan Valley. There are also numerous Buddhist temples in these mountains.

Emei Wushu includes the essence of both Shaolin and Wudang Wushu. As early as the Ming Dynasty, there had been written documentation of Emei Wushu. During the Qing Dynasty, more and more styles began to surface from the Emei Mountains. There are over 300 Emei Wushu styles with over one thousand barehanded and weapon routines. Many of the specific Emei styles are introduced under their own heading.

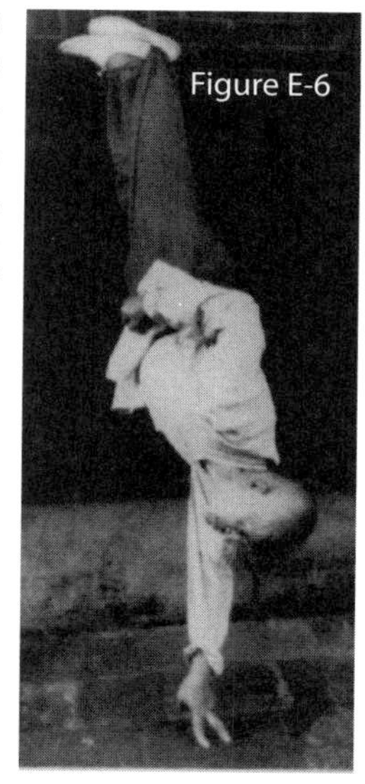

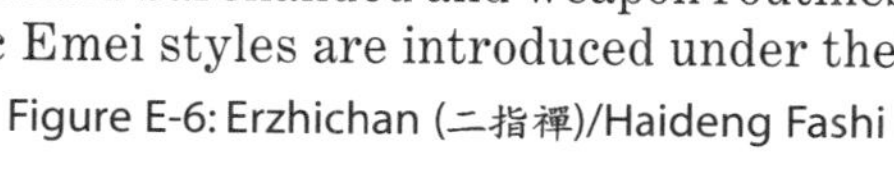

Figure E-6: Erzhichan (二指禪)/Haideng Fashi

Figure E-7: Emei Eagle Claw/Lu Xiaoling
Figure E-8: Libaishiyijian (李白詩意劍)/Chen Jian
Figure E-9: Emei Jingangquan (金剛拳)/He Tao
Figure E-10: Emei Shequan (蛇拳)/Maria Liang
Figure E-11: Emei Kuaishuaiquan (峨嵋快摔拳)/He Tao
Figure E-12: Emei Spear/Lu Xiaoling
Figure E-13: Emei Sword/Lu Xiaoling
Figure E-14: Emei Double Swords/Li Rong
Figure E-15: Chuanlinjian/Li Rong

Drawing E-1

Emeici 峨嵋刺 Translated as Emei Piercer. This was a weapon used in ancient water combat. It is a short piece of metal which is thick in the middle and tapered to sharp ends. It has a spinable ring in the middle for the fingers to fit through (Drawing E-1). Emeici are usually used in a pairs.

Figure E-16: Emeici/Kelly Maclean

Emeipai Quanshu Dantaolu 峨嵋派拳術單套路 Translated as Individual Wushu Routines of the Emei Mountains. There have been many well-known routines taught in the Emei Mountains. Many of these routines are practiced by practitioners of other styles and have been incorporated into other styles. They have lasted for a long time and have spread all over China.

These routines include: Shisantaibaoquan (十三太保拳), which was taught in the palace of the Qing Dynasty and combined the essence of 72 different routines into one; and Liuchengquan (六乘拳), which was created over 200 years ago by a Emei Mountain monk by imitating the movements of white crane and the legendary green dragon. There are many others including: Jianzhuangquan (劍樁拳), Emei Luohanquan (峨嵋羅漢拳), Jiji Sanshiliufa (技擊三十六法), Sanhuaquan (三花拳), Emei Meihuaquan (峨嵋梅花拳), Emei Zuibaxian (峨嵋醉八仙), Xiaofuhu (小伏虎), Emei Neijiaquan (峨嵋内家拳), Songxi Sanshou (松溪散手), Emei Xiaohongquan (峨嵋小洪拳), Jianzhuangquan (箭莊拳), Emei Shazhou (峨嵋殺肘), Xiaojinganquan (小金剛拳), Emei Gongliquan (峨嵋功力拳), Emei Taiquan (峨嵋傣拳), Kongmen Ruanshou (孔門軟手), Manjianghong (滿江紅), and Sipingdazhenquan (四平大鎮拳).

F

Fangmen 方門 Translated as Fang Family Style. This is an Emei Style. Fang Shunyi (方順懿) created Fangmen by combining Shaolin with Xingyiquan and "Xiao (肖)" style. There are twelve known barehanded routines and five weapon routines.

Fanziquan 翻子拳 Translated as Turning Body Fist. It was recorded as Bashanfan (八閃翻) during the Ming Dynasty (1368-1644) by General Qi Jiguang (戚繼光). Fanziquan is classified as Changquan. Its movements are described as "Two fists are fast like the falling rain drops, and fast like a snapping whip". Fanziquan routines are usually short and fast.

In the 1860's, after a failed revolt against the Qing empire, Fanziquan and Chuojiao practitioner, Zhao Shanyi (趙灿益), retreated to Hebei Province and taught Fanziquan and Chuojiao there. It was then that Fanziquan also spread to Shenyang (沈陽). Yu Boqiang (于伯謙) was a well-known Fanziquan practitioner from Shenyang. In the 1930's, it spread to Sichuan Province.

Some of the known traditional routines include: Chuibafan (翠八翻), Kaoshoufan (靠手翻), Caishoufan (採手翻), Qinshoufan (擒手翻), Liushoufan (六手翻), Yanqingfan (燕青翻), Yingzhuafan (鷹爪翻), Gunbangfan (滾膀翻), Sanshoufan (散手翻), and Jianzhongfan (健中翻).

Figure F-1: Fanziquan/Guo Jianhua
Figure F-2: Fanziquan/Wu Wen-Ching
Figure F-3: Fanziquan/Hui Mo

Farrands, Barry He has been studying Wushu since 1995 with Wu Wen-Ching. He is an assistant instructor at The Way of the Dragon School. He is also a long distance runner and medal winner in many races. *See* his photo demonstration under Shaolin Wushu.

Fenghuolun *see* Quan

Finger, Steve He has been studying martial arts since 1971 and began his Wushu training in 1986 with many leading Wushu practitioners in the United States. He is a database applications developer. He is currently based in Connecticut, U.S.A. *See* his photo demonstration under Wushu Bingqi.

Fontaine, Bruce He is a prominent Wushu practitioner. He was a member of the Canadian Wushu team in 1986. He began his Wushu studies with Cailifoquan. In the middle of the 1980's, he began studying Wushu from Liang Shou-Yu. He received two Bronze medals in the Second World Wushu Invitational Championships. He is a member of the Board of Directors and Wushu Form Chairman of Wushu B.C. He has appeared in many Hong Kong action movies. He currently teaches in Canada. *See* his photo demonstration under Xiandai Wushu.

Fu 斧 An ax. Fu usually refers to a short handled ax (Drawing F-1). Long handled axes are referred to as yue (鉞, Drawing F-2). Short axes are practiced singularly or in a pair. In ancient times, long axes were used by practitioners on horseback.

Drawing F-1

Drawing F-2

Fu, Zhongwen 傅鐘文 (1907-1997) One of the best disciples of Yang Chengfu (楊澄甫), and one of the most prominent representatives of Yang Style Taijiquan. He was the founder of the Yongnian Taijiquan Club (永年太極拳社) in 1944, a Shanghai City Taijiquan instructor from 1958-1971, and the Vice Chairman of the Shanghai Wushu Association in 1979. His whole life was dedicated to the teaching and promotion of Taijiquan. He has taught many outstanding Taijiquan students. He the author of an authoritative book, *Yang Style Taiji Saber*. *See* his photo demonstration under Taijiquan.

Fujian Hequan 福建鶴拳 Translated as Fujian Crane Style. This is one of three major crane styles. Fujian Hequan includes four unique characteristics. They are the Zonghequan (宗鶴拳, Ancestral Crane), Shihequan (食鶴拳, Ravaging Crane), Feihequan (飛鶴拳, Flying Crane), and Minghequan (鳴鶴拳, Shrieking Crane). The more predominant characteristics of each are: the vibrating power of Zonghequan, the hooking and clawing movements of the Shihequan, the flapping arms of the Feihequan, and the loud shrill sound emitted along with the applications of the Minghequan.

Also see Baihequan and Wuzuquan.

Fujian Province 福建省 A Chinese province located at the southeastern part of continental China which borders the Taiwan Strait to its southeast. It covers over 121 thousand square kilometers with a population of over 32 million people as of 1999.

Fujian Shaolin Temple 福建少林寺 *see* Shaolin Temple

Funk, Jon He was a Chairman of the Western Canada Chinese Martial Arts Association. He is a promoter of Tiger Balm International Karate-Kung Fu Championships, and has a monthly column in *Black Belt Magazine* titled "Legends of Kung Fu". He is an 8th generation practitioner of Tanglangquan. He is a member of the Board of Directors and the Traditional Wushu Form Chairman of Wushu B.C. He teaches Seven Star Preying Mantis Kung Fu in Vancouver, British Columbia, Canada. *See* his photo demonstration under Tanglangquan.

Fushi Wushu 傅氏武術 Fu Style Wushu. Towards the end of the 1920's, five northern Wushu practitioners traveled south to Guangdong and other southern provinces to teach Wushu. They were known as the "Five tigers that went south of the Yangtze River (五虎下江南)". One of them was Fu Zhensong (傅振嵩). He was a native of Henan Province and studied under many prominent Wushu instructors. He was the head coach of Guangdong and Guangxi, and the head coach at the Nanjing Central Guoshu Institute. Yang Chengfu (楊澄甫) and Sun Lutang (孫祿堂) were his good friends and training partners. Fu Zhengsong absorbed the essence of the other styles and founded Fushi Wushu. Some of the well-known Fushi Wushu routines include: Fu Style Taijiquan, Taiji Shandianzhang (太極閃電掌), Bagua Longxingzhang (八卦龍形掌), Chongfengquan (沖鋒拳), Xianrenzhang (仙人掌), Liangyiquan (兩儀拳), Sixiangquan (四象拳), Taiji Shandianchui (太極閃電錘), Bagua Xunfengdao (八卦旋風刀), Zhanshenqiang (站神槍), Wudang Feilongjian (武當飛龍劍), Luanpijian (亂劈劍), Bagua Qimengun (八卦奇門棍), and many sparring routines.

Fu Zhensong had many prominent disciples including: Fu Yonghui, Sun Baukang, Lin Chaozhen, Liang Richu, Liang Qiangya (梁強亞), Cui Rongji (崔榮基), and Li Huangsheng. His son, Fu Yonghui (傅永輝) continued his father's legacy and by continuing Fushi Wushu in Guangdong Province for over 60 years. Today, there are many other well-known Fushi Wushu practitioners in the U.S., they include: Johnny Kwong Ming Lee (勵光明), Mark Bow-Sim (麥寶嬋), Nick Gracenin, Jose Johnson, Joel Timons, etc.

Figure F-4: Fu Style Taijiquan Lightning Palm/Liang Qiangya
Figure F-5: Fu Style Bagua Dragon Palm/Liang Qiangya
Figure F-6: Fu Style Spear/Liang Qiangya
Figure F-7: Fu Style Bagau Staff/Liang Qiangya
Figure F-8: Lianyiquan/Nick Gracenin
Figure F-9: Fu Style Baguazhang/Jose Johnson

G

Gacki, Tadeusz (1954-) One of the most significant figures in the promotion of Wushu in Poland. He began his martial arts training in 1967. He was the Vice President of the first Polish Commission of Kung Fu/Wushu. He was the first person to organize Polish national Wushu competitions. In 1994, he assisted in the founding of the Polish-Chinese Association of Wushu (Nanbei) and was its first vice president. He has authored three Qigong books. Many of his students are Polish and U.S. national and international Wushu champions. *See* his photo demonstration under Changquan.

Gansu Province 甘肅省 A Chinese province located upstream of the Yellow River which borders Inner Mogol to its northeast. It covers over 453 thousand square kilometers with a population of over 25 million people as of 1999.

Gao, Xian 高西安 A graduate of Xian Sports Institute in Shanxi with a masters degree in sports science, specializing in martial arts. He was a China national Fanziquan and Tongbeiquan champion in 1982 and 1983. He has appeared in over thirty movies. He has over 20 years of teaching experience. Many of his students are now famous athletes and action stars. He currently teaches in New York, U.S.A. *See* his photo demonstration under Piquaquan.

Goh, Anthony 吳庭貴 One of the most significant organizers and contributors of Wushu in the United States. He is currently the President of the United States Wushu-Kung Fu Federation (U.S.A.W.K.F.), the President of the Pan American Wushu Federation (PAWF), and an organizer of the International Wushu-Kung Fu Festival and Championships. In 1995, he organized the Third World Wushu Championships in Baltimore, Maryland, U.S.A. It was the first world Wushu championship in North America. He is a prominent practitioner of several Wushu styles and known for his Sanshou abilities. For more information about him and U.S.A.W.K.F. please visit *www.usawkf.org*. *See* his photo demonstration under Kejiaquan.

Goldberg, Herb He is a prominent Taijiquan practitioner in Atlanta, Georgia. He is an advisor of the U.S.A. Wushu Kung Fu Federation, a national judge of Taijiquan and Push Hands. He currently teaches in Atlanta, Georgia. *See* his photo demonstration under Taijiquan.

Gongfu 功夫 1. The pinyin romanization of Kung Fu. 2. An attainment gained through the input of time and effort into a particular discipline.

Gong, Henry He is a prominent Wushu instructor in the New York area. He has been teaching Wushu for over twenty-eight years. He has taught his unique concepts on Lower Spinal Rotation at the Massachusetts Institute of Technology and the University of Delaware. His past and present affiliations include the Amateur Athletic Union and the National Association of Asian American Professions. He currently teaches in New York City. *See* his photo demonstration under Changquan.

Drawing G-1

Figure G-1

Gou 鈎 A hook sword. It is a narrow blade sword with a hook at the tip of the sword, a moon shaped blade next to the handle of the sword, and a sharp end (Drawing G-1). It is an ancient short weapon that can be practiced singularly or as a pair. There are many well-known gou routines including: Chagou (查鉤), Xinggou (行鉤), Shiersugou (十二速鉤), Xuepiangou (雪片鉤), and Juanjiangou (卷帘鉤).

Figure G-1: Double Hook Swords/Liu Yu

Gracenin, Nick He is a prominent all-around martial artist in the United States. He studied Fushi Wushu from Mark Bow-Sim. He has also studied many other Wushu styles and routines, especially the International Wushu competition routines. He has taught many outstanding students, and is a significant contributor to the development of Wushu in the U.S.A. Prior to studying Wushu, he had already attained a fifth level black belt in Karate. He was the third place all-around champion at the Second World Wushu Invitational Tournament. He was also an executive member of the International Wushu Federation. *See* his photo demonstration under Fushi Wushu.

Great Accomplishment Fist *see* Dachengquan

Drawing G-2

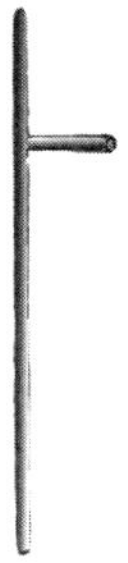

Ground Style *see* Ditangquan

Gu, Daijuan 古岱娟 Also known as, Jennifer Gu. She graduated from the Guangzhou Athletic University (廣州體育學院) in 1987. She was a former instructor at Huanan Normal University (華南師範大學). She was a Canadian national Taijiquan champion and a member of the Canadian National Wushu team. She currently teaches in Canada. See her photo demonstration under Taijiquan.

Guai 拐 A cane. This is also referred to as Guaizi (拐子). It is a crutch or cane that can be used to assist in walking. A traditional guai looks like a rod with a smaller piece extending from the upper part (Drawing G-2).

Figure G-2

Figure G-2: Guai/Tony Bujas

Guangdong Province 廣東省 A Chinese province located at the southeastern part of continental China which borders the South China Sea to its south. It covers over 178 thousand square kilometers with a population of over 71 million people as of 1999.

Guangxi Zhuangzu Zizhiqu 廣西壯族自治區 An autonomous region in southern China which borders Guangdong to its east and Beibu Gulf to its south. It covers over 236 thousand square kilometers with a population of over 46 million people as of 1999.

Figure G-3

Guizhou Province 貴州省 A Chinese province located south of the Yangtze River which borders Sichuan to its north and Guangxi to its south. It covers over 176 thousand square kilometers with a population of over 36 million people as of 1999.

Guoshu 國術 Another term for Chinese martial arts. It literally means national art of China. It is also romanized as Kuo Shu.

Gun 棍 A pole. It is also referred to as a bang (棒). It is a pole (Drawing G-3) made from a piece of wood or metal. It is known as the *head of all weapons* (百兵之首). A gun is a long weapon that is usually about the height of person from their feet to their eyebrows or taller. Often times, when the term *gun* is used, it refers to a cylindrical

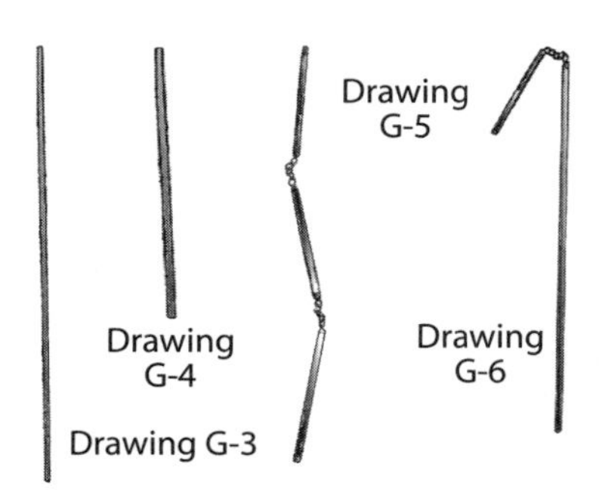

stick that is tapered from one end to the other, such as, the trunk of a small tree. When the term *bang* is used, it refers to a cylindrical pole having the same diameter throughout its length.

A pole longer than the distance between the practitioner's feet and eyebrows is considered a long weapon. Shorter poles are known as duanbang (短棒, Drawing G-4), short staff. It is also referred to as biangan (鞭杆). Short staffs are used singularly and as a pair. The shorter length makes it an easy weapon to carry around. Some well-known short staff routines include: Shisanbian (十三鞭), Sanshiliubian (三十六鞭), Tuolobian (陀螺鞭), and Liupanbian (六盤鞭).

There are also poles that are connected with chain links such as the Sanjiegun (三節棍) and Dashaozigun (大梢子棍). Sanjiegun is a three sectioned staff chain-linked together (Drawing G-5). It is classified as a flexible weapon. Dashaozigun is a two sectioned staff chained-linked together (Drawing G-6). It is also classified as a flexible weapon. The well-known pole routines include: Shaolingun (少林棍), Ziweigun (紫微棍), Qingtiangun (青田棍), Zhaotaizu Tengshegun (趙太祖騰蛇棍), Bazigun (巴子棍), Yudayougunfa (俞大猷棍法), and many others.

There is a legend that during the peaceful and prosperous period of the Tang Dynasty, even the Shaolin Temple had lost the original nature of the Shaolin pole applications. A Ming Dynasty general, Yu Dayou (俞大猷), went to the Shaolin Temple and taught the practical pole applications to the Shaolin monks. General Yu also selected two martial monks from the Shaolin Temple to study pole techniques in the military. Three years later, the monks returned to the temple and reestablished the fierce and practical nature of the Shaolin pole techniques. Later, Cheng Chongdou (程沖斗) went to the Shaolin temple to study Shaolin pole techniques and wrote about it. Cheng's book is the well-known, *Shaolin Gunfa Chanzong* (少林棍法闡宗).

Figure G-3: Carrying a Staff in Resting Stance/Li Wenqi
Figure G-4: Hougun/Wu Wen-Ching
Figure G-5: Monkey Staff/Hu Jianqiang
Figure G-6: Biangan/Lu Biao
Figure G-7: Three Sectional Staff/Derek Cheng
Figure G-8: Staff/Katrina Leung
Figure G-9: Staff/Hilbert Yiu, Jr.

Guo, Jianhua 郭建華 He began his Wushu training at the age of seven in Hubei, China. He studied under the direction of Professor Wen Jinmin and Liu Yuehua. He trained and competed professionally for both Wuhan Institute Professional Team and the Hubei Professional Team. He was the head coach of the Wuhan Institute of Physical Education and Hubei Provincial Team from 1972 to 1986. He has published several research articles on the study and training of martial arts for teenagers. He came to the U.S. in 1987 as a professor at Ball State University in Indiana. In 1991, he founded the Championship Martial Arts Academy in Chicago, Illinois. He has taught many martial arts champions and movie stars, including: Chris Farley, Anthony Marquez, and Daniel Pesina. *See* his photo demonstrations under Fanziquan and Yumenquan.

H

Haideng Fashi 海燈法師 (1902-1989) Also known as Fan Wubing (范無病). He was a prominent practitioner in the recent past. At age 21, he became a monk in the Emei Mountains and trained in Yizhijin (一枝金), Erzhichan (二指禪), Tongzigong (童子功), and Shaolin Wuquan (少林五拳). He was the former Henan Shaolin Temple Abbot and Vice Chairman of the China Buddhist Association. *See* his photo demonstration under Emei Wushu.

Hainan Province 海南省 A Chinese island province located off the southern part of continental China. It covers over 34 thousand square kilometers with a population of over 7 million people as of 1999.

Halberd *see* Ji

Hammer *see* Chui

Hao, Zhihua 郝志華 A former member of the Beijing Wushu team and a Wuyin (武英) title recipient. She has attained forty-five top three places in China national Wushu championships, including nineteen gold medals. She was a member of the China Wushu team that performed in many countries. She is a graduate of the Beijing Physical Education University. Upon graduation she remained on as a Wushu instructor for the university. She currently lives in the United States. *See* her photo demonstration under Xiandai Wushu.

Hard Whip *see* Bian

He, Fusheng 何福生 (1910-1998) A prominent Wushu practitioner in China. He inherited his Wushu from his family and also learned from many prominent Wushu practitioners. He learned Chaquan from Wang Ziping (王子平) and Ma Liang (馬良); Bajiquan from Ma Yingtu (馬英圖); Xingyiquan from Huang Bonian (黄柏年), Jiang Rongqiao (姜容樵), and Zu Guofu (朱國福); and Shuaijiao from Hong Wu (洪武). He was the Assistant Dean of Education at the Central Guoshu Institute in 1938. He was well-known for his fast takedown ability, and was nicknamed "Maqiansandao Hekuaijiao (馬前三刀何快跤)". He was the Wushu coach of the Yunnan Provincial team. He was a committee member of the Chinese Wushu Association and a Chairman of the Yunnan Wushu Association. In 1988, he received the "Wushu Contribution (武術貢獻)" award. Later, he also received the "Sport Pioneer Award of New China (新中國體育開闊)" award. *See* his photo demonstrations under Huaquan and Taijiquan.

He, Tao 何濤 A former head coach of the Guangdong Dongguan City Sports Association (廣東東莞市體委). He began his Wushu studies under Liang Shou-Yu in 1970 and continued until Liang Shou-Yu immigrated to North America in 1981. He is a Seventh Level Black Belt in Wushu and a Sixth Level Black Belt in Sanshou Dao. He has trained many gold medalists for provincial and national Wushu competitions in China. He was also an all-around champion in the 1983 Sichuan Provincial Wushu Competition, and gold medalist in 1987 for his sword performance in a China National Competition. He received his Wuyin (武英) title in 1987, became a world competition fighting judge in 1996, and became a national level coach and judge for lion and dragon dancing competitions. He currently teaches in San Francisco, California. *See* his photo demonstrations under Tongbiquan, Emei Wushu, Yuanyangyue, and Dao.

He, Weiqi 何偉琪 One of three prominent female swordsmen in the 1970's. In 1974, she was the featured performer in the first official Wushu Delegation to the United States and performed at the White House. She was the senior Wushu coach for the youth at the Shanghai Sports Palace from 1976 to 1989. Her team won the first place honor for seven years in a row at the Shanghai National Junior Wushu competitions. She has received numerous awards from China and abroad, including the prestigious China's Coaches of Excellence award. She has taught thousands of students all over the world. She has both appeared in and been the action choreographer for many action movies. She is the cofounder of the 18-form system of Taiji Qigong now practiced around the world. In August 2000, she was featured on the Friday Evening News with Peter Jennings. *See* her photo demonstrations under Jian, Quan, Taijiquan, and Wudang Wushu.

Hebei Province 河北省 A Chinese Province located downstream and north of the Yellow River which borders Shandong, Tianjin, Bejing, and Liaoning to its east, and borders Shanxi to its west. It covers over 183 thousand square kilometers with a population of over 65 million people as of 1999.

Heilongjiang Province 黑龍江省 A Chinese Province located at the most northeastern part of China which borders Russia to its north and east, and borders Jilin to its south. It covers over 543 thousand square kilometers with a population of over 37 million people as of 1999.

Henan Shaolin Temple 河南少林寺 *see* Shaolin Temple

Henan Province 河南省 A Chinese province located downstream and to the south of the Yellow River and borders Jiangsu to its east. It covers over 167 thousand square kilometers with a population of over 93 million people as of 1999.

Ho, Fred 何偉中 A gold and silver medalist in western U.S. international Wushu competitions. He has been a judge at Canadian National Wushu competitions. He is a S.Y.L. Wushu Institute instructor. He is also included in the book, *China's Contemporary Wushu Masters* (中國當代武林名人志). *See* his photo demonstrations under Yanqingquan and Wushu Sanshou Dao.

Holmes, Michael He is a Second Degree Black Belt in Wado Kai Karate, a First Degree Black Belt in Nisei Karate, and a First Level Black Belt in Wushu Sanshou Dao. *See* his photo demonstration under Wushu Sanshou Dao.

Hong, Yijiao 洪一姣 A member of the U.S. Wushu team. She was a U.S. National Grandchampion in Internal Styles many times. In 1998, she was named Athlete of the Year in the U.S.A. In the 1999 World Wushu Championships held in Hong Kong, she attained seventh place in the compulsory Taiji Sword category. She is a graduate of Zhejiang University with a degree in Physical Education and a majored in Wushu. She was also a former Wushu teacher at Zhejiang University. She was a chief instructor of the Wushu team and former faculty member at the Zhejiang College of Traditional Chinese Medicine. In 2001, she was certified by the International Wushu Federation as an International Wushu Forms Judge. She currently teaches in Seattle, Washington, USA. *See* her photo demonstrations under Xiandai Wushu and Taijiquan.

Hongjiaquan 洪家拳 Translated as Hong Family Fist. It is one of the major Southern Styles. This style was created by Hong Xiguan (洪熙官) of Fujian Province during the Qing Dynasty. It is also popular in Guangdong Province and Southeastern Asian nations. Hong learned his Wushu from Zhishan (至善禪師), a Chan Buddhist monk from Fujian Shaolin Temple. Hong Xiguan was also the character featured in the novel *Wangnian Qing* (萬年青) written in the later part of the Qing Dynasty. Some of its rotuines include: Sipingliuzhen (四平六鎮), Sanjian (三箭), Tiejian (鐵箭), Shixing (十形), Huhe Shuangxinguan (虎鶴雙形拳), Gongzifuhuquan (工字伏虎拳), Wuxingquan (五行拳), Shixingquan (十行拳), Huquan (虎拳), and Hequan (鶴拳). Its characteristics include using sounds to assist in power emission. Some well-known practitioners in Hongquan include: Tie Qiaosan (鐵橋三), Huang Feihong (黃飛鴻), and Lin Shirong (林世榮).

Figure H-1: Hongjiaquan/John Leong

Figure H-2: Hongjiaquan/Ken Low

Figure H-3: Hongjiaquan/Saleem Alamudeen

Figures H-4 and H-5: Hongjiaquan Matching Set/Purdy Cheung and Kerry Cheung

Hong Kong 香港 A Special Administrative Region in China, located in the South China Sea which includes Hong Kong Island. The total area is about one thousand square kilometers. Hong Kong means *fragrant harbor* in Chinese. It was originally part of the Guangdong Province until after the Opium War in 1842, when it was ceded to British rule. Hong Kong was under British rule for nearly one and a half centuries until 1997, when it was returned to China and became a Special Administrative Region of China. Hong Kong has a population of over 7 million people.

Hongmen 洪門 There are two legends to the origin of this style. The first legend believes that it was created by Emperor Zhao Taizu (趙太祖). His face was always hong (紅) or red. Therefore, the style was named Hongquan (紅拳) and later became known as Hongmen.

The second legend believes that in the year 1661, the defeated Ming Dynasty general, Zheng Chenggong (鄭成功), organized a counterrevolutionary force against the new Qing Dynasty. The organization used the name Hongmen because the first emperor of the Ming Dynasty was known as Hongwu (洪武). It gradually evolved into two distinct divisions, the Northern and the Southern Hongmen. There are over forty-five known barehanded routines, over seventeen weapon routines, and eight application training methods.

Hongquan 紅拳 Translated as Red Fist. Hongquan is popular in Shanxi and Sichuan. Legend has it, that it was passed down by Jueyuanshangren (覺遠上人) during the Yuan Dynasty. Hongquan is classified as Changquan.

Figure H-6: Xiaohonguqan (小紅拳)/Maria Liang

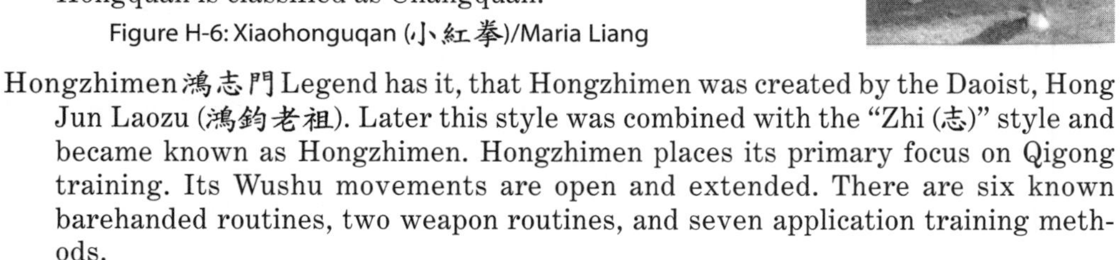

Hongzhimen 鴻志門 Legend has it, that Hongzhimen was created by the Daoist, Hong Jun Laozu (鴻鈞老祖). Later this style was combined with the "Zhi (志)" style and became known as Hongzhimen. Hongzhimen places its primary focus on Qigong training. Its Wushu movements are open and extended. There are six known barehanded routines, two weapon routines, and seven application training methods.

Hook Sword *see* Gou

Hoover, Paul He began his Wushu training in 1977 and has been studying from Wu Wen-Ching since 1990. He is a computer consultant. He currently teaches Taijiquan at the Community College of Rhode Island and in the New England area. *See* his photo demonstration under Nanquan.

Houquan 猴拳 Translated as Monkey Style. Houquan is believed to have existed several thousand years ago. It was recorded in the Ming Dynasty book, *Jixiaoxinshu* by Qi Jiguang. Houquan is an imitation style mimicking the movements of a monkey It is also known as Dashengmen (大聖門).

Figure H-7: Monkey Staff/Hu Jianqiang

Howey, Ayron He is an instructor at the S.Y.L. Wushu Institute and the University of British Columbia Sanshou class. In 1999, he was the gold medalist in the Pan American Wushu Championships and silver medalist in the Canadian National Wushu Competition in the 65-70 Kg Sanshou division. In 2001, he was the gold medalist in the 65 to 70 Kg Canadian National Sanshou competition. He was selected to represent Canada at the 6th World Wushu Championships. He is a Third Level Black Belt in Wushu Sanshou Dao. *See* his photo demonstrations under Wushu Sanshou Dao and Cha.

Hsing Yi Chuan *see* Xingyiquan

Hsu, Adam 徐紀 (1941-) A prominent Wushu practitioner known for his vast knowledge about many traditional Wushu styles. His principal teacher was the late Liu Yun-Chiao (劉雲樵). He has a master's degree in Chinese literature from Taiwan. He was the General Secretary of the National Kung Fu Federation of Taiwan, Instructor to the Republic of Liberia, and Member of the Republic of China National Kung Fu Delegation. He was the editor and publisher of Wu Tang Martial Arts Magazine, and a senior editor of the Kung Fu Library of Wu Chow Publishing Company. He has written several books and over one hundred articles in English and Chinese. He has been featured and honored by numerous magazines throughout the world. He is the founder of the Traditional Wushu Association. More about him can be found at *www.adamhsu.com*. See his photo demonstration under Bajiquan.

Hu, Jianqiang 胡堅強 He is a famous movie star and Wushu practitioner. He is best known for his starring role in the movie, *Shaolin Temple*. He became a choreographer in Hong Kong for various movies. He has also appeared in, *Kids From Shaolin, North and South Shaolin*, and *Shogun*. He was a member of the Zhejiang Provincial Wushu Team, and won numerous all-around titles. He represented China eleven times and performed Wushu in over thirty nations. He is one of the most outstanding athletes, coaches, and performers in China. He has demonstrated in numerous TV shows that were well received by the audience. He currently teaches and operates a successful school in Connecticut, U.S.A. *See* his photo demonstrations under Shaolin Wushu, Houquan, and Gun.

Hu, Zehua 胡澤華 Also known as Simon Hu. He began his Wushu studies at age twelve under the legendary Wang Ziping; and Wang Jurong, Wu Chengde, and many other prominent Wushu practitioners in China. He is well-versed in all areas of Wushu including the ti, da, shuai, and na components. Under the guidance of Wang Ziping and Wu Chengde, he has also excelled in Qigong and traumatology. He has been a judge at U.S. and Canadian National Wushu competitions and is a founding member of the Confederation of Canadian Wushu Organizations. He currently teaches in Toronto, Canada. *See* his photo demonstration under Wangshi Wushu.

Huakoumen 化口門，化門 This is an Emei Style. Huakoumen focuses on one handed applications, neutralization training; and utilizes Yin-Yang, Five Elements, and Bagua as its training philosophy. There are sixteen known routines in this style and various weapons training.

Huang, Rena 黄雪 A 1991 graduate of the Beijing Academy of Performing Arts (北京舞蹈學院). She is a first class actor in China. She has received several outstanding performance awards for her performances in Chinese National and Beijing dance competitions. She has starred in several major dance productions and represented China in good will performances overseas. She has also appeared in many movies and TV shows. After immigrating to Canada, she began studying Wushu at the S.Y.L. Institute. *See* her photo demonstration under Xiandai Wushu.

Huang, Wei-Lun 黄慰倫 Born in Guangzhou, China where he began his studies of Taijiquan since he was a child. He is a prominent Taijiquan practitioner in the United States. He has been teaching and giving workshops in the U.S., South America, and Europe since 1984. His Taijiquan teachers were Lu Zi Ling, a student of Yang Chengfu, and Ou Yong Ju, the President of the Foshan Wushu Association. His Liuhebafa teacher was Wang So Ting of Shanghai. He currently teaches in Florida, USA. *See* his photo demonstration under Taijiquan.

Huanglinpai 黄林派 Translated as the Yellow Forest Style. This is an Emei Style. It is credited to an old Taoist priest of the Wannian Temple (萬年寺) in the Emei Mountains. During the reign of the Qing Emperor, Yongzheng (雍正, 1723-1735), the emperor gave an order to arrest all nonmilitary martial artists. As a result many martial art practitioners gathered at Jiufeng Mountain (九峰山) as a sanctuary to practice their Wushu and to share their Wushu with youngsters that came to learn.

The leaves of the ginkgo or the maidenhair trees in the Jiufeng Mountains turn a golden yellow color in the Fall. Thereby, the style was named Huanglin, meaning Yellow Forest. The known barehanded routines include: Sipingquan (四平拳), Dengzhuangquan (等樁拳), and three Hulongquan (火龍拳), a weapon routine known as Yanlindao (燕林刀), and a training method referred to as Meirenzhuang (美人樁).

Figure H-8: Huolongquan/Derek Cheng

Huaquan 花拳 Translated as Flower Fist. According to legend, this style was created by Gan Fengchi (甘風池) of the Qing Dynasty. It is a short range style. Huaquan focuses on offensive and defensive techniques. There are over eighty-eight specific fighting and takedown techniques.

Huaquan 華拳 Translated as Hua Mountain Fist. Legend has it, that this style was created by the Cai (蔡) brothers during the Song Dynasty in the Sandong area. The Cai brothers were prominent Wushu practitioners who taught their relatives their Wushu. Because their ancestors were originally from the Hua Mountains, their style was later named Huaquan.

Another explanation for the naming of the style is believed to be from the training of jing (精), qi (氣), and shen (神). Jing, qi, and shen are also known as the three hua (華), or three *pure essences*. By combining the three hua into one it becomes Huaquan. Huaquan is classified as Changquan.

Figures H-9 and H-10: Huaquan/He Fusheng

Figure H-11: Huaquan/Michael Li

Huatao Wuyi 花套武藝 A term referring to the performance art derived from traditional Wushu, and practiced for the purpose of entertaining audiences. It is also referred to as Huaquan Xiutui (花拳繡腿), which literally means "flowery fist and embroidered feet". That is, of no combat value.

Since the Ming Dynasty, peace and raising prosperity in the cities brought about a greater need for cultural entertainment. Some of these needs were met by Wushu practitioners wandering into the cities from the countryside. In order to make a living, many Wushu practitioners became street performers. Their amazing abilities were warmly received and further promoted the increase in the artistic value of Wushu. As a result, more and more artistically expressive Wushu routines were created. The Chinese opera and ethnic dances had also been significantly influenced by Wushu. The popularity of combat performances in the Chinese opera and ethnic dances pushed the popularity of Huatao Wuyi to its height.

From an artistic perspective, it was a wonderful development. From the Wushu standpoint, Huatao Wuyi had lost its original nature. For this reason, the Ming Dynasty military officer, Qi Jiquang, forbade his troops to learn it. However, for people that didn't know Wushu, it was very entertaining. Therefore, the development of Huatao Wuyi continues even today.

Hubei Province 湖北省 A Chinese province located at the mid-stream of the Yangtze River and borders Sichuan to its west. It covers over 185 thousand square kilometers with a population of over 59 million people as of 1999.

Huen, Siu Hung 禤小虹 A member of the Canadian Wushu team in 1985. He began studying Internal and External Style Wushu from Liang Shou-Yu in 1982. He has attained many gold and silver medals in several international Wushu championships, and was included in the book, *China's Contemporary Wushu Masters* (中國當代武林名人志). He is a S.Y.L. Wushu Institute instructor. He has trained many Wushu athletes that have attained outstanding marks in international competitions. *See* his photo demonstration under Wuji Xiaoyaopai.

Huheshuanxingquan 虎鶴雙形拳 Translated as Tiger-Crane Routine. This is a southern style routine created by Lin Shirong (林世榮) during the end of the Qing Dynasty and the beginning of the republic. Lin was from Pingzhou (平州), Nanhai (南海). Lin studied his family Wushu then studied from Wu Quanmei (吳全美), Huang Feihong (黃飛鴻), etc. He based his creation on Hongiaquan (洪家拳) and Foquan (佛拳), with the characteristics of the tiger and crane. Thereby, the name Huheshuanxingquan, meaning Tiger-Crane Paired Shaped Routine. This routine consists of 108 postures.

Figure H-12

Figure H-12: Huheshuanxingquan/Tony Bujas

Hui, Mo 許無方 A gold medalist in the 1997 U.S. National Wushu championships in Nine Sectioned Chain, and a Silver medalist in the Canadian National Sanshou competition. He is an instructor at the S.Y.L. Wushu Institute. He is a graduate of the University of British Columbia with a degree in Computer Science. He is also included in the book, *China's Contemporary Wushu Masters* (中國當代武林名人志). *See* his photo demonstrations under Tongbiquan, Fanziquan, Bian, and Xiandai Wushu.

Huimen 慧門 This style was created by Song Luhua (宋魯華) of Shandong Province. Huimen training includes: meditation, visualization, and intention training. The movements are usually accompanied with small steps and lower stances. The known routines include: Yangjianquan (楊戩拳), Nazhaquan (哪吒拳), Hamaquan (蛤蟆拳), Hudiequan (蝴蝶拳), Shetouquan (蛇頭拳), and Rope Dart.

Hunan Province 湖南省 A Chinese province located south of the Yangtze River which borders Hubei to its north and Guangdong to its south. It covers over 204 thousand square kilometers with a population of over 65 million people as of 1999.

Hung Gar *see* Hongjiaquan

Huquan 虎拳 Translated as Tiger Routine. This term refers to an imitation routine that mimics the characteristics of a tiger or leopard. There are many Huquan routines including: Huquan (虎拳), Heihuquan (黑虎拳), Huxingquan (虎形拳), Xingyi Hubaoquan (形意虎豹拳), Menghu Xiashanquan (猛虎下山拳), Ehuquan (餓虎拳), Baihuquan (白虎拳), and Huzhuaquan (虎爪拳).

Huxingquan 虎形拳 Translated as Tiger Style. This is one of the imitation type Southern Styles. It imitates the tiger's characteristics in its movements. It was created by Zhou Zihe (周子和) of Fujian Province. It focuses on short range applications emphasizing the strength of the fingers or the claws. Some of the known routines include: Sanzhan (三戰), Simen (四門), Wufei (五飛), Bagua (八卦), Qixing (七星), Xiashanhu (下山虎), and Yibailinbashi (一百零八式).

I

Inner Mongolia *see* Nei Mongol Zizhiqu

Internal Style *see* Neijiaquan

I.W.S.D. *see* Wushu Sanshou Dao

J

Jay, Bok Tong 謝宇雲 Also known as Tony Jay. He is a prominent instructor of Lamapai Kung Fu, Taijiquan, and Qigong. He currently teaches in Vancouver, British Columbia, Canada. *See* his photo demonstration under Lamapai.

Jeet Kune Do *see* Jiequandao

Ji 戟 A halberd or lance. It is like a spear with an additional moon shaped blade along one or both sides of the spear head. A ji with a single moon shape blade is referred to as a Qinglongji (青龍戟, Drawing J-1). A ji with moon shape blades on both sides of the spear head is referred to as a Fangtianji (方天戟, Drawing J-2).

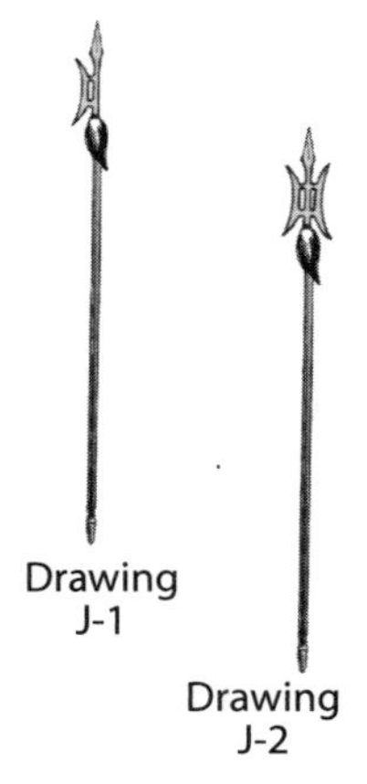
Drawing J-1

Drawing J-2

Jian 劍 A narrow blade sword (Drawing J-3). It is known as the *king of blades* (白刃之君) and is regarded by both scholars and martial artists as the most distinguished of all weapons. It is not just the "king of blades"; in ancient China, sword ownership represented power and prestige. For example, the Emperor's Sword, which ancient emperors presented to their royal subjects, had the authority to execute prisoners without first acquiring permission. Swords were also ceremonial tools used in Taoist ceremonies for getting rid of evil. The wearing of a sword at official gatherings represented prestige and rank. Scholars also wore a sword to be distinguished and elegant.

During the Spring-Autumn era, bronze and iron weapons were the most lethal war weapons. Tl ability to produce quality swords and the ability fight with the sword were significant factors in wi

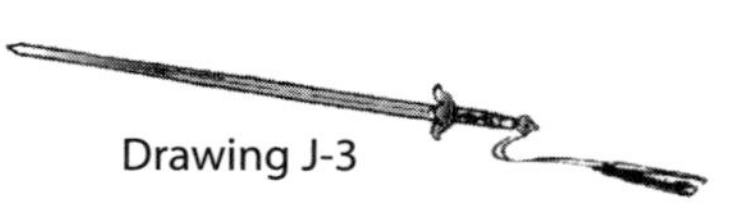
Drawing J-3

ning or losing a war. This was especially true in the area south of the Yangtze River where the land was filled with rice paddies, streams, and rivers. The war machines of the time were nearly useless. The primary military strength was the soldiers' ability to fight with a sword. For this reason, the quality of sword production and sword fighting techniques advanced significantly in this era.

The kings of all territories hired expert swordsmen to teach their army *jiandao*, the way of the sword. There have been many famous swordsmen in ancient China. One of the most famous historical figures was Yuenu, the Lady of the Yue Kingdom. Yuenu was a swordswoman that taught the way of the sword to the Yue army and gave them victory over their nemesis. Yuenu was also one of the most significant people in the ancient development of swordsmanship.

To improve the fighting abilities of their soldiers, it was customary for kings to employ master swordsmen to teach their soldiers. On a chance encounter, the king's consul met Yuenu, and he recommended Yuenu to Jujian, the King of Yue. King Jujian requested Yuenu to demonstrate her sword skills and to teach his soldiers. Yuenu complied. In Jujian's palace ten of his most elite bodyguards attempted to close in on Yuenu at the same time. None of them were able to touch her. In just a few moments, with the chilling sounds of slicing and jabbing blades, followed by falling bodies and the sounds of the swords hitting the palace floor, it was all over. Yuenu's superior skill was obvious to all present.

King Jujian asked Yuenu to explain the principles of her sword skills. Yuenu explained that her way of the sword was based on the *Book of Changes*, *Laozi*, and *Sunzi's Art of War*. She explained the technical, strategic, and psychological components of swordsmanship; and how they applied to movement and stillness, fast and slow movements, defense and offense, consequential and inconsequential movements, internal energy and external expression, following and opposing movements, and inhalation and exhalation. With Yuenu's expertise and teaching, Jujian's army became more and more powerful and defeated his nemesis. Legend has it, that Yuenu gained her extraordinary sword skill by practicing her stick-sword fighting with a white ape, since she was a child. The *White Ape Sword* and *Yuenu Sword* are credited to have been the creation of Yuenu.

As early as the Han Dynasty, a thirty-eight chapter book on *Jiandao* or the *Way of the Sword* was compiled. Today, there are many types of swords and many well-known sword routines. Different styles also have their own training methods and routines.

Figure J-1: Long Sword Exits the Scabbard/Pan Qingfu

Figure J-2: Group Double Swords/S.Y.L. Wushu Institute Students: Mo, Derek, Francis, Chanelle, Cheryl, and Tiffannie

Figure J-3: Fingers with No Sword/ Jiang Haoquan

Figure J-4: Sword with Scabbard/ Liang Shou-Yu

Figure J-5: Long Tassel Sword/ He Weiqi

Figure J-6: Eight Immortal Sword/ Helen Liang

Figure J-7: Sword/Zhang Lingmei

Figure J-8: Double Long Tassel Sword/He Weiqi

Figure J-9: Three Incense Points at the Heaven/Liang Shihong

Figure J-10: Group Long Tassel Sword/ S.Y.L. Wushu Institute Students: Kelly, Shona, Sarah, Chanelle, Cheryle, Katrina, and Tiffannie

Figure J-11: Group Double Sword/S.Y.L. Wushu Institute Students: Mo, Derek, Francis, Chanelle, Cheryl, and Tiffannie

Figure J-12: White Ape Sword/Helen Liang

Figure J-13: Sancaijian/Wu Wen-Ching

Figure J-14: Sword Points at Mount Kunlu/Li Jinheng

Figure J-15

Figure J-16

Figure J-17

The well-known sword routines include: Taijijian (太極劍), Taiyijian (太乙劍), Wudangjian (武當劍), Kunlunjia (昆侖劍), Kunwujian (昆吾劍), Emeijian (峨嵋劍), Qixingjian (七星劍), Baxianjian (八仙劍), Baguajian (八卦劍), Damojian (達摩劍), Baiyaunjian (白猿劍), Chuanlinjian (穿林劍), Tongbeijian (通背劍), Qingpingjian (青萍劍), Longfengjian (龍鳳劍), Tanglangjian (螳螂劍), Panlongjian (蟠龍劍), Chunyangjian (純陽劍), Sancaijian (三才劍), Sanhejian (三合劍), Tipaojian (綈袍劍), and Qinghongjian (青虹劍).

Figure J-15: Double Swords/Zhang Hong Mei

Figure J-16: Sword Matching/Zhang Hong Mei and Liu Yu

Figure J-17: Sword/Phillip Wong

Jian 鐧 A short weapon, usually made of metal, with a handle and a rod extension (Drawing J-4). The cross section of the rod extension is usually shaped like a square, an octagon, or a pentagon. It is practiced singly or in pairs.

Drawing J-4

Jiang, Haoquan 蔣浩泉 (1917-) The first person to receive a Ph.D. in Wushu in China. He is a Wushu professor and was the head coach of many provincial, military, and police training centers. He began swimming lessons at age three and started his Wushu studies at age 4. He is a graduate of the Central Guoshu Institute (1932-1936). In his youth, he defeated many foreign and Chinese boxers. He attained many awards and nicknames, including "China and Asia Boxing King (中國,亞洲拳王)", "China Fitness Champion (中國健美冠軍)", "Living Huo Yuanjia (活著的霍元甲)", "The Great Fighter (技擊泰斗)", "Chinese National and Shanghai Diving Champion", and many others. He currently teaches at Jiang Haoquan Chinese Martial Arts College in California, U.S.A. *See* his photo demonstrations under Jian and Xiandai Wushu.

Jiang, Jianye 姜建業 A prominent Wushu practitioner and calligrapher. He was a former instructor at Shandong Qufu Athletic University (山東曲阜體育學院). He is a graduate of Shandong Teachers University, and holds a master degree in Physical Education from the Shanghai Physical Education Institute. He has also produced numerous instructional Wushu videotapes. He currently teaches in Albany, NY and gives workshops throughout the United States. *See* his photo demonstrations under Shequan and Shandongjiao.

Jianghequan 江河拳 Translated as River Style. It originated from Kaifeng (開封) in Henan Province. There are four known routines in this style.

Jiangsu Province 江蘇省 A Chinese province located on the eastern coast of continental China. It is located downstream of the Yangtze River and borders the Yellow Sea to its east. It covers over 102 thousand square kilometers with a population of over 71 million people as of 1999.

Jiangxi Huimen 江西會門 Translated as the Huimen Style of Jiangxi. This style originated in the Jiangxi Province by Liu Jiangxi (劉江西). It focuses on offensive applications. There are seven barehanded routines and one bench routine.

Jiangxi Province 江西省 A Chinese province located south of the Yangtze River and borders Fujian Province to its southeast and borders Hunan to its west. It covers over 167 thousand square kilometers with a population of over 41 million people as of 1999.

Jiequan 節拳 Translated as Sectional Fist. It utilizes Tantui (潭腿) as its foundation. It is a style developed during the Qing Dynasty.

Jiequandao 截拳道 Also known as, Jeet Kune Do. This is a new martial arts style created by Bruce Lee (李小龍,李振藩, 1940-1973). Bruce Lee was born in San Francisco, California while his parents were traveling in the United States. He started his Wushu training under his father at age seven in Hong Kong. At thirteen, he began studying Yongchunquan under his teacher Yip Man (葉問) and older classmate Huang Chunliang (黃淳樑). At age eighteen, he returned to the U.S. and in 1961, he entered the University of Washington and majored in philosophy. While in the U.S., he continued his Wushu training and absorbed other eastern and western fighting arts into his own practice and created Jiequandao. He was the star in many martial arts films and his movies jolted the movie industry, bringing Chinese martial arts to an all time high in awareness and popularity in the west.

Jiequandao can be translated as the *way of intercepting fist*. However, Bruce Lee, himself, regarded Jiequandao more as a philosophy and concept rather than a style. Jiequandao is deeply rooted in ancient Chinese philosophy.

Jilin Province 吉林省 A Chinese province located in the middle of the northeastern part of China. It borders Heilongjiang to its north, North Korea to its southeast, and Liaoning to its southwest. It borders Russia to its north and east, and borders Jilin to its south. This province covers over 187 thousand square kilometers with a population of over 26 million people as of 1999.

Jinbashou 緊八手 Translated as Tight Eight Hands. This was a popular style during the middle of the Qing Dynasty around the Hubei Province. The known training includes: eight routines, sixteen kicking methods, and eight punching methods.

Jingpo Wushu 景頗武術 This refers to the Wushu developed by the Jingpo tribe of ancient China. They lived in deep forests and were under a constant threat from animals. To protect themselves they developed effective blade techniques. Today, the descendants of the Jingpo still practice their Wushu. Their saber techniques tend to be more offensive than defensive in applications. They have many saber routines including: Sanbukanbao (三步砍豹), Wugejiaobu (五個腳步), Qigejiaobu (七個腳步), and several double saber routines. Performances of saber techniques are often seen during the Jingpo ethnic holiday celebrations.

Jinjiagong 金家功 This was created during the reign of the Qing Emperor, Daoguang (道光), between 1823 and 1850. After a failed revolution against the Qing Empire, Ji Yiwang (姬一旺) changed his name to Jin Daoren (金道人) and created Jinjiao

Shiershi (金家十二式). They have two special training methods and five characteristics. The special training methods are Kaihe Qigong (開合氣功) and Caojin Wucidi (操勁五次弟). There are twenty-eight known routines in this style.

Jinwu Tiyuhui 精武體育會 This athletic association was founded in 1910 by Chen Gongzhe (陳公哲). It was originally named the Shanghai Jinwu Ticao Xuexiao (上海精武體操學校) which was founded in 1909. In 1909 Huo Yuanjia (霍元甲, 1857-1909) of Hebei Province was invited to Shanghai to teach his Wushu. He defeated foreign challengers during the later part of the weakened Qing Dynasty and became a prominent practitioner of the time. Unfortunately, he died six months after he arrived, due to an illness. Some people believe he was poisoned. However, the spirit of Huo Yuanjia and Jinwu continue until today. His legacy still continues in the Jinwu Athletic Associations all over the world.

Jixiaoxinshu 紀效新書 A Wushu book written by Qi Jiquang (戚繼光, 1528-1587). Qi was a Ming Dynasty general and author of *Jixiaoxinshu* (紀效新書)—*The New Book of Effective Disciplines*. His book was one of the earliest records of the different styles of Wushu available. He was a prominent practitioner in Wushu and military strategy. His book and teachings had a significant influence on the development of Wushu and the military. This book was originally published in 1584 and has been repeatly reprinted in subsequent centuries until today. It has also been reprinted under many other titles in Imperial China, Japan, and Korea.

Johnson, Jared A member of the Canadian Wushu team and a student of the S.Y.L. Wushu Institute. In 1998, he was a gold medalist in the Pan American Wushu Championships and Canadian National Wushu Competition in the 90 kilogram Sanshou division. *See* his photo demonstration under Wushu Sanshou Dao.

Johnson, Jerry Alan A Doctor of Traditional Chinese Medicine. He is well-known for his work in the field of Qigong, Taijiquan, and Baguazhang. He has written and published numerous books and videos on martial arts and Qigong. He is the Executive Director and Founder of the International Institute of Medical Qigong with branches in the U.S.A., Canada, South Africa, and Europe. More about him and his school can be found at *www.qigongmedicine.com*. *See* his photo demonstration under Baguazhang.

Johnson, Jose He was the Internal Style Grandchampion in the 1995 U.S. National Wushu Championships. He has also been the grandchampion at A Taste of China Internal Style competitions. He is a student of Nick Gracenin. He currently teaches in Harrisburg, Pennsylvania, U.S.A. *See* his photo demonstration under Fushi Wushu.

K

Karate-do 空手道 A Japanese system of martial arts that combined Chinese martial arts with the native Okinawan martial arts. In the 1920's it spread to the Japanese mainland from Okinawa. The original characters used were 唐手道, pronounced as *tangshoudao* in Chinese. The original characters implied that the art came from the martial arts of the Chinese Tang Dynasty. In the 1930's, it was changed to the current characters, meaning *barehanded ways*, without changing the Japanese pronounciation.

Figure K-1: Karate/Wang Yu Wa (1978)

Keele, Calvin A many time Push Hands gold medalist at the West Coast U.S. and Canadian Wushu competitions. He has completed Level Two Taijiquan Instructor training at S.Y.L. Wushu Institute. *See* his photo demonstrations under Taijiquan and Wushu Sanshou Dao.

Kejiaquan 客家拳 A term referring to Southern Styles practiced by the Kejia (客家, Hakka) speaking people in China. More specifically, it refers to the Southern Styles of Guangdong Province; namely, Diaojiaquan (刁家拳), Zhujiajiao (朱家教), Niujiajiao (牛家教), Zhangjiajiao (張家教), etc.

Figure K-2

Figure K-2: Zhangjiajiao/Anthony Goh

Kexingzhang 克星掌 This style was created by Cheng Kexin (程克欣). Cheng combined Wushu with the Yijing (易經). He incorporated bagau (八卦), yinyang (陰陽), wuxing (五行), energy channels, and Daoist and Emei Wushu. Kexingzhang is a Wushu, Qigong, energy healing technique, and probability prediction style. In recent years, it has been warmly received by Wushu and Yijing practitioners alike. Its training content includes: Baguawuxing Kexingzhang (八卦五行克星掌), Wanshouzhuangong Kexingzhang (萬壽轉宮克星掌), Wanshoupaibing Caiqigong (萬壽排病採氣功), and Kexingzhang Xinlidafa (克星掌心力大法).

Figure K-3

Figure K-4

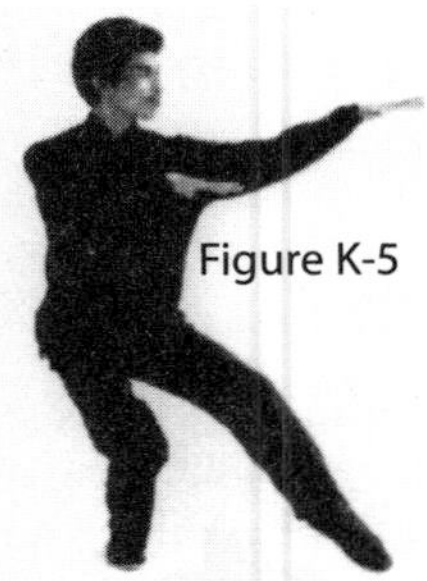

Figure K-5

Figures K-3, K-4, and K-5: Kexingzhang/Cheng Kexin

Khow, Malee 許瑪麗 She is the president and head instructor of Malee's School of Tai Chi and Kung Fu. She is a certified international Wushu Kung Fu instructor and judge. She was born in Thailand and has trained in the martial arts for over twenty-five years. She has won the annual Thailand Wushu Competition five times since 1985. She was a gold medalist in numerous international Wushu competitions. She was the director of the First New England International Chinese Martial Arts Championships. More about her and her school can be found at *www.malees-tai-chi-kung-fu.com*. *See* her photo demonstration under Dao.

King, Declan He has completed his Level One Taijiquan Instructor training at S.Y.L. Wushu Institute. *See* his photo demonstration under Wushu Sanshou Dao.

Kongmenquan 孔門拳 Translated as Confucius Style. This style is popular in Wuhan (武漢) City in Hubei Province. It was created by Hu Tielu (胡鐵鏕) during the beginning of the Qing Dynasty. Hu competed in a fighting competition and lost. After his defeat, he traveled around China in search of teachers and friends to improve his ability. His ability grew during his travels. Hu began to teach his Wushu to his villagers upon returning from his travels. Because he was a devotee of Kongzi's (Confucius) teachings, his Wushu was named Kongmenquan. The known routines include: Longshi (龍式), Hushi (虎式), Fengshi (風式), Yunyan (雲燕), Longhudou (龍虎斗), Huzhanshan (虎占山), Bilongzhu (逼龍珠), and Laocuchudong (老粗楚洞). This style is also popular in the Guangdong Province.

Kung Fu 功夫 A generic term referring to Chinese martial arts. *Also see* gongfu.

Kunlunpai 昆侖派 Translated as Kunlun Mountain Style. This style originated in the Kunlun Mountains. Legend has it, that the Taoist ancestor, Hongjun (鴻鈞老祖) taught three disciples. They were: Laozi (老子), Yuanshi (元始), and Tongtian (通天). Among the three, Tongtian was credited as the originator of Kunglunpai. Yuanshi had 12 disciples. Later, Kunlunpai was divided into two branches—Eastern and Western Kunlunpai.

In its long history, there have been many legendary practitioners of Kunlunpai. During the Eastern Jin Dynasty, the Taoist, Tieleng (鐵棱), was well-known and had many prominent students. Legend has it, that during the Tang Dynasty, Shentianyun (聖天雲), Tianfeng (天風), and Tianlei (天雷) were known for their Kunlunjian (昆侖劍), Qianyuangong (乾元功), and Tiangangzhang (天罡掌). During the Song Dynasty, Wang Long (王龍) was known for his Bagua Longxingjian (八卦龍行劍). During the Ming Dynasty, there were seven Taoists of Kunlun, known as the Kunlun Qijian (昆侖七劍) who were well-known at that time. During the Qing Dynasty, there were three Taoists known for their Qianyuan Qixingjian (乾元七星劍).

Since the five dynasties mentioned, there have been over 105 generations of Kunlunpai practitioners. There are eight known barehanded routines and many weapon routines.

Kunlunquan 昆侖拳 It is believed, that this style has been around for over 200 years. The eight key words to this style are: diao hua (刁滑), xiong meng (凶猛), tun tu (吞吐), and fu chen (浮沉).

Kwok, Alex 郭其聰 He is a prominent Mizhongquan practitioner. He has been a champion in many major tournaments and was rated as the number one forms competitor in North America in 1974. In 2001, he was certified by the International Wushu Federation as an International Wushu Forms Judge. He currently teaches in Calgary, Alberta, Canada. *See* his photo demonstration under Mizongquan.

Kwok, Fred 郭英華 He is the Vice President of the Canadian National Chinese Martial Arts Federation and the President of the Western Canada Chinese Martial Arts Association. He is a prominent Yongchunquan instructor in Vancouver, Canada. He is noted for his powerful street techniques demonstrated by breaking the limbs off many wooden dummies. *See* his photo demonstration under Yongchunquan.

L

Lai, William 賴偉立 A gold medalist in U.S. Tae Kwon Do competitions. He is a student of the S.Y.L. Wushu Institute. *See* his photo demonstration under Zuiquan.

Lamapai 喇嘛派 This is a style developed by the Xizang (Tibet) Mizong Lama (西藏密宗喇嘛). Legend has it, that this style was developed in the 14th century by a Lama who witnessed a fight between a white crane and an ape. The Lama mimiced the movements of the white crane and the ape, and developed this style.

Figure L-1: Mizong Lama Staff/Tony Jay

Langzi Yanqingquan 浪子燕青拳 This is the name of a routine that includes high, medium, and low stances, along with many hand techniques. Power is often generated from the shoulders and back. Its movements are agile and constantly turning, and utilizes an offensive approach in its applications.

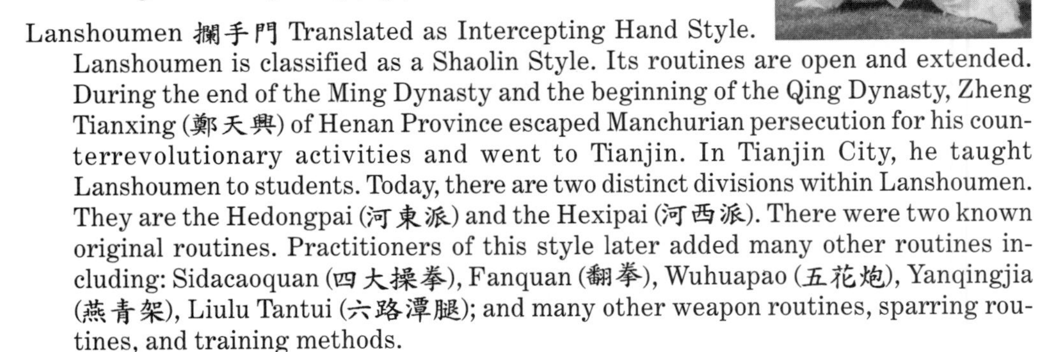

Figure L-2: Langzi Yangqingquan/Fremont Woo

Lanshoumen 攔手門 Translated as Intercepting Hand Style. Lanshoumen is classified as a Shaolin Style. Its routines are open and extended. During the end of the Ming Dynasty and the beginning of the Qing Dynasty, Zheng Tianxing (鄭天興) of Henan Province escaped Manchurian persecution for his counterrevolutionary activities and went to Tianjin. In Tianjin City, he taught Lanshoumen to students. Today, there are two distinct divisions within Lanshoumen. They are the Hedongpai (河東派) and the Hexipai (河西派). There were two known original routines. Practitioners of this style later added many other routines including: Sidacaoquan (四大操拳), Fanquan (翻拳), Wuhuapao (五花炮), Yanqingjia (燕青架), Liulu Tantui (六路潭腿); and many other weapon routines, sparring routines, and training methods.

Latecki, Narcyz A. 賴鐵客 He has won the title of all-around champion many times in national and international Wushu competitions in Poland and the U.S. He began his martial arts studies in 1983 and attained over thirty-two gold medals from 1986 to 1997. He has studied extensively with several prominent Wushu masters in China, Poland, and North America. He has been featured in five instructional videotapes on Chinese martial arts. On numerous occasions, he has appeared as a guest performer for the Commonwealth Civic Ballet and the American Chinese Art Society. He is the founder and head instructor of the Chinese Martial Arts Health and Fitness Center of Acton. *See* his photo demonstration under Xiandai Wushu.

Lau, Francis A S.Y.L. Wushu Institute instructor and a black belt in Sanshou Dao. *See* his photo demonstration under Liuhequan.

Lee, Hansen 李鋼 He is a former member of the Sichuan Physical Education College Wushu team (四川體校武術隊) and a graduate of the Beijing Physical Education University. He is a film action director for over 20 action movies and he has also starred in many movies himself. He currently teaches in Vancouver, Canada. *See* his photo demonstration under Bian.

Lee, Johnny 勵光明 Also known as Lee Kwong Ming. He is a prominent practitioner of Taijiquan, Baguazhang, Mizongquan, and hard Qigong. He is one of the first instructors to introduce traditional Wushu into mainstream America. He has been featured on the covers of many national martial arts magazines. He was also named Instructor of the Year and inducted into the Black Belt Hall of Fame. In 1998, he co-directed with Jeff Bolt, the World Kung Fu/Wushu Championships in Florida, one of the largest International Kung Fu tournaments held in America. He currently teaches at Lee's White Leopard Kung Fu School in Dallas, Texas, U.S.A. *See* his photo demonstration under Mizongquan.

Lee, Kam P. 李佳保 He began his training in Wuzuquan in Malaysia when he was fifteen. He is a licensed Acupuncture Physician in Florida; and is the director of the Chinese Medical Center in Orange Park, Florida. He began teaching Wuzuquan in 1993. He is the lineage holder of Wuzuquan in the U.S. *See* his photo demonstration under Wuzuquan.

Lee, Sanford 李相燁 He is a Way of the Dragon school instructor, a student of Wu Wen-Ching, and a black belt in Wushu Sanshou Dao. He has been a gold medalist in U.S. national and international Wushu competitions many times. He holds a masters degree from Rhode Island School of Design and is a graduate of the New England School of Acupuncture. He now teaches Wushu and practices acupuncture in Rhode Island and Massachusetts, U.S.A. See his photo demonstration under Changquan.

Lee, Santos He is a top student of Hilbert T.S. Yiu and an instructor at the Choy Lee Fut Shung Ying School in Canada. He has been a gold medalist in many tournaments in Northwestern U.S.A. and Canada. He is a committee member of Wushu B.C. *See* his photo demonstration under Nanquan.

Leong, John 梁崇 He is a prominent Wushu practitioner and a pioneer of Kung Fu in the Pacific Northwest. In 1963, he founded the Seattle Kung Fu Club. He has taught many students in his Seattle Chinatown location. He has been featured in many martial arts magazines, and represented the United States in demonstrating Kung Fu at the First International Wushu Championships in Xian, China in 1985. He has organized many charity events that have featured numerous high profile martial artists. He is the current Chairman of the United Kung Fu Federation of North America. *See* his photo demonstration under Hongjiaquan.

Leung, Howie 梁念中 He began studying Wushu from Liang Shou-Yu at age eight, learning different styles of Internal and External styles, Qinna, Shuaijiao, Sanshou, and Hard Qigong. He has been a gold medalist and all-around champion of U.S. and Canadian national and international Wushu championships many times. He is included in the book, *China's Contemporary Wushu Masters* (中國當代武林名人志). He is a Third Level Black Belt in Wushu Sanshou Dao. In 2001, he was the gold medalist in the 75 to 80 Kg Canadian National Sanshou competition. He was selected to represent Canada at the 6th World Wushu Championships. He is certified by the International Wushu Federation as a coach and an International Sanshou Judge. He is also the Sanshou Chairman of Wushu B.C. *See* his photo demonstrations under Nanquan, Wushu Sanshou Dao, and Xiandai Wushu.

Leung, Katrina 梁嘉靜 She is a many time U.S., Canadian, and Pan American Wushu all-around champion. She began studying from Liang Shou-Yu at age 5. In the 1995 World Wushu championships held in the U.S.A., she attained fifth place in the compulsory staff category. In the 1997 World Wushu Championships held in Rome she attained fourth place. In the 1999 World Wushu Championships held in Hong Kong, she attained third place in the compulsory staff category and seventh in the compulsory Changquan category. At age 13, she was one of the youngest and most accomplished Wushu athletes in the world. She is included in the book, *China's Contemporary Wushu Masters* (中國當代武林名人志). She has been featured on the CCTV in China. In 2001, she was selected as a member of the Canadian Wushu team to compete in the Sixth World Wushu Championships to be held in Armenia. *See* her photo demonstrations under Xiandai Wushu, Changquan, and Gun.

Levenston, Michael (1951-) He is one of the founding members of the International Wushu Sanshou Dao Association and an Instructor at the S.Y.L. Wushu Institute. He has been a student of Liang Shou-Yu since 1981. He has learned many Internal and External Styles, and Qigong. He began his martial arts training in 1971 from Yuwa Hedrick-Wong. He has also trained Yang Style Taijiquan with Raymond Chung, Fu Style Internal Arts with Ken Chung, and trained Okinawan weapons with Koyabo Shihan. He is a Sixth Level Black Belt in Wushu Sanshou Dao; and is the Chairman of the Vancouver Affliate of I.W.S.D. Since 1978, he has been the Executive Director of City Farmer - Canada Urban Agriculture. *See* his photo demonstration under Wushu Sanshou Dao.

Lew-Watson, Betty She began her study of Wushu in 1982. In 1989, she met Dr. Wu Chengde and Professor Wang Jurong. Since 1990, she has studied Beiquan (Chaquan system) Taijiquan, and short weapons. Currently, she teaches Taijiquan and Wushu several days a week, as well as, continues her training under Professor Wang and Dr. Wu in group and private classes. She has been actively involved in promoting Wushu in the U.S.A., and in developing judging standards and methods for Wushu competitions. *See* her photo demonstration under Chaquan.

Li, Enjiu 李恩久 A native of Shandong Province. He was the coach of Licheng County (厲城縣), principle of Jinanshi Jiaoqu Tixiao (濟南市郊區體校), and Jinan City Wushu Head Coach. He has been a gold medalist in China national competitions. He is a prominent representative of Chen Style Taijiquan. His students have attained over eighteen gold and five silver medals in China national Taiji Push Hands competitions. He has been invited on numerous occasions to give workshops in the U.S. and Japan. He is also a prominent practitioner of Chaquan, Paoquan, Sunbinquan, Tanglangquan, and Two Handed Sword. *See* his photo demonstration under Taijiquan.

Li, Jinheng 李金恆 He is a former member of the Beijing Wushu team. He was also a member of the China Wushu Youth Representative (中國少年武術代表) that performed in many countries. He was a gold medalist in Rope Dart in a China national Wushu championship. He has organized several Wushu competitions in the Phoenix, Arizona area, where he currently teaches. *See* his photo demonstrations under Jian and Xiandai Wushu.

Li, Michael 李永謙 Also known as Li Yongqian. He has been the chief judge of U.S. national and international Sanshou competitions. He graduated from Beijing Physical Education University in 1984. He has been the gold medalist many times in forms and Sanshou categories during Gansu provincial and China national Wushu competitions. He was the 1993 U.S. Wushu team coach, and an advisor of the U.S.A. Wushu Kung Fu Federation. *See* his photo demonstrations under Xiandai Wushu, Chuojiao, Huaquan, Piguaquan, Bajiquan, and Xibei Difangquan.

Li, Rong 李蓉 (1962-) She began her Wushu training in 1974 from Liang Shou-Yu. Later, she entered Chengdu Physical Education University. She became a Wushu instructor of Sichuan Provincial Wushu school in 1985. She was instrumental in the compilation of Wushu books about Sichuan Wushu styles and weapons; and received an individual award for her pioneering efforts in organizing and rediscovering Wushu. In 1990, her teacher, Liang Shou-Yu, assisted her in coming to Canada. She received a gold medal both for her double sword and Chen Style Taijiquan in the 5th World Cup International Championships. She is a Seventh Level Black Belt in Wushu. She is included in the book, *Biography of China's Prominent Wushu Practitioners* (中華武林著名人物傳). *See* her photo demonstration under Emei Wushu.

Li, Sam He is a many time U.S. and Canadian national Wushu competition grandchampion. He was a member of the 1999 Canadian Wushu team. He is an instructor at the Canadian Chinese Martial Arts Training Center, and one of Ken Low's top students. In 2001, he was selected as a member of the Canadian National team to compete in the Sixth World Wushu Championships to be held in Armenia. *See* his photo demonstration under Bian.

Li, Wenqi 李文啓 He is also known as Wayland Li. He has been the gold medalist many times in individual competitions in China. He was the head coach of the National Wushu team for the Republic of Mongolia, and was the head coach for the Canadian National Wushu team in 1995 and 1997. He currently operates a successful Modern Wushu Centre in Toronto, Canada. *See* his photo demonstration under Gun.

Liang, Helen 梁好 Also known as Liang Hao. Liang Shou-Yu's eldest daughter. She began studying Wushu from her father, Liang Shou-Yu at age 4. She is a former Sichuan provincial athlete, and a S.Y.L. Wushu Institute instructor. She has received numerous gold medals in international competitions. She is a graduate of the University of British Columbia with a degree in Economics. Her Liuhebafa performance has been broadcast on numerous TV stations in the United States, and her Shequan performance with her sister, Maria, has been broadcast on TV stations in China. She has been featured numerous times in Chinese and English Wushu magazines. She is also included in the book, *China's Contemporary Wushu Masters* (中國當代武林名人志). *See* her photo demonstrations under Baguazhang, Xingyiquan, Liuhebafa, Shequan, and Shan.

Liang, Maria 梁爽 Also known as Liang Shuang. Liang Shou-Yu's youngest daughter. She has received numerous gold medals in international Wushu competitions. She is a graduate of the University of British Columbia with a degree in Computer Science. She is a S.Y.L. Wushu Institute instructor. She is also included in the book, *China's Contemporary Wushu Masters* (中國當代武林名人志). *See* her photo demonstrations under Hongquan (紅拳), Shequan, Xiandai Wushu, and Dao.

Liang, Qiangya 梁強亞 He is a formal disciple of Fu Zhensong (傅振嵩). When Fu Zhensong traveled to southern China for the second time in 1945, he stayed in the home of Liang Qiangya and taught his Wushu to Liang Qiang-Ya. He is the director of the Guangzhou Wushu Committee; the Executive Director, Vice President, and Chief Training Officer for the Guangzhou Wudang Association; advisor and guest coach of Hong Kong Association for Advancement of Bagua Martial Arts; and the coach for the Martial Arts Association of Guangzhou Herbal University, Martial Arts Association of Guangzhou Institute of Medicine, and Martial arts Association of Guangzhou Foreign Trade College. He is a prominent practitioner of Fushi and Wudang Wushu. *See* his photo demonstrations under Fushi Wushu and Wudang Wushu.

Liang, Shihong 梁士洪 (1946-) In 1962, he was the all-around champion of the Guangdong Provincial championships. From 1974-1983, he was the coach of the Guangdong Wushu team, and a judge at China national Wushu competitions. In 1980, he was the coach of the Guangdong Hard Qigong and Wushu Performance team that visited all over Asian countries. He also taught Qigong and Wushu in Australia. He has written a book about Liuhebafa. He currently has an acupuncture and Qigong healing practice in Vancouver, Canada. *See* his photo demonstrations under Liuhebafa and Jian.

Liang, Shou-Yu 梁守渝 (1942-) He began his Wushu and Qigong studies at age 6. He is a *Coaches of Excellence* recipient from China. In his youth, he received many gold medals in provincial and national Wushu, Shuaijiao, and weight lifting competitions. He has published over 20 books and videos. He has been the Wushu Chairperson and faculty member of the U.B.C. since 1984. He has been the Head Coach of the Canadian Wushu team many times. He is the founder of the I.W.S.D. Association, and the Vice President of the Confederation of Canadian Wushu Organizations. He has been the Referee General in international Wushu competitions many times. He is included in the books *The Biography of China's Prominent Wushu Practitioners* (中華武林著名人物傳), *China's Contemporary Wushu Masters* (中國當代武林名人誌), *Who's Who in the World* (世界名人錄), and *The Record of Prominent Chinese Descendants in the World* (世界華人精英錄). *See* his photo demonstrations throughout this book.

Lianmenquan 聯門拳 Translated as the United Fist. It was known to have existed since the 1850's in eastern Sichuan Province. The known routines include: Lianbachui (連八捶), Huzichiu (虎子捶), and Bifengdandao (碧風單刀).

Lianshouduanda 連手短打 Translated as Connected Hands and Short Strikes. It is also known as Gouguaizi (勾拐子). Its origin can be traced back to Cangzhou (滄州), Hebei Province.

Liaoning Province 遼寧省 A Chinese province located on the lower part of northeastern China. It borders the Bohai Sea to its south, North Korea to its southeast, and Jilin to its northeast. It covers 145 thousand square kilometers with a population of over 41 million people as of 1999.

Lin, Siyan 林思彥 He is a former member of the Washington University Wushu team. See his photo demonstration under Xiandai Wushu.

Lintunen, Juha A. He was the 1995 Canadian national Karate invitational free fighting and forms grandchampion. In 1993, he was the bronze medalist at the Wado Kao Karate invitational free fighting competition. He has been studying Taijiquan and Sanshou for many years. In 1994, he received a gold medal at the Shanghai International Wushu Festival/Competition. He is a Third Level Black Belt in Sanshou Dao. *See* his photo demonstration under Wushu Sanshou Dao.

Liquan 李拳 Translated as Li Family Fist. This style was created by Li Ci (李錫), a monk from Fujian Shaolin Temple. It spread to Guangdong Province and became one of the popular Southern Styles in Guangdong today.

Liu, Shawn 劉向陽 Also known as Liu Xiangyang and De Ru. He is the 31st generation disciple of the Shaolin Temple in Henan Province. He has often been the chief judge of U.S. national Sanshou competition, and the head coach of the U.S. Sanshou team. He is the president of the East-West Health and Wellness Center and the East-West International Culture and Arts Exchange, Inc. *See* his photo demonstrations under Luohanquan and Shaolin Wuquan.

Liu, Weixiong 劉偉雄 He was a member of the 1986 and 1996 Canadian Wushu team. He was a silver medalist in the First Pan American Wushu Championship. He received his diploma for the 2000 International Wushu Coach Training Course. He is the coach of the Montreal Wushu Institute. *See* his photo demonstration under Zuiquan.

Liu, Yu 劉玉 A former member of the Jiangsu Wushu Professional team. She attained the title of National Collegiate Taiji Champion in 1987. She graduated from the Beijing Physical Education University in 1989. She has served as a coach of the U.S.A. Wushu team in 1997, 1998, and 1999. She has been the chief judge at many U.S. national and international Wushu championships. She is a Seventh Level Black Belt in Wushu, awarded by the Chinese Wushu Institute. She currently teaches San Luis Obispo, California, U.S.A. *See* her photo demonstrations under Changquan, Jian, and Gou.

Liuhebafa 六合八法 Also known as Water Boxing. This is an Internal Style Wushu translated as Six Unities and Eight Principles. Legend has it, that it was created by Chen Bo (陳博) of the Hua (華) Mountains during the Song Dynasty. This style utilizes power similar to Xingyiquan as its center; utilizes the similar stepping patterns of Baguazhang for its turning and spinning; and utilizes the similar neutralizing power of Taijiquan for its variations. Its movements are sometimes high, sometimes low, sometimes fast, and sometimes slow. These movements resemble that of floating clouds and flowing water, in that they are sometimes calm and sometimes surging. This is why Liuhebafa is also known as Water Style. The movements of Liuhebafa are constantly fluctuating with clearly defined forward, backward, upward, downward, and lateral motions. Each and every movement is led by the mind (心意). The mind initiates and the movements follow which is why it is also known as Xinyi Liuhebafa (心意六合八法).

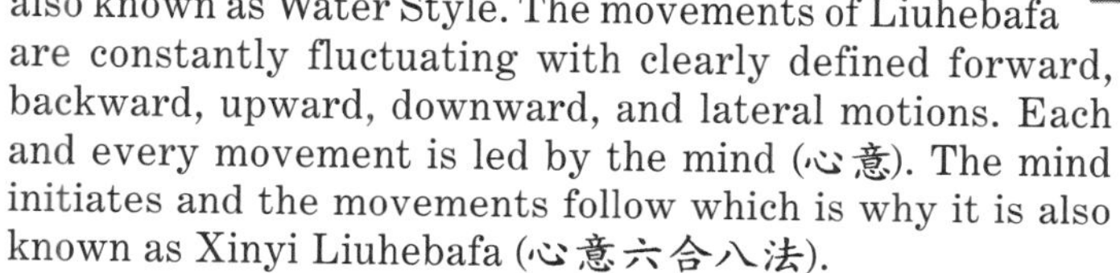

Liuhe (六合) refers to: the unity of the heart (心) and the mind (意); the unity of the mind and qi (氣); the unity of qi and shen (神); the unity of shen and movement (動); and the unity of movement and emptiness (空). Bafa refers to: circulating qi to gather the spirit (氣); condensing the power to the bones (骨); disguising the obvious and mimicking the shapes (形); being flexible in strategy (隨); elevating into a state of emptiness (提); continuous without stopping (還); calm in protecting one's disadvantage (勒); and illusive in hiding one's advantage (伏).

There are two Liuhebafa routines: Liuhebafaquan (六合八法拳) and the Sanpan Shiershi (三盤十二式) routine. The Liuhebafaquan consists of sixty-six postures including over five hundred martial applications. It is divided into two sections, and each section can be practiced as a routine. The Sanpan Shiershi routine is for foundation training; and includes advancing, retreating, rising, and lowering movements, which are designed to develop reaction skills for combat.

Because this style contains characteristics of Taijiquan, Baguazhang, and Xingyiquan, practitioners of the different lineages may practice Liuhebafa with the characteristics of either Taijiquan, Baguazhang, or Xingyiquan.

Figure L-3: Close the Door and Push the Moon Posture/Liang Shou-Yu

Figure L-4: Turn Over the River and Empty the Sea Posture /Liang Shihong

Figure L-5: Liuhebafa/Helen Liang

Figure L-6: Liuhebafa/Liang Shou-Yu

Figure L-7: Liuhebafa/Wu Wen-Ching

Liuhemen 六合門 Translated as Six Harmony Style. This style has been around for over 400 years. It was already noted in the book, *Jixiaoxinshu* (紀效新書, *The New Book of Effective Discipline*) by the Ming Dynasty General, Qi Jiguang (戚繼光). Liuhe refers to the six directions north, east, south, west, up, and down. It also refers to the unity of internal and external components. The three internal unities are: the heart (心) and mind (意) unite; yi and qi (氣) unite; and qi and shen (神) unite. The three external unities are: upper arms and waist unite; the elbows and knees unite; and the shoulders and thighs unite. There are over eleven known barehanded routines, nineteen weapons routines, three sparring routines, and several hard Qigong methods for iron shirt training.

Figure L-10: Liuheqiang (六合槍)/Bill Chen

Liuhequan 六合拳 Translated as Six Harmony Fist. Liuhe refers to the focus of the six directions: east, west, north, south, up, and down; the unity of hands (手) and eyes (眼); the unity of stepping (步) and body movements (身); and the unity of strategy (智) and power delivery (力). Some the the known routines and training include: Tantui (潭腿), Yingmenpao (迎門炮), Xinglongquan (行龍拳), Huagongquan (化功拳), Xingquan (行拳), Liujiashi (六家式), Babuxingzou (八步行走), Meihua Bian Silukaoda (梅花變四路拷打), Qishierba Qinna (七十二把擒拿), and many weapon and shuaijiao.

Figure L-8: Liuhequan/Francis Lau

Figure L-9: Group Liuhequqan/S.Y.L. Wushu Institute Students: Tana, Audrey, Jacob, Emily, Cynthia, Jacob, Bonnie, James, Sandy, Davis, Gabe, Gabe, and Kevin

Liujiaquan 劉家拳 Translated as Liu Family Fist. This style was created by Liu Shen (劉生) of Guangdong Province. Liu is also known as Liu Sanyan (劉三眼) and Liu Qingshan (劉青山). It is one of the popular Southern Styles in Guangdong.

Liuxingchui 流星錘 Translated as Comet Hammer. This is also referred to as feichui (飛錘), flying hammer. It is classifed as a concealed weapon and it usually consists of a roped section with a heavy object tied to one end (Drawing L-1). It is used to wrap around an opponent to immobilize them and to strike opponent from a distance.

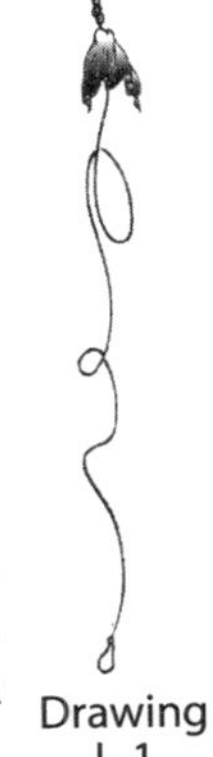
Drawing L-1

Lo, Ken 羅興貴 Also known as Lo Shing Kwei. He is a prominent practitioner of Wumeipai in the U.S.. He is the disciple of Peng Hseih (彭俠). He currently teaches at the Wu Mei Kung Fu Association in New York. More information about him and his school can be found at *www.wumei.com*. *See* his photo demonstration under Wumeipai.

Lo, Perry A many time gold, silver, and bronze medalist in U.S. and Canadian international Wushu competitions. He is a S.Y.L. Wushu Institute instructor. *See* his photo demonstrations under Xiandai Wushu and Wushu Sanshou Dao.

Long Fist *see* Changquan

Long River *see* Yangtze River

Longxingquan 龍形拳 Translated as Dragon Style. This is an imitation type and a Southern Style. This style utilizes the legendary dragon characteristics in its movements and applications. It is popular in Hong Kong and Fujian Province. Some of the known routines include: Angfengpilan (昂峰劈擱), Qichuibagan (七錘八趕), Simen (四門), Ershibasu (二十八宿), and Taizao (台棗).

Figure L-11: Longxingquan/Zou Fu

Low, Ken 劉勁錚 The founder of the Western Canada Martial Arts Association. He is a prominent practitioner of many Wushu styles, the vice president of the Confederation of Canadian Wushu Organizations, and an advisor for the International Wushu Sanshou Dao Association. He was the leader for the Canadian National Wushu team. He has organized 21 annual West Coast Canadian-American Championships. He is one of the most significant Wushu contributors in Canada. He is the President of Wushu B.C. *See* his photo demonstrations under Baimeiquan, Hongjiaquan, and Mizongquan.

Lu, Biao 呂彪 A disciple of the Shaolin Temple. His Buddhist name is Xingbiao (行彪). He is a former member of the Henan Provincial Wushu team. He graduated from Wuhan Physical Education College (武漢體育學院); is a board member of the International Shaolin Medical Study (少林國際醫學理事); and has organized three International Shaolin Wushu Festivals (國際少林武術節). He currently teaches in San Gabriel, California, U.S.A. *See* his photo demonstration under Gun.

Lu, Fenglin 呂鳳林 A native of Shanghai City. He is an instructor at the China Grand View International Wushu Competition Center (中國大世界國際武術競技中心). He is known for his Liuhebafa, Wujiquan, Taijiquan, Baguazhang, and Yuejiaquan. He currently teaches in Los Angeles, California, U.S.A. *See* his photo demonstration under Xiliangquan.

Lu, Xiaoling 呂小林 A former member of the Sichuan Wushu team. She is a graduate of the Beijing Physical Education University and has a master's degree in Wushu. She has published several martial arts books and has won numerous gold medals in Chinese national Wushu competitions. She served as the coach of the U.S. Wushu team in 1993, 1995, and 1996. She is an International Wushu Forms Judge, certified by the International Wushu Federation, and is one of the significant contributors of Wushu in the United States. She is a Seventh Level Black Belt in Wushu, awarded by the Chinese Wushu Institute. *See* her photo demonstration under Emei Wushu.

Lu, Yuzhi 陸玉芝 A former instructor of the Shandong Qufu Athletic University (山東曲阜體育學院). She has produced numerous instructional Wushu video tapes. She has been a judge at U.S. national and international Wushu competitions. She currently teaches in Albany, NY. *See* her photo demonstration under Nanquan.

Lulinpai 綠林派 Translated as the Green Forest Style. Legend has it, that Liu Zhong (劉中) attempted to assassinate the Qing Emperor Yongzheng (雍正, 1723-1735), but failed. Liu escaped to the Qingcheng Mountains (青城山) and studied Wushu there. Later, he exchanged techniques with Wushu practitioners all over the country and absorbed the essence of different styles, and created Lulingpai.

Luo, Cindy A member of the Canadian Wushu team and is a Canadian national Wushu champion. In the 1999 World Wushu Championships held in Hong Kong, she attained seventh place in the compulsory saber category. In 2001, she was selected as a member of the Canadian National Wushu team to compete in the Sixth World Wushu Championships to be held in Armenia. *See* her photo demonstration under Xiandai Wushu.

Luo, Hongyuen 羅宏元 He graduated from the Guangzhou Physical Education University (廣州體育學院) in 1983. He is a former instructor at Huanan Teacher's University (華南師範大學). He is the founder of Ji Hong Tai Chi College of Canada. He was one of the people instrumental in the formation of the Confederation of Canadian Wushu Organizations where he served as the Vice President for the first term. In 1999, he served as the Sanshou team manager of the Canadian Wushu team. In 2001, he was certifed by the International Wushu Federation as an International Wushu Forms Judge. *See* his photo demonstration under Taijiquan.

Luohanquan 羅漢拳 This is a type of Shaolin Wushu. The known routines include: Sishiba Luohan (四十八羅漢), Liushiba Luohan (六十八羅漢), and Yilingba Luohan (一百零八羅漢).

Figure L-12: Shaolin Luhanquan/Shawn Liu

Luomen 羅門 Translated as Luo Family Style. Legend has it, that during the end of the Sui Dynasty and the beginning of the Tang Dynasty, General Luo Yi (羅藝) and his son General Luo Cheng (羅成) created this style. The style taught by Luo Yi was known as the large frame old Luomen. In addition to learning from his father, Luo Cheng also learned from his teacher, Hong Daoren (洪道人). Luo Cheng later created the small frame new Luomen.

The characteristics of Luomen include the flavors of both Northern and Southern Style Wushu. There are seventeen known barehanded routines, fourteen weapon routines, and several training methods.

Lykins, Jeffrey He began his Wushu training in 1975 and has been studying from Wu Wen-Ching since 1999. He is an assistant instructor at The Way of the Dragon School; and he is an architect in Rhode Island. *See* his photo demonstrations under Baguazhang and Wushu Bingqi.

M

Maclean, Kelly A many time U.S. and Canadian national and international grandchampion in Internal Styles. She began studying Internal and External Style Wushu and Qigong from Liang Shou-Yu in 1988. She attained 6th place in the 1999 World Wushu Championships held in Hong Kong in the southern staff category, and three gold medals in the Sixth World Cup International Championship. She is the first non-Chinese decent person to be included in the book, *China's Contemporary Wushu Masters* (中國當代武林名人志). She is an instructor at the S.Y.L. Wushu Institute and University of British Columbia in Vancouver, Canada and is the Tai Chi Chairperson of Wushu B.C. *See* her photo demonstrations under Emeici, Taijiquan, Xiandai Wushu, and Wushu Sanshou Dao.

Mak, Hin Fai 麥顯輝 A champion of many full contact competitions in Hong Kong. He is a protege of Koon Hung Lee. He currently teaches Cailifoquan in Seattle, Washington, U.S.A. See his photo demonstration under Cailifoquan.

Manshouquan滿手拳 Translated as Full Hand Fist. The origin of this style is unknown. There are fourteen known barehanded routines and one weapon routine known as Nanyangdao (南陽刀).

Mao 矛 A spear like weapon (Drawing M-1). It is basically the same as a spear with the exception of the metal tip. The metal tip is longer than the spear tip, and has a snake like shape.

Drawing M-1

Masich, Sam He has been training and teaching Internal Arts for over 20 years. In 1985, he began studying Taijiquan and other Internal and External Style Wushu with Liang Shou-Yu. He has also studied from Yang Jwing-Ming, Jou Tsung Hwa, Yang Zhenduo, Chen Xiaowang, and Chung Yam Man. He was many times a multiple gold medalist in national competitions. He was a member of the Canadian National Wushu team in 1985. He has been the Chief Referee in the U.S. All Taijiquan Championships since 1989. He currently teaches in Canada and travels around the world giving workshops. He has produced 14 instructional videos about Taijiquan, Qigong, Push Hands, and Xingyiquan. *See* his photo demonstrations under Taijiquan and Baguazhang.

May, Ryan He started his martial arts training with Kempo in 1993. He has been studying Wushu from Wu Wen-Ching since 1998. He is a way of the Dragon School assistant instructor. *See* his photo demonstrations under Baguazhang and Wushu Bingqi.

Mazloum, Naji He is a prominent medical doctor with a specialty in surgery. Currently Dr. Mazloum has his practice in the New England area. He started his martial arts training in 1970 with Karate, Judo, Aikido, Iaido, and Kenjiutsu. He began his Taijiquan, Xingyiquan, Baguazhang, and Qigong studies with Wu Wen-Ching in 1997. *See* his photo demonstration under Xingyiquan.

McKay, Gord He completed his Level One Taijiquan Instructor training at S.Y.L. Wushu Institute. *See* his photo demonstration under Wushu Sanshou Dao.

Means, Howard He started his Wushu training in 1994. He has been studying with Wu Wen-Ching since 1999; and is an assistant instructor at The Way of the Dragon School. *See* his photo demonstrations under Baguazhang and Wushu Sanshou Dao.

Meehan, J. Justin He is a St. Louis trial attorney. He is the Central State Missouri Representative of Feng Zhiqiang's U.S.A. Taijiquan Academy under Zhang Xuexin. He is the President of the Chinese Internal Arts Center and Missouri Director of the Chinese Culture Society, and is a nationally recognized writer on the martial arts, especially Taijiquan. He is an advisor for the U.S.A. Wushu-Kung Fu Federation. He has studied the martial arts for 40 years and Taijiquan specifically for over 33 years. He has studied Qigong from Liang Shou-Yu for more than 10 years. More about him can be found at *www.stltaiji.com*. See his photo demonstration under Taijiquan.

Meihuaquan 梅花拳 Translated as Palm Flower Fist. Legend has it, that Meihuaquan was created at the end of the Ming Dynasty and the beginning of the Qing Dynasty. There have been over 16 generations of this style. It is classified as Changquan. Its training is often done on posts partially buried in the ground in a palm flower pattern, thereby, the name Palm Flower Fist.

Meishiquan 梅氏拳 Translated as Mei Family Style. Legend has it, that this style was taught by a nun during the reign of the Qing Emperor, Guangxu (光緒), between 1875 and 1908. Since the nun's last name was Mei, the style was named Meishiquan. This style focuses on the applications of the legs. There are eight known barehanded routines, three weapon routines, and a training method known as Shierliangongfa (十二練功法).

Meng, Xiantang 孟憲堂 One of the major representatives of Sunbinquan. He is a student of Sun Wenbin (孫文賓). He organized three Sunbingquan Wushu competitions in China. He is the author of *Sunbinquan of China* (中國孫臏拳). *See* his photo demonstration under Sunbinquan.

Meridian Ax Couple *see* Yuanyangyue

Mianquan 綿拳 Translated as Cotton Fist. Practitioners of this style are required to attain a high level of flexibility. It is also known as Yanshou (延手), referring to the characteristics of extending the arms during its applications. Their traditional routines include: Liujiashi (六家勢) and Bazhe (八折).

Mianzhang 綿掌 Translated as Cotton Palm. This style primarily utilizes the palms in its applications. There are three known routines and many weapon training. Shisantaibaogong (十三太保功) is one of their foundation training. This style is also known for its spear techniques.

Miaoquan 苗拳 This style focuses heavily on internal cultivation and sticking training. The known training includes: Sanshiliugong (三十二攻) and Qishierfang (七十二防). The known barehanded routines include: Simen (四門), Dasimen (大四門), Xiaosimen (小四門), Kaisimen (開四門), Bisimen (閉四門), and Zangshanzhuang (藏山樁). There are also many weapon routines.

Minghaiquan 明海拳 This is an Emei Style, created by a monk named Minghai (明海). Minghai was a Shaolin Temple monk who migrated to Sichuan Province and studied Sichuan Wushu. Later, he combined Shaolin Wushu with the indigenous Sichuan Wushu and became Minghaiquan. There are seven known barehanded routines and two Pudao (扑刀) weapon routines.

Figure M-1

Figure M-2

Figure M-3

Mizongquan 迷蹤拳 Translated as Lost Track Style. Legend has it, that this style was created by Cheng Juxiao (程君俠). Cheng's maternal grandfather and mother were practitioners of Mizongyi (迷蹤藝). His maternal grandfather and his mother immigrated from northern China to Guangdong Province. Cheng learned from his grandfather and his mother and further developed his family style into Mizongquan. There are over thirty-six different basic routines referred to as Mizong Luohanquan (迷蹤羅漢拳).

Some people believe that Mizongquan and Yanqingquan came from the same origin. It is believed that they were taught by Sun Tong (孫通) of Shandong Province during the reign of the Qing Emperor, Qianlong (乾龍) between 1736 and 1795. Sun taught his Wushu to the grandfather of Huo Yuanjia (霍元甲). This branch became known as Mizongquan. Another of Sun's lineage was taught by Zhang Yaoting (張耀庭). Zhang's branch became known as Yanqingquan.

Also see Yanqingquan.

Figure M-1: Mizong Luohanquan/Johnny Lee
Figure M-2: Mizong Luohanquan/Ken Low
Figure M-3: Mizong Luohanquan/Alex Kwok

Modern Wushu *see* Xiandai Wushu

Monkey Style *see* Houquan

Moquan 莫拳 Translated as Mo Family Fist. This style was created by a Buddhist Chan priest, Zhishan (至善禪師) of the Fujian Shaolin Temple. It is a popular Southern Style in Guangdong Province. Some of the known routines include: Mojia Zhengzongquan (莫家正宗拳), Zhuangquan (樁拳), Sanzhibi (三支筆), Suishou (碎手), Shuanlongchuhai (雙龍出海), and Zhishiquan (直式拳).

Figure M-4

Mulanquan 木蘭拳 A derivative of Huatao Wuyi. This style was created by Ying Meifeng (應美鳳) of Shanghai. It is an exercise that combines Wushu with modern calisthenics. It utilizes the yin-yang philosophy and Qigong breathing in its practice. It also utilizes appropriate music to assist the practitioner in achieving a tranquil state. This allows the body to attain a proper energetic balance to prevent illness, heal diseases, and attain longevity. There are six Mulanquan routines, including: two barehanded routines, one single fan rou-

Figure M-5

Figure M-6

Figure M-7

tine, one single sword routine, one double fan routine, and one double sword routine.

Information provided by Zang Lijuan.

Figures M-4 and M-6: Mulanquan/Zang Lijuan
Figure M-5: Mulan Fan/Cheng Aiping
Figure M-7: Mulan Single Sword/Zang Lijuan

N

Nanquan 南拳 Translated as Southern Style. Nanquan is not one particular style, but a classification of styles with their origin primarily south of the Yangtze River. Generally, all the Wushu styles originating in the southern provinces of China are considered Nanquan or Southern Style. We have introduced many of the Nanquan styles under their own heading. Here we will list the popular Nanquan styles in Southern Chinese provinces including those we have already introduced, as well as, many that we have not.

Figure N-1

Guangdong Nanquan (廣東南拳): Hongjiaquan (洪家拳), Caiquan (蔡拳), Liquan (李拳), Moquan (莫拳), Cailifoquan (蔡李佛拳), Huheshuanxing (虎鶴雙形), Xiaquan (俠拳), Yongchunquan (詠春拳), Baimeiquan (白眉拳), Nanzhiquan (南枝拳), Ruquan (儒拳), Fojiaquan (佛家拳), Diajiaquan (刁家教), Zhujiajiao (朱家教), Yuejiajiao (岳家教), Zhongjiajiao (鐘家教), and Kunlunquan (昆侖拳).

Guangxi Nanquan (廣西南拳): Zhoujiaquan (周家拳), Tulongquan (屠龍拳), Hongmen Fuhuquan (洪門伏虎拳), and Xiaocheda (小策打).

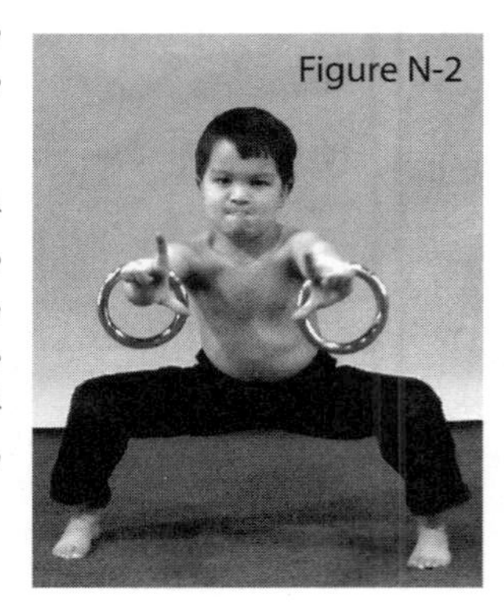
Figure N-2

Fujian Nanquan (福建南拳): Nanshaolin Wuxingquan (南少林五形拳) including Dragon, Tiger, Leopard, Snake, and Crane; Wuzuquan (五祖拳), Luohanquan (羅漢拳), Meihuazhuang (梅花樁), Lianchengquan (連城拳), Diquanquan (地犬拳), Yongjiafa (泳家拳), Wumeiquan (五梅拳), Shiquan (獅拳), Houquan (猴拳), Yufa (魚法), Jifa (雞法), Rufa (儒法), and Fangwuji (防烏跡).

Hunan Nanquan (湖南南拳): Wujiaquan (巫家拳), Xuejiajiao (薛家教), and Yuejiajiao (岳家教).

Hubei Nanquan (湖北南拳): Hongmen (洪門), Kongmenquan (孔門拳), Yuemenquan (岳門拳), Yumenquan (魚門拳), Sunmenquan (孫門拳), Wujiayi (巫家藝), Naimen (奈門), Fomen (佛門), Yinxianmen (隱仙門), Shuihumen (水滸門), Zhengmen (蒸門), Yanmen (嚴門), and Xiongmen (熊門).

Sichuan Nanquan (四川南拳): Cengmen (曾門), Yuemen (岳門), Zhaomen (趙門), Dumen (杜門), Hongmen (洪門), Huamen (化門), Zimen (字門), and Huimen (會門).

Jiangxi Nanquan (江西南拳): Sanshiliulu Songjiangquan (三十六路宋江拳).

Zhejiang Nanquan (浙江南拳): Heihuquan (黑虎拳), Jingangquan (金剛拳), Wenzhouquan (溫州拳), and Taizhaoquan (台州拳).

There are also Suzhou Nanquan (蘇州南拳), Wuxi Nanquan (無錫南拳), Shanghai Difanquan (上海地方拳), and Changzhouquan (常州拳). Among all these Nanquan styles, there are over one thousand barehanded and weapon routines.

Figure N-1: Hongjiaquan/Raymond Cheung
Figure N-2: Nanquan/Andrew Wu
Figure N-3: Dayanquan (大雁拳)/Lu Yuzhi
Figure N-4: Competition Nanquan/Howie Leung
Figure N-5: Southern Saber/Santos Lee
Figure N-6: Fujian Hequan/Paul Hoover
Figure N-7: Nanquan/Kit Poon
Figure N-8: Southern Praying Mantis/Andrew Chung
Figure N-9: Nanquan/Rick Sue

Nanzhiquan 南枝拳 Legend has it, that Nanzhiquan was created by Nanzhu (南枝), a monk from the Fujian Shaolin Temple. Nanzhi escaped from the Southern Shaolin Province after the temple was burned by the Qing army. Nanzhi escaped to Guangdong Province and taught his Wushu to his students. There are over twenty different barehanded and weapon routines.

Narrow Blade Sword *see* Jian

Naughton, Dianne A senior disciple of Pan Qingfu. She is a many time gold medalist in U.S. and Canadian international and national Wushu competitions. She has been featured with her teacher in numerous TV programs. She currently teaches in the Toronto area, Canada. *See* her photo demonstration under Ditangquan.

Nei Mongol Zizhiqu 内蒙古自治區 A autonomous region in northern China, also known as Inner Mongolia Autonomous Region. It covers over 1.1 million square kilometers with a population of over 23 million people as of 1999.

Neijiaquan 内家拳 Translated as Internal Fist. Legend traces its origin back to Zhang Sanfeng (張三丰). One of the predominant representatives of Neijiaquan was Zhang Songxi (張松溪) of the Qing Dynasty. Therefore, this style is also known as Songxi Neijiaquan to distinguish it from the generic term Neijiaquan, referring to all Internal Style Wushu. After Zhang Songxi, the prominent practitioners of this style included Ye Jimei (葉繼美), Dan Sinan (單思南), and Wang Zhengnan (王征南).

Neijiaquan 内家拳 A generic term referring to all Internal Style Wushu such as Taijiquan, Xingyiquan, Baguazhang, and Liuhebafa. It is a term used in contrast with Waijiaquan (外家拳), External Style.

Nine Sectioned Chain *see* Bian

Ningxia Huizu Zizhiqu 寧夏回族自治區 An autonomous region around central China which borders Shaanxi to its east and Inner Mogol to its north. It covers over 66 thousand square kilometers with a population of over 5 million people as of 1999.

Ng, Paul 吳錦新 A 1985 Canadian National Wushu team member. He is a practitioner of Mizongquan. In the early 1980's, he began studying Internal and External Style Wushu from Liang Shou-Yu. In recent years, he began an in-depth study of Qigong and Taijiquan achieving high attainments. He currently teaches in Canada. *See* his photo demonstration under Taijiquan.

Ng, Sam 伍紹華 He is the Vice-Chairman and Treasurer of the International Choy Lay Fut Kung Fu Federation of America. He is a fifth generation practitioner of Cailifoquan. He has been practicing Cailifoquan for over 29 years and has been teaching publicly for over 10 years. In 1997, he founded the Ng Family Chinese Martial Arts Association with his son, Philip Ng. He has been involved in both organizing and performing in numerous martial arts demonstrations in the Chicago area. *See* his photo demonstration under Cailifoquan.

Ngu, Augustin 吳家文 He is a prominent Baihequan practitioner in Canada with many schools in the Toronto, Canada area. He is a Sanshou judge certified by the International Wushu Federation. Currently, he is the President of the Canadian Guo Shu Federation; Chairman of the United Wushu Federation of Canada; President of the White Crane Kung Fu Society of Canada; and Kung Fu instructor of the Buddhist progress Society of Toronto. *See* his photo demonstration under Baihequan.

Nojiri, Yumi She was the 1997 all-around champion at A Taste of China Internal Wushu competition. She is a student of Kelly Maclean and Liang Shou-Yu. *See* her photo demonstration under Taijiquan.

Northern Shaolin Temple *see* Shaolin Temple

Northern Style *see* Beipai

O

Ott, Rudi A member of the U.S. Sanshou team participating in several world Wushu competitions. He is a many time U.S. national Sanshou competition gold medalist. He is a black belt in Sanshou Dao. He studied Xingyiquan and Dapeng Qigong from Liang Shou-Yu. He was a Sanshou instructor at S.Y.L. Wushu Institute. He is currently in the U.S. training Sanshou with Cung Le. See his photo demonstration under Wushu Sanshou Dao.

P

Pa Kua Chang *see* Baguazhang

Painter, John He was one of the first Americans to introduce Baguazhang to the West through his articles and video tapes. He began his training in 1957 under the tutelage of Li Longdao of Sichuan Province in the family style of Jiulong Baguazhang. He has a Ph.D. in naturopathic medicine. He is listed in the book, *Who's Who in the Chinese Martial Arts, Master, Founders, and Leaders of the Chinese Martial Arts.* He was elected three times to the Inside Kung-Fu magazine Hall of Fame and is a member of the Texas Martial Arts Hall of Fame. He presently operates the Gompa Center, the oldest Chinese martial arts school in Texas and seven Baguazhang schools worldwide. *See* his photo demonstration under Baguazhang.

Pan, Qingfu 潘清福 A prominent international Wushu practitioner. His nickname is *Iron Fist.* He was the former Wushu coach for the Liaoning Provincial Wushu team (遼寧省武術隊), for the Shenyang Physical Education Institute (沈陽體育學院), for the Hunan Provincial Wushu team (湖南省武術隊), for the Tianjin City Wushu team (天津市武術隊), and the head coach of the China Wushu Good Will team (中國武術訪問團). He was awarded one of the "Pioneers in the Development of Sports in New China 新中國體育運動開拓者". He has starred in many Wushu movies. He has been the referee general for Canadian national and Pan American Wushu Championships. He is a honorary chairman and honorary head coach of the Confederation of Canadian Wushu Organizations. He currently teaches in Toronto, Canada. *See* his photo demonstrations under Jian and Qiang.

Panpomen 盤破門 This is a style that originated in Sichuan Province. It is popular in the eastern and southern parts of Sichuan. Their stances are generally high; hand movements are small, but constantly changing; kicks are low and fast; and steps are quick and agile. There are sixty-six known barehanded routines, sixteen weapon routines, two sparring routines, and thirteen training methods.

Paochui 炮捶 Translated as Cannon Hammer. Pauchui is also known as Sanhuang Paochui (三皇炮捶). Sanhuang refers to the ancient emperors of China: Fuxi (伏羲), Shennon (神農), and Huangdi (黃帝), implying the ancient nature of the style. Paochui refers to the cannon like power of the style. Pauchui can be traced back to the Song Mountain Shaolin Temple. It was taught by the Shaolin monk, Pu Zao (普照) to Gan Fengchi (甘風池), and to other students. There are over 9 generations in the Pauchui lineage. Paochui is classified as Changquan.

Peng, Youlian 彭友連 He is a graduate from the Department of Physical Education at Beijing Teacher's University. He is the President of the Peng You Taijiquan Association; Chairman of the Thunder Bay International Tai Chi Festival; and the Chief Taiji Instructor of the Thunder Bay 55 Plus Centre. He is the recipient of the 2001 Best Chinese Canadian Entrepreneurs Award; and the Best Community Service Award. *See* his photo demonstration under Taijiquan.

Piguaquan 劈挂拳 Translated as Splitting and Hooking Fist. Legend has it, that this style was created by Zuo Baohai (左寶海), a Shaolin monk. Some believe that it was created by Li Linbiao (李林彪) of the Hebei Province. It is believed that this style has existed since the Ming Dynasty. Towards the end of the Qing Dynasty, Pan Wenxue (潘文學) was known to have taught this style.

Piguaquan uses both short and long range applications. It utilizes the waist and back as the pivot point to turn the body from side to side. The arms and hands are trained until they are fast like falling "rain drops" in a storm, for a continuous attack. It is also known as Tongbei Piquaquan.

In its movements, the arms are relaxed and swift with power connected throughout the body, and the chopping power, like an explosion going off. It emanates the soft-hard characteristic. Piquaquan emphasizes the chest's opening and closing movements, the turning of the waist, along with the swinging of the arms; to attain large opening and closing applications.

Figure P-1

Figure P-2

Figure P-3

Figure P-4

Figure P-1: Piguaquan/Gao Xian
Figure P-2: Piguaquan/Michael Li
Figure P-3: Piguaquan/Tjhie Wie Hong
Figure P-4: Fengmogun (風魔棍)/Michael Li

Pole *see* Gun

Poon, Kit He is a student of Lu Hongyuen and Gu Daijuan. He has been a gold medalist many times in Wushu competitions. In 2001, he was selected as a member of the Canadian National team to compete in the Sixth World Wushu Championships to be held in Armenia. *See* his photo demonstration under Nanquan.

Praying Mantis Style *see* Tanglangquan

Pyne, William He began his Wushu training with Wu Wen-Ching in 1992. He is an instructor at The Way of the Dragon School; and is a data base programer and computer consultant. *See* his photo demonstration under Wushu Bingqi.

Q

Qi 氣 1. Energy. 2. Breath. 3. The intrinsic substance that makes up the cosmos. 4. In traditional Chinese Medicine, it refers to the intrinsic substance that flows in the human body and is the impelling force for all living activities. 5. In Wushu, it is the component of internal strength developed by the practitioner for accomplishing what seems to be incredible tasks.

Qi, Ke Bao 齊克寶 (1944-) A graduate of Anhui College of Traditional Chinese Medicine (安徽中醫學院). He has been practicing Wushu since a young age. He is a disciple of Wu Chongguang (吳重光), a sixth generation practitioner of Yang Style Taijiquan, and a practitioner of Baguazhang and Chuojiao. He is also a successor of Feng Jinsheng (馮金升) from the Chinese Daoist Hunyuanpai (中國道教混元派) lineage. He currently has his healing practice and teaches Taijiquan in Columbia, South America. *See* his photo demonstration under Xiyangzhang.

Qiang 槍 A spear (Drawing Q-1). It is known as the *king of all weapons* (百兵之王). The basic applications of qiang are lan (攔), a parrying movement to the outside; na (拿), a controlling movement to the inside; and zha (扎), a spearing forward movement. Qiang movements are often described as "qiang zha yitiaoxian (槍扎一條線)", meaning that the movements are even, straight, and fast. It is said that a straight spearing movement is the ultimate movement in spear maneuvers because it is the hardest to defend when going straight for the center of an opponent.

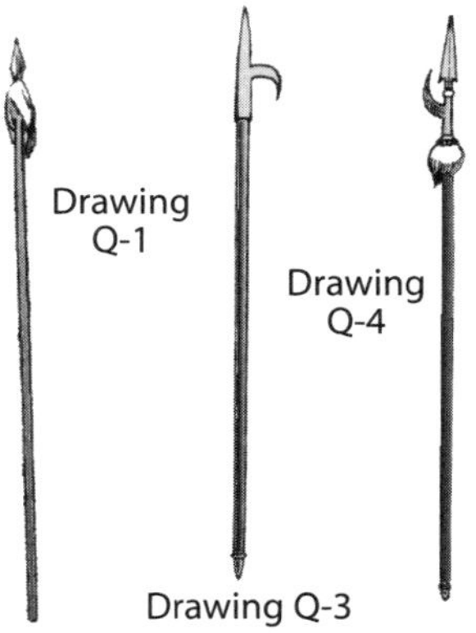

Drawing Q-1

Drawing Q-4

Drawing Q-3

Drawing Q-2

There are many different types of qiang including: Daqiang (大槍), Biaoqiang (標槍), Huaqiang (花槍), Biqiang (筆槍), Zhuaqiang (爪槍), Shuangtouqiang (雙頭槍, Drawing Q-2), Shuangtou Shuangqiang (雙頭雙槍), Goulianqiang (鉤鐮槍, Drawing Q-3), Qurenqiang (曲刃槍), Huanziqiang (環子槍), Guiziqiang (拐子槍), Huntieqiang (渾鐵槍), Longtouqiang (龍頭槍), Longdaoqiaong (龍刀槍, Drawing Q-4), Huyaqiang (虎牙槍), Dangouqiang (單鉤槍), Shuangouqiang (雙鉤槍), Liuyeqiang (柳葉槍), and Jumaqiang (柜馬槍).

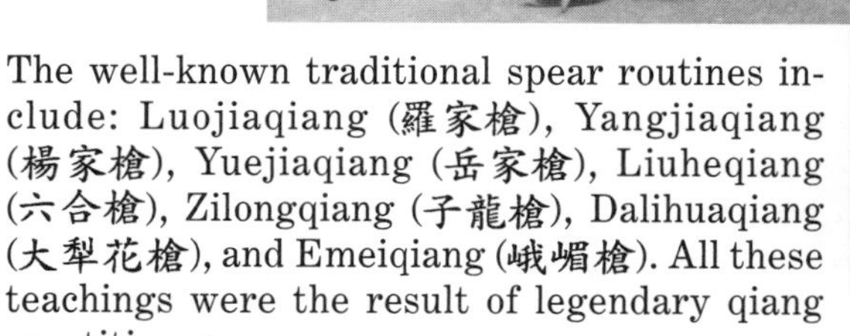

The well-known traditional spear routines include: Luojiaqiang (羅家槍), Yangjiaqiang (楊家槍), Yuejiaqiang (岳家槍), Liuheqiang (六合槍), Zilongqiang (子龍槍), Dalihuaqiang (大犁花槍), and Emeiqiang (峨嵋槍). All these teachings were the result of legendary qiang practitioners.

Figure Q-1: Carrying the Spear/Pan Qingfu
Figure Q-2: Spear vs Saber/Xie Qingcai and Tan Shunlu
Figures Q-3 and Q-4: Double Headed Spear/Candice Wong

Qigong 氣功 1. Any set of breathing and energy circulation techniques that are capable of improving health, preventing illness, strengthening the body, and for spiritual development. 2. The attainment of qi.

There are many different types of Qigong. They include: Medical, Taoist, Buddhist, and Wushu Qigong. Please refer to the book, *Qigong Empowerment* for more information about the different types of Qigong.

Figure Q-5: Taiji Walking Qigong/Xu Junheng
Figure Q-6: Five Animal Frolics/John Du Cane

Qingchengbuqimen 清淨布氣門 This style was created by Lin Xiao (凌霄) during the reign of the Qing Emperor, Qianlong (乾龍) between 1736 and 1795. Lin was a royal palace bodyguard. This style absorbed the essence of Shaolin, Emei, and Wudang Wushu. It is popular in Sichuan, Shanxi, Yunnan Province, etc. The known routines include: Yinyang Lianhuanquan (陰陽連環拳), Bagua Jiugongquan (八卦九宮拳), Chaoyangquan (朝陽拳), Huxiaoquan (虎嘯拳), Yingzhaoquan (鷹爪拳), Rouyinquan (柔陰拳), Hudiezhang (蝴蝶掌), Bianfushou (蝙蝠手), Yuanyantui (鴛鴦腿), and Yinyang Taiji (陰陽太極). This style also has many weapon, Qinna, cavity press, fast take down, hidden weapon, hard Qigong, Sanshou, and life nourishing training.

Qingchengpai 青城派 Translated as Qingchen Mountain Styles. This is a term referring to the styles originated from the Qingcheng Mountains (青城山). The known barehanded routines include: Qingcheng Hongquan (青城洪拳), Liuhe Sanshou (六合散手), Qingcheng Baguazhang (青城八卦掌), Gubajiquan (古八極拳), Xuanmen Jiushi (玄門九式), and Erlu Hongquan (二路洪拳). The known weapon routines include: Qixingjian (七星劍), Baxianjian (八仙劍), Qingchengjian (青城劍), Zimugun (子母棍), Daqinglongdao (大青龍刀), and Qiankunquan (乾坤圈). Training methods include: Jianshen Yanshougong (健身延壽功) and Liuhe Neigong (六合内功).

Qinghai Province 青海省 A Chinese province which borders Gansu to its north, and Sichuan and Tibet to its south. It covers over 721 thousand square kilometers with a population of over 5 million people as of 1999.

Figure Q-7

Qinglongquan 青龍拳 Translated as Green Dragon Fist. This style focuses on the application of the palms and fingers. These movements are described to look like a swimming dragon. Thereby, the name Qinglongquan was coined. There are three known barehanded routines and several weapon routines.

Drawing Q-5

Figure Q-8

Quan 圈 Refers to any ring shaped weapon. Many of these weapons consist of sharp edges and sharp protrusions, such as, the Qiankunquan (乾坤圈) and the Fenghuolun (風火輪, Drawing Q-5). They are usually handheld weapons, but can also be used as throwing weapons.

Figure Q-7: Double Quan/He Weiqi

Figure Q-8: Wind and Fire Wheels/Steve Sun

R

Ren, Guang Yi 任廣義 He is the president of the International Chen Style Taijiquan Association. He represented Chen Village in the International Taiji Push Hands Competition and attained the gold medal in the heavyweight division. He is a disciple of Cheng Xiao-Wang (陳小旺). More about him and his school can be found at *www.chentaijiquan.com*. *See* his photo demonstration under Taijiquan.

Renjiajiao 任家教 Translated as Ren Family Teaching. It is also known as Renmenquan (任門拳). This style was passed down by Ren Sizhen (任思鎮), a Qing Dynasty officer of the Sichuan area. Ren utilized his understanding of *Sunzi's Art of War* (孫子兵法) and the Yijing (易經), and combined it with several martial styles, to create this style. The known routines include: Jinjiduli (金雞獨立) and Qiufengsaoluoye (秋風掃落葉) Saber routine.

Renmenquan *see* Renjiajiao

Rope Dart *see* Shengbiao

Ricci, Bedry He is an exceptional practitioner of Ninjutsu, Karate, Qinna, and Sanshou. *See* his photo demonstration under Wushu Sanshou Dao.

Rice, Pat She is the Director of *A Taste of China*. She has organized over 18 national Taijiquan and other internal arts competitions. She is one of the most significant figures in the promotion of Taijiquan in the United States. She currently teaches in Virginia, U.S.A. *See* her photo demonstration under Taijiquan.

Ritchie, David He began his martial arts training in 1969 and he has been practicing Taijiquan since 1973. He has studied from prominent practitioners from both Asia and the U.S. He is the owner and director of Central Connecticut Tai Chi Chuan in Meriden, Connecticut where he teaches Taijiquan, weapons, and Qigong. He is also an Assistant Professor at Quinnipiac University in Hamden, Connecticut. *See* his photo demonstration under Taijiquan.

Ross, Robert He began his martial arts training with Kempo in 1980 and has been studying Wushu and Qigong since 1992 from Wu Wen-Ching. He is an instructor at the Way of the Dragon School and also teaches Taijiquan and Qigong in the New England area. He is a black belt in Wushu Sanshou Dao. *See* his photo demonstrations under Taijiquan and Baguazhang.

S

Saber Usually refers to a short handled dao. *Also see* Dao.

Sai *see* Cha

Sanhuang Paochui *see* Paochui

Sanjiegun *see* Gun

Drawing S-1

Sengmen 僧門 Translated as Monastery Style. This is one of the most well-known Emei Styles. Emei region of China is a Buddhist utopia filled with temples. Thereby, the name Sengmen was coined. Legend has it, that this style was based on Shaolin Wushu. After the Shaolin Wushu migrated to the Emei Mountains, it gradually developed into what is known as Sengmen. This style focuses on Qinna and short range applications. There are over forty known barehanded routines and over twenty weapon routines and many training methods.

Figure S-1

Sengmen training routines include: Huolongquan (火龍拳), Lianbuquan (練步拳), Dalianhuanquan (大連環拳), Hubaoquan (虎豹拳), and Liutongquan (六通拳).

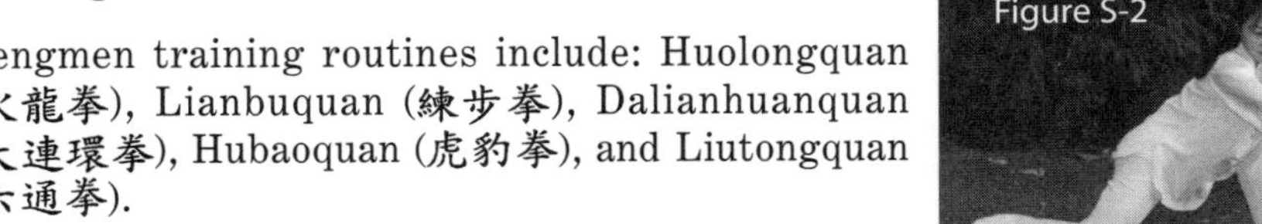

Figure S-2

Shan 扇 A fan. Weapon grade fans (Drawing S-1) are commonly made with metal spokes. Fans are used singularly or as a pair. Well-known fan routines include: Xiaoyaoshan (逍遙扇), Taijishan (太極扇), Baiyishushenshan (白衣書生扇), Luohandapushan (羅漢大撲扇), and Mulanshan (木蘭扇).

Figure S-1: Taiji Double Fan/Helen Wu

Figure S-2: Xiaoyaoshan (逍遙扇)/Helen Liang

Shandong Province 山東省 A Chinese province located around the lower part of the Yellow River. The eastern part of Shandong is a peninsula extending into the Bohai Sea and the Yellow Sea. It covers 153 thousand square kilometers with a population of over 88 million people as of 1999.

Shandongjiao 山東教 Translated as Shandong Teaching. Legend has it, that it was created by General Qin Shubao (秦叔寶) in the beginning of the Tang Dynasty (618-907). Qin was a hero to the Tang empire who helped the Tang emperor defeat the Sui Dynasty. There are five known routines in this style.

Figure S-3: Shandongjiao Saber/Jiang Jianye

Figure S-3

Shanghai City 上海市 One of China's four municipalities that is under the direct jurisdiction of the central government. It is a port city located at the mouth of the Yangtze River in the eastern part of China. It covers over 6 thousand square kilometer with a population of over 14 million people as of 1999.

Shaanxi Province 陝西省 A Chinese province located in the middle of continental China. It is intentionally romanized with a double "a" to distinguish it from Shanxi (山西) Province. It is located above the midpoint of the Yellow River, with the river at most of its eastern and southern provincial border. It borders Hebei to its east. It covers over 205 thousand square kilometers with a population of over 35 million people as of 1999.

Shanxi Province 山西省 A Chinese province located at the midpoint and north of the Yellow River. It borders Shandong to its east and Shaanxi to its west. It covers over 156 thousand square kilometers with a population of over 31 million people as of 1999.

Shaolin Huimen 少林會門 This style was created by the Henan Shaolin priest, Huang Fazhuang (黃法莊). There are four barehanded routines, one crutch routine, and eight application training methods.

Shaolin Temple 少林寺 A Buddhist temple located in Henan Province. It is also referred to as the Songshan Shaolin Temple. Songshan (嵩山) is the specific location where the temple was actually built. It was built in the year 495 A.D. during the height of Buddhism. A Buddhist priest, Batuo, came to preach Buddhism in China. He was warmly received by the emperor of China. The emperor built the Shaolin Temple as a place for Batuo to teach Buddhism. In the year 527, another Buddhist priest came to China. His name was Damo. Legend has it, that Damo meditated in a cave for nine years and popularized Buddhism in China. The Shaolin Temple is not only known for its Buddhist teachings, but it is also known for its Kung Fu.

During the course of history, Shaolin martial monks assisted the leaders of the empire in solidifying their control of the empire. This was especially significant during the Tang Dynasty, when thirteen martial monks assisted the Tangtaizong (唐太宗) Emperor, Li Shimin (李世民), in solidifying his control of the empire by defeating the tyrannical Wang Sichong (王世充) of the Sui Dynasty. From then on, the Shaolin martial ability was known throughout the empire. As time went on, Shaolin monks continued to refine their martial skills, while absorbing skills from Wushu practitioners that sought refuge at the temple.

There are many other Shaolin Temples in China. They include the Fujian Shaolin Temple, Shanxi Shaolin Temple, Hebei Shaolin Temple, Luoyang (洛陽) Shaolin

Temple, and Changan (長安) Shaolin Temple. The Henan Shaolin Temple is the original Shaolin Temple and is also referred to as the Northern Shaolin Temple. The Fujian Shaolin Temple is also known as the Southern Shaolin Temple.

Shaolin Wuquan 少林五拳 Legend has it, that this style was created by the prominent Yuan Dynasty (1260-1368) Shaolin Wushu practitioner, Bai Yufeng (白玉峰). He imitated the movements of the dragon, tiger, leopard, snake, and crane; and created this style. He believed in training the five components of the body: the essence, strength, energy, bones, and spirit, to attain a high level. Therefore, the characteristics of this style are to use the dragon routine to train the spirit; the tiger routine to train the bones; the leopard routine to train for strength; the snake routine to train the energy; and the crane routine to train the essence.

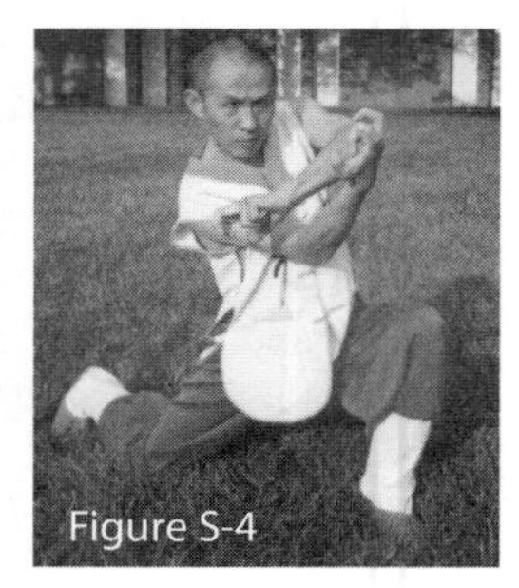
Figure S-4

Figure S-4: Shaolin Dragon Fist/Shawn Liu

Shaolin Wushu 少林武術 A term referring to all the styles of Wushu that can trace their origin back to the Song Mountain Shaolin Temple. It is one of the oldest and most well-known Chinese martial arts systems. It is also one of the most influential Chinese martial arts that has had the greatest impact in the world today.

Figure S-5

Figure S-6

For lack of a better choice and to honor Bodhidharma, the father of Chinese Chan, later generations gave Bodhidharma credit for the martial arts originating from the Shaolin Temple. Today, it is generally believed that Shaolin martial arts were the result of the many martial artists who sought spiritual sanctuary and martial skills, throughout the history of the Shaolin Temple, and who in turn shared their martial arts with the monks. Over the centuries Shaolin martial arts and other styles have mutually influenced and benefited each other.

Figure S-7

Shaolin Wushu is further divided into Northern Shaolin and Southern Shaolin styles. Northern Shaolin refers to the styles that can trace their origins to the Song Mountain (嵩山) Shaolin Temple in the Henan Province. Southern Shaolin refers to the styles that can trace their origins to the Jiulian Mountain (九蓮) in the Fujian Province. Both Northern and Southern Shaolin Wushu styles have spread all over the world today.

Figure S-8

Figure S-5: Southern Shaolin Wushu/Hu Jianqiang
Figure S-6: Dahongquan (大洪拳)/Wu Wen-Ching
Figure S-7: Gunshu/Barry Farrands
Figure S-8: Quanshu/Sam Carroll

Shaolin Xingyi Liuhe 少林形意六合 Translated as Shape-Intent Six Harmony of Shaolin. This is a derivative of Shaolin Wushu. It is practiced in Hunan, Jiangxi, and Sichuan Provinces. This style was based on the jumping, flying, nesting, and hunting characteristics of animals. It focuses on the unity of the internal jing (精), qi (氣), and shen (神); as well as, the unity of the external hands, eyes, and body movements. There are two known barehanded routines, one Lianhuanziwu Panlonggun (連環子午盤龍棍) weapon routine, and three training methods.

Shape and Intent Fist *see* Xingyiquan

Shenda 神打 Translated as Spiritual Strike. There are many Shenda branches including: Maoshan (茅山), Fo (佛), Dao (道), and Qirijiao (七日教). Shenda was popular for several decades in China after the failed revolt by the Yihetuan (義和團) during the Boxer's Rebellion in China. Shenda relies heavily on chanting to increase the ability and strength of its practitioners.

In the year 1900, Yihetuan was the Chinese organization that led an unsuccessful uprising against foreign powers and foreigners in China. As a result, China was forced to make economic and territorial concessions.

Shengbiao 繩鏢 Translated as Rope Dart. It is classified as both a flexible weapon and as a concealed weapon. It usually consists of a roped section with a sharp dart tied to one end (Drawing S-2). It is used to wrap around an opponent to immobilize them or to strike an opponent from a distance.

Figure S-9: Rope Dart/Narcyz Latecki

Figure S-9

Drawing S-2

Shenmenquan 生門拳 An Emei Style. It is also known as Jinjiaquan (金家拳) or Jin Family Teaching. There are over ten known barehanded and weapon routines, including Daluandao (大鸞刀).

Shequan 蛇拳 Translated as Snake Fist. Shequan routines are based on the movements of a snake. It is part of some Shaolin and Emei styles.

Figure S-10: Green Dragon Leaves Its Hole Posture/Maria Liang
Figure S-11: White Snake Spits Its Tongue Posture/Helen Liang
Figure S-12: Shandong Shequan/Jiang Jianye

Figure S-10

Figure S-11

Figure S-12

Short Staff *see* Gun

Shuo 槊 There are many different variations of shuo. Generally, it consists of a pole and attached at one end of the pole is a heavy object with multiple spikes or sharp blades. The most well-known weapon of this type is the Lanyabang (狼牙棒, Drawing S-3), or the Wolf Tooth Pole.

Drawing S-3

Sichuan Huimen 四川會門 This style utilizes the Five Elements to name its routines. The keys to this style are: tun (吞), tu (吐), feng (封), hua (化), and tie (貼). There are ten barehanded routines and six application training methods.

Sichuan Lijiaquan 四川李家拳 Translated as Li Family Style of Sichuan. This style originated from the Gaozui Mountain (高嘴山) area of Sichuan Province. Their routines are usually short with low stances. There are six known barehanded routines, three weapon routines, and two training methods. Since the Qianlong (乾龍) era of the Qing Dynasty, there have been over eight generations of practitioners.

Sichuan Province 四川省 A Chinese province located upstream of the Yangtze River which borders Tibet to its west and Hubei to its east. It covers over 560 thousand square kilometers with a population of over 84 million people as of 1999.

Sichuan Ziranmen 四川自然門 Translated as Natural Style of Sichuan. Legend has it, that in the Sichuan Nanchong (四川南充) area there were two families, the Tang and the Liu families, who were in constant conflict for land. Sichuan Ziranmen was the result of the Tang family's struggle with the Liu family. There are two known routines in this style.

Sigman, Mike He is a prominent Internal Style instructor in the U.S. He has over thirty-six years of experience in several styles of martial arts, including Judo, Okinawan Karate, Aikido, Taijiquan, Xingyiquan, and Baguazhang. He has written many magazine articles and has officiated at many national and international competitions. He is well-known in North America and Europe for his Internal Strength workshops. *See* his photo demonstrations under Dao and Wushu Sanshou Dao.

Simpson, Jacob He completed his Level One Taijiquan Instructor training at S.Y.L. Wushu Institute. *See* his photo demonstration under Wushu Sanshou Dao.

Sinclair, Ian A many time Taijiquan and Push Hands gold medalist in West Coast U.S. and Canadian Wushu competitions. He completed his Level Two Taijiquan Instructor training at S.Y.L. Wushu Institute. He currently teaches in Canada. *See* his photo demonstrations under Taijiquan and Wuji Xiaoyaopai.

Sit, Chun Man 薛振民 (1950-) He has been practicing Wushu for over 30 years. He is a prominent practitioner of Wu Style Taijiquan and Taixuquan. He has written numerous articles on applications, power development, and Taiji Sword. *See* his photo demonstration under Taixuquan.

Six Unities and Eight Principles *see* Liuhebafa

Songxi Neijiaquan *see* Neijiaquan

Southern Shaolin Temple *see* Shaolin Temple

Southern Style see Nanquan

Spear *see* Qiang

Spence, Peter He is a First Degree Black Belt in Wado Karate and a Wushu practitioner. See his photo demonstration under Wushu Sanshou Dao.

Staff *see* Gun

Sue, Rick H.Y. 蘇浩源 He is the Vice President of the United Wushu Federation and a District Chairman of the United Wushu Association of Ontario. He was a gold medalist at the 1990 Canadian Kung Fu Championships, 1991 World Martial Arts Championships, and 1992 Canadian Kung Fu Championships. *See* his photo demonstration under Nanquan.

Sujiajiao 蘇家教 Translated as Su Family Teaching. This style was created by Su Caifeng (蘇裁縫) during the Ming Dynasty. There are over thirty-one known barehanded routines, fourteen weapon routines, and thirteen training methods.

Sun, Jie 孫杰 A former member of the Beijing University Wushu Sanshou team. He is a student of Shou-Yu Liang. He is a practitioner of Wuji Xiaoyaopai, Liuhebafa, Dapeng Qigong, and several other Internal and External Styles of Wushu. He was also a Chinese consul stationed in Vancouver, British Columbia, Canada. *See* his photo demonstration under Wuji Xiaoyaopai.

Sun, Steve L. 孫樹霖 He is a 31st generation disciple of the Henan Shaolin Temple. He began his Wushu training under the guidance of his father and many other teachers at age ten. He is a graduate of the University of Pennsylvania with a Ph.D. in Civil and Environmental Engineering. He the author of the *Tai Chi Wind and Fire Wheels*, and *Advanced Tai Chi Chuan Wind and Fire Wheels*. In 1999, he was inducted into the U.S.A.W.K.F. Hall of Fame. In September 1999, he received the "World Outstanding Achievement in Martial Arts Golden Award" from the International Martial Arts Kung-Fu Federation, U.S.A. In 2000, he received the Life Time Achievement Award from the U.S.A.W.K.F.. He currently teaches in Pennsylvania, USA. *See* his photo demonstration under Quan.

Sunbinquan 孫臏拳 Legend has it, that this style was created by Sun Bin (孫臏) during the Spring-Autumn and Warring Kingdoms era. Sun Bin was the descendent of Sun Wu (孫武), the greatest military strategist in ancient China. Sun Wu, also known as Sunzi (孫子), wrote the *Sunzi's Art of War* or *Sunzi Binfa* (孫子兵法). *Sunzi Binfa* consists of thirteen chapters. It is considered one of the greatest military strategy books in the world.

After studying his family Wushu, Sun Wu studied under the hermit, Guiguzi (鬼谷子) to further his Wushu and military understanding. Historical records indicate that Sun Bin wrote over 39 chapters on the art of war. Sunbinquan became popular towards the end of the Qing Dynasty. Whether or not, it was actually created by Sun Bin is unknown. However, the style did contain a lot of Sun Bin's military thinking.

In the past, practitioners of Sunbinquan wore long sleeves that extended towards their fingers when they trained. Therefore, it was also known as Changxiuquan (長袖拳), meaning long sleeved style. There are over fourteen known routines in this style.

Figure S-13: Sunbingquan/Meng Xiantang

Sunmenquan 孫門拳 Translated as Sun Family Fist. Legend has it, that this style was based on the Southern Shaolin of Fujian Province. It was created by Sun Chunan (孫楚南) of Sichuan Province. Sun absorbed the essence of several styles plus his personal experience and characteristics, to create this style. This style includes mostly arm strikes and very little kicks, relying on short range applications in combat. There are over twenty known barehanded and weapon routines. It is classified as an Emei Style.

Sunzi Bingfa 孫子兵法 A military strategy book written by Sunzi during the Spring-Autumn (722-481 B.C.). It is considered one of the greatest strategy books ever written.

Sunzi's Art of War see Sunzi Bingfa

Sword *see* Jian

T

Tae Kwon Do 跆拳道 A Korean system of martial arts that combined the Tang Dynasty's Shaolin Wushu with native Korean martial arts. It was officially named Tae Kwon Do between 1955-1957. Tae Kwon Do became an Olympic Exhibition event in 1988 and officially became an Olympic medal event in the 2000 Olympics.

Tai Chi Chuan *see* Taijiquan

Taijiquan 太極拳 An Internal Style Wushu, also romanized as Tai Chi Chuan, and translated as the Grand Ultimate Fist. This is one of the most influential Wushu styles in the world today. There are participants of Taijiquan in over 100 nations throughout the world today. The five major traditional Taijiquan styles include: Chen Style (陳式), Yang Style (楊式), Wu Style (吳式), W'u Style (武式) also known as Hao Style (郝式), and Sun Style (孫式).

Legend has it, that a Daoist priest, Zhang Sanfeng (張三丰) of the Northern Song Dynasty (960-1126 A.D.) created Taijiquan after observing a fight between a crane and a snake. The theoretical foundation of Taijiquan is based on the ancient Yin-Yang philosophy.

Martial arts historians today believe that the movements in Taijiquan originated from Chen Wangting (?-1719). Many people now believe that Chen Wangting combined the *Martial Classics in Thirty-Two Postures* (拳經三十二式) with the *Taoist Yellow Court Classic* (黃庭經) to become what is known as Taijiquan today.

In Taijiquan practice, physical symmetry and balance are accomplished with condensing and extending movements. These movements are enhanced with the regulation of your mind and deep relaxed breathing to attain internal energetic symmetry. It has been proven, by the test of time, to be an effective life prolonging, nourishing, healing, and rejuvenating exercise. The practice of Taijiquan also increases mental awareness and centering, develops coordination, and builds good habits for proper body alignment. The benefits from Taijiquan practice have been realized by millions of people all over the world. Today, Taijiquan is still trained as a martial art by countless practitioners, but it is also a well-known healing art practiced all over the world.

In addition to the above five styles there are also many other Taijiquan routines known today. They include: Sanfeng (三丰) Taiji, Wudang (武當) Taiji, Songxi (松溪)

Figure T-1

Figure T-2

Figure T-3

Figure T-4

Figure T-5

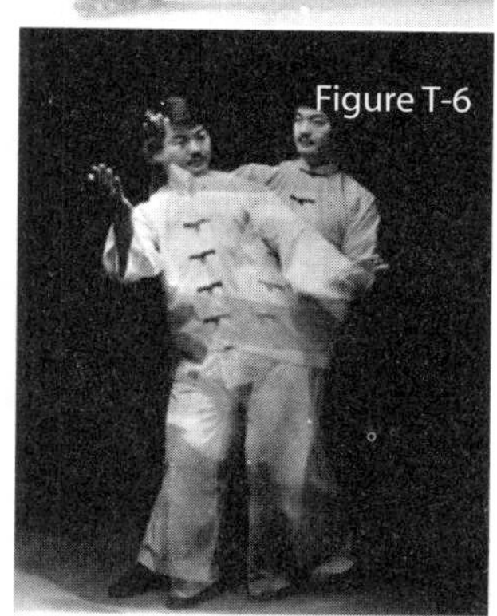
Figure T-6

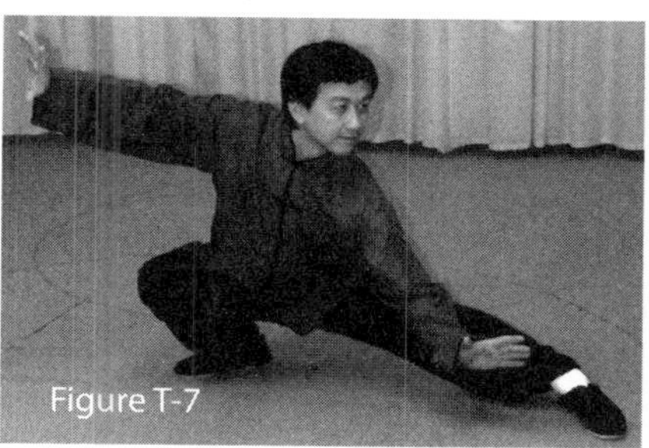
Figure T-7

Figure T-8

Figure T-9

Taiji, Yang Style Small Frame (楊式小架) Taiji, W'u Style Fast (武式太極快拳) Routine, Taiji Cotton Fist (太極綿拳), Simplified Taijiquan (簡化太極), Simplified Wu (吳) Taijiquan, Simplified Sun (孫) Taijiquan, Simplified Chen (陳) Taijiquan, 48 Posture Taijiquan, 88 Posture Taijiquan, 42 Posture International Competition Routine (國際比賽套路), Zhengzi Taiji (鄭子太極), and Daoist (道家) Taiji in Canada, and many others.

Figure T-1: Yang Style Single Whip/Yang Zhenduo
Figure T-2: Chen Style Taijiquan/Chen Xiaowang (photo supplied by Justin Meehan)
Figure T-3: Yang Style Taijiquan/Fu Zhongwen
Figure T-4: Chen Style Taijiquan/Zhu Tian Cai
Figure T-5: Chen Style Taiji/Zhang Xuexin (photo supplied by Justin Meehan)
Figure T-6: Wu Style Taijiquan/Eddie Wu
Figures T-7 and T-9: Chen Style Taijiquan Small Frame/Chang Chung-Jen
Figure T-8: Yang Style Taijiquan/Pat Rice

Figure T-10: Yang Style Taijiquan/Yang Chengfu
Figures T-11, T-12, and T-13: Yang Style Taijiquan/Yang Zhenduo
Figure T-14: W'u (武) Style Taijiquan/Luo Hongyuen
Figure T-15: Taiji Single Fan/Helen Wu
Figure T-16: Wu Style Taiji Sword/Yu Wen Mei
Figure T-17: Yang Style Taijiquan Fast Routine—Playing the Lute/Huang Wei-Lun
Figure T-18: Sun Style Taijiquan/Cheng Aiping
Figure T-19: Yang Style Taijiquan/Herb Goldberg
Figure T-20: Zhengzi Taijiquan/David Ritchie
Figure T-21: Taiji Spear/Daniel Y. Wang
Figure T-22: Wu Style Taijiquan/Yumi Nojiri
Figure T-23: Chen Style Taijiquan/Cheng Aiping

Figure T-24: Yang Style Small Frame/Daniel Y. Wang
Figure T-25: Yang Style Taijiquan and Sword/Yang Zhenduo and Yang Jun
Figure T-26: Taiji Double Fan/Helen Wu
Figure T-27: Wu Style Taijiquan/Yu Wen Mei
Figure T-28: Wu Style Competition Taijiquan/Kelly Maclean
Figure T-29: Chen Style Kick/Yang Yang (photo by David Riecks, www.riecks.com)
Figure T-30: Taiji Saber/Gu Daijuan
Figure T-31: Chen Style Taiji Saber/Ren Guang Yi
Figure T-32: Yang Style Taijiquan/Peng Youlian
Figure T-33: 42 Posture Taijiquan/Hong Yijiao
Figure T-34: 48 Posture Taijiquan/Kelly Maclean

Figure T-35: Yang Style Push Hands/ Liang Shou-Yu & Wen-Ching Wu

Figure T-36: Chen Style Taijiquan Push Hands/Zhu Tian Cai & Ren Guang Yi

Figure T-37: Chen Style Taiji Push Hands/Zhang Xuexin & Justin Meehan (photo supplied by Justin Meehan)

Figure T-38: Taiji Push Hands/ Liang Shou-Yu (R) & Li Enjiu (L)

Figure T-39: Wu Style Peng Lu Ji An Push Hands/Ian Sinclair and Calvin Keele.

Figure T-40: Taiji Push Hands and rooting training/Liang Shou-Yu and Wu Wen-Ching

Figure T-41: Taiji Sanshou/Frank Whitsitt-Lynch (R) and Robert Ross (L)

Figure T-42: Official Push Hands Competition/Ian Sinclair, referee

Figure T-43: Taiji Flexibility Push Hands/Sam Masich and Chang Chung-Jen

Figure T-44: Taiji Push Hands/Paul Ng and student

Figures T-45, T-46, and T-47: Yang Style Taijiquan—Snake Creeps Down Posture/Huang Wei-Lun

Figure T-48: Taiji Push Hands/Fu Zhongwen & He Weiqi

Figure T-49: Taiji Practice/He Fusheng & He Weiqi

Figure T-50: Taiji Pengjin Demonstration/Liang Shou-Yu & students

Figure T-51: Taiji Push Hands Individual Drill/Sam Masich

Figure T-52: Group Chen Style Taijiquan/S.Y.L. Wushu Institute Students: Simon, Chris, Charles, Itamar, Hal, Michael, Bob, Jimmy, Rein, Vasara, Paula, Virginia, James, Jason, Michael, Nelson, Jacob, Ken, Gordon, Brigitte, Mary Lynn, Kelly, Joan, and David

Figure T-53: Group Push Hands/S.Y.L. Wushu Institute Students

Taiwan Province 台灣省 A Chinese island province located about 100 kilometers off the coast of Fujian Province. It covers over 36 thousand square kilometers with a population of over 22 million people as of 1999.

Taixuquan 太虛拳 Translated as the Ultimate Void Fist. It was created by Wu Rongyu (伍榮羽，伍榮祖) during the Qing Dynasty and was based on the Taixu (太虛), Taiji (太極), Sancai (三才), Sixiang (四象), Wuyun (五運), Liuqi (六氣), Bagua (八卦), and Tuwenluoshu (圖紋洛書) philosophies.

Figure T-54

*Wu Rongyu was a merchant from Guandong during the 1800's. He traveled to Bejing to sell herbs. During a chance meeting, he sold his herbal formula to the then royal uncle of the emperor. This chance meeting also landed him royal treatment at the residence of the royal uncle. As a token of appreciation, the royal uncle's teacher taught Wu Rongyu his family style. Taixuquan continued for four generations in the Wu family. In the 1930's, the fourth generation descendent, Wu Xuepo (伍雪波), broke the tradition and taught outside of his family when his own son didn't want to learn Taixuquan.

*Information supplied by Sit Chun Man.

Figure T-54: Taixuquan/Sit Chun Man

Figure T-55

Figure T-57

Taizuquan 太祖拳 Translated as Grand Ancestor Fist. Legend has it, that this style was created by Emperor Zhao Kuangyin (趙匡胤) of the Northern Song Dynasty who reigned between 960 and 975. Taizuquan was recorded in the book, *Jixiaoxinshu* (紀效新書) by Qi Jiguang (戚繼光) in the Ming Dynasty. Taizuquan focuses on the five key words: gang (剛), meng (猛), jin (緊), wen (穩), and xiao (小).

Figure T-56

Figures T-55 and T-56: Taizuquan/Zhang Zhi Bin

Figure T-57: Taizuquan/Benson Xiao

Tang, Alan A member of the Canadian Wushu team. He has been an all-around champion in the compulsory categories during Canadian national Wushu competitions many times. He was the all-around champion three times at the Pan American Wushu championships. He has many times been the bronze medalist and in the top six places at World Wushu Championships. In 2001, he was selected as a member of the Canadian National Wushu team to compete in the Sixth World Wushu Championships to be held in Armenia. *See* his photo demonstration under Xiandai Wushu.

Tang, Sunny 鄧華 The First Vice President of the Confederation of Canadian Wushu Organizations; Vice President of the Pan American Wushu Federation (P.A.W.F.); Director and Organizer of the East Coast Canadian National and Pan American Wushu championships. He currently teaches in Toronto, Canada. *See* his photo demonstrations under Yongchunquan and Dao.

Figure T-59

Tanglangquan 螳螂拳 Translated as Praying Mantis Style. This is an imitation style mimicking the movements of a mantis. Legend has it, that Wang Lang (王朗) created this style in the later part of the Ming Dynasty into the beginning of the Qing Dynasty. In the legend, after Wang Lang completed his training in the Shaolin Temple, he went to travel around the country. One day as he was wandering in the country, he met a martial artist named Dan Tong (單通) who had long arms. They sparred for three days and three nights. Wang Lang was unable to touch Dan Tong. As Wang Lang was resting under a tree and contemplating a strategy to win the match, he observed a preying mantis on the grass.

Wang Lang poked the mantis with a long stem of grass. The mantis was able to evade the stem by turning its head and deflecting the stem with its leg. Even though the stem was long, the mantis was able to skillfully neutralize the attack. From his observation, Wang Lang figured out a way to use his shorter range application against the longer range of Dan Tong, and successfully defeated Dan Tong.

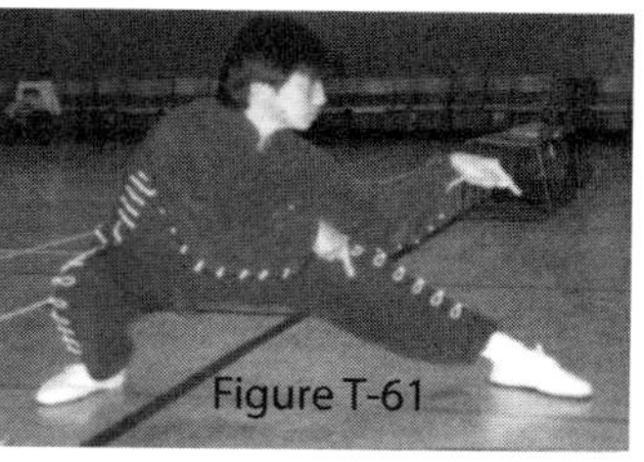

Wang Lang took the mantis back to the Shaolin Temple and tested it with the grass stem to observe and imitate its movements. After a few months, he understood and learned the many characteristics of the mantis. On another day as he was practicing the mantis movements, an ape took the clothes that he left on a branch. He chased the ape. Every time he got close to the ape, the ape was able to maneuver out of his grab. As he came close to grabbing the ape, again the ape, was able to get away. After several hours, the ape gave up and put his clothes down and went away. Wang Lang was dumfounded. He thought that he was fast and good in martial arts, yet he was unable to catch the ape. He observed the angles of the tracks made by the apes, he practiced them daily, and attained the agility of the ape's maneuvers. He then combined the mantis movements with the ape's stepping pattern, and created the Tanglangquan.

During the course of its development, practitioners of Tanglangquan continued to absorb the essence of other styles and created many variations of Tanglangquan. Today, there are several different styles of Tanglangquan including: Mimen (秘門) Tanglangquan, Babu (八步) Tanglangquan, Meihua (梅花) Tanglangquan, Shuaishou (摔手) Tanglangquan, Liuhe (六合) Tanglangquan, Guangban (光板) Tanglangquan, Yuhuan (玉環) Tanglangquan, Yin (硬) Tanglangquan, Qixing (七星) Tanglangquan, and Nan (南) Tanglangquan.

Figures T-58 and T-59: Mantis Catches the Cicada/Wu Wen-Ching and Sanford Lee
Figure T-60: Tanglang Moon Tooth Saber/Tony Chen
Figure T-61: Meihua Tanglangquan/Solen Wong

Figure T-62: Preying Mantis Application/Jon Funk and partner
Figure T-63: Tanglangjian/Hassan Bishil
Figure T-64: Tanglangquan/Yang Chen-Han

Tangpingquan 湯瓶拳 This style is also known as Tangpingqishi (湯瓶七式). It originated from within the Hui ethnic Chinese and is popular in Shanxi and Henan Provinces. Archeological findings indicate that it has existed since the Tang Dynasty (618-907). Traditionally, this style was only taught to male children, not female.

Tantuimen 潭腿門,彈腿門 Translated as Springy Leg Style. One legend believes that Tantuimen originated from the Longtan Temple (龍潭寺) in Shandong Province. This style utilizes powerful, spring like kicks, thereby, the style was known as Tantui. Tan from Longtan and tui for its kicks. Another legend believes that it originated from the Tan Family Village in Henan Province.

Tantuimen is popular among the Hui ethnic Chinese. Tantui training has also been adopted into the foundation training in many other Changquan styles. It is believed that originally there were only ten Tantui routines. Later, two more were added to the original ten and became twelve routines. Tantuimen also has a weapon routine known as Liuhe Single Saber (六合單刀).

Figure T-65: Silu Tantui/Wang Jurong
Figure T-66: Tantui/Grace Wu
Figure T-67: Jiulu Tantui/Wu Wen-Ching

Thomas, Vingrove The founder and chief instructor of the Six Harmony Martial Arts Academy. He has studied several Chinese martial arts styles including: Tiger Claw, Yongchunquan, Chen Style Taijiquan, and Xinyi Liuhequan, since the early 1970's. He serves regularly as a judge at annual U.S. national Chinese martial arts competitions. Since 1993, he has been invited to conduct biennial instructional tours in Italy and Switzerland. In 1997, he was celebrated as a cross-cultural role model in the New Yorker series produced by the N.H.K. for Japanese television. In 1998, he received a lifetime achievement award from the U.S.A. Wushu-Kung Fu Federation. *See* his photo demonstration under Yongchunquan.

Tianjin City 天津市 One of China's four municipalities that is under the direct jurisdiction of the central government. It is a port city located in the northeastern part of China and is about 120 kilometers northwest of Beijing. It covers over 11 thousand square kilometers with a population of over 9 million people as of 1999.

Tibet *see* Xizang Zizhiqu.

Timons, Joel A many time gold medalist and grandchampion in U.S. national and international Wushu competitions. He is a student of Nick Gracenin. He is also a black belt in Sanshou Dao. He currently teaches in Florida, U.S.A. *See* his photo demonstrations under Ditangquan and Chain.

Tjhie, Wie Hong 徐維豐 In 1992, he was the North American all-around Wushu champion in the youth division. He began his Wushu training at a young age from Liang Shou-Yu, and is now an instructor at the S.Y.L. Wushu Institute. In 1993, he was a member of the Canadian Wushu team that competed in the World Wushu Championships. In 1995, he entered Beijing Physical Education University. He is a certified practitioner of Traditional Chinese Medicine by the Xiamen University in China; and is a member of the Board of Directors of Wushu B.C. *See* his photo demonstration under Piguaquan.

Tjhie, Wie Tjong 徐維崇 He began his Wushu training with Liang Shou-Yu in 1982. He is an instructor at the S.Y.L. Wushu Institute, and a black belt in Wushu Sanshou Dao. In 2001, he was the gold medalist in the 60 to 65 Kg Canadian National Sanshou competition. He was selected to represent Canada at the 6th World Wushu Championships. *See* his photo demonstrations under Changquan and Wushu Sanshou Dao.

Tongbei Piquanquan *see* Piquaquan

Tongbiquan 通臂拳 Translated as Connected Arm Fist. Legend has it, that this style was created by the Taoist Baiyuan Daoren (白猿道人) in Sichuan Emei Mountain during the Spring-Autumn and Warring Kingdom era (770-221 B.C.). Its movements resemble the swinging arms of the ape. *Tongbei* literally means connected arms, implying that the arms are very integrated in its movements.

Today, there are several different types of Tongbeiquan. They include: Baiyuan (白猿) Tongbeiquan, Pigua (劈挂) Tongbeiquan, Shaolin (少林) Tongbeiquan, Wuxing (五行) Tongbeiquan, Tanglang (螳螂) Tongbeiquan, Liuhe (六合) Tongbeiquan, Guanzhong (關中) Tongbeiquan, Liangyi (兩翼) Tongbeiquan, and Liangyi (兩儀) Tongbeiquan.

Tongbeiquan mimics the fighting characteristics of the ape. It utilizes long range strikes; generates power with the assistance of rounding the back and arcing the chest; and uses the swinging and shaking of the arms and hands in its applications. Both arms alternate in splitting movements.

Figure T-68

Figure T-69

Figure T-68: White Ape Tongbiquan—White Ape Offers the Fruit Posture/He Tao
Figure T-69: Emei Pigua Tongbiquan/Hui Mo

Tujiazu Wushu 土家族武術 This is a term referring to the Wushu developed by the Tujiazu ethnic people living in the mountain range between Hunan, Hubei, and Sichuan Province. Ancient Tujiazu people had been known to be stubborn and brave. Chinese history indicates that the Tujiazu had revolts against the Tang, Song, and Yuan Dynasties. The emperors of the time had to make truces with them. Tujiazu Wushu is known for its close range combat abilities and its ability to engage in combat in narrow paths, and cliffs.

U, V, W

Uva, Thomas He began his martial arts training in 1973 and has continued his Wushu training with Wu Wen-Ching since 1996. He is a Way of the Dragon School assistant instructor; and is a chemical Engineer and a Pretreatment Manager at the Narragansett Bay Commission. *See* his photo demonstrations under Baguazhang, Wushu Bingqi, and Wushu Sanshou Dao.

Wang, Daniel Y. 王宇 A prominent practitioner of Wushu with over 40 years of experience. He is a prominent practitioner of all major styles of Taijiquan, Taiji weapons, Taiji Sanshou, and Taiji Neigong. He was a member, then a team leader of a prestigious martial arts team in Beijing, where he won many gold medals in martial arts competitions, and coached many champion athletes. He is a judge for international competitions. He has been featured multiple times on Fox Television, in the Los Angeles Times, and in several magazines including People, Tai Chi, Inside Kung Fu, and Black Belt. He currently teaches in Los Angeles, California, U.S.A. *See* his photo demonstration under Taijiquan.

Wang, Jurong 王菊蓉 A Wushu Professor Emeritus of the Shanghai Physical Education University. She is the first female Wushu professor in Chinese history. She began her Wushu and traumatology medical training at age five from her father, Wang Ziping. At age 18, she competed in a national competition and attained the level of champion. In 1959, she was instrumental in the first compilation of the *Bare-handed Compulsory Routine* and *Sword Compulsory Routine.* She was personally responsible for the compilation of the *Narrow Blade Sword* and the *Double Sword*, all of which were part of the required Wushu curriculum. In 1960, Shanghai Physical Education University officially began the first Department of Wushu ever in China and she was appointed head of this department. More about her can be found under Wangshi Wushu. *See* her photo demonstrations under Chaquan, Tantuimen, and Wangshi Wushu.

Wang, Shutian 王樹田 (1918-) A Professor of Wushu at the Chengdu Physical Education University (成都體育學院). He is a committee member of the Chinese Wushu Association, Chairman of the Sichuan Wushu Association, and head coach of the Sichuan Provincial Wushu School. He is a graduate of the prestigious Central Guoshu Institute (中央國術館). He has written eight authoritative books about Wushu. He is an advisor of the International Wushu Sanshou Dao Association. *See* his photo demonstrations under Xingyiquan and Baguazhang.

Wang Xuezhi 王學治 (1945-) A Professor of Traditional Chinese Medicine at Beijing University. He was born into a family with a long history of medical, martial arts, and fine arts practices. He began his training when he was six years old and studied under many prominent instructors in Shaolin and Wudang styles, medicine, herbs, painting, and calligraphy. He is the author of *The Encyclopedia of Chinese Herbs.* He is the Chairman of the 5th Generation Wudangmen. He specializes in Li Style Taijiquan, Baguazhang, Xingyiquan, Qigong, and qi healing. He currently lives in Seattle, Washington, where he has started the Qi Gong Longevity Association to teach people how to live a long, healthy life. *See* his photo demonstration under Wudangmen.

Wang, Yu Wa 王月魂 Also known as, Yuwa Hedrick-Wang. He is one of the founders of the International Wushu Sanshou Dao Association (I.W.S.D). He is a black belt instructor in Karate, Jujutsu, Tae Kwon Do, and Kick Boxing. He is also well-versed in Wushu, Taijiquan, hard and soft Qigong, boxing, and Thai Boxing. He has trained many outstanding black belt students. He was one of the first to be invited to China to promote Karate. He has given workshops in the U.S., France, Italy, Western Europe, the Philippines, and Southeast Asia. He is also a well-known economic advisor to many nations around the world. See his photo demonstrations under Karate-do and Wushu Sanshou Dao.

Wang, Ziping 王子平 (1881-1973) He was known for his patriotism, great strength, martial skills, and as a doctor of traumatology. He started his Wushu training at age 6, and became a prominent practitioner in both Internal and Exeternal Styles of Wushu. He was an expert in Qinna, Shuaijiao, free fighting, hard Qigong, soft Qigong, and light body skill. He defeated numerous foreign challengers that claimed to be undefeated in the world. He was also a prominent practitioner in traumatology. He combined his adept knowledge of Qinna with his bone setting skills and originated a well-known system of treatment for sports and Wushu related injuries in Northern China. He was the head of the Shaolin Division at the Central Guoshu Institute (中央國術館). He was the chairman of the Chinese Wushu Association. In 1960, at age 80, he was the first head coach to lead a Wushu team to perform outside of China. *See* his photo demonstrations under Chan and Wangshi Wushu.

Figure W-1

Wangshi Wushu 王氏武術 Founded by Wang Ziping and his daughter Wang Jurong. Both Wang Ziping and Wang Jurong are prominent practitioners of many Internal and External Styles of Wushu. In 1960, Wang Ziping and Wang Jurong were appointed to lead the Wushu team, along with Premier Zhou Enlai's diplomatic delegation, to visit Burma. Wang Ziping was the head coach. Wang, Jurong was the women's coach. This was a historic event because it was the first time, since New China, that a Wushu team ever performed outside of China.

Wang Jurong came to the United States in 1989, after retiring for a few years. At the time, the United States and China had recently normalized diplomatic relations. She was one of the first Wushu professors to venture into the United States from mainland China, to teach Wushu. Since her arrival in the United States, she has actively engaged in the promotion and organization of Wushu competitions. She has personally worked in the Chief Arbitrator and Referee General positions at U.S. National Competitions. Her many efforts made it possible for the U.S. to host the succesful Third World Wushu Championships.

Wang Jurong fulfilled her life dream of promoting Wushu in China and became a leading Wushu practitioner in China. Upon retirement, she has continued her efforts in the United States, using Wushu to strengthen the bridge between the Chinese people and Americans. She has done a tremendous job. Her influence and contribution to the development of Wushu in the United States is next to none. She is an advisor of the International Wushu Sanshou Dao Association. She was awarded the Lifetime Achievement Award by the U.S.A.W.K.F. in 1997, and she was twice voted the Women of the Year by Inside Kung Fu Magazine.

Wangshi Wushu includes: traditional Taijiquan, Xingyiquan, Baguazhang, Chaquan, Tantui, Paoquan, and many others. It also includes the new routines created by

Figure W-2 Figure W-3 Figure W-4 Figure W-5 Figure W-6 Figure W-7 Figure W-8 Figure W-9 Figure W-10 Figure W-11 Figure W-12

Figure W-13

Wang Ziping and Wang Jurong. These new routines include: Green Dragon sword, Taiji Sword, the Flying Rainbow Fan Series, and Wangshi Traumatology. Currently, the already compiled Wangshi Wushu books include: *Qubingyannian Ershishi* (祛病延年二十勢), *Longfeng Double Swords* (龍鳳雙劍), *Quanshu Ershifa* (拳術二十法), *Wang Ziping and Wushu* (王子平與武術), *Wushu and Trauma* (武術與傷科), *Training and Life Nourishing* (練功與養生), and the *Flying Rainbow Fan Series* (飛虹扇功系列).

Also see Wang Ziping and Wang Jurong.

Figure W-14

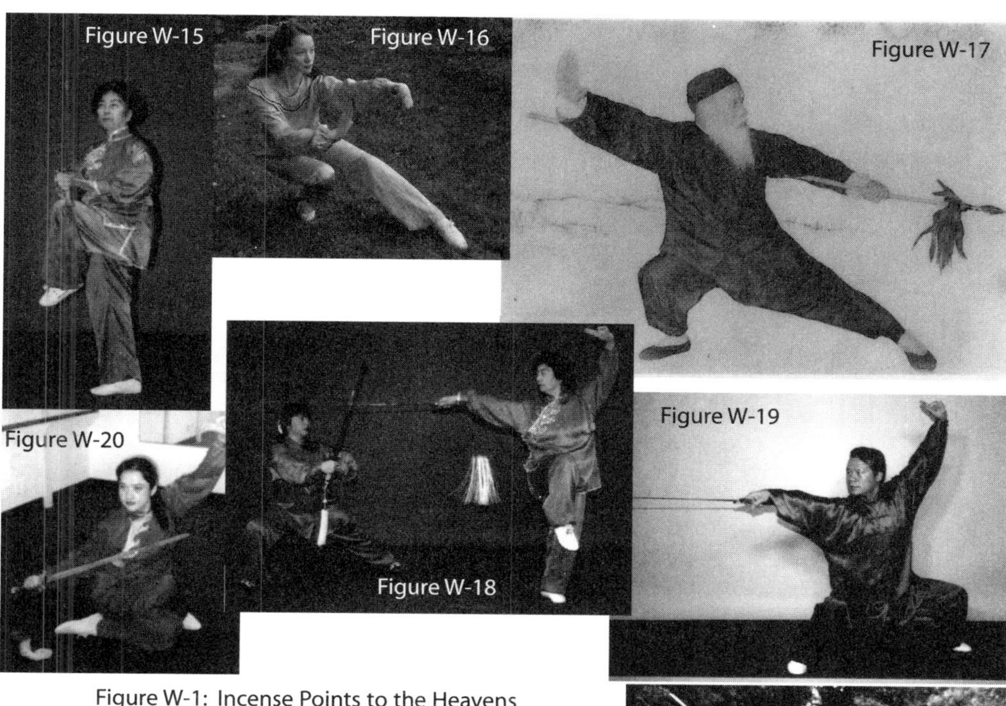

Figure W-15

Figure W-16

Figure W-17

Figure W-18

Figure W-19

Figure W-20

Figure W-1: Incense Points to the Heavens (朝天一柱香)/Wang Ziping
Figure W-2: Spear/Wang Jurong
Figure W-3: Traumatology/Wang Ziping
Figure W-4: Chaquan/Wang Jurong
Figure W-5: Shuaijiao/Wu Chengde
Figure W-6: Green Dragon Sword/Wang Ziping
Figure W-7: Taiji Single Fan/Helen Wu
Figure W-8: Kick to the Heaven/Simon Hu
Figure W-9: Green Dragon Sword/Wang Jurong and Andrew Wu
Figure W-10: Sword/Greg Watson
Figure W-11: Toubupingheng (偷步平衡)/Grace Wu
Figure W-12: Flying Phoenix Double Sword (飛鳳雙劍)/ Helen Wu
Figure W-13: Bajiquan/Wang Jurong (C), Denise Breiter-Wu (L), Helen Wu (R)
Figure W-14: Traditional Zhuanggong (傳統樁功)/Simon Hu
Figure W-15: Saber/Wang Jurong
Figure W-16: Wulu Chaquan (五路查拳)/Grace Wu
Figure W-17: Spear/Wang Ziping
Figure W-18: Green Dragon Sword Sparring/Wang Jurong And Helen Wu
Figure W-19: Green Dragon Sword/Wu Wen-Ching
Figure W-20: Jianshu/Wu Xiaoping
Figure W-21: Taiji Lianhuan Double Sword (太極連環雙劍)/Helen Wu
Figure W-22: Quanshuershifa (拳術二十法)/Grace Wu
Figure W-23: Rainbow Fan Sparring/ Helen Wu and Denise Breiter-Wu

Figure W-21

Figure W-22

Figure W-23

Watson, Greg He began studying Wushu in 1976. In 1981, he began his study of Taijiquan. In 1989, he met Dr. Wu Chengde and Professor Wang Jurong. A short time later, he became a formal student of Professor Wang and Dr. Wu. Since 1990, he has studied Beiquan (primarily from the Chaquan system) emphasizing long weapons, Taijiquan, Jian, Fan, and Qigong. Currently, he teaches Taijiquan and Wushu several days a week, as well as, continues his training under Professor Wang and Dr. Wu in group and private classes. He has been actively involved in promoting Wushu in the U.S.A., and in developing judging standards and methods for Wushu competitions. *See* his photo demonstration under Wangshi Wushu.

Weapons *see* Wushu Bingqi and specific Wushu weapon names.

Whiting, Fred A member of the Canadian Wushu team in 1985 and 1986. He was a student of Liang Shou-Yu from 1982-1990; and was an instructor at the S.Y.L. Wushu Institute. In 1986, he attained a silver medal in the Xingyiquan category at the International Wushu Invitational Tournament held in China. He has been to Beijing and Sichuan on numerous occasions to continue his Wushu training. He has been a judge and chief judge for many Canadian national Wushu competitions. He is an International Wushu Federation certified coach. In 2001, he was also certified by the International Wushu Federation as an International Wushu Forms Judge. He currently teaches at his school in Vancouver, Canada. *See* his photo demonstration under Xiandai Wushu.

Whitsitt-Lynch, Frank He was a wrestler on his high school and college wrestling teams from 1964 to 1969. He began his martial arts training in Tae Kwon Do in 1969 where he attained a black belt level. He began his Chinese martial arts studies in 1974. In 1992, he began studying Wushu and Qigong from Wu Wen-Ching. He is an instructor at The Way of the Dragon School, a black belt in Wushu Sanshou Dao, and an engineer with the Department of the Navy. *See* his photo demonstrations under Baguazhang, Taijiquan and Xingyiquan.

Wing Chun *see* Yongchunquan

Wong, Candice She is a student of Ken Low and an assistant instructor under him. Through the introduction from her teacher, she also began to study from Liang Shou-Yu in 1999. She is a many time gold medalist and all-around champion in U.S. & Canadian Wushu competitions. *See* her photo demonstration under Qiang.

Wong, Ivan He is a former member of the Canadian National Wushu team. He has been a silver and bronze medalist in World Wushu competitions; and a gold and silver medalist in Pan American Championships. He is also a certified coach by the International Wushu Federation. *See* his photo demonstration under Changquan.

Wong, Phillip He has over 25 years of teaching experience. He attained 13 national and international Grand Championships. He was also the all-around silver medalist at the Second International Wushu Invitational Tournament. He was an Inside Kung Fu Competitor of the Year. He has been the character motion capture for numerous video games, and has appeared most notably in Tekken 1, 2, and 3 as Lei Wu Long. He is the cofounder and teacher of the Pacific Wushu and the Stanford Wushu Club. *See* his photo demonstration under Jian.

Wong, Solen 王深寰 He is a native of Taiwan. In 1982, he became a student of Liang Shou-Yu. He has studied many different styles of Wushu, Qigong, Shuaijiao, Sanshou, and short weapon sparring. He was a gold medalist in the Canadian-American martial arts competition in the black belt division. He is currently in the business field. *See* his photo demonstration under Tanglangquan.

Wong, Tat-Mau 王達謨 President of the International Choy Lay Fut Kung Fu Federation of America. He was a Southeast Asian forms and fighting champion. He has over 35 years of extensive experience. He was named "Man of the Year" and "Instructor of the Year" by the Inside Kung Fu Magazine's Hall of Fame and he was named "Kung Fu Artist of the Year" by the Black Belt Magazine's Hall of Fame. He is the sponsor of one of the most acclaimed tournaments in Kung Fu history, the International Chinese Martial Arts Championship. He currently operates three schools in the San Francisco area and two schools in Sao Paulo, Brazil. More information about him and his schools can be find at *www.tatwong.com*. *See* his photo demonstration under Cailifoquan.

Wu, Andrew 吳鼎文 (1995-) Wu Wen-Ching and Denise Breiter-Wu's son. He began his Wushu training under his parents' tutelage at age two and a half. His first major performance was at Professor Wang Jurong's seventieth birthday celebration when he was only three years old. His matching set performance and one-handed pushups amazed the audience and received loud applause. *See* his photo demonstrations under Emei Shaolin, Wangshi Wushu and Nanquan.

Wu, Chengde 吳誠德 (1930-) A Professor Emeritus of the Shanghai Traditional Medicine and Herbology University. Dr. Wu is a disciple and the son-in-law of Wang Ziping. He was the first coach of the Shanghai Wushu team. He is a prominent practitioner in Shuaijiao, many Wushu styles, and a highly acclaimed professor and doctor of Traditional Chinese Medicine. He is an advisor of the International Wushu Sanshou Dao Association. Dr. Wu has over a half century of Wushu, Taijiquan, and Qigong experience, as well as, clinical experience in Chinese medicine. From 1959 to 1989 he served as the Director and professor for the Shanghai College of Traditional Chinese Medicine, and a Doctor-in-Chief of the Longhua Hospital in Shanghai. He currently teaches and has his medical practice in Houston, Texas, USA. *See* his photo demonstration under Wangshi Wushu.

Wu, Eddie Kwong Yu He is the 5th Generation Wu Style Taijiquan descendent and is currently the Chief Instructor of the Wu Style Tai Chi Chuan Toronto Academy and Head of the North American and European Academies. He is the great grandson of Wu Chuan Yau (吳全佑, 1834-1902). He began his training at age 6 under the tutelage of his grandfather, Wu Kung Yi, and his father Wu Tai Kwei. He has produced and directed several instructional videos about Wu Style Taijiquan. He is a founding member of the Canadian Chinese Kuo Sho Federation (1987), and served as President for four years. He is also on the Board of Directors on the Confederation of Canadian Wushu Organizations and the Vice President of the United Wushu Federation of Canada. *See* his photo demonstration under Taijiquan.

Wu-Monnat, Grace X. 吳小高 Also known as Wu Xiagao. She is a prominent Wushu practitioner. She is the granddaughter and student of Wang Ziping, and the daughter of Wang Jurong and Wu Chengde. She received a B.A. in Physical Education at the Shanghai Teacher's University, and a Master's degree in Sports Administration at the Wichita State University. She is a certified Wushu judge. By dedicating countless hours of her time and serving conscientiously as a judge to the U.S.A. team trials and numerous regional, national, and international tournaments, she shares her contribution to the promotion of Wushu and wellness. She is an instructor and administrator of the Grace Wu Kung Fu School in Wichita, Kansas, U.S.A. *See* her photo demonstrations under Chaquan, Wangshi Wushu, and Tantuimen.

Wu, Helen X. 吳小蓉 (1956-) She is a prominent Wushu practitioner. At age three, she began her traditional Wushu training from her grandfather, Wang Ziping; her mother, Wang Jurong; and her father, Wu Chengde. She has been judging competitions and teaching Kung Fu, Tai Chi, and Qigong since 1975. She graduated from Shanghai Teacher's University and remained on as a teacher of sports medicine. She has also studied and practiced traditional Chinese Medicine under the direction of her father. She is the author and co-author of several books and videos including: *Tai Chi Single Fan* and *Tai Chi Double Fan*. She was noted as, the "Great pioneer martial woman that singly ventured into North America" in the *Great Changes in the Course of Time*. More about her can be found at www.masterhelenwu.com. *See* her photo demonstrations under Shan, Taijiquan, and Wangshi Wushu.

Wu, Wen-Ching 吳文慶 A prominent practitioner of Wushu and Qigong. He has written and coauthored many books about Chinese martial arts, Taijiquan, and Qigong. He has a BSME degree from Northeastern University. In 1990, he was a U.S. National Chinese Martial Arts Competition Grandchampion in both Internal and External Styles where he competed in eight events and was ranked first in every event he competed in. In 1998, he was awarded three gold medals at the Fourth Shanghai International Wushu Festival/Competition. In the same year, he was also included in the book, *China's Contemporary Wushu Masters* 中國當代武林名人志. He is the Vice Chairman of the International Wushu Sanshou Dao Association and currently teaches in the Providence, Rhode Island area. *See* his photo demonstrations throughout this book.

Wu, Xiaoping 吳小平 Also known as Lucy Wu. She began her traditional Wushu training at age three from her grandfather, Wang Ziping; her mother, Wang Jurong; and her father, Wu Chengde. She is a graduate of the prestigious Shanghai Teacher's University and the Shanghai College of Traditional Chinese Medicine. She is a prominent Wushu practitioner and a highly skilled instructor and lecturer in a wide range of Internal and External Style Wushu and sports medicine. She was the recipient of the "Outstanding Employee of all Shanghai" award and currently teaches at the Houston Taiji Kung Fu Health Academy in Houston, Texas, U.S.A. *See* her photo demonstration under Wangshi Wushu.

Wudang Hongmenquan 武當洪門拳 The earliest records indicate that this style spread from Sichuan Province to Hubei Province. It was then influenced by Wudang (武當) Wushu and gradually became a style of its own. This style utilizes many sounds to assist in its power emission. Sounds, such as: sha (嗄), zhi (吱), hei (嘿), and ha (哈), are often used. Some of the known routines include: Zhongshou (總手), Fengshou (封手), Hongmenshou (洪門手), Jingangshou (金剛手), Qinglongshou (青龍手), Badashou (八大手), Jiugongshou (九宮手), Shizishou (十字手), Laojuntang (老君堂), Chuhai (出海), Panjjiao (盤腳), and many training methods.

Figure W-25

Figure W-26

Wudang Wushu 武當武術 This is a term referring to all of the styles that originated from the Wudang Mountains. The Wudang Mountains are also known as Taiheshan (太合山). This is a famous Daoist Mountain range, as well as, the core of Daoist Wushu. There have been many legendary stories about Wudang

Najiaquan (武當内家拳) and Zhang Sanfeng (張三丰). During the end of the Qing Dynasty and toward the beginning of the Republic, the last Abbott of Jinshan (金山), Xu Benshan (徐本善), was known to possess nearly incredible skills. In 1931, General He Long (賀龍元帥) studied Wudang Wushu from him. Wudang Wushu includes many styles which have been introduced under their own headings.

Figure W-27

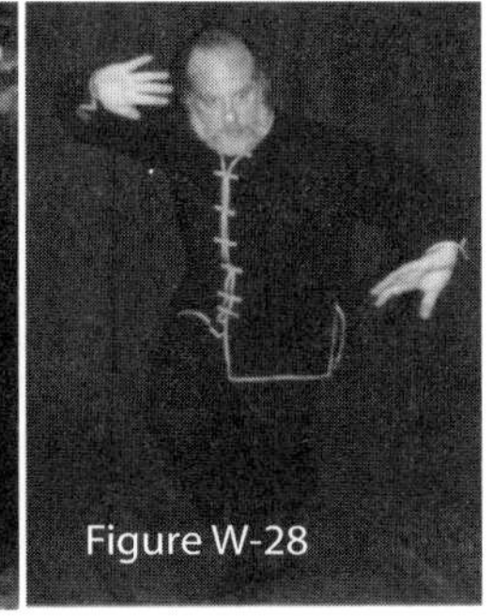
Figure W-28

Figures W-25 and W-26: Wudang Lianhuanjian (武當連環劍)/Liang Qiangya
Figure W-27: Wudang Jian/He Weiqi
Figure W-28: Snake and Hawk Boxing/Kenneth Cohen (photo by Rebecca D. Cohen)

Wudangmen 武當門 Translated as Wudang Gate, also known as, Lipai Gongfu (李派功夫). It was created by Li Ruidong (李瑞東) during the Qing Dynasty. Li was the director of training for the imperial guards, a position he held for over twenty years. Li was a prominent practitioner in Chuojiao, Shaolin, Tantui, Xinyi, Bagua, and Wudang Jinchanpai Taijigong (武當金蟾派太極功). Li taught his style to his top student Zhang Tao (張濤). Zhang taught it to Chen Yuefang (陳月舫). Chen taught it to Wang Youyu (王友虞). Wang taught it to his son, Wang Xuezhi (王學治), the fifth generation chairman. The training content of this style includes: Wudang Wuxiu Jinchanpai Taiji (武當悟修金蟾派太極), Taiji Bagua Qimenquan (太極八卦奇門拳), Taiji Baba Shenna Luanchaquan (太極八把神拿亂插拳), Taiji Wuxingchui (太極五行捶), and many other barehanded and weapon routines. This training also includes traumatology and traditional healing methods.

Figure W-29

Figure W-30

Information provided by Wang Xuezhi.

Figure W-29: Wudang Jinchanpai Taijigong/Wang Xuezhi
Figure W-30: Wudang Bagua Double Sabers/Wang Xuezhi

Wuji Xiaoyaopai 無極逍遙派 The complete name for this style is Shusan Wuji Xiaoyaopai (蜀山無極逍遙派). Shushan is a term referring to the region in China that includes current day Sichuan and northern parts of Yunnan and Guizhou, and part of Shaanxi. The term Xiaoyao implies the state of free expression at its highest level. The term Wuji implies the unlimited and unrestricted nature of the style. In order for a practitioner to attain a state of absolute freedom in utilizing one's martial ability, it is necessary that one have a solid foundation and broad martial arts knowledge and ability, and is able to integrate the usefulness of the different styles. When the practitioner is able to express and assimilate the characteristics of different styles, and digest them into useful forms to make them one's own, then the practitioner will have attained the state of "extend from the rule, yet in accord with the rule" in every movement.

Figure W-31 Figure W-32 Figure W-33 Figure W-34 Figure W-35 Figure W-36 Figure W-37 Figure W-38 Figure W-39 Figure W-40 Figure W-41

This style is inspired by the Wuji and Xiaoyao styles that existed during the Song Dynasty. It was founded by Liang Shou-Yu and is based on his extensive Wushu background and experience in many Wushu styles. The requirements of the Wuji Xiaoyaopai are for the practitioner to learn the well-known styles, to absorb the essence of these different styles, and to charge up one's knowledge and ability. The practitioner should not be restricted to any particular style's strengths or limitations. From the dedicated practice of the different styles, the practitioner will be able to attain a state of truly free expression of the different styles.

The Wuji Xiaoyaopai is a fusion of Emei, Wudang, Shaolin Wushu, and Qigong into one exceptional style. The style's foundation training includes the essence of traditional routines from well-known Wushu styles. Practitioners are required to be well-versed in the styles' characteristics and principles governing the style's barehanded and weapon routines, and free fighting.

The training content of Wuji Xiaoyaopai consists of routines from thirty-six different styles and eighteen categories of weapons; and the Xiaoyao routines created by

Figure W-42

Figure W-43

Liang Shou-Yu. They include: Shaolin Fuhuquan (少林伏虎拳), Liuhequan (六合拳), Yanqingquan (燕青拳), Chaquan (查拳), Emei Shaolin Bafa (峨嵋少林八法), Tiangangquan (天罡拳), Qixingquan (七星拳), Heihuquan (黑虎拳), Hongquan (洪拳), Hongquan (紅拳), Fanziquan (翻子拳), Tongbiquan (通臂拳), Yingzhuaquan (鷹爪拳), Tanglangquan (螳螂拳), Chuojiaoquan (戳脚拳), Tuokaoquan (脱拷拳), Emei Shequan (峨嵋蛇拳); the Baguazhang System (八卦掌系列), the Xingyiquan System (形意拳系列); Chen (陳), Yang (楊), Wu (吳), and Sun (孫) Style Taijiquan; Huayue Xinyi Liuhebafa (華岳心意六合八法) and Sanpan Shiershi (三盤十二式); the Wujiquan System (無極拳系列); Xiaoyaoquan (逍遙拳), Xiaoyaoshuai (逍遙摔), Xiaoyaona (逍遙拿), Xiaoyaotui (逍遙腿), Xiaoyaozhang (逍遙掌), Xiaoyaodianxue (逍遙點穴), and Push Hands methods.

Their practical fighting training includes: traditional Shuijiao (摔跤), Sanshou Kuaijiao (散手快跤), Qinna (擒拿), cavity press, competition Sanshou training, self-defense and street Sanshou training; and Taiji basic, free, and Sanshou Push Hands. Their internal strength and Qigong training includes: Iron Shirt, Dapeng (大鵬) and Golden Bell Cover Qigong, Medical Qigong, External Qi Healing Qigong, Buddhist Qigong, and Daoist Jinguang Xuanlin (道家金光玄靈) Qigong.

Figure W-31: Xiaoyaoquan/Liang Shou-Yu
Figure W-32: Tiangangquan/Wu Wen-Ching
Figure W-33: Wujiquan/Liang Shou-Yu
Figure W-34: Xiaoyaona/Sun Jie
Figure W-35: Xiaoyaozhang/Liang Shou-Yu
Figure W-36: Xiaoyaoshuai/Liang Shou-Yu
Figure W-37: White Ape Sword/Wu Wen-Ching
Figure W-38: Xiaoyaoshui Application/Liang Shou-Yu and Ian Sinclair
Figure W-39: White Ape Sword/Huen Siu Hung
Figure W-40: Rooting Training at the Beach/Liang Shou-Yu and Wu Wen-Ching
Figure W-41: Xiaoyaotui/Sun Jie
Figures W-42 and W-43: Xiaoyaoquan and Applications/S.Y.L. Wushu Institute Students: Michael, Matthew, Terry, Michael, Patti, Itamar, Tony, Mo, Gordon, Jacob, Michael, Ken, Brigitte, Shona, Kelly, Chen-Han, Chris, Ron, Derek, and Tjong

Wujiaquan 巫家拳 This is a Southern Style originally from the Fujian Shaolin Temple. The known training includes: Liuluquan (六路拳), six elbow techniques, eight fist techniques, twelve palm techniques, and many kicking techniques.

Wumeipai 五梅派 Legend has it, that Wumeipai was created by Wu Mei, the daughter of a general in the Ming imperial court. Thus, she had the benefits of imperial tutors in all aspects of knowledge, art, and culture. She was an advocate of strong and rigorous training to improve military readiness. Wu Mei sought refuge at the White Crane Shaolin Temple in Guangxi when the Qing Dynasty took control of the empire. Wu Mei taught her Wushu to the monks and nuns at the temple, and helped the Ming loyalists raise an army against the Qing rulers. Her art was only taught at the temple so that her methods would not fall into enemy hands. She innovated wooden posts training—logs driven into the ground in a huge matrix in patterns of five. Individuality, improvisation, and unpredictability are the hallmarks of Wumeipai.

Figure W-44

Information provided by Ken Lo.

Figure W-44: Wumeipai/Ken Lo

Wushouquan 五手拳 Translated as Five Handed Fist. This is a popular Wushu trained by the people of Qingdao City (青島市) of Shandong Province. The focus of this style is on practical applications rather than on forms. Each of their routines contains only a few techniques that are practiced individually or together as a short routine. The power expression of this style resembles Xingyiquan.

Wushu 武術 The official term for Chinese martial arts. It is also a general term meaning martial arts.

Wushu Anqi 武術暗器 Anqi generally refers to any weapon that can be concealed on a person. Anqi can be used from a few feet to one hundred feet away to strike an opponent. Wushu practitioners of old learned not only barehanded and weapon combat skills, but they also learned anqi skills. It was almost impossible to travel around the countryside without the ability to use anqi. Anqi skills were often used when one's ability was not as good as their opponent. To surprise an opponent and to avert a life or death situation, fighters often resorted to anqi to save themselves. Generally, there are thirty-six different kinds of traditional Wushu anqi including throwing anqi, roped anqi, projectile activated anqi, blow darts, etc.

Wushu Bingqi 武術兵器 This term refers to all Wushu weapons. Since ancient times, there has not been a consistent record of how many Wushu weapons there are. The way the numbers are used in Chinese is very intriguing with multiple context and meaning. It is known that there are more than eighteen Wushu weapons, but there is a figure of speech that states, "eighteen types of weapons". Generally speaking, the term simply means "all the weapons". Today, Wushu weapons are typically classified into either long, short, flexible, small, or concealed weapons.

Typically, long and short weapons are used as primary weapons, flexible and short weapons are used as secondary weapons, and hidden weapons are used as ambushing weapons.

Long weapons typically refer to all weapons that have a long rod or an extension of a long rod. Weapons like the staff, spear, and trident, are typical long weapons. They are usually about as long as the distance from the practitioner's feet to his eyebrows. Long weapon movements are generally held with both hands when used.

Short weapons typically refer to weapons that are longer than the practitioner's arm, but shorter than the distance between the practitioner's feet and eyebrows. Weapons like the sword, saber, and short rods, are typical short weapons. Many short weapons are easily converted into long weapons by adding a pole extension.

Flexible weapons typically refer to weapons that bend. Weapons such as the chain, three section staff, and rope dart, are typical flexible weapons. Flexible weapons are often used as secondary weapons when the primary weapon is not available or breaks during combat. Some flexible weapons are also considered concealed weapons or anqi (暗器). Small weapons typically refer to weapons that are shorter than the practitioner's arm. Weapons like the deer hooks, dagger, and Emei piercer, are typical short weapons. Concealed weapons are known as Wushu Anqi and are described under their own heading.

Also see specific types of Wushu weapons.

Figure W-45: Staff/William Pyne
Figure W-46: Spear/Jeffrey Lykins
Figure W-47: Pudao/Fred Barbosa
Figure W-48: Saber/Ryan May
Figure W-49: Double Sabers/Tom Uva
Figure W-50: Sword/Gordon Yiu
Figure W-51: Staff/Steve Finger

Figure W-52: Group Saber/S.Y.L. Wushu Institute Students: Billy, Desmond, Trylon, Kerry, Leslie, Tjong, Derek, Hong, and Howie

Figure W-53: Group Staff/S.Y.L. Wushu Institute Students: Eric, Francis, Derek, Leslie, Jonathan, Chelsia, and Hong

Figure W-54: Group Spear/S.Y.L. Wushu Institute Students: Billy, Kerry, Desmond, Chen-Han, Dora, Eli, Shona, and Sarah

Wushu Qigong 武術氣功 A part of the martial arts' internal energy training that develops the physical body's ability to withstand attacks, and develops a strong offensive application potential.

Wushu Sanshou Dao 武術散手道 Officially called the International Wushu Sanshou Dao (I.W.S.D.) Association. An organization founded in the 1980's by martial arts practitioners from Canada, U.S.A., China, and Russia. It is not a style of martial arts, rather it is an organization dedicated to preserving and training well-rounded martial artists. Wushu Sanshou Dao utilizes Chinese Wushu as a foundation, while incorporating the advantages from other martial arts systems into its training outline. Wushu Sanshou Dao encourages its members to participate in different martial arts competitions to learn and familiarize themselves with other systems of martial arts. It supports all international martial arts movements and does not discriminate against any style of martial arts. If it is a practical and useful martial

art, it is a good martial art. Since its conception, members of the Wushu Sanshou Dao organization have participated in Wushu, Sanshou, Karate, Judo, and Taiji Push Hands competitions with outstanding achievements in both the routines and the application categories.

Wushu Sanshou Dao has enlisted many advisors in its organization. These advisors are all outstanding and prominent practitioners in the martial arts community with remarkable contributions to the promotion of martial arts around the world. They receive the highest admiration and respect from the Wushu Sanshou Dao members.

Wushu Sanshou Dao ranking is very demanding. To attain each level of black belt, the practitioners must go through rigorous training and testing. Only the well-rounded practitioners with exceptional knowledge and skills are granted black belt status. The general requirements for each level of Wushu Sanshou Dao are listed on the following pages.

Figure W-55: Qinna/Liang Shou-Yu and student
Figure W-56: Sanshou Application/ Wang Yu Wa
Figures W-57, W-60, and W-61: Sanshou Training/Tjhie Wie Tjong and Howie Leung
Figure W-58: Sanshou Training/Jared Johnson and Ayron Howey
Figure W-59: Sanshou Training/Ayron Howey and Derek Cheng
Figure W-62: Conditioning the Abdomen with a Log/Howie Leung
Figure W-63: Breaking bricks with the head/Yang Wei
Figure W-64: Holding and breaking two bricks with the palm/Yang Wei

Figure W-65: Breaking five bricks with the palm/Sun Xiaodong

Figure W-66: Push Bricks in Horse Stance 1000-1500 times in ten minutes/ Vancouver, Canada I.W.S.D. Members

Figure W-65: Minimum of Twenty One Handed Push Up/Vancouver, Canada I.W.S.D. Members

First Level Black Belt

1. Five routines:
   a. One Northern or Southern Chinese Wushu routine
   b. One Internal Style Chinese Wushu routine
   c. One other routine that can be from any accepted martial arts style
   d. One short weapon routine from any accepted martial art style
   e. One long weapon routine from any accepted martial arts style
2. Ten Qinna techniques.
3. Ten take down techniques.
4. Basic Taiji Push Hands ability including Peng, Lu, Ji, An, Cai, Lie, Zhou, Kao.
5. Twenty one step fighting techniques.
6. Proficiency in free style sparring.
7. Men must be able to do 20 one handed push ups (feet placed on a foot high bench), with each arm. Women must be able to do 30 standard two handed push ups (feet placed on a foot high bench).

Many of the Wushu Sanshou Dao First Level Black Belt recipients have also attained the top three rankings in international competitions held in the United States and Canada. Some have also attained the top three rankings in world competitions. Wushu Sanshou Dao does not require its members to compete in competitions, however, participants that are interested in competition are encouraged to do so. The primary goal of Wushu Sanshou Dao is to nurture the all-around martial artist.

Second Level Black Belt

1. Ten additional Qinna techniques.
2. Ten additional take down techniques.
3. Ten ground fighting techniques.

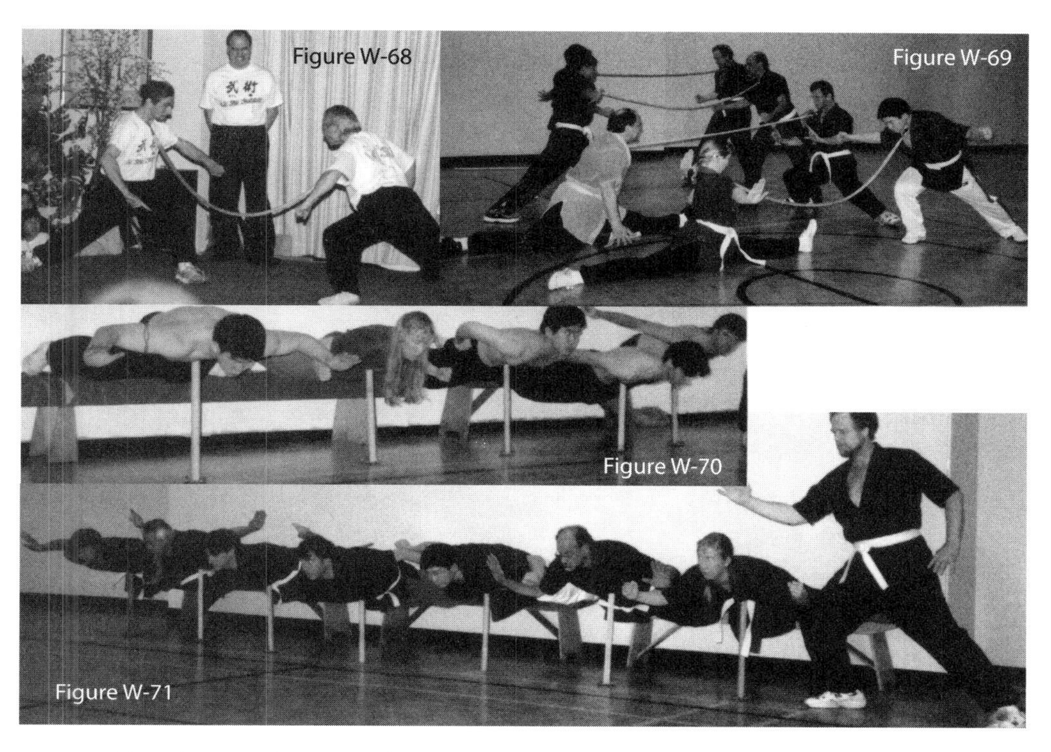

Figure W-68 and W-69: Hard Qigong-Spear to the Throat/Vancouver, Canada I.W.S.D. Members

Figures W-70 and W-71: Supporting Body weight with a stick on the solar plexus (30 seconds to 2-1/2 minutes)/Tony Bujas, Ron Case, Peter Spence, Michael Young, Gord McKay, Calvin Keele, Jacob Simpson, Howie Leung, Barry Luqer, Declan King, Derek Cheng, Michael Holmes, and Kelly Maclean

4. Free Taiji Push Hands ability.
5. Internal energy (Qigong) attainment, such that strikes to the arms, abdomen, chest, sides of the torso, and head can be withstood without injury. Women are exempt from strikes to the chest and waist.
6. Breaking techniques with the hands, feet, and head, which indicate strength and power for martial application.
7. Free sparring incorporating Push Hands skills which indicate the ability to use neutralization skills against an opponent's muscular strength.

Third Level Black Belt

1. Two advanced External and/or Internal Style routines.
2. Ten additional take down techniques.
3. Ten additional ground fighting techniques.
4. Ten additional Qinna techniques incorporating ten effective pressure point attacks.
5. Barehanded free sparring training against weapons
6. Combined free sparring with take down, Qinna, and Push Hands skills.
7. A qualified Second Level holder may be exempt from all of the above requirements, if he or she has achieved recognition as an all-around routine champion or a Sanshou champion in a recognized national competition.

Figure W-72: Sanshou Training/Liang Shou-Yu (R) and Mike Sigman (L)
Figure W-73: Sanshou Dao/Michael Levenston
Figure W-74: Sanshou Ready Posture/Wang Yu Wa
Figure W-75: Sanshou/Yang Wei
Figure W-76: Sanshou Training/Juha Lintunen and Bedry Ricci
Figure W-77: Ground Control/Al Arsenalt (R) and Jared Johnson (L)
Figure W-78: Sanshou/Rudi Ott, Ayron Howey, and Howie Leung
Figure W-79: Leg Conditioning/Fred Ho and Perry Lo

Fourth Level Black Belt — Master Level 1

1. Proficiency in more than ten routines.
2. A minimum of 10 years of teaching experience in the martial arts.
3. Advanced achievement in internal energy training.
4. A university degree or equivalent life experience.
5. A free fighting champion in a recognized world competition may be considered for this level without testing. First place all-around routine champion in a recognized world competition may also be considered for this level without testing.

Fifth Level Black Belt — Master Level 2

1. Experienced in judging a national and/or an international martial arts events.
2. Published pieces of work in the field of martial arts (books, magazine or journal articles, videos, audiotapes ...).
3. Further advancement achieved in internal energy training.
4. Contributions in teaching and promoting martial arts.

Figure W-80: Staff vs. Staff/Howard Means and Thomas Uva
Figure W-81: Sanshou Competition/Ayron Howey (Canadian National Champion, 65 Kg)
Figure W-82: Sanshou Competition/Howie Leung (Canadian National Champion, 80 Kg)
Figure W-83: Sanshou Competition/Derek Cheng (Canadian National Champion, 70 Kg)

Sixth Level Black Belt — Master Level 3

1. Continuous contribution in teaching and promoting martial arts.
2. Has positive national (country of permanent residence) recognition in the martial arts community.

Seventh Level Black Belt — Master Level 4

1. Continuous contribution in teaching and promoting martial arts and Wushu Sanshou Dao.
2. Has positive international recognition in the martial arts community.

Eighth Level Black Belt — Honorary Level 1

1. Honorary Level 1 recipients must be a person of great martial arts accomplishment, recommended and approved by the I.W.S.D. Association Headquarters.
2. This individual must be at least 55 years of age and have over 30 years of martial arts experience.

Ninth Level Black Belt — Honorary Level 2

1. Honorary Level 2 recipients must be a founding member of the I.W.S.D. Association with continuous contribution in promoting Wushu Sanshou Dao or be an individual with an extraordinary contribution to Wushu Sanshou Dao.
2. This individual must be at least 60 years of age and have over 40 years of martial arts experience.

Wuxing Dunshumen 五行遁術門 In ancient times, in addition to combat training, practitioners also learned many other techniques to evade enemy pursuit or to trick their opponents. These techniques and tricks utilized the environment and concealed weapons, to mislead and to distress their opponents, and to achieve self-preservation. These types of techniques and tricks are referred to as dunshu (遁術) or elusive techniques. Training in dunshu also includes: camouflage within the natural environment, climbing techniques up walls, crossing techniques from building to building, etc. The style that specifically focuses on these elusive techniques is known as Wuxing Dunshumen.

Wuzuquan 五祖拳 Translated as Five Ancestor Fist. It is also known as Wuzuheyangquan (五祖鶴陽拳), and romanized as Ngor Chor in Fujian Chinese dialect. It is classified as a Southern Style that is popular in Southern China, Malaysia, Singapore, and the Philippines. Wuzuquan was developed by Li Chun-Jen (李俊仁) during the reign of the Qing Emperor, Yongzheng (雍正), between 1723 and 1735.

Figure W-84

In his youth, Li studied Taizuquan (太祖拳), Baihequan (白鶴拳), and Houquan (猴拳). After many years of study and contemplation, he realized that all martial art styles have their own strengths and weaknesses. He decided to further his skills by traveling around China to learn and exchange skills with practitioners of different styles. After his travels, Li settled in Southern China and taught his Wushu to many students. Li organized his Wushu into five categories. They were: Taizuquan, Luohanquan (羅漢拳), Baihequan, Hoquan, and Xuanuquan (玄女拳). One of the most noted students of Li was Kan Te-Yen (干德源). Kan was the nephew of Li's wife. Kan studied the five styles taught to him by his teacher and further unified the styles into one.

Wuzuquan is noted for its effective close range combat methods, including joint-locks and leg sweeps. Its movements are simple and direct. Wuzuquan consists of a total of one hundred and eight barehanded, weapon, sparring, and Green Lion against weapon routines. Wuzuquan's emphasis is on the development of an individual's martial skill according to their adaptability, body type, and personal strength. Its training focus lies within the requirements of stability, strength, speed, subtleness, and softness.

Information provided by Kam P. Lee

Figure W-84: Wuzuquan/Kam P. Lee

X

Xiandai Wushu 現代武術 Translated as Contemporary or Modern Wushu. This is also referred to as Sports Performance Wushu. It has the appeal of Huatao Wushu of the Ming Dynasty, but surpassed Huatao Wushu's degree of difficulty. The level of difficulty in Contemporary Wushu is very demanding on the practitioners' endurance, speed, jumping ability, flexibility, balance, coordinated power, and the overall quality of the physical body. It is suitable for sports competitions, performance, and for youngsters to practice. Most Contemporary Wushu routines are not suitable for combat, but they are very good for foundation training for combat.

During the ten years of the Cultural Revolution (1966-1976) in China, all traditional culture was ravaged. Traditional Wushu was also restricted. Sanshou (散手) and practical applications were not allowed to be practiced or shown in public. Even sports Shuaijiao (摔跤), boxing, and weight lifting, were eliminated from formal competition categories.

When the Cultural Revolution ended, Wushu performances had become Huajiazi (花架子), or dance-like without martial intent. These Wushu routines included many dance, ballet, and acting movements and became known as Zixuan Taolu (自選套路), individual creation routines.

These routines included very graceful and highly difficult movements and were very entertaining to the audience. Since they didn't include any violent expressions, they were warmly received by many parents who sent their children to study. When these charismatic Wushu routines were taken outside of China on friendship tours around the world, they also captivated foreign audiences. People around the world began to view Wushu as a healthy, body strengthening, and artistic sport training.

The contribution of Contemporary Wushu has been significant to the popularity of Wushu around the world today. However, at the time, people outside of China thought of Wushu as "it looks good, but is not useful". The newer generation of performers were only trained for performance, without actual combat experience. The performers, shortly after the Cultural Revolution, were unable to accept fighting challenges. Wushu practitioners outside of China condemned the performance Wushu. It wasn't until more and more traditionally trained coaches started to immigrate outside of China, accepting and defeating challenges, that Wushu from mainland China regained its respect. Towards the end of the 1990's, Wushu Sanshou (武術散手) teams from China challenged fighters from around the world. They defeated many of these fighters and proved to the world that the fighting ability of Wushu is still thriving in China.

Wushu had come to another crossroad. Many practitioners of Wushu either practiced routines only and ignored the combat training, or practiced combat training and ignored the routine training. Realizing this deviation, the International Wushu Sanshou Dao (I.W.S.D.) was formed. Practitioners from China, Canada, United States, and Russia, got together and developed this organization with the objective to foster a versatile martial artist, not one that was proficient only in routines or only in fighting.

Today, the trend is very encouraging. The younger generation of Wushu practitioners have become well-versed in both routines and combat. There have been many young versatile Wushu practitioners in recent years.

Due to the tireless work of Wushu enthusiasts around the world, Wushu has become an international competition event. After 1985 and two world competitions held in China, Wushu has steadily increased its popularity. There have been five world Wushu competitions held around the world and Wushu enthusiasts are working to make it an Olympic event in the year 2008.

Today, the competition categories for Wushu include routine and Sanshou categories along with exhibition components and matching sparring set competition components. The routine component includes separate divisions for men and women. They include: the International Compulsory Changquan, Nanquan, 42 Posture

Taijiquan, Saber, Spear, Staff, Sword, 42 Posture Taiji Sword, Southern Staff, and Southern Saber.

In the Sanshou category, there are 11 divisions. They are: 48 kg, 52 kg, 56 kg, 60 kg, 65 kg, 70 kg, 75 kg, 80 kg, 85 kg, 90 kg, and over 90 kg subcategories. The matching sparring set categories include: Sword vs. Saber, Barehanded vs. Barehanded, Staff vs. Staff, Staff vs. Spear, and Three Section Staff vs Staff.

Figure X-1: Butterfly with a 360 Degree Twist/Hui Mo
Figure X-2: Jumping Side Kick/Lin Siyan
Figure X-3: Opening the Door Posture/Jiang Haoquan
Figure X-4: Wushu Basics/Bruce Fontaine
Figure X-5: Compulsory Saber Routine/Maria Liang
Figure X-6: Saber/Narcyz Latecki
Figure X-7: Shuaijiao/Jiang Haoquan and Wang Weizhang
Figure X-8: Sanshou Competition/Michael Li, referee
Figure X-9: Daggers vs. Spear/Li Jinheng (L) and Hao Zhihua (R)
Figure X-10: Sword Compulsory Routine/Kelly Maclean
Figure X-11: Nanquan Compulsory Routine/Howie Leung
Figure X-12: Saber Compulsory Routine/Douglas Chin
Figure X-13: Saber Compulsory Routine/Cindy Luo
Figure X-14: Sword Compulsory Routine/Chris Chin
Figure X-15: Southern Saber Compulsory Routine/Perry Lo
Figure X-16: Spear Compulsory Routine/Alan Tang
Figure X-17: Taiji Sword Compulsory Routine/Hong Yijiao
Figure X-18: Staff Compulsory Routine/Fred Whiting
Figure X-19: Changquan Compulsory Routine/Katrina Leung

Figure X-8
Figure X-9
Figure X-10
Figure X-11
Figure X-12
Figure X-13
Figure X-14
Figure X-15
Figure X-16
Figure X-17
Figure X-18
Figure X-19

Figures X-20 and X-21: Coaching Students/Liang Shou-Yu and Students
Figure X-22: Balance Training/Rena Huang, Kelly Maclean, Sandy, Emily, and Bonnie
Figure X-23: Qinna Matching Set/Narcyz Latecki and Eva Latecki

Xiangmen 向門 Translated as Xiang Family Style. It was created by Xiang Kui (向奎), a Security Guard in Bejing during the Qing Dynasty. Xiangmen's movements are close and continuous. There are seven known barehanded routines and a Nanzhenggun (南征棍) staff routine.

Xianhumen 弦虎門 This is an Emei Style. There are three known barehanded routines, a Zheshoujian (折手劍) sword routine, and a Nuanhuafu (煖花斧) ax routine.

Xiao, Benson 蕭濱生 Also known as Xiao Binsheng. He was a former member of the Heilongjiang Provincial Wushu team. He was a gold medalist many times in city, provincial, and national Wushu competitions. He is a graduate of Beijing Physical Education University with a degree in Wushu. He was the former editor of China Wushu Magazine, a first class judge, and Wushu coach of the China National Sports Committee. In 2001, he was certified by the International Wushu Federation as an International Wushu Forms Judge. He currently teaches in Vancouver, British Columbia, Canada. *See* his photo demonstration under Taizuquan.

Xiaquan 俠拳 Translated as Xia Style. Legend has it, that Li Huzi (李胡子) of Sichuan taught it to students in Guangdong during the Qing Dynasty. Li Huzi was also a Chan Buddhist priest, known as Jingo (肖). He taught his Wushu to Huang Yinlin (黄隱林). When Huang taught his students, he named the style Xiaquan, out of respect and in remembrance of his teacher who was known as Da Xia, meaning great and ethically upright martial artist.

It is classified both as an Emei Style and a Southern Style. Some of the known routines include: Huheshuandou (虎鶴雙斗), Daluohan (大羅漢), Xiajia Dandao (俠家單刀), and Zuoshougun (左手棍).

Xibei Difangquan西北地方拳 Translated as Northeast Regional Style. It is also known as Lanzhoudifang Laobashi (蘭州地方老八式) and Bamen (八門). This style is an embodiment of many other styles. These famous styles include: Paoquan (炮拳), Siquan (撕拳), Jiuhuanzi (九環子), Tongbeiquan (通背拳), and Fengshoubakuai (封手八快). Among them, Paoquan is the *mother*, including twelve routines. Siquan is the *son*, including six routines. There are many kicking and takedown methods. The primary palm technique is an expression of power to the finger tips to distress an opponent. The practitioners also used to put coins in the ends of their sleeves to increase the effectiveness of their strikes. Within the movments are constant opening and closing moves which both can be offensive techniques.

Figure X-24

Information provided by Michael Li.

Figure X-24: Sipaoquan (撕炮拳)/Michael Li

Xie, Qingcai 解慶才 He is a first class China Wushu judge. He is a committee member and director of the Sichuan Wushu Association, and the Principal of the Chongqing Yunyang Teacher's College (重慶雲陽師範學校). He is the Chairman of the Changjiang Sanxia Affiliate of the International Wushu Sanshou Dao Association. During the 1960's to the 1980's, he studied Wushu from Liang Shou-Yu. *See* his photo demonstration under Qiang.

Xiliangquan 西涼拳 Legend has it, that during the Three Kingdom era, General Ma Chao (馬超), created Xiliangquan. General Ma used Xiliangquan to train his troops. His troops became one of the most feared groups of warriors. In the Qing Dynasty, a prominent Wushu fighter, Tang Dianxiang (唐殿鄉) was well-known for Xiliangquan.

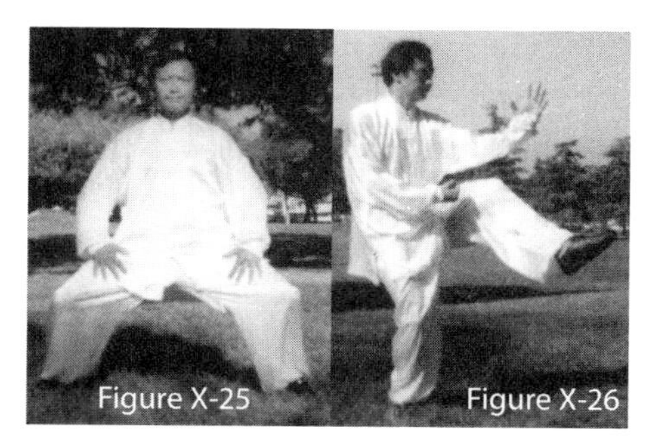
Figure X-25 Figure X-26

Information provided by Lu Fenglin

Figures X-25 and X-26: Xiliangquan/ Lu Fenglin

Xingyiquan 形意拳 An Internal Style Wushu, also romanized as Hsing Yi Chuan, and translated as Shape and Intent Fist. This is a Wushu style known for its dynamic and explosive movements. *Xing* or shape, is derived from the characteristics of the fighting movements of 12 different animals. *Yi* or intent, refers to the elevated spirit of the animals in action. Legend has it, that Marshal Yue Fei (岳飛) (1103-1142 A.D.) of the Southern Song Dynasty created Xingyiquan and taught it to his troops.

Xingyiquan basics include: Santishi (三體式), Wuxingquan (五行拳), and Shierxing (十二形). Santishi or Three Body Posture, is the basic stance, referring to the three powers of the universe: heaven, earth, and men. Wuxingquan or Five Element Routine, are the basic punching methods referring to Piquan (劈拳, Splitting Fist), Zuanquan (鑽拳, Drilling Fist), Bengquan (崩拳, Crashing Fist), Paoquan (炮拳, Exploding Fist), and Hengquan (橫拳, Shearing Fist). Shierxing or Twelve Animal Shapes, refer to the fighting movements and spirit of the animals. The Twelve animals are: dragon (龍形), tiger (虎形), monkey (猴形), horse (馬形), water lizard (鼉形), chicken (雞形), sparrow hawk (鷂形), swallow (燕形), snake (蛇形), heavenly bird (鮐形), eagle (鷹形), and bear (熊形).

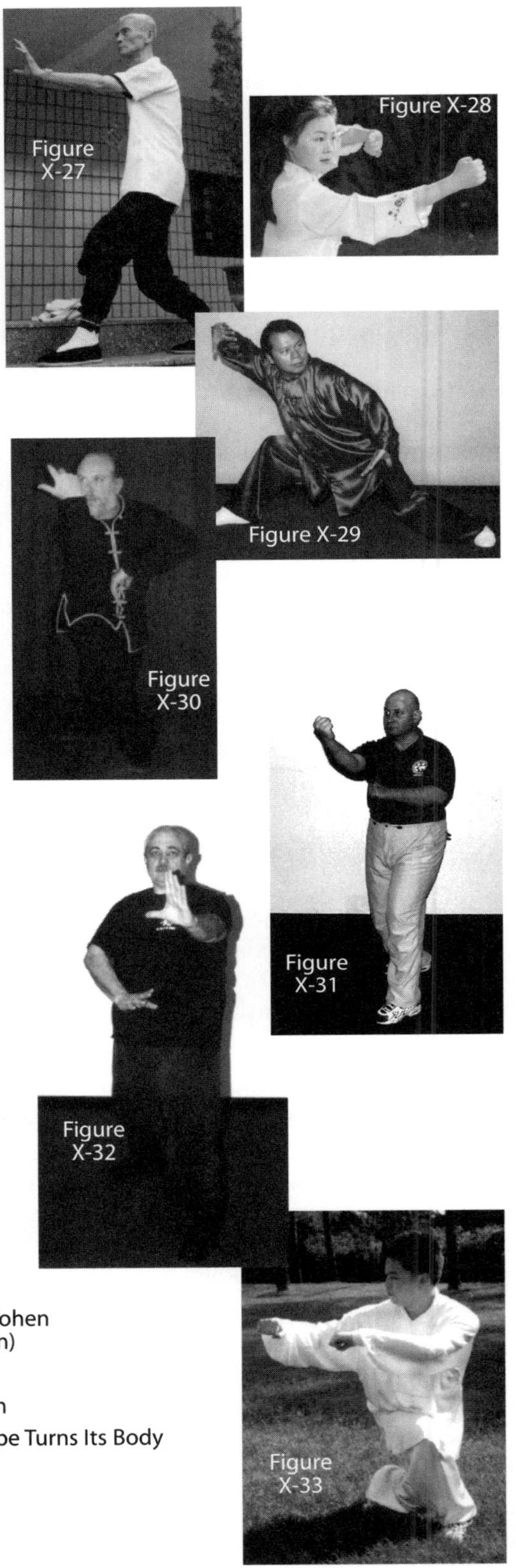

Figure X-27: Santishi (三體式)/ Wang Shutian

Figure X-28: Paoquan (炮拳)/ Helen Liang

Figure X-29: Sparrow-Hawk Posture/ Wu Wen-Ching

Figure X-30: Monkey Posture/Kenneth Cohen (photo by Rebecca D. Cohen)

Figure X-31: Zhuanquan/Naji Mazloum

Figure X-32: Piquan/Frank Whitsitt-Lynch

Figure X-33: Shashi Xingyiquan-White Ape Turns Its Body Posture/Cheng Shaoming

Xinjiang Uygur Zizhiqu 新疆維吾爾自治區 An autonomous region in northwestern China that borders Russia and Mongolia. It covers over 1.6 million square kilometers with a population of over 17 million as of 1999. It is the region/province with the largest land mass in China.

Xiyangzhang 曦陽掌 This style was passed down from Tang Dianqing (唐殿青) of the Anhui Province. Tang was a martial arts hero during the later part of the Qing Dynasty. Legend has it, that he was the bodyguard for Li Hongzhang (李鴻章), a high royal officer of the Qing Emperor. Tang's disciple, Wu Chongguang (吳重光) was the head instructor of the Wuhu City Guoshu School (蕪湖市國術館).

Figure X-34 Figure X-35

Xiyangzhang movements are open and extended, but require a lot of effort to perform. The foundation routines are the ten Tantui routines (十趟彈腿); Xiyangzhang is to develop a practitioners' internal strength; and the Upper and the Lower Shitouquan (西藏自治區) are the fighting application training. Practitioners must be accepted as a disciple before they are allowed to learn this style.

Information provided by Qi Ke Bao.

Figures X-34 and X-35: Xiyangzhang/Qi Ke Bao

Xizang Zizhiqu 西藏自治區 An autonomous region in southwestern China, also known as, Tibet. It borders Nepal, Bhutan, and India to its south. It covers over 1.2 million square kilometers with a population of over 2 million people as of 1999.

Xu, Junheng 徐均亨 He is a prominent Taijiquan and Qigong practitioner, and an outstanding swimming athlete for the Shanghai Swimming team. He served as the Director and Coach-in-Chief for the Division of Swimming for the Shanghai Municipal Government. In 1971, he began to practice Yang Style Taijiquan with Fu Zhongwen; and started his serious study of Chinese medicine, acupuncture, and therapeutic massage. He has been teaching Taiji Walking Qigong to maximize general health and to help cancer patients. He currently teaches at the Ross Institute in Long Island, New York. He serves as the Director of the Asian Exchange Program at the Ross Institute where he teaches the 18-form Taiji Qigong and his unique Taiji Walking Program. See his photo demonstration under Qigong.

Y

Yaan Yujiaquan 雅安余家拳 Translated as Yu Family Fist of Yaan. It was created by Yu Zhenggang (余正剛) of Yaan (雅安). Yaan Yujiaquan was only taught to their family members. This style focuses on both the healing, as well as, the fighting components of Wushu. The known routines include: Sanshiliuzhou (三十六肘) and Shisangun (十三棍).

Yang, Chen-Han 楊承翰 A member of the alternate Canadian Sanshou team in 1998. He received two gold medals in the 1995 U.S. National Competitions. He is a S.Y.L. Wushu Institute instructor. He is also included in the book, *China's Contemporary*

Wushu Masters (中國當代武林名人志). In 2001, he was the first place winner at the Canadian National Sanshou competiton in the 124 to 132 pound category. *See* his photo demonstration under Tanglangquan.

Yang, Chengfu 楊澄甫 (1883-1936) He is the grandson of the founder of Yang Style Taijiquan, Yang Luchan (楊露禪). He was the head coach of the Wudang division at the Central Guoshu Institute (中央國術館). The modern version of Yang Style Taijiquan is based on his teachings. He had many students. The notable ones include his sons; and students Cui Dianshi (崔殿士), Li Yaxuan (李雅軒), Wu Huichuan (武匯川), Fu Zhongwen (傅鐘文), and Dong Yinjie (董英杰). *See* his photo demonstration under Taijiquan.

Yang, Fukui 楊福奎 A graduate of Tianjin College of Physical Education. He was a professional Wushu coach in Tianjin and Japan from 1984 to 1996. He won numerous prizes in China and the U.S. for Xingyiquan, Chen and Yang Style Taijiquan, Push Hands, and Wushu forms. He is certified in China to practice qi healing and tuina. He was the director of the Tianjin Qigong Institute from 1994 to 1996. He is the founder and head coach of Heart Mind Chinese Martial Arts in Manhattan, New York, U.S.A. He is also a member of the adjunct faculty at the Pacific College of Oriental Medicine, where he teaches tuina. *See* his photo demonstration under Baguazhang.

Yang, Jun 楊軍 A prominent sixth generation representative of Yang Style Taijiquan. He lived and studied with his grandfather, Yang Zhenduo (楊振鐸) since childhood. He has traveled extensively with his grandfather, giving workshops around world. He currently teaches in Seattle, Washington, U.S.A. *See* his photo demonstration under Taijiquan.

Yang, Wei 楊維 (1966-) Vice Chairman of the International Wushu Sanshou Dao Association. He was the gold medalist in the 70 kilogram division at the Heilongjiang China national Sanshou competition. He has written many books on hard Qigong and Sanshou training. He is an outstanding young martial artist in the Wushu community. *See* his photo demonstration under Wushu Sanshou Dao.

Yang, Yang 楊揚 (1961-) He began his Chen Style Taijiquan study at age twelve. He studied from Gu Liuxin (顧留馨), Chen Zhaokui (陳照奎), and Feng Zhiqiang (馮志強). He is a formal disciple of Feng Zhiqiang. He was a gold medalist at the Shanghai University Gongfu Tournament for three straight years (1981-1983), and was voted Best Overall Martial Artist in 1983. He was an instructor at the Shanghai Chen Style Research Association. He has a law degree and an engineering degree from China, a Master's degree in economics from Illinois State University, and is currently working on his doctorate in kinesiology at the University of Illinois. He is the director of the Feng Zhiqiang Martial Academy of North America and the Qiu Zhen Yi Center for Taiji Studies in Illinois. *See* his photo demonstration under Taijiquan.

Yang, Zhenduo 楊振鐸 (1926-) He is the great-grandson of the founder of Yang Style Taijiquan, Yang Luchan (楊露禪). He is one of the most prominent fourth generation representatives of Yang Style Taijiquan today. He began his Taijiquan study with his father, Yang Chengfu (楊澄甫). He currently teaches in Seattle, Washington, U.S.A., and gives workshops around the world. *See* his photo demonstration under Taijiquan.

Yangbalangquan 楊八郎拳 This is a style practiced in the Chongqing City area. There are six known barehanded routines, six weapon routines, five training methods, and sparring methods.

Yangtze River 楊子江 The longest river in China, and the fourth longest in the world. It is also known as Changjiang (長江) or Long River. It is also one of the most important water transportation routes in China. Wushu styles originating above the Yangtze River are considered Northern Styles and Wushu styles originating below the Yangtze River are considered Southern Styles.

Yaojia 瑤家 This is a style developed by the Yao ethnic people living in the mountain range between Hunan and Guangxi. Over one thousand years ago, this area was infested with bandits and thieves. To protect themselves, the Yao people had to absorb other styles and develop their Wushu skills. Their routines tend to be short with only about ten movements. The known weapon routines include: Qimeigun (齊眉棍), Biandan (扁擔), Shuangdao (雙刀), and Huba (虎鈀).

Yanqingquan 燕青拳 A Changquan type Wushu. Legend has it, that Lu Junyi (盧俊義) of the Tang Dynasty created this style and taught it to Yan Qing (燕清). Another legend has it, that Yan Qing, a Song Dynasty hero of the people, created this style based on the agile movements of the monkey. The type of monkey was a macaque, which is referred to as mizong (獼猔,猊猔) in Chinese.

The term Mizong also sounds like many other Chinese words. One of the popular Mizong characters used to refer to this style literally means "secret ancestry", implying the secrecy of the origin. Since Yan Qing was an outlaw who was wanted by the government at the time, the practitioners of this style would not advertise their ties to Yan Qing. Therefore, they referred to their style as the "secret ancestry" style.

Also see Mizongquan.

Figure Y-1: Yanqingquan/Fred Ho

Yaxingquan 鴨形拳 Translated as Duck Style. This is a style based on the movements of a duck. According to legend, this style was created by the Taoist, Luya Daoren (綠鴨道人), of the Emei Mountain during the Tang Dynasty.

Yingzhuaquan 鷹爪拳 Translated as Eagle Claw Style. This is an imitation style mimicking the movements of an eagle. It is believed that Yingzhuaquan was created by Liu Sijun (劉士俊) of the Qing Dynasty. In the early 1900's, Chen Zizheng (陳子正) taught at the Shanghai Jinwu Athletic Association (上海精武體育會). The characteristics of Eagle Claw include many Qinna (擒拿) techniques in its applications. It is described as "Rapid, explosive, and continuous when in motion; alert and brisk as an eagle waiting for a rabbit when still."

Figure Y-2: Yingzhuaquan/Derek Cheng

Yiquan *see* Dachengquan

Yiu, Gordon He began his Cailifoquan studies at age 5 from his father, Hilbert Yiu. He also learned modern competition routines and was the gold medalist and all-around champion many times in major Wushu competitions. *See* his photo demonstration under Wushu Bingqi.

Yiu, Hilbert, Jr. 姚博熙 He is the eldest son of Hilbert Yiu. He is an instructor of Choy Lee Fut Shung Ying School in Canada. He has been a gold medalist in many Northwestern Canada tournaments. *See* his photo demonstration under Gun.

Yiu, Hilbert T.S. 姚崇英 A member of the Canadian National Wushu team in 1986. He is a prominent practitioner of Cailifoquan, international Wushu competition routines, and lion dancing. His lion dancing team has received several gold medals in Canadian national Wushu championships. He was instrumental in the organization of several east coast U.S.A. and Canadian national Wushu championships. He is the Vice President of Wushu B.C. and the Confederation of Canadian Wushu Organizations. *See* his photo demonstrations under Cailifoquan and Cha.

Yizu Wushu 彝族武術 This term refers to the Wushu developed by the Yizu ethnic people. It is believed, that during the reign of the Qing Emperor, Daoguang, between 1823 and 1850, Wushu spread to the Yizu people. They have many routines, over twenty different weapon routines, and Sanshou training. Fifty years ago, there was an old man named Pu Chaoqing (普朝青) who was said to have extraordinary Wushu ability. Once he performed a jumping toe kick to the ceiling. Before he came down, he gently nudged his wife off the chair she was sitting on with his other leg and landed on the chair in a crossed leg sitting position. His light-body ability had to be amazing to be able to do so.

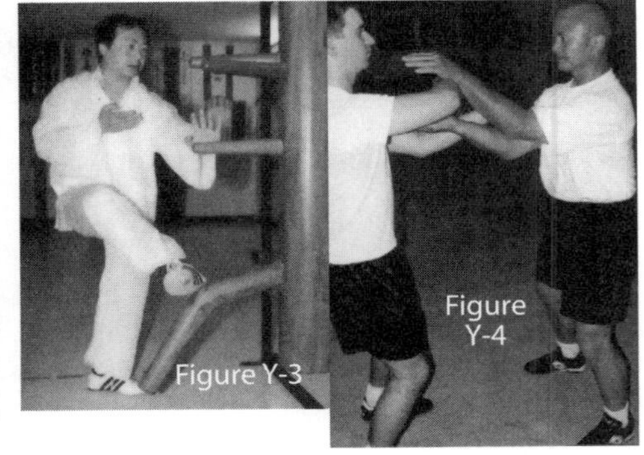

The Yizu people had often won Shuaijiao (摔跤) and fighting competitions during the annual Southwestern ethnic competions that included over thirty divisions. In the 1960's, Liang Shou-Yu (梁守渝) was the first Han ethnic person to win against a Yizu competitor. Liang was still in college at the time. The Han ethnic people were traditionally not as strong as the Yizu competitors and had never won Shuaijiao competitions.

Yongchunquan 詠春拳 Legend has it, that it was created by Yan Sanniang (嚴三娘) in Yongchun (永春) County, Fujian Province. Many believed that its name was derived from the location where it was created. Others believed that Yan Sanniang's other name was Yongchun, therefore, the style was called Yongchunquan. The movements of Yongchunquan require that the hand movements do not go higher than the eyebrows and not lower than the crotch; and left and right movements do not go wider than shoulder width. It attacks an opponent's center while protecting its own center. Its emphasis is on close range applications. Traditional routines include: Xiaorentou (小稔頭), Biaozi (標字), and Xunqiao (尋橋).

Figure Y-3: Wooden Dummy Drills/Sunny Tang
Figure Y-4: Sticky Hands/Fred Kwok and partner
Figure Y-5: Butterfly Knives/Vingrove Thomas

Yu, Wen Mei 郁文美 Recognized as a Top Instructor in Taijiquan in the Wushu division of China in 1983. She was a former professor at Jin Wu Athletic College and a former General Secretary of the Shanghai Physical Culture Association for the elderly. As a competitor, she has won many tournaments in China and the United States. She also received numerous awards including the "Award of Excellence" presented to her by the National Women's Martial Arts Federation. She has published more than 40 articles in the Inside Kung Fu Magazine. She was recognized as the 1994 "Writer of the Year" and as the 1997 "Women of the Year" by Inside Kung Fu magazine. She currently teaches at the Jian Mei Association in Burbank, California, U.S.A. *See* her photo demonstration under Taijiquan.

Yuan, Shaoliang 袁紹良 A physician at Beijing Hospital of Chinese Medicine. He is a professor of Taiji and Qigong at the Chinese University of Hong Kong, Academy for Performing Arts, and various institutions in Hong Kong. Since his youth, he has studied under many prominent Wushu teachers in Beijing. He is known for Dabeiquan and several other Wushu styles. He is an antique collector; and he has been featured in numerous Chinese newspapers in Hong Kong. *See* his photo demonstration under Dabeiquan.

Yuanyangyue 鴛鴦鉞 Deer Hooks or Meridian Ax Couple (Drawing Y-1). It is a Baguazhang weapon, usually used in pairs.

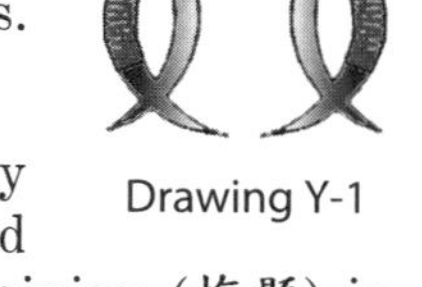

Drawing Y-1

Figure Y-6

Figure Y-6: Yuanyanchan/He Tao

Yuejiajiao 岳家教 Translated as Yue Family Teaching. Legend has it, that it originated in Hunan Province and spread to Meixian (梅縣) in Guangdong Province. There is a known routine called Yipenzhu (一盆珠).

Yuemenquan 岳門拳 Translated as Yue Family Fist. This is one of the most well-known Emei Styles. Legend has it, that it was created by Marshall Yue Fei (岳飛). There are over seventy known barehanded routines, over twenty weapons routines, and many matching routines and training methods.

Yueshilianquan 岳氏連拳 Translated as Yue Family Connected Fist. It is believed to have been created by Marshall Yue Fei (岳飛) during the Song Dynasty. It was known as Yushi Sanshou (岳氏散手), meaning Yue Family free fighting techniques. During the Qing Dynasty, Liu Sijun (劉仕俊) created additional short routines into this style and connected the short routines into a longer routine for training. Thereby, the style was later named Yue Family Connected Fist. It is classified as Changquan.

Yujiaquan 余家拳 Translated as Yu Family Fist. It is known in eastern Sichuan Province. Yujiaquan combined the philosophies of Taoist and Confucius thinking into their style. There are sixteen known barehanded routines, eight weapon routines, and eight training methods.

Yumen 于門 Translated as Yu Family Style. This style was created by Yu Qian (于謙) during the Ming Dynasty. Yumen is characterized by the Empty Stance, it utilizes defensive-offense as a strategy, and uses soft-neutralizing against hard attacks. The known barehanded routines include: Zhiziquan (支子拳), Mianzhangquan (綿掌拳), and Bangeyanqing (半個燕青). Its known weapon routines include: Nanyangdao (南陽刀), Gunlongdao (滾龍刀), Wumingdao (無名刀), and Gunlu (棍路).

Yumenquan 余門拳 Legend has it, that it was derived from the Wuqinzi (五禽戲) Qigong created by Hua Tuo (華佗). In the 1770's, Yu Youfu (余有福) continued this style and taught it to his students. Thereby, the style was later named Yumenquan. Yumenquan has many changing hand techniques and a few kicking techniques. There are over thirty known barehanded routines and fourteen weapon routines.

Yumenquan 魚門拳 Translated as Fish Style. Legend has it, that in Hubei Province there were six Wushu companions that were inspired by observing swimming fish and fishermen casting their nets. Yumenquan is also known as Liujiayi (六家藝). This style has many similar characteristics as in Taijiquan. The known routines include: Bazhentu (八陣圖), Baguafan (八卦番), Youchang (游場), Liuhe (六合), and Luhechangquan (六合長拳).

Figures Y-7 and Y-8: Yumenquqan/ Guo Jianhua

Yunnan Province 雲南省 A Chinese province located at the southeastern border of China. It borders Vietnam and Laos to its south. It covers 394 thousand square kilometers with a population of over 41 million people as of 1999.

Z

Zang, Lijuan 藏麗娟 A native of Cangzhou, Henan Province. She inherited her family's Wushu styles. She is a prominent practitioner in many Wushu styles including Mulanquan and Dunhuangquan. She currently teaches in San Gabriel, California, USA. *See* her photo demonstrations under Mulanquan and Dunhuanquan.

Zangqiang Wushu 藏羌武術 This term refers to the Wushu developed from the Xizhang (西藏) and Qiang (羌) area. The Qiang ethnic Chinese had its own Wushu. For ten years, between the years 136 and 165, the Han (漢) people were at war with the Qiang people. Qiang had to develop their Wushu to combat the Han.

In the Tang Dynasty, to attain peace, the King of Xizang and the Emperor of Tang arranged for the marriage between Princess Wencheng (文成) of Tang and the Prince of Zang. Princess Wencheng brought with her, her Han culture and bodyguards that were Wushu experts. Han Wushu spread to Zang and assisted in furthering the development of Wushu for the Zang.

The Zang people also absorbed the Qiang Wushu and developed what was known as Quanba (拳巴). During the Qing Dynasty, the royal family often employed the services of the Xizang Mizong Lama (西藏密宗喇嘛) to protect the palaces.

Zen *See* Chan. The Japanese romanization of Chan.

Zhang, Hong Mei 張紅梅 She was born in Beijing, China. She began studying Wushu at age 9. She was a member of the Beijing Wushu Team. She was a Chinese National Champion in Baguazhang, Double Sword, and Sparring Routines. At the First International Wushu Games, she won a gold medal in the Straight Sword category. She has traveled around the world performing and teaching Wushu, including the Yokohama Wushu Society. She is currently the teacher and cofounder of the Pacific Wushu and the Stanford Wushu Club. *See* her photo demonstrations under Baguazhang and Jian.

Zhang, Li 張莉 She was an Associate Professor of Physical Education at Hunan Medical University. She is a Chinese National Wushu Judge, and a Fifth Degree Black Belt Wushu Instructor. She came to the United States in 1996. In 1997, she was awarded the "Top One Hundred Wushu Practitioners" award at the 1997 World Cup Wushu Championships. She currently teaches in Seattle, Washington, U.S.A. *See* her photo demonstration under Baguazhang.

Zhang, Lingmei 張玲妹 One of three prominent female swordsmen in the 1970's. She was the former head coach for the Shanxi Provincial team (山西省武術隊). She has represented China many times as a performer, coach, and leader, for China Wushu teams performing around the world. She is a certified Senior Coach and National Judge of Wushu. She is one of two women to receive the Wushu Contribution Award from the Chinese Wushu Research Institute. She is a Seventh Level Black Belt in Wushu awarded by the Chinese Wushu Institute. She is also included in the book, *Biography of China's Prominent Wushu Practitioners* (中國武林著名人物傳). She currently teaches in San Francisco, California, U.S.A. *See* her photo demonstration under Jian.

Zhang, Peng 張鵬 A former member of the Shaanxi Provincial Wushu team. He is a Wuyin (武英) title recipient. He was also a member of the China Wushu team that performed in many countries around the world. He attained many gold and silver medals in China's national Wushu competitions. He is a graduate of the Beijing Physical Education University and was a Wushu instructor at the Beijing Artillery Command Center. He has also appeared in many Wushu movies and TV programs. He has been judging in Canadian National Wushu competitions. *See* his photo demonstration under Dao.

Zhang, Shu-Fang 張樹芳 A graduate of the Beijing Physical Education University (北京體育學院) In the 1960's, he was a professional coach of Wushu, weight lifting, and Shuaijiao, for the Beijing City Sports Committee Association (北京市體育運動委員會). He was a gold medalist in the Beijing Physical Education University Shuaijiao competition. He was a professor at Beijing Qigong University (北京氣功學院), and a professor of Traditional Chinese Medicine. He was a student of Wang Shichuan (王十川) and Yao Zongxun (姚宗勛). Yao was a disciple of Wang Xiangzhai (王鄉齋), the founder of Danchengquan. *See* his photo demonstrations under Dachengquan and Duanbin Boji.

Zhang, Xuexin 張學信 (1928-) A senior disciple of Feng Zhiqiang and studied under Chen Zhaokui. He is a prominent Chen Style Taiji practitioner in the United States. Prior to immigrating to the United States, he taught Taijiquan in China for over ten years and was certified by the Chen Style Taiji Association. He currently teaches in San Francisco, California and gives workshops around the world. *See* his photo demonstration under Taijiquan.

Zhang, Zhi Bin 張植彬 In 1953, at age 8, he was the youngest practitioner to represent Northeast China in the China National Wushu Competitions. In 1958, he became a member of the Heilongjiang Provincial Wushu Team. In 1960, he was a member of the Wushu delegation that accompanied Premier Zhou Enlai to Burma. He is a graduate of the Wuhan Physical Education University, and the Wushu coach for Harbin City. In the past 36 years or more, he has trained many outstanding Wushu athletes. In 1989, 1993, and 1995, he traveled to Russia, Korea, and Japan to teach Wushu. He is a prominent Wushu practitioner in Harbin, China with over 50 years of Wushu experience. In 1999, he was awarded an Eight Degree Black Belt. He currently teaches in Canada. *See* his photo demonstration under Taizuquan.

Zhao, Li-Ying 趙麗英 She graduated from the Beijing Physical Education University in 1964. She was the former coach of short weapons and sword fighting for the Beijing City Sports Committee Association (北京市體育運動委員會). She currently teaches in Richmond, British Columbia, Canada. *See* her photo demonstration under Duanbin Boji.

Zhao, Ziqiu 趙子虬 (1904-1998) A graduate of the Central Guoshu Institute. In the 1930's, Zhao Ziqiu defeated three prominent foreign challengers. He was also a prominent practitioner of Chinese language and medicine. Since Wushu, language, and martial arts, are three Chinese national arts, he was also nicknamed, Mr. Three Nationals (三國先生). He wrote the *Emei Huamen Nanquan* (峨嵋化門南拳). He was the Vice Chairman of the Chongqing Wushu Association and was an advisor of the International Wushu Sanshou Dao Association. *See* his photo demonstration under Baguazhang.

Zhaomenquan 趙門拳 Translated as Zhao Family Fist. Legend has it, that it originated from the first Northern Song Dynasty Emperor, Zhao Kuanyin (趙匡胤). There are two major groups within this style. One is the Sanyuanpai (三原派) that migrated to Sanyuan County in Shanxi Province during the middle of the Qing Dynasty. The other is the Zhilipai (直隸派) that migrated to Zhili during the middle of the Qing Dynasty by Zhang Tianhu (張天虎). Zhaomenquan focuses on kicking applications, and tends to use offense as a defense. They have many barehanded routines, weapon routines, and training methods.

Zhejiang Province 浙江省 A Chinese province located south of Shanghai City and Jiangsu Province. It borders the East China Sea to its east. It covers over 101 thousand square kilometers with a population of over 44 million people as of 1999.

Zhimen 智門 This style originated in the 1850's by Deng Dingguo (鄧定國). Deng taught it to his son, Deng Jida (鄧繼達). Deng Jida taught it to his son. The grandson of Deng Dingguo taught it to the general public when he became the head instructor of the Fengdu Guoshu School (丰都國術館). Zhimen movements are open and extended. The known routine includes: Xuanfeng Saoluoye (旋風掃落葉) and a training method known as Baiyunzuojingong (白雲座勁功).

Zhoujiaquan 周家拳 Translated as Zhou Family Fist. This style was created by Zhou Yufeng (周玉峰) of Chongqing City during the reign of the Qing Emperor, Qianlong (乾龍), between 1736 and 1795. There are four known barehanded routines, two weapon routines, and two sparring routines.

Zhu, Tian Cai 朱天才 An official 19th generation Chen Taiji successor and renowned as one of the "Great Fours". He has traveled all over China and around the world to teach and promote Taijiquan. He was the former president of the Chen Village

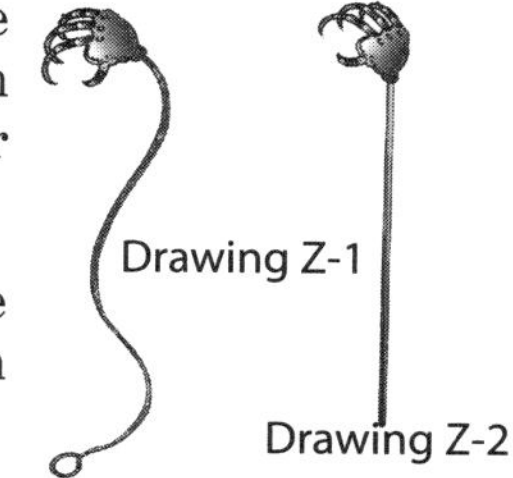

Taijiquan School (陳家溝太極拳專修院院長). Currently, he is an advanced instructor at the Singapore Tiancai Taijiquan Training Centre. *See* his photo demonstration under Taijiquan.

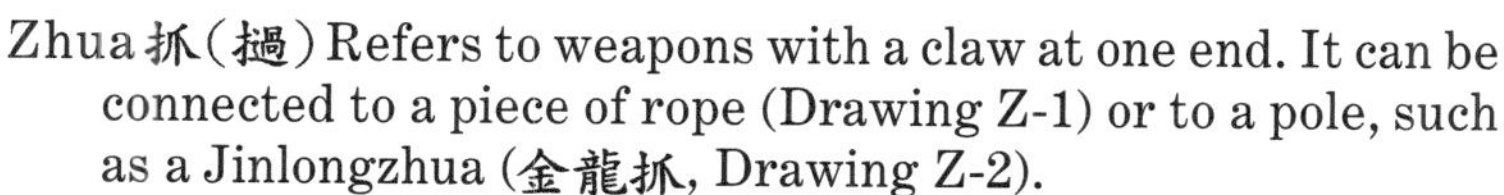

Zhua 抓(撾) Refers to weapons with a claw at one end. It can be connected to a piece of rope (Drawing Z-1) or to a pole, such as a Jinlongzhua (金龍抓, Drawing Z-2).

Zhuangzu Wushu 壯族武術 This term refers to the Wushu developed by the Zhuangzu ethnic people. There have been many legendary Zhuangzu Wushu practitioners in China. On the Huashanyai (花山崖) cliff drawing in Guangxi, there is a vivid drawing representing the fighting abilities of the Zhuangzu people. Historical records describe that the Zhuangzu people were so fierce in battles that they made their enemies drop their shields and armor, and run for their lives.

Lady Washi (瓦氏) in the Ming Dynasty was described to have led her young warriors into battle with double sabers, right into the core of the enemy camp, and killed the enemy commander. During the Qing Dynasty, Xiao Chaogui (肖朝貴) and Tan Shaoguang (潭紹光) were prominent Wushu practitioners that served the Qing Dynasty and were awarded high royal positions.

Zhujiajiao 朱家教 Translated as Zhu Family Teaching. This style is popular in Xingning (興寧) in Guangdong Province. Some of the known routines include: Sanbujian (三步箭), Dane (單蛾), Shuangquan (雙拳), Huaquan (花拳), and Jianliquan (箭李拳); and many fighting methods.

Zimen-1 字門 In 1838, Luo Baishanye (羅跰三爺) of Sichuan was 12 years old, when he went to Henan to study Zimen Wushu. Later, he traveled all over China absorbing a vast amount of other style's essences into Zimen Wushu. Zimen has no routines to speak of. Each zi or word is an application and/or a training method. Each zi could consist of one or several movements.

Zimen-2 字門 There are three legends to the origin of this style. Some believe that it was created by Chen Yu (陳鈺) of Henan Province. Others believe it was created by Zhou Daxia (周大俠) of Guilin (桂林) after he learned his Wushu in the Emei Mountains. Yet, others believe it was created by Li Quanshi (李拳師), a military general of the Qing Dynasty. The beginning and end of the routines from the Zimen Style of Henan resembles specific characters. There are over thirty known barehanded routines, one Liuhe Qimeigun (六合齊眉棍), one Fenghuang Shuangdao (鳳凰雙刀), and eleven Sanshou and training methods.

Zimu Nanquan 子母南拳 Translated as Mother and Son Nanquan. This style was created by Peng Ying (彭瑛) who was a Wudang Taoist. He participated in the Keju (科舉), an imperial China civil service examination where he passed the martial examination. During the reign of the Emperor Guangxu (1875-1908), the emperor sent him to represent the Qing Dynasty in Europe and America for seven years. When he returned, he was awarded a military office in Beijing. There are six known barehanded routines, three weapon routines, and two training methods.

Ziranmen 自然門 Translated as Natural Style. One legend states that this style was created by Xu Xiake (徐俠客). Xu taught Ziranmen to Jin Chanzi (金禪子), and then two generations later it was taught to Yang Wenzhao (楊文釗) of Sichuan. Xu also taught Ziranmen to Du Xinwu (杜心五), and Du taught it to Wan Liasheng (萬籟生).

Ziranmen is considered an internal style. Some of the known routines include: Xinyiquan (心意拳), Bazhenquan (八陣拳), Baluquan (八路拳), Feilongjian (飛龍劍), Huolonggun (火龍棍), and Baxianguai (八仙拐). They also have numerous fighting techniques and training methods. Practitioners start with a specific training and gradually go beyond the forms and shapes, into unrestricted and natural expressions of fighting movements.

Ziwumen 子午門 Translated as Midnight and Noon Style. This is an Emei Style. During the end of the Qing Dynasty, two Emei Buddhist high priests, Taikong Fashi (太空法師) and Shendeng Fashi (神燈法師), traveled to the four famous mountains in China. They exchanged their techniques with practitioners of Shaolin and Wudang, and absorbed both the Internal and the Externals Styles' essence. Twenty years later, they created the style named Ziwumen.

Ziwu refers to the time of the day. Zi refers to midnight and wu refers to noontime. Much of the Buddhist training is around midnight or noontime, thereby the style's name was coined. This style utilizes the philosophy of Yin-Yang as its principle. There are six known barehanded routines, several weapon routines, and six training methods.

Zou, Fu 鄒福 A prominent Longxingquan teacher in Hong Kong. *See* his photo demonstration under Longxingquan.

Zou, Yinghui 鄒映輝 She has a master's degree from the Beijing University of Physical Education. She was the team captain of the Hunan Provincial Wushu team; and has been a silver and bronze medalist in China National Wushu Competitions. From 1976 to 1986, she was a coach for the Hunan Provincial Wushu team. Many of her students attained gold, silver, or the top six places in China National Wushu Competitions. Since 1978, she has judged in over 60 China National and International Wushu Competitions. She was the assistant Referee General in China National Wushu Competitions; and is a certified International Wushu Forms Judge. She was the assistant dean of the Physical Education Department at the Hainan Teacher's University; and a Professor of Wushu. She has written five Wushu instructional materials and over twenty Wushu articles. *See* her photo demonstration under Changquan.

Zuiquan 醉拳 Translated as Drunken Style. Its routines are based on a drunkard's intoxicated movements. A well-known Zuiquan routine is Zuibaxian (醉八仙), which imitates the drunken movements of the legendary Eight Immortals. Another well-known routine is the Drunkard Captures the Monkey (醉漢擒猴) matching routine.

Figures Z-1 and Z-2: Zuiquan/ William Lai

Figure Z-3: Zuiquan/ Liu Weixiong

Glossary Addendum-1: Practitioners around the world

The continuation of Wushu and the promotion of Wushu is the responsibility of all practitioners of Wushu. There are numerous practitioners around the globe that are actively engaged in promoting Wushu. This addendum consists of practitioners not listed in the main section of the glossary. These practitioners have or are continuing their efforts in teaching and promoting Wushu around the world. Individuals on this list include the authors's teachers, authors' top students, many outstanding newcomers to Wushu, friends and acquaintances of the authors, and many world champion athletes and practitioners from around the world that the authors have had the chance of meeting during World Wushu Championships. The authors are certain that there are many other outstanding practitioners around the world that the authors have not had the good fortune to meet. Therefore, they are not included in this list. There may also be some other practitioners that the authors have forgotten and not included, due to losing touch with each other. The authors apologize for not including them in this list. In this list we have categorized the practitioners under U.S.A., Canada, Taiwan, Other Countries, and China. Chinese practitioners in China are mostly listed in Chinese and are not listed in any particular order.

U.S.A.

Austin, Sidney — NJ
Bracy, John, — U.S.A.
Barry, Michael — U.S.A.
Best, Joe — MA
Brown, Tony — OH
Burr, Martha — CA
Chambers, Dean — IL
Chan, Pui 陳培 — FL
Chen, John — U.S.A.
Chen, William C.C. 陳至誠 — NY
Cheng, Jin Cai 程進才 — TX
Cheng, Man-Ching 鄭曼青 — NY
Cheng, Ping-Zhen 程平眞 — U.S.A.
Cheung, Michael 張煒光 — CA
Chu, Gin Soon — MA
Chu, Vincent — MA
Chung, Kenneth 鐘萬年 — CA
Choi, Wai-Lun — IL
Chow, Amy — U.S.A.
Clifford, Rosey — MA
Crawford, Bruce — MA
D'Agostino, Art — FL
Derosa, Susanna — NJ
Dillon, Paul — U.S.A.
Dixit, Ravi — MA
Dufresne, John — KY
Dunbar, Jay — NC
Dunphy, Joe — MD
Faulise, Joseph — AK
Feng, Qiuying 馮秋英—U.S.A.
Fong, Augustine — U.S.A.
Fong, Bryant — CA
Frantzis, B.K. — CA
Fu, Gao — WA
Gracenin, Kathy — PA
Hallander, Jane — CA
Harn, Lin-Lin — MA
Huang, Chien-Liang 黃乾量 — MD
Hui, Gerald 許瑞麟 — U.S.A.
Israel, Stan — NY
Jacobs, Gary — AK
Jones, Calvin — U.S.A.
Jones, Michael — PA
Jou, Tsung Hwa 周宗華 — NY
Jung, Chul-Woo — CO
Kiesel, Alex — MA
Lai, Brandon 黎達沖 — CA
Lai, Xueying 賴雪英 — U.S.A.
Latecki, Eva — MA
Lau, Lily 劉莉莉 — CA
Le, Cung — U.S.A.
Lee, Bin — U.S.A.
Lee, Daniel 李愷 — CA
LeLievre, Faith — HI
Leung Kay-Chi 梁紀慈 — MA
Li, Baiqing — MA
Li, Jet 李連杰— U.S.A.
Ji, Junfeng 李俊峰 — U.S.A.
Li, Pei Yun 李沛雲 — PA
Li, Yao — MA
Liang, Beiping 梁北平 — CO
Liang, Jeffrey D.S. 梁德馨 — WA
Liang, Eva (Tang, Ying-Hua) 唐應華 — WA
Liang, T.T. — CO
Liu, Abraham — U.S.A.
Liu, Ji Rong 劉紀榮 — NY
Liu, Ming-Der — CO
Lo, Benjamin Pang-Jeng 羅邦楨 — CA
Look, Henry — U.S.A.
Loriaux, Alan — U.S.A.
Luo, Li 羅禮 — East Coast
Luth, Chris — CA
Mark, Bow-Sim 麥寶嬋 — MA
Martin, Louisa — AL
Meng, Benny — OH
Miller, Dan — CA
Miller, Don — MA
Napoli, Mario — NY
Niler, Timothy — DE

Ng, John — KY
Ngo, Tai 吳東才 — MA
Oh, Gigi Chien 吳簡琪 — CA
Olson, Stuart — MN
Pang, Simon — MA
Park, Bok-Nam — U.S.A.
Rhodes, Steve — CA
Rones, Ramel — MA
Rosen, Bob — MA
Sauer, Ed — IL
Schilling, Rick — IL
Shearer-Best, Carol — MA
Shi, Yan Ming — NY
Shih, T.K. — NY
Smalheiser, Marvin — CA
Staford, William — TX
Stier, Gary — TX
Tai, Yim — U.S.A.
Trescott, Leon — U.S.A.
Torres, Pete — CO
Tsai, David Juon Haw — TX
Tsang, Robert — U.S.A.
Wang, Tao 王濤 — U.S.A.
Waters, Elaine — AR
Wiederhold, Michael — AZ
Weng, Daniel Chi-Hsiu 翁啓修 — U.S.A.
Wong, Doc-Fai — CA
Wong, Jimmy — TX
Wong, Rick — MA
Wong, Woody — U.S.A.
Yang, James 楊志堅 — MA
Yang, Jwing-Ming 楊俊敏—MA
Yang, Kathy 楊愷怡 — MA
Yang, Nicky 楊志豪 — MA
Yang, Shu-Ton 楊曉東 — OH
Yao, Jane 姚培靜 — U.S.A.
Yee, Jason — MA
Yu, Shaowen 喻紹文— U.S.A.
Xu, George 徐谷鳴 — CA
Xu, Jane 許宛音 — IL
Xu, Tingsen 許廷森 — GA
Xu, Xiantang 徐獻堂 — WA
Yu, Cheng-Hsiang — NY
Zhu, Hong-Po 朱洪波 — TX
Zhang, Luping 張璐平 — MA
Zhang, Xiu 張秀 — U.S.A.
陳道雲 — CA

Canada

Arsenault, Gordon — B.C.
Case, Matthew — B.C.
Cheng, Al 鄭龍川 — B.C.
Chan, Nelson 陳就祥 — Ontario
Chin, Erika 陳銘怡—Vancouver
Ching, Raymond Y. 程一鵬 — Canada
Choy, Ava — Vancouver
Chow, Phipipman 周至鋒 — Ontario
Chu, Gary — B.C.
Chung, William — Canada
Clausen, Diana — B.C.
Cooper, Ed — Ontario
Fafard, Chantal — B.C.
Falk, Andrea 霍安娣— Canada
Fan, Harry — B.C.
Fu, Shenlong 傅盛龍 — Vancouver
Gallagher, Brien — Vancouver
Ha, Paul 夏智權 — Canada
Henderson, Paul — B.C.
Ho, Yep 何志業 — Toronto
Hong, Kee 熊景光 — Canada
Hu, Xining 胡西寧 — Canada
James, Andy — Toronto
Kelly, Patrick — Canada
Lee, Arthur — B.C.
Lee, Chi Wai 李智偉 — Toronto
Lee, David 李培富 — Toronto
Leung, Gordon 梁卓崑 — B.C.
Li, Qiang 李強 — Canada
Li, Yuwen 李宇文 — Canada
Liang, Xinxin 梁欣欣—Canada
Lumhoist-Smith, Sonya — B.C.
Luqer, Barry — Vancouver
Mark, Hugh 麥耀庭 — B.C.
Mcnab, Joan — Vancouver
Morford, Robert — B.C.
Niu, Huailu 牛懷祿 — Canada
Osmachenko, Graig — B.C.
Sanchez, Rene Hugo — B.C.
Sang, Anthony 岑擎天 — B.C.
So, York-Ming 蘇約明 — B.C.
Sun, Ying 孫穎 — Canada
Tchoung, Raymond 鐘蔭民 — Vancouver
Tchoung, Ta Tchen 鐘大政 — Canada
Wang, Taisun 鄭大蓀— Canada
Wang, Xia 王蝦 — Vancouver
Webb, Carla — B.C.
Wong, Amy — Toronto
Wong, Jack 黄幼璋 — Canada
Wong, Peter 黄碧海 — B.C.
Wong, Long 王龍 — Ontario
Wong, Marvin — Toronto
Woo, Fremont — Vancouver
Yamanaka, Derrick — B.C.
Yang, Guo Tai 楊國泰 — Vancouver
Young, Michael — Vancouver
Xu, Gong Wei 徐功偉—Canada
Zhang, Alice 張國紅 — Canada
Zhong, Po 鐘波 — Canada
Zhou, Po 周波 — Canada
湯玉蘭 —Vancouver
李劍青 —Vancouver
朱典新 —Vancouver
馬均耀 —Vancouver
洪鼎生 — Toronto
胡偉坤 — Canada

Taiwan

Chang, Dong-Sheng (1909-1986) 常東昇 — Taiwan
Chang, En Huang 張育誠 — Taiwan
Chang, Shi Po — Taiwan
Chen, Jong-Sheng 陳榮盛 — Taiwan
Chen, Rosa 陳修姚 — Taiwan
Chiu, Wen Hsu — Taiwan
Fu, Shuyun 傅淑雲— Taiwan
Kuo, Chien-Cheng 郭建成 — Taiwan
Li, Mao-Ching 李茂清 — Taiwan
Lin, Mu-Huo 林木火— Taiwan
Lin, Kuo Hsiung — Taiwan
Lo, Ching-Hsiang 羅清香 — Taiwan
Soo, Roger C. 蘇成 — Taiwan
韓慶堂 — Taiwan
劉雲樵 — Taiwan
張詳三 — Taiwan
賀順定 — Taiwan

Other Countries

Abolghasemi, Naser — Iran
Akbari, Abbasali — Iran
Alexandrovitch, Borodinov Anton — Russia
Alves, Marcus V.F. — Brazil
Amador, Enrique — Andorra
Amiryan, Ashot — Armenia
Arai, Shinji 蘆井伸次— Japan
Aryal, Ganesh — Nepal
Athanassiou, Dimitrios — Greece
Aubakirov — Kazakhstan
Ayredin, Awoi — Ethiopia
Azuma, Takashi — Japan
Bai, Li Juan — England
Barroso, Nelson — Portugal
Benea, Ion — Romania
Bezabih, Binyan — Ethiopia
Boudagov, D. — Azerbaijan
Bouyakoubi, Aicha — Morocco
Borisovitch, Turavlev Evgeny — Russia
Boveri, Carlos — Argentina
Castro, Leopoldo — Mexico
Chan, Kam Fai 陳錦輝— Venezuela
Chavez, Manuel — Mexico
Cherkaoui, Abdelgheni — Morocco
Chin, Hoong Lap — Malaysia
Chobanyan, Ruben — Armenia
Cruz, Eduardo C. — Mexico
Davodipanah, Housain — Iran
Eckert, Manfred — Germany
Fernandes, Rui — Portugal
Fouad, Samir — Egypt
Frenkel, Alexander — Israel
Garcia, Orlando—New Zealand
Gleb, Muzrukov — Russia
Gomez, Daniel E. — Argentina
Grindeanu, Petru — Romania
Hallden, Fredrik — Sweden
Han, Jing Song — Australia
Hee, Bae Kyoung 裴耿嬉 — Korea
Heroin, Daniel — France
Hoang, Vinh Giang — Vietnam
Hui, Hin Yee — Malaysia
Igor, Kreimer — Russia
Ishihara, Yauhiko 石原泰彦 — Japan
Islamuddin, Mohd — India
Jayaneera, Prasanna — Sri Lanka
Jung, Yong Man — Korea
Kalayci, Ali — Turkey
Karutyunyan, Korhannes — Armenia
Keith, Glen — New Zealand
Khadka, Bina — Nepal
Kigan, Alla — Turkmenistan
Kilichan, Aybars — Turkey
Li, Li — Philippines
Li, Rongmei — Italy
Li, Xia 李霞 — Japan
Liang, Ya Dong — Vietnam
Lu, Jian Cheng — Vietnam
Lvovna, Vereshchagina Elena — Russia
Lyudmyla, Solodylina — Ukraine
Makraf, Belkacem — Algeria
Magamedovna, Ussaeva Vladlena — Russia
Mansuy, Charlie — Switzerland
Mishiro, Masahior — Japan
Morita, Hisako 森田久子 — Japan
Mvkola, Matulevsky — Ukraine
Nguyen, Xuan Thi — Vietnam
Ninomiya, Hideo 二宮秀夫 — Japan
Nseir, Georges — Lebanon
Nuy, Manfred — Germany
Ong, Chiuo Hing — Philippines
Osvch, Piotr — Poland
Ou, Bo 偶波 — England
Palonen, Sirkka — Finland
Panjaitan, Moskos — Indonesia
Petrov, Alexey — Russia
Phan, Poh Ngean — Malaysia
Ping, Lin Quan — Spain
Piwowarsai, Darivsz — Poland
Poyton, Robert — England
Quenon, Roland — Belgium
Rabadanov, Kamil — Russia
Resnianski, Ilia — Turkmenistan
Rinaldi, Salvatore — Italy
Ryser, Xiaojuan — Switzerland
Saade, N. — Lebanon
Sanchez, Julian — Spain
Shi, Mian M. 施棉棉 — Philippines
Sinch, M. Biramani — India
Smith, Raymond — England
Suuntala, Liisa — Finland
Swanson, Anthony — England
Tavares, Firmino — Brazil
Thakuri, Diwas S. — Nepal
Theeboom, Marc — Belgium
Toh, Cheng Hai — Singapore
Tumurbaatar, T. — Mongolia
Tung, Patricia — Argentian
Turneber, Jan — Czech
Vagil, Dumenno — Ukraine
Vasiljevic, Mile — Yugoslavia
Wang, Dong Lian 王冬蓮— Singapore
Warr, Peter — England
Wewhinda, Priya — Sri Lanka
Wu, Yongmei 吳詠梅 — Switzerland
Wiranata, Alim — Indonesia
Xu, Hao 徐浩 — Italy
Young, Peter 楊良方—England
Yu, Zhibo — Philippines
Yue, Liming 岳黎明 — England
Yurevitch, Sergeev Michail — Russia
Zhang, Xiaoyan 張小燕 — France
Zhou, Shusheng 周樹聲 — Singapore
藤井久子 — Japan
廣田成 — Japan
木村豐彦 — Japan
馬劍臣 — Thailand
傅聲遠 — Australia
許榮安 — Australia
池方盛 — Singapore
霍錫山 — Germany

Mainland China, Hong Kong & Macau

張文廣 - 北京
蔡龍雲 - 上海
邱丕相 - 上海
謝雨生 - 上海
黃劍君 - 河北
佟慶輝 - 遼寧
鄭懷賢 - 四川
徐才 - 北京
前中國，國際武協主席
張耀庭 - 北京
前中國，國際武協主席
李杰 - 北京
中國，國際武協主席
梁芷箱 - 四川
梁作風 - 四川
張騰蛟 - 重慶
顧留馨 - 上海
李沛然和尚 - 重慶
鄒德發 - 四川
陳秉仕 - 河北滄州
江雲國 - 重慶
溫佐惠 - 成都
吳信祥 - 四川
夏斯俊 - 湖北
王一甫 - 重慶
曹德勇 - 四川
鄧昌宜 - 四川
習雲太 - 四川
郭洪海 - 四川
周文富 - 四川江津
吳彬 - 北京
何傳民 - 重慶
綦爲華 - 四川萬州
靳立勤 - 廣東
劉濤 - 四川萬州
潘小麗 - 重慶
錢莉 - 四川雲陽
劉靜 - 重慶萬市
鄭興榮 - 重慶奉節
徐家春 - 四川雲陽
周子樸 - 四川成都
賴永全 - 重慶萬市
王榮生 - 成都
李高兵 - 重慶萬市
劉一鳴 - 重慶萬市

張原民 - 四川
鄭家元 - 四川雲陽
魏慶榮 - 四川雲陽
何傳蓉 - 四川雲陽
向道兵 - 四川雲陽
高萬生 - 四川雲陽
林信群 - 四川萬州
周惠瓊 - 四川雲陽
何克民 - 四川雲陽
曹士蘭 - 四川萬州
黃國政 - 四川萬州
陳代玲 - 重慶
劉天富 - 重慶
林遠志 - 成都
肖應鵬 - 成都
王永川 - 四川
熊長貴 - 四川
彭英 - 四川
李殿芳 - 四川
任剛 - 四川
曹科潤 - 四川
鐘承宇 - 四川
王平 - 四川
沙國政 - 雲南
蔡鴻祥 - 上海
郝心蓮 - 甘肅
李晃生 - 江西
門惠豐 - 北京
劉萬福 - 天津
朱國福 - 重慶
吳翼翬 - 東北
陳照奎 - 河南
李雅軒 - 成都
趙長軍 - 陝西
周永福 - 山東
穆秀杰 - 沈陽
楊國忠 - 重慶
黃少華 - 四川雲陽
史思汗 - 廣東東莞
黃立偉 - 香港
陽亞雄 - 重慶
李紅 - 四川
馮素君 - 重慶
王培生 - 中國
潘友茂 - 廣東
教安寧 - 中國
馬福林 - 黑龍江

于小蘭 - 四川雲陽
胡蓉 - 四川雲陽
鐘家全 - 四川雲陽
聶剛全 - 四川雲陽
向磊 - 四川雲陽
馮志強 - 北京
康戈武 - 北京
陳正雷 - 河南
馮華蓉 - 四川
凌躍華 - 浙江
鄭家龍 - 重慶
況偉生 - 四川雲陽
黃建剛 - 廣東
于立光 - 香港
張培蓮 - 重慶
全汝忠 - 雲南
黃俊敏 - 寧夏
楊柏林 - 重慶
肖長根 - 河北
馬賢達 - 西安
奚潘良 - 上海
武淑清 - 河北
杜月屏 - 香港
鄭寶林 - 香港
李德印 - 北京
劉成 - 四川雲陽
呂紫劍 - 重慶
戈春艷 - 北京
汪福興 - 中國攀枝花市
趙洪軍 - 黑龍江
楊曉軍 - 吉林
孫曉東 - 黑龍江
孟凡艷 - 黑龍江
朱旦標 - 浙江
臧曉忠 - 江蘇
黃晶忠 - 福建
王彥儒 - 北京
朱玉軍 - 雲南
趙幼生 - 重慶江北
雷大燮 - 四川
周德潛 - 四川
王國輝 - 廣東
陳昌棉 - 廣東
陳思坦 - 福建
張玉平 - 山東
龐林太 - 山西
費玉俠 - 南京

王小川 - 中國攀枝花市
李宗儒 - 北京
曾向陽 - 重慶
王向紅 - 四川
蔣薀麗 - 重慶
鄢行輝 - 福建
趙科 - 廣東
王敬峰 - 遼寧
梅長江 - 湖北
李文森 - 浙江
孔凡偉 - 黑龍江
李士信 - 北京
陸慧心 - 香港
孫劍群 - 中國
鄧昌成 - 香港
胡桂珍 - 香港
王二平 - 廣東
曾廣鍔 - 廣東
張山 - 北京
趙斌 - 重慶萬市
劉太福 - 四川
葉道清 - 四川
李毅立 - 重慶
林文洁 - 重慶
成傳鋭 - 北京
田回 - 北京
邵善康 - 上海
任崇德 - 中國
黄明生 - 四川
李天驥 - 北京
李青山 - 浙江
愛新覺羅.傅偎 - 浙江
周通勇 - 重慶
任德 - 四川
曾揚 - 四川
劉偉 - 四川
冉學東 - 四川
艾澤秀 - 四川
闞桂香 - 北京
夏柏華 - 北京
馬雷 - 北京
馬淑芳 - 四川
唐玉清 - 成都
周繼勉 - 溫江
宋麗 - 四川
胡亞渝 - 江北
肖顯容 - 樂山

寥沛然 - 成都
呂立 - 四川
陳龍驤 - 成都
朱興榮 - 成都
付尚勛 - 四川
譚偉 - 重慶萬縣
付小艾 - 重慶
方琴 - 重慶
張小琴 - 北京
胡一林 - 四川
高正誼 - 吉林
曾鐵明 - 廣西
王金寶 - 江蘇
張耀寧 - 江蘇
白文祥 - 陕西
馬振邦 - 陕西
王劍軍 - 北京
李志洲 - 北京
徐其成 - 遼寧
林泉 - 廣東
嚴廣才 - 吉林
王新武 - 寧夏
于海 - 山東
王常凱 - 山東
劉玉華 - 湖北
高佳敏 - 福建
溫敬銘 - 湖北
馬岳梁 - 上海
馬禮堂 - 北京
吳圖南 - 中國
黄漢勛 - 香港
于伯謙 - 遼寧
張之江 - 中國
原中央國術館館長
萬籟聲 - 中國
孫劍雲 - 中國
傅振嵩 - 中國
譚順祿 - 四川
姜容樵 - 中國
王薌齋 - 北京
梁挺 - 香港
李林寧 - 澳門
劉綏濱 - 青城
倪憲章 - 雲陽
馬教官 - 雲安鎮
朱志雄 - 雲安
籃素貞 - 四川

彭善思 - 内江
馬鎮岱 - 重慶
萬漢奎 - 奉節
安天榮 - 武漢
陳盛甫 - 山西
趙瑞章 - 山東
徐星俊 - 福州
古前昌 - 永川
郭燕京 - 重慶
蘇自芳 - 昆明
陳振安 - 重慶
何少華 - 重慶
李代鉞 - 重慶
徐連生 - 上海
楊振江 - 深圳
徐功保 - 上海
李吉成（釋德修）- 深圳
王肇基 - 上海
王國琪 - 北京
劉新 - 北京
曾美英 - 上海
李明中 - 四川
蕭承東 - 重慶
程劍良 - 江北
烏樹堂 - 陕西
周元龍 - 上海
錢源澤 - 江蘇
朱興雲 - 成都
傅尚勛 - 成都
栗子宜 - 成都
黄加達 - 香港
何天祺 - 成都
Lau, Tak - 香港
Lei, Man Lam - 澳門
Zhang, Guangsheng - 中國
Zeng, Tie Ming - 澳門

Glossary Addendum-2: World Champions

This addendum includes a list of champions of the First and Second World Wushu Invitational Tournament, and the Fifth World Wushu Championships. At the First World Wushu Championships, China dominated the competitions. The Chinese athletes took all the first places. During the Second World Wushu Championships, China again dominated the competitions. The Chinese athletes took all but one first place. Based on the top six places, China had 16 top six places, all 16 were gold medals; Canada took 13 top six places, including 6 silver and 3 bronze medals; U.S.A. took 11 top six places, including 4 silver and 3 bronze medals; Japan took 13 top six places, including 3 silver and 5 bronze medals; and Britain took 11 top six places, including 1 gold, 1 silver, and 2 bronze medals.

The standards of U.S., Canadian, and English athletes were high at the First and Second World Wushu Invitational Tournaments. After 1986, the regular Wushu competitions in the Asian nations and at the Asian games had significantly raised the standards of the athletes in the region. Since 1990, the athletes in the Western Hemisphere began to fall behind the Asian athletes. Since the two Invitational Tournaments, there have been five World Wushu Championships held around the world. In the Fifth World Wushu Championships held in Hong Kong in 1999, the standards of the Asian athletes were very high. Comparatively, the standing of the Western nations only ranked around tenth place, especially that of U.S. and Canada. In the Sanshou competitions, the lighter divisions were dominated by the Chinese athletes. The other weight divisions winners were from Korea, Russia, Azerbaijan, Iran, Egypt, and Ukrain.

First World Wushu Invitational Tournament — 1985

Xian, China

All-Around First Place (Men)	Zhao, Changjun	China
All-Around First Place (Women)	Zhang, Yuping	China
All-Around Second Place (Men)	Ninomiya, Hideo	Japan
All-Around Second Place (Women)	Bertrand, Paule	Canada
All-Around Third Place (Men)	Vecchiolla, Richard	U.S.A.
All-Around Third Place (Women)	Yen, Chi-Ching	U.S.A.
First Place Taijjiquan (Men)	Chen, Xiaowang	China
First Place Taijiquan (Women)	Lin, Qiupin	China
First Place Nanquan (Men)	Yang, Shiwen	China
First Place Daoshu (Men)	Zhao, Changjun	China
First Place Daoshu (Women)	Zhang, Yuping	China
First Place Jianshu (Men)	Jia, Ping	China
First Place Jianshu (Women)	Zhang, Hongmei	China
First Place Qiangshu (Men)	Jia, Ping	China
First Place Gunshu (Men)	Zhao, Changjun	China
First Place Gunshu (Women)	Zhang, Yuping	China

Second World Wushu Invitational Tournament — 1986

Tianjin, China

All-Around First Place (Men)	Zhao, Changjun	China
All-Around First Place (Women)	Zhang, Yuping	China
All-Around Second Place (Men)	Wong, Phillip	U.S.A.
All-Around Second Place (Women)	Chang, Alice	Canada
All-Around Third Place (Men)	Gracenin, Nick	U.S.A.
All-Around Third Place (Women)	Barber, Gillian	England
First Place Jianshu (Men)	Jia, Ping	China
First Place Jianshu (Women)	Fang, Jian	China
First Place Gunshu (Men)	Zhao, Changjun	China
First Place Gunshu (Women)	Zhang, Yuping	China
First Place Changquan (Men)	Zhao, Changjun	China
First Place Changquan (Women)	Zhang, Yuping	China
First Place Qiangshu (Men)	Jia, Ping	China
First Place Qiangshu (Women)	Fang, Jian	China
First Place Daoshu (Men)	Zhao, Changjun	China
First Place Daoshu (Women)	Zhang, Yuping	China
First Place Xingyiquan	Zhang, Chengzhong	China
First Place Nanquan	Yang, Shiwen	China
First Place Taijjiquan (Men)	Ding, Jie	China
First Place Taijiquan (Women)	Lin, Qiuping	China
First Place Baguazhang	Sutton, Nigel	England

Fifth World Wushu Championships — 1999
Hong Kong, China

First Place Changquan (Men)	To, Yu Hang	Hong Kong
First Place Changquan (Women)	Nguyen, Thi Thuy Hien	Vietnam
First Place Nanquan (Men)	Chen, Lun	China
First Place Nanquan (Women)	Ng, Siu Ching	Hong Kong
First Place Taijjiquan (Men)	Zou, Yunjian	China
First Place Taijiquan (Women)	Qiu, Huifong	China
First Place Daoshu (Men)	Jian, Zengjiao	China
First Place Daoshu (Women)	Liu, Xiaolei	China
First Place Jianshu (Men)	Cheung, Man Keung	Hong Kong
First Place Jianshu (Women)	Chen, Be	China
First Place Nandao (Men)	Ho, Ro Bin	Malaysia
First Place Nandao (Women)	Huang, Chunni	China
First Place Taijijian (Men)	Kong, Xiangdong	China
First Place Taijijian (Women)	Li, Fai	Hong Kong
First Place Qiangshu (Men)	Chow, Ting Yu	Hong Kong
First Place Qiangshu (Women)	Lei, Fei	Macau
First Place Gunshu (Men)	Park, Chan Dea	Korea
First Place Gunshu (Women)	Dam, Thanh Xuan	Vietnam
First Place Nangun (Men)	Cheng, Ka Ho	Hong Kong
First Place Nangun (Women)	Nguyen, Thi Phung Lan	Vietnam
First Place 48 Kg Sanshou	Chen, Long	China
First Place 52 Kg Sanshou	Wang, Wenjun	China
First Place 56 Kg Sanshou	Zheng, Kunyou	China
First Place 60 Kg Sanshou	Kim, Gwee Jong	Korea
First Place 65 Kg Sanshou	Ahhadov, Murat	Russia
First Place 70 Kg Sanshou	Djanpolad, Boudagov	Azerbaijan
First Place 75 Kg Sanshou	Ojaghi, Housain	Iran
First Place 80 Kg Sanshou	Ataev, Bozigit	Russia
First Place 85 Kg Sanshou	Elkena, Basel Ibrahim	Egypt
First Place 90 Kg Sanshou	Mogomedov	Ukrain
First Place 90+ Kg Sanshou	Mirmiran, Sayyedali	Iran

References used in this Glossary

1. 《大悲拳》 *Dabeiquan*. Provided by Yuan, Shaoliang. 2000.
2. 《中國年鑑》1981年香港京士威國際出版有限公司。
3. 《中國武術史》1985年人民體育出版社。習雲太。
4. 《中國大百科全書》1982年中國大百科全書出版社。姜椿芳等。
5. 《中國清淨布氣門正宗絕技》北京體育學院出版社。徐星俊。
6. 《中國萬壽系列功法》廣西南宇東方人體研究所。程克欣，三峽醫學氣功武術易經研究學會。
7. 《中華武林著名人物傳》1998年百花洲文藝出版社。張文廣，蔡龍雲，郝心蓮，王國輝。
8. 《王子平與武術》1992年上海教育出版社。王菊蓉，吳誠德。
9. 《六合螳螂拳》1970年五洲出版社。張詳三。
10. 《木蘭拳》 *Xiliangquan*. Provided by Zang, Lijuan. 2000.
11. 《五梅派》 *Wumeipai*. Provided by Lo, Ken. 2000.
12. 《五祖拳》 *Wuzuquan*. Provided by Lee, Kam. 2000.
13. 《太虛拳》 *Taixuquan*. Provided by Sit, Chun Man. 2000.
14. 《六合八法拳》1985年科學普及出版社。梁士洪。
15. 《六合八法圖說》1979年麒麟圖書公司。陳亦人。
16. 《世界武術錦標賽論文》中國武術協會等。
17. 《四川武術大全》1987年四川科學技術出版社。四川省武術挖整組。
18. 《西涼拳》 *Xiliangquan*. Provided by Lu, Fenglin. 2000.
19. 《武術匯宗》香港錦華出版社。萬籟聲。
20. 《武術》人民體育出版社。體育學院教材編審委員會。
21. 《武當門》 *Wudangmen*. Provided by Wang, Xuezhi. 2000.
22. 《神打》九龍武叢出版社。雄師編著。
23. 《神奇的武術》1991年廣西人民出版社。鄭勤，田雲清。
24. 《迷蹤派拳功》九龍武叢出版社。雄師編著。
25. 《國際武術散手道聯盟會員手册》The Way of the Dragon Publishing. IWSD.
26. 《梁守渝武術筆記》手抄本
27. 《敦煌拳》 *Dunhuangquan*. Provided by Zang, Lijuan. 2000.
28. 《戳腳》1983年河北人民出版社。劉景山。
29. 《曦陽掌》 *Xiyangzhang*. Provided by Qi, Ke Bao. 2000.
30. 《鶴拳》1984年華聯出版社。楊景崎。
31. Short biographies submitted by practitioners. 2000.

Appendix B: Herbal Formulas

The application of herbal liniments during training is very important in body conditioning where intentional, repeated pounding actions, are required to *harden* the training area (such as the palms, fists, and forearms). However, in the process of hardening the palm, fist, or arm, blood-stasis may occur. If blood-stasis is not removed after every training session, the results could be detrimental to the body. Without the proper types of herbs to help treat injuries or to condition the body, bones and tendons may be damaged and an arthritic condition may creep up after a period of time. It is imperative that proper herbal liniments are applied to the injured or conditioned area to prevent problems.

Herbal liniments and internal herbal medicine are also an important treatment for healing injuries. Injuries occur for many reasons. Although, we should be careful not to get injured, sometimes it is unavoidable to get occasional black and blue marks during training by ourselves or with a partner. These injuries need to be treated properly to reduce blood-stasis and to improve qi (energy) circulation, so that training can be resumed without delay. A long delay in one's training will reduce one's attainment.

Traditional herbal liniments used to treat minor bruises will generally include:

1. Diaphoretics — herbs to increase perspiration in order to dispel pathogenic factors from the exterior of the body.
2. Antirheumatics — herbs for preventing and relieving painful conditions of the joints and muscles, by removing dampness, eliminating coldness, and activating blood circulation in the collaterals.
3. Herbs for invigorating blood circulation and eliminating blood-stasis.
4. Herbs for invigorating qi (energy) circulation and for relieving pain.

In body conditioning training, such as, Iron Arm, Iron Sand Palm, Iron Fist training, etc., the liniment will generally include all four types of herbal mixtures listed above, plus additional herbs to strengthen the bones and tendons, to heal fractures to the bones and tendons, and to reduce inflammation.

There are many prepared herbal liniments that can be purchased from various locations. Here, we will list a few herbal liniment formulas that you can make yourself. The herbs are listed in Chinese. You can buy most of them in herbal stores, especially in Chinatown. All of the formulas listed can be used for treating bruises and for body conditioning; and are for external use only.

Formula 1: Palm Conditioning Liniment

掌 功 外 洗 方：

歸尾，紅花，乳香，沉香，沒藥，血述，虎骨，赤芍，枝子，
桃仁，荆介，丹皮，枳殼，桔梗，木香 。

Get an equal amount of each herb listed above. If they are not already in small pieces, chop them into small pieces or grind them into a thick powder. Place the herbs in a glass jar with an airtight cover and immerse the herbs with enough rice wine to cover all the herbs. The liniment is ready to be used in 7 days. However, the longer you soak the herbs in the wine, the more potent the liniment will be. Before training, pour some on your hands and massage it into your hands. After training, pour some more on your hands and massage again.

Note: Shake well before use. This liniment is for external use only. Don't use it on open wounds and don't drink it.

Formula 2: Training Liniment

洗 手 單 - 1：

三棱一兩， 莪術一兩， 赤芍一兩， 桃仁一兩， 紅花八錢， 枳實六錢，
生南星一兩， 生半夏一兩， 生二烏一兩， 胡交一兩， 花交一兩，
狼毒二兩， 血余一兩， 白螞蟻窩二兩，八楞麻一兩， 北前葉二兩，
一支蒿二兩 。

Get the amount of each herbs listed above. If they are not already in small pieces, chop them into small pieces or grind them into a thick powder. Place the herbs in a glass jar with an airtight cover and immerse the herbs with enough rice wine to cover all the herbs. The liniment is ready to be used in 7 days. However, the longer you soak the herbs in the wine, the more potent the liniment will be. This liniment is used for palm, fist, arm, and feet conditioning. Before training, pour some on your hands and massage it all over the area being conditioned. You may also immerse your hands in the liniment for a few minutes before use. After training, pour some liniment on your hands and massage the area that has just been conditioned.

Note: Shake well before use. This liniment is for external use only. Don't use it on open wounds and don't drink it.

Formula 3: Training Liniment

洗 手 單 - 2：

桃仁，紅花，青鹽，血倚，血騰，狼毒，生南星，生半夏，生二烏，土別，制蘆，乳沒，姜黄，伏岭，象皮，古石灰，地骨皮，枳殼 ○ 各五錢 ○

Get the amount of each herbs listed above. If they are not already in small pieces, chop them into small pieces or grind them into a thick powder. Place the herbs in a glass jar with an airtight cover and immerse the herbs with enough rice wine to cover all the herbs. The liniment is ready to be used in 7 days. However, the longer you soak the herbs in the wine, the more potent the liniment will be. Before training, pour some on your hands and massage it all over the area being conditioned. You may also immerse your hands in the liniment for a few minutes before use. After training, pour some liniment on your hands and massage the area that has just been conditioned.

Note: Shake well before use. This liniment is for external use only. Don't use it on open wounds and don't drink it.

Formula 4: Iron Finger Liniment

指 功 外 洗 方：

硫磺一兩，透骨草一兩，狼毒一兩，青鹽四兩，紫花地丁一兩，花椒一兩，蛇床子一錢，地皮骨一兩，海牙一兩，劉寄奴二兩，黎蘆一兩，龍骨一兩，秦艽蒂一錢 ○

Get the amount of herbs listed above and place them in a clay pot. Add 5 cups of vinegar and 5 cups of water. Simmer the herbs until there is only 7 cups of liquid left. When the liniment cools down, place it in a glass jar. Before training, warm up the liniment slightly, then immerse your hands in the liniment for 30 minutes, before beginning your session of finger conditioning. After training, massage your hands and fingers with the liniment.

Note: Shake well before use. This liniment is for external use only. Don't use it on open wounds and don't drink it.

About the Author:

Shou-Yu Liang

Shou-Yu Liang was born in 1942 in Sichuan, China. At age six, he began his training in qigong, under the tutelage of his renowned grandfather, the late Liang, Zhi-Xiang. He was taught esoteric qigong and the martial arts of the Emei Mountain region, including Emei Dapeng Qigong. At age eight, his grandfather also made special arrangements for him to begin training Emei Qigong and Wushu with other well-known masters of the time.

By the time he was twenty, Shou-Yu Liang had already received instruction from 10 of the most well-known legendary grandmasters of both Southern and Northern systems. His curiosity inspired him to learn more than one hundred sequences from many different styles. As he grew older, through and beyond his college years, his wide background in various martial arts helped form his present character, and led him to achieve a high level of martial arts and qigong skills. Some of the training he concentrated on included: the Emei Styles, Shaolin Long Fist, Praying Mantis, Chuojiao, Qinna, vital point striking, many weapons systems, and qigong methods.

Shou-Yu Liang received a university degree in biology and physiology in 1964. He was then transferred to a remote village in China where he taught high school. This relocation was part of the *reeducation* program enforced on him by the government during the political structure of the time, for having been born in a bourgeois family. His dedication to his own training and helping others to excel didn't stop during the years he was in the remote village. He began to organize Wushu and wrestling teams to compete in provincial tournaments.

During the years of the Cultural Revolution, all forms of martial arts and qigong were suppressed. To avoid conflict with the Red Guards, Shou-Yu Liang left his teaching position and used this opportunity to tour various parts of the country. He visited and studied with great masters in Wushu and qigong, and made many friends with people who shared his devotion. His mastery of qigong and martial arts, both technically and philosophically grew to new horizons.

Shou-Yu Liang traveled through numerous provinces and cities, visiting many renowned and revered places where Wushu and qigong originated, was developed, and refined. Among the many places he visited were Emei Mountains, Wudang Mountains, Hua Mountains, Qingcheng Mountains, Chen's Village in Henan, the Changzhou Territory in Hebei Province, Beijing, and Shanghai.

At the end of the Cultural Revolution, the Chinese government again began to support the martial arts and qigong. During the reorganization and categorizing of the existing martial arts, research projects were set up to seek out living masters and preserve their knowledge. It was at this time that the Sichuan government appointed Shou-Yu Liang as a coach for the city, the territory, and the province. Many of Shou-Yu Liang's students were among the top martial artists of China. In 1979, he received the title of *Coach of Excellence* since 1949, by the People's Republic of China.

With his wealth of knowledge, Shou-Yu Liang was inspired at an early age to compete in martial arts tournaments where he was many times a noted gold medalist. During his adolescence, Shou-Yu Liang won titles in Chinese wrestling (Shuaijiao), various other martial arts, and weight lifting. After the Cultural Revolution, despite his many official duties, Shou-Yu Liang continued to participate actively in competitions both at the provincial and national level. Between 1974 and 1981, he won numerous awards, including four gold medals. His students also performed superbly both in national and provincial open tournaments, winning many medals. Many of these students are now professional Wushu coaches in colleges, in the armed forces, or have become movie stars. In 1979, Shou-Yu Liang received several appointments, including committee membership in the Sichuan Chapter of the Chinese National Wushu Committee and Coaches Committee.

In 1981, Shou-Yu Liang visited Seattle, Washington. This trip marked another new era in the course of his life. His ability immediately impressed Wushu devotees. The Wushu and Taiji Club of the Student Association, at the University of Washington, retained him as a Wushu Coach. At the same time, Shou-Yu Liang taught at the Taiji Association in Seattle. In the following year, Shou-Yu Liang went to Vancouver, Canada, and was appointed Taiji Coach by the Villa Cathy Care Home. During the same year, he was appointed Honorary Chairman and Head Coach by the North American Taiji Athletic Association. He also began to teach classes in the Physical Education Department at the University of British Columbia (UBC).

In 1984, Shou-Yu Liang was certified as a national First Class Ranking Judge by China. He was also appointed Chairperson and Wushu Coach by the University of British Columbia. In 1985, Shou-Yu Liang was elected coach of the First Canadian National Wushu Team, which was invited to participate in the 1985 World Wushu Invitational Competition that took place in Xian, China. The Canadian team took Third Place after competing against teams from 13 other countries. The following year, he was again elected coach of the Second Canadian National Wushu Team, that competed in the 1986 World Wushu Invitational Competition held in Tianjin, China. A total of 28 countries participated. This time, the Canadian team took Second Place, which was only second to China. Shou-Yu Liang and the Canadian success story shocked the Chinese nation, and news of their outstanding accomplishment spread throughout China.

In 1994, Shou-Yu Liang led the North American Martial Arts Exhibition Team for a friendship performance tour to ten major cities in China where his team received a warm welcome by the people and government of China. While in China, the team also competed in the International Wushu Competition held in Shanghai. This competition was represented by 32 nations. Shou-Yu Liang's students received 42 gold medals. Canadian premier, Mr. Jean Chretien, also wrote a letter of encouragement to the team. Many Chinese television stations, radio stations, and newspapers spread the news of the Exhibition Team all over China.

Since the beginning of the 1960's, Shou-Yu Liang has personally taught over 10,000 students. He has touched the lives of tens of thousands of students in his affiliate schools and the schools of his students' students. His students have received hundreds of gold medals in national and international competitions. Many of his students are currently teaching all over the world.

Shou-Yu Liang continues to gain recognition in China and abroad. In the past few years, he was selected as "The Instructor of the Year" by Inside Kung Fu Magazine and selected by the China Wushu Magazine in the "Biography of Today's Extraordinary Martial Artists". He has been awarded the "World's Top 100 Outstanding Martial Artists Professional Award", "World's Greatest Contribution Award" and "World's Outstanding Accomplishment Award." He is included in the books: *The Biography of China's Prominent Wushu Practitioners* (中華武林著名人物傳), *China's Contemporary Wushu Masters* (中國當代武林名人誌), *Who's Who in the World* (世界名人錄), and *The Record of Prominent Chinese Descendants in the World* (世界華人精英錄). The chairman of the China Wushu Association wrote this about him, "Uses his martial arts to teach people, and uses his morals to inspire people."

Since the beginning of his advantageous martial arts life, Shou-Yu Liang has been featured by scores of newspapers and magazines in China, Europe, the USA, and Canada. He has also been interviewed by many television stations in China, the USA, and Canada, including the recent interview by CNN.

Currently Shou-Yu Liang is the Advisor or Honorary Advisor for over 20 national and professional Wushu organizations in China, the United States, and Canada. He has been the Wushu Chairperson and faculty member of the UBC, since 1984. He has been the Head Coach of the Canadian Wushu team, is the founder of the I.W.S.D. Association, and the Vice President of the Confederation of Canadian Wushu Organizations. He has been the Referee General in international Wushu competitions.

Shou-Yu Liang has written and published over 20 books and videotapes including, *Hsing Yi Chuan*, *Simplified Tai Chi Chuan with Applications*, *Baguazhang*, *Qigong Empowerment*, *Chinese Fast Wrestling for Fighting*, *Xiaoyaoshuai*, and *Kung Fu Elements*.

梁守渝簡介

（號：逍遙子）

1942 年出身中國重慶市。六歲開始跟隨爺爺梁芷箱先生學習大鵬氣功，鐵布衫功和峨嵋派武功。後又在爺爺的介紹下向十多位前輩老師學習少林派，峨嵋派其它多種功夫。猶愛散手。17 歲開始學習太極拳，八卦掌，形意拳與武當派功夫和練習摔跤，太極推手等。

1960 年重慶市第 29 中畢業。學習優秀被政府保送進入西南民族學院生物系。

1960-1964 年參加成都體育學院武術訓練。被選爲成都市武術代表隊成員。任西南民族學院武術隊隊長兼教練。參加各級武術比賽，摔跤比賽和舉重比賽。獲得多次第一名和前幾名好成績。開始學習佛家密宗修煉氣功。

1965 年由於家庭出身不好，被分配到山峽地區雲陽縣。參加一年社會主義教育運動後被分配到高陽中學教書。

1966 年開始文化大革命運動。四處流浪，遍尋名師武友學習各種武術。

1974 年中國恢復武術，被政府調到體育運動委員會當專職武術教練。任第一任雲陽縣武術教練。

1975 年任第一任萬州地區武術教練。又開始參加四川省和全中國的武術比賽和表演，獲得多次金牌，也在全國比賽中作裁判員。

1978 年被評選爲四川省優秀教練員，先進工作者，獲獎。

1979 年被評選爲全國優秀教練員，獲獎。被指定爲第一屆全國武術協會四川省協會委員，和教練委員會委員。

1981 年任美國華盛頓大學武術俱樂部教練。

1982 年任加拿大溫哥華市華宮太極和氣功教師。溫哥華北美太極聯誼會名譽主席兼教練。

1984 年任加拿大哥倫比亞大學體育學院正式教師，後任武術專業主任直到現在（1999）。是第一個進入美，加大學中正式編制的中國武術教師。

1985 年被選爲第一任加拿大國家武術隊總教練，到中國參賽，加拿大隊總分第三。

1986 年再作加拿大國家武術隊教練到天津參加國際武術邀請賽，加拿大總分僅次中國獲第二。

1987 年成立加拿大 SYL 武術學院，任院長，旗下有十多名教練員。

1988 年和加拿大，美國，蘇聯，中國的同道一起創建國際武術散手道聯盟，任第一任主席。目的是在各國推行以中國武術爲基礎的，培養全面武術人材的計劃。

1994 年任北美洲綜合武術代表團團長，訪問表演中國十 大城市，得到加拿大總理支持並題詞。在中國時受到中國政府和觀眾熱情接待和歡迎。

1995 年被美國雜誌(Inside Kung Fu)選爲當年國際最佳教練員(Instructor of the Year)。

1996 年被中國百花洲文藝社出版的《中華武林著名人物傳》選爲傳主之一。1998 年 9 月在中國正式出版。

1996 年中國全國武術協會主席張耀庭先生題詞："守渝先生，以技教人，以德感人"。

1997 年第六屆世界杯，被選爲："世界傑出百名武術名人金牌獎"。

1998 年被全美武術協會 (USAWKF) 選爲國際三名最優秀武術大師之一 (Outstanding Master)。

1998 年被選入《中國當代武林名人志》。

1999 年第七 屆世界杯，被選爲："世界最佳武術貢獻金牌獎"和"世界傑出武術成就獎"。

1999 年被選入《世界名人錄》。(由香港世界文化藝術研究中心，世界人物出版社，中國國際交流出版社正式出版)

1999 再次被選爲加拿大國家武術隊教練參加在香港舉辦的武術錦標賽。

2000 加拿大全國比賽和美加國際比賽總裁判長。

2001 加拿大全國武術選拔賽總裁判長。被評爲 2001 年最佳教練員，再次被選爲國家隊領隊和散手教練。準備參加在亞美利亞的第六屆世界武術錦標賽。在第八屆世界杯國際武術比賽中被選爲大會最高榮譽主席，並獲得最高武術成就金牌獎（日本舉行）。

1995-2001 在加拿大，美國全國性武術比賽，泛美洲武術比賽和多次國際武術比賽中作仲裁，副總裁判長和總裁判長。

其它任職和名譽任職：

加拿大國際總會副會長

加拿大聯合武術協會名譽主席，名譽總教練

加拿大武術團體聯合總會顧問，副主席

美國全國武術協會(USAWKF)顧問

美國全國氣功學會顧問

美國全國氣功協會理事

世界武術歷史學會第一任名譽主席
中國四川省武協委員(1979-)
中國重慶市武協顧問(1994-)
中國黑龍江省武術館名譽館長(1986-)
中國上海市硬氣功功法研究會顧問(1988-)
中國《防身與制敵》雜誌顧問
中國三峽易經研究學會名譽主席

曾被中國，美國，加拿大，歐州，日本，幾十份報刊雜誌介紹，包括中國的《人民日報》。被七份國內外雜誌選爲封面人物。幾十次被中國，加拿大，美國，英國，墨西哥等電視節目報道，多次接受中國，美國，加拿大國家電視台專訪，包括CNN世界廣播電台。

由於參與社會活動和在社會上的知名度，曾會見加拿大總理Jean Chretien。八十年代會見過中國總理趙紫陽，也榮幸代表華人會見中國國家主席江澤民先生和副主席李瑞環先生等…近四十年來，梁守渝在中國，美國，加拿大和歐洲各大城市親自教授過的學生(包括公開課，講座等)有數萬人之多。如包括學生的學生，那就更多了。訓練的運動員中，獲得全國性和各種國際比賽的金牌數有幾百塊之多。很多學生已經成爲有名的武術大師，氣功大師，武術專職教練員，軍隊和警察中的武術教官，功夫演員，大學的教授講師等。有十幾位學生都被選入了《中國當代武林名人志》。

出版過的書籍有：

八卦掌理論及運用
形意拳理論及實用
24，48式太極拳理論及實用
散手快摔
氣功能
蜀山無極逍遙摔
中國武術

教學錄影帶：

八卦掌三卷
形意拳三卷
24式太極拳一卷
24式太極拳及其運用
(包括48式太極拳套)
孫式太極拳及其運用一卷
吳式太極拳及其運用一卷
32式太極劍一卷
無極逍遙摔一卷
醫療健康氣功一卷
小周天功法一卷
密宗九節佛風一卷
無極逍遙拿一卷
無極逍遙一掛鞭一卷
陳式太極拳老架一路一卷

About the Author:

Wen-Ching Wu

Wen-Ching Wu was born in Taiwan, China in 1964. He loved Wushu and other sports since a young age. Like all other youngsters his age, he dabbled in Southern Wushu with his family and relatives. During high school he was on the school's basketball and softball teams. He graduated from high school as a salutatorian. He came to the U.S. in 1983 to study Mechanical Engineering and in 1988, he graduated with honors from Northeastern University, with a BSME degree.

Wen-Ching Wu is the son of Mr. and Mrs. Yu-Kuang Wu. With the support of his parents, Wen-Ching Wu was given an incredible opportunity to experience the world—from Asia to Africa, to North America... He is the protege of Shou-Yu Liang. With the guidance of Shou-Yu Liang, Wen-Ching Wu has excelled in both the Internal Styles, External Styles, and Qigong. Wen-Ching Wu is the adopted son of Professor Ju-Rong Wang and Dr. Cheng-De Wu. With their guidance, Wen-Ching Wu has also excelled in Chaquan, Taijiquan, and Qigong.

In 1990, he competed in the United States National Chinese Martial Arts Competition where he was awarded the Grandchampion award in both Internal and External Styles. He competed in eight events in 1990 and was ranked first in every event he competed in.

Since then, he has focused his efforts on learning, teaching, and writing. In 1991, he and his wife, Denise, founded The Way of the Dragon, Ltd. He then began teaching and writing full time, and traveling to other states and countries to offer seminars. Below are some of Wen-Ching Wu's accomplishments and appointments:

1993—Published *A Guide to Taijiquan* book.

1994—Published the *Baguazhang* book.

1995—Published *A Complete Tai Chi Chuan Workout Tape* and *Qi Permeating Technique Audio Tape*

1997—Awarded Master Level II Instructor by the International Wushu Sanshou Dao Association (I.W.S.D.).

1997—Published the *Qigong Empowerment* book, *Health Maintenance qigong* video, *Microcosmic Circulation Qigong* video, and *Nine Segment Buddhist Breathing Qigong* video.

1998—Awarded three Outstanding Performance awards at the Fourth Shanghai International Wushu Festival/Competition.

1998—Published *Feel the Qi* video, *Tai Chi Beginning Workout Partner* video, and *Tai Chi Beginning* book.

1998—Selected to be included in the book, *China's Contemporary Wushu Masters.*

1999—Appointed as a United States of America Wushu-Kung Fu Federation (USAWKF) Advisor.

1999—Published *Xiaoyaoshuai* book.

2000—Published *Tai Chi Single Fan* book.

2001—Awarded Master Level III Instructor by the International Wushu Sanshou Dao Association (I.W.S.D.).

2001—Appointed as Vice Chairman of the International Wushu Sanshou Dao Association.

2001—Published *Kung Fu Elements* book.

1991-2001—Served as a judge in U.S. National and International Wushu competitions.

Wen-Ching Wu has been giving workshops in Internal Style, External Style, and Qigong throughout the U.S. and Europe. His workshops have been very well received by participants. He has also been featured many times on TV programs. To date, he has written and coauthored over 15 books and videos. Currently, he is working on several other books about Chinese martial arts and Qigong, to be published by The Way of the Dragon Publishing in the near future.

吳文慶簡介

(號: 逍遙客)

吳文慶出身中國台灣省。從小就熱愛武術和其它體育運動。小學時隨家長練過南拳。高中時代表學校棒球隊和籃球隊。從師梁守渝大師學習峨嵋，少林，武當派武術，摔跤，和氣功修煉。是梁師在美國的得意大弟子。他從師王菊蓉教授和吳誠德教授學習查拳，太極，和氣功。是王老和吳老的義子。以下是吳文慶的一些簡歷。

1964 年出身台灣省。父親吳餘光。母親范秋妹。祖先從廣東梅縣移民台灣。

1983 以優秀的成績高中畢業。畢業後進美國東北大學機械工程系。

1988 年以優秀的成績畢業於美國東北大學機械工程系獲學士學位。

1990 年在休士頓的全美武術大賽中獲得八項金牌。奪得內家拳術，外家拳術兩項總冠軍。

1991 年成立美國龍道武學院，任院長。同時也在美國麻州大學任武術，太極和氣功教師。

1993 年出版了《24，48 式太極拳理論及實用》。

1994 年出版了《八卦掌理論及運用》。

1995 年出版了一卷太極拳教學錄影帶和一卷貫氣法錄音帶。

1997 年出版了《氣功能》和三卷氣功教學錄影帶。

1997 年任職國際武術散手道聯盟行政辦公室主任，美國羅德島主席，和大師級教練。

1998 年參加第四屆國際博覽會比賽表演三項都得到特別優秀奬。獲得金牌。

1998 年被選入《中國當代武林名人志》。

1999 年被聘爲全美武術協會(USAWKF)顧問。

1999 年出版了《蜀山無極逍遙摔》

2000 年出版了《飛虹太極單扇》

2001 年當選國際武術散手道聯盟副主席

2001 年出版了《中國武術》

1991-2001 在美國和國際武術比賽中作裁判員。

吳文慶對內家和外家拳術都有很高的照詣。他全面的學習各門各派的武術，包括少林派，峨嵋派與武當派多種功夫。對武術的踢打摔拿和多種武器都有很高的功力。練拳時能剛能柔，虛實分明。發勁時眼到手到力道十足。做到意動身隨形意並重充分的表現出武術的精，氣，神。對道家佛家醫療和武術氣功也有很深的研究。

他經常在北美和歐洲各地演講傳授武術和氣功受到學生們的愛戴。他也多次接受美國電視台的採訪報道。1993年到今他著有十五種武術，氣功書藉和教學錄影帶深受各地讀者歡迎。

Bibliography

(English References)

1. Barham & Wooten. *Structural Kinesiology.* New York: Macmillan Publishing Co., Inc., 1973.

2. Gray, Henry. *Gray's Anatomy.* Philadelphia, PA: Running Press, 1974.

3. Memmler & Wood. *The Human Body in Health and Disease*, Sixth Ed. Philadelphia, PA: J.B. Lippincott Company, 1987.

4. Liang & Wu. *Qigong Empowerment.* Rhode Island: The Way of the Dragon Publishing, 1997.

5. Liang & Wu. *Xiaoyaoshuai.* Rhode Island: The Way of the Dragon Publishing, 2000.

Bibliography

(Chinese References)

1. 《中國武術史》1985年人民體育出版社，習雲太。
2. 《中醫啓蒙》安徽科學技術出版社，金天衡。
3. 《中國醫學診法大全》1991年台灣中華書局印行，麻仲學等。
4. 《中醫學概論》1991年知音出版社，孟景春，周仲瑛。
5. 《中國大百科全書》1982年中國大百科全書出版社，姜椿芳等 。
6. 《中國清淨布氣門正宗絕技》北京體育學院出版社，徐星俊。
7. 《少林點穴法》北京體育學院出版社，德虔。
8. 《四川武術大拳》1987年四川科學技術出版社，四川省武術挖整組。
9. 《武術》人民體育出版社，體育學院教材編審委員會。
10. 《武術匯宗》香港錦華出版社，萬籟聲 。
11. 《孫子兵法》1983年時報文化出版企業有限公司，徐瑜。
12. 《梁守渝武術筆記》手抄本。
13. 《跌打損傷驗方總論》手抄本，沈萬春。
14. 《實用針灸選穴手册》1990年金盾出版社，楊兆民，鞠傳軍。
15. 《點穴秘訣》香港陳湘記書局，五台山靈空禪師。
16. 《藥酒藥茶》1994年廣東人民出版社，顧奎琴。

Index